Education Research in African Contexts

Traditions and New Beginnings for Knowledge and Impact

Edited by
Paul Webb, Mathabo Khau and
Proscovia Namubiru Ssentamu

**AFRICAN
MINDS**

Published in 2024 by African Minds
4 Eccleston Place, Somerset West, 7130, Cape Town, South Africa
info@africanminds.org.za | www.africanminds.org.za

ISBN (paper): 978-1-0672535-0-9
eBook edition: 978-1-0672535-1-6
ePub edition: 978-1-0672535-2-3

Copies of this book are available for free download at: www.africanminds.org.za

ORDERS:
African Minds
Email: info@africanminds.org.za
To order printed books from outside Africa, please contact:
African Books Collective
PO Box 721, Oxford OX1 9EN, UK

Email: orders@africanbookscollective.com

Contents

Acknowledgements

The production of *Education Research in African Contexts: Traditions and New Beginnings for Knowledge and Impact* has been a long-cherished goal for many students, faculty, and project staff involved with the East and South African-German Centre of Excellence for Educational Research Methodologies and Management (CERM-ESA). Established in 2014, CERM-ESA and its partner institutions in Germany (University of Oldenburg), Kenya (Moi University), South Africa (Nelson Mandela University), Tanzania (University of Dar es Salaam), and Uganda (Uganda Management Institute) recently celebrated a decade of impactful collaboration. This milestone was marked by a conference at Moi University, CERM-ESA's physical home, on the future of educational research in African contexts.

The realization of this book would not have been possible without the contributions of many individuals. First and foremost, we express our deepest gratitude to the CERM-ESA master's and doctoral students, who, together with their supervisors, are the primary authors of the chapters in this book. These students, many of whom have dedicated years to teaching in East and Southern African schools, pursued further study with the ambition of improving the education of children and transforming educational institutions. Their commitment and determination have been truly inspiring.

Our thanks also go to the supervisors who guided these students throughout their research journeys, often encouraging them to explore new and unfamiliar methodologies, contributing significantly to their academic and professional growth.

A special thank you is extended to the CERM-ESA project leaders and coordinators, whose vision, dedication, and collaborative spirit fostered a partnership based on trust and shared goals. This strong foundation enabled CERM-ESA to flourish, resulting in the graduation of approximately 70 master's and 15 PhD students by 2024. We would like to acknowledge the former and current CERM-ESA project coordinators and leaders, namely Professors Susan Kurgat, John Chang'ach, Anne Kisilu, Jonah Kindiki, and Julius Tanui at Moi University; Professors Karsten Speck, Bernd Siebenhüner, and Dr Malve von Möllendorff at the University of Oldenburg; Professor Paul Webb, Kholisa Papu, and Dr Ayanda Simayi at Nelson Mandela University; Dr Eugenia Kafanabo and the Honourable Professor Kitila A. Mkumbo (MP) at the University of Dar es Salaam; and Professor Proscovia Namubiru Ssentamu at the Uganda Management Institute. The unwavering support from the leadership and Schools/Faculties of Education at all host institutions has been invaluable—CERM-ESA's achievements would not have been possible without this institutional backing.

Finally, we are immensely grateful for the generous support provided by the German Academic Exchange Service (DAAD) with funds from the Federal Foreign Office (AA). The sustained funding, material and non-material support, particularly from Dr Dorothee Weyler, Dr Helmut Blumbach, Isabell Mering, and Eva Rothenpieler-Dione, have been instrumental in ensuring the success and longevity of CERM-ESA's activities. Your solidarity and team spirit has been truly appreciated.

Introduction

Paul Webb, Editor in chief

The Centre for Educational Research Methodologies and Management in East and South Africa (CERM-ESA) has evolved as an exemplar of collaborative innovation and transformative impact across the African continent. Anchored by the partnership of five universities from Germany (University of Oldenburg), East Africa (Moi University, the University of Dar es Salaam, and the Uganda Management Institute) and South Africa (Nelson Mandela University), CERM-ESA is committed to nurturing a future-oriented educational culture while fostering mutual learning and growth among its stakeholders.

At the heart of CERM-ESA's mission lies a dedication to strengthening higher education at postgraduate level. Positioned within the overall network of 'Centres of African Excellence,' supported by the German Academic Exchange Service (DAAD) with funds from the Federal Foreign Office of Germany, CERM-ESA provides a model of strategic intervention aimed at elevating the quality of education and expanding research capacities on the African continent.

With a rich tapestry of achievements encompassing higher education research projects, ongoing capacity-building initiatives, and a continuum of professional development opportunities, CERM-ESA stands as an example of what collaborative scholarship and collective vision can achieve. As it continues to redefine educational paradigms and empower future generations, CERM-ESA strives to exemplify the transformative potential of education as a catalyst for positive change. Over time, CERM-ESA has earned acclaim as a trusted advisor to education policymakers, actively contributing to shaping the trajectory of educational reform. Specifically, through collaborative initiatives with the Ministry of Education in Kenya and the establishment of a Dean's Forum across the country (Kenya), CERM-ESA has earned its status as a respected player in shaping educational policy and practice.

As one of thirteen Centres of Excellence in sub-Saharan Africa, each tailored to address the disciplinary focus area of the Centres in each host university, CERM-ESA distinguishes itself with its primary focus on modernising educational paradigms. The chapters in this book highlight some of the work done by CERM-ESA (DAAD) scholarship holders that are the result of cultivating robust networks across German, East African and South African partners.

In the realm of higher education, CERM-ESA scholarship holders embarked on a journey of exploration and innovation, delving into diverse facets of educational practice, research and pedagogy through collaborative inquiry and scholarly reflection, including co-supervision of postgraduate research across the participating universities. The work of the scholarship holders in this book (all but Chapter 15) illuminates an evolving landscape of academia and its impact on society. The first part of the book focuses on current issues in higher education at African universities, while the second part presents findings from school-based research and school–society interactions. Several of the chapters explore research methods that specifically respond to the contextual conditions of the East and South African education sites, in order to increase the relevance for these contexts. The final review chapter by Michael Anthony Samuel critiques the portrayal of Africa as needing saviours, emphasising that solutions already exist within local projects that go beyond elitist and external agendas.

Issues in higher education at African universities

Noel Japheth and Mercy Chemutai Barasa, with John Chang'ach and Susan Kurgat, CERM-ESA Project Leader and Project Coordinator at Moi University respectively, examined the case of the East and South African-German Centre of Excellence for Educational Research Methodologies and Management (CERM-ESA) through the lens of collaborative teaching and learning in higher education postgraduate research.

Janet Ronoh and I explored the intricate interplay between traditional wisdom and contemporary education. Our study investigated the efficacy of an indigenous methodology with teacher educators. The findings shed light on the potential of indigenous wisdom to enrich and contextualize educational experiences, fostering a deeper understanding of cultural heritage and identity.

In the field of engineering education, Curwyn Mapaling and colleagues interrogated the resilience of students in the face of academic challenges. Through quantitative inquiry, they tried to understand the factors that contribute to academic resilience among engineering students at a South African university. Their findings inform strategies for fostering student success and well-being, empowering future generations of engineers to thrive in a rapidly evolving world.

Beyond the confines of the university campus our scholarship holders engaged with pressing environmental issues, exploring the intersections of education, climate change, and sustainability. At Makerere University in Uganda, David Ssekamatte et al. collaborated with faculty and students to examine training and research interventions aimed at addressing climate change and promoting sustainability. Through participatory inquiry, they examined the perspectives and experiences of stakeholders, informing holistic approaches to environmental education and advocacy. Nelson Mandela and his co-investigators explored university-community engagement opportunities to address climate change issues in African contexts.

Cornelius Kipleting Rugut grappled with the dynamics of the student–supervisor relationship as doctoral students navigate the complexities of their academic journey.

Through qualitative inquiry, he explored the experiences of doctoral candidates in African universities, shedding light on the challenges and opportunities inherent in the supervision process. His insights inform strategies for enhancing support structures and fostering academic success.

Findings from school-based research and school–society interactions

In the broader context of society and education, Dorothy Nakiyaga and her fellow researchers examined the complex dynamics of school management and community engagement. Through exploratory factor analysis they investigated stakeholder participation in school management and its impact on academic achievement in Ugandan secondary schools. Lily Yego and her co-researchers investigated the effectiveness of participatory visual methods in broaching sensitive topics such as sexuality, HIV and AIDS education, and fostering inclusive and empowering learning environments in Kenyan classrooms.

Annah Atuhaire et al. delved into the perceptions of children in street situations in Kampala, Uganda, advocating for their inclusion in mainstream education and challenging societal stereotypes and prejudices. Naomi Mworia confronted the scourge of gender-based violence in Nairobi's informal settlements, seeking to amplify the voices of marginalised girls and promote pathways to safety and empowerment. Through innovative pedagogies and culturally appropriate approaches, Simon Ekiru and his co-authors deconstructed gender stereotypes in order to promote gender equity in the classroom.

Evans Mos Olao, Bernard Misigo and Karsten Speck used participatory visual methods to teach character education in early childhood in Kenya and concluded that participatory visual methods are innovative approaches which are child-friendly and offer an alternative for better teaching and learning of character education in early childhood settings.

In the realm of primary education, Sarah Jemutai explored the transformative potential of play-based learning in developing digital literacy among pupils in Kenyan schools. She deduced that, through the play way method, educators can empower students to become active participants in their learning, fostering creativity, critical thinking, and technological fluency.

Finally, in the context of teaching biology, Ayanda Simayi and I navigated the complexities of taboo issues, exploring culturally appropriate linguistic responses to sensitive topics. Simayi's research underscores the importance of cultural sensitivity and inclusivity in educational practice, fostering dialogue and understanding across and within cultural contexts.

Michael Anthony Samuel's review chapter critiques the portrayal of Africa as needing saviours outside the continent, emphasising that solutions already exist within local projects that go beyond elitist and external agendas. He questions the design, purpose, and beneficiaries of educational research, highlighting the need for collaborative efforts at various levels of the education system.

The chapter is divided into two parts. Part A reviews the anthology "Education research in African contexts" within the context of the African Union's Agenda 2063, showing how the CERM-ESA project supports continental transformation. Part B examines CERM-ESA's institutional research, focusing on higher education and school–society studies.

He notes that the CERM-ESA project addresses the goals of the African Union's Agenda 2063, particularly through its collaborative and evidence-based research efforts across Africa. He also highlights the importance of people-centred, localised research that challenges traditional and external models, recognising that the CERM-ESA project respects diverse pedagogical traditions and advocates for gender equity and youth empowerment. However, he also points out the need for broader systemic support and macro-level interventions to sustain meaningful change and calls for more critical, locally relevant research that transcends imitation of external models and promotes deep, transformative dialogue within the African context.

Collectively, the narratives in this book offer a rich tapestry of African scholarship and inquiry, illuminating the multifaceted intersections of education, society, and culture. Through the CERM-ESA approach to research, our scholarship holders were able to strive to advance knowledge, promote equality, and empower individuals and communities to thrive in an ever-changing world.

CHAPTER 1

A reflection on collaborative teaching and learning in higher education: The case of the East and South African-German Centre of Excellence for Educational Research Methodologies and Management

Noel Japheth, John K. Chang'ach, Susan Kurgat, Mercy Chemutai Barasa

Introduction

In sub-Saharan Africa, institutions of higher learning are advocating for a paradigm shift in graduate teaching and research, emphasising the need for increased partnerships, support and adherence to international standards (Skupien & Rüffin, 2020; Beaudry et al., 2018). This chapter explores a partnership, facilitated over ten years by the East and South African-German Centre of Excellence for Educational Research Methodologies and Management (CERM-ESA), and which is aligned with collaborative learning principles.

One may ask, 'why should one explore such partnerships?'. The answer is that they set the stage for examining the educational initiatives facilitated by four African and one German higher education institution, namely Moi University, Nelson Mandela University, Uganda Management Institute, University of Dar es Salaam and University of Oldenburg under the umbrella of the CERM-ESA project (2014–2023). These partnerships are examined through the lens of collaborative learning theory with its social constructivist principles of peer learning, reciprocal teaching, shared knowledge and resources, interdependence and group processing. (O'Donnell & Hmelo-Silver, 2013). Through that lens we aim to reflect on the question of whether the CERM-ESA activities that leverage collaborative learning theory to address the teaching and research capacity challenges in sub-Saharan Africa can be successful. By exploring the integration of collaborative learning principles in CERM-ESA teaching and learning designs, one can evaluate their effectiveness in enhancing teaching and research skills, improving research outcomes, and addressing capacity gaps in African higher education institutions. This analysis contributes to a deeper understanding of the role of collaborative learning theory in shaping educational practices and promoting research capacity development in sub-Saharan Africa. Evaluating the outcomes and impact of the activities enables us to judge whether the framework can be further refined by others and adapted to different contexts, contributing to improved research, education and development in the region.

As such, this chapter aims to examine the educational practices and partnerships established by CERM-ESA. Analysing these initiatives allows one to assess the extent to which CERM-ESA's educational programmes, partnerships, and activities facilitate peer interaction, reciprocal teaching, knowledge sharing, and other collaborative work among students and faculty members.

CERM-ESA expected outcomes

The expected outcomes of the CERM-ESA activities encompass a range of benefits, including enhanced teaching and research capacity at the postgraduate level, improved research quality and completion rates among graduate students, the cultivation of a collaborative learning culture in higher education, and increased scholarly interaction and knowledge exchange. These outcomes can be assessed through various means, such as tracking students' success and research outputs, monitoring completion rates, evaluating skills development, and assessing the impact of CERM-ESA activities on research capacity and scholarly interaction.

Aligned with collaborative learning theory, which posits that collaborative learning enhances students' higher-level thinking, oral communication, self-management, and leadership skills (Johnson & Johnson, 1999), CERM-ESA initiatives aim to foster deeper understanding and critical thinking. This is achieved by encouraging participants to actively engage with course material through peer-to-peer and peer-to-educator interactions. Both students and lecturers, who meet in that collaborative space, come from a variety of institutional, national and cultural backgrounds.

In practice, CERM-ESA focuses on several key areas and activities to promote collaborative learning principles. Capacity building workshops and training sessions aim to equip lecturers and supervisors with enhanced supervision skills and innovative didactics. Additionally, jointly developed academic master's and doctoral programmes provide support for students, exposing them to diverse perspectives and research methodologies. Seminars and colloquiums offer platforms for knowledge sharing and discussions between students, alumni and faculty, facilitated mainly by online technologies.

Research schools provide intensive training in research methodologies, while co-supervision and cohort supervision practices involve multiple supervisors from different universities, encouraging diverse perspectives and collaboration among students and academics. Peer mentorship activities further support collaboration and mutual assistance among students through peer-to-peer interactions. Overall, these initiatives align with collaborative learning theory by promoting active engagement, peer interaction, knowledge sharing, reciprocal teaching, communication, and leadership skills within the academic community.

Collaborative learning theory

Collaborative learning theory, as elucidated by Johnson and Johnson (1999), posits that group learning serves as a catalyst for the development of students' higher-level cognitive skills, oral communication abilities, self-management competencies, and leadership qualities. This approach to learning is grounded in the principle that collaborative interactions among peers facilitate deeper understanding and critical thinking.

In the context of higher education, collaborative learning emphasises active engagement with course material through peer-to-peer interactions. By working together in groups, students can exchange ideas, challenge assumptions, and collectively solve problems. This process not only enhances their comprehension of the subject matter but also cultivates essential skills that are valuable beyond the classroom.

Research supports the efficacy of collaborative learning in promoting higher order thinking skills. For example, a study by Slavin (1995) found that students engaged in collaborative learning activities demonstrated greater gains in critical thinking abilities compared to those in traditional instructional settings. This finding underscores the value of peer-to-peer interactions in stimulating intellectual growth and fostering analytical reasoning. Furthermore, De Hei et al. (2020) found that intercultural competence can be enhanced through collaborative group activities in international higher education settings, if the quality of collaboration is perceived as high, meaning that all group members can contribute, which depends on the nature of the task.

Moreover, collaborative learning fosters the development of oral communication skills. Through discussions, debates, and presentations within group settings, students learn to articulate their ideas effectively, listen actively to their peers, and engage in constructive dialogue. These communication skills are essential not only for academic success but also for professional advancement in diverse fields (Aliyu, 2017).

Self-management is another key area of growth facilitated by collaborative learning experiences. Working collaboratively requires students to take responsibility for their contributions to group tasks, manage their time effectively, and coordinate efforts with team members. By assuming these roles, students develop self-discipline, organizational skills, and the ability to work autonomously – a crucial aspect of lifelong learning and professional development (Sharan & Sharan, 2021).

Furthermore, collaborative learning provides a platform for the cultivation of leadership skills. Within group settings, students can take on leadership roles, delegate tasks, and motivate their peers towards common goals. This experience nurtures leadership qualities such as effective communication, decision-making, conflict resolution, and teamwork – attributes that are highly prized in academic, professional, and social contexts (Johnson et al., 2000).

In summary, collaborative learning theory is said to underscore the transformative potential of group interactions in education by engaging students in peer-to-peer and peer-to-lecturer activities. Collaborative learning fosters deeper understanding, critical thinking, oral communication, self-management, and leadership skills. These skills are said to not only enhance academic performance but also empower students and staff to thrive in an increasingly complex and interconnected world.

Activities

As noted earlier, the expected outcomes of CERM-ESA activities include enhanced teaching and research capacity at postgraduate level, cultivation of a collaborative learning culture in higher education and increased scholarly interaction and knowledge exchange. The activities, all of which have components of collaborative learning, are described below.

Academic programme

CERM-ESA established academic programmes aim at addressing the research capacity gaps in African higher education institutions (Gaillard, 2010). The Master of Education in Research and Doctor of Philosophy in Educational Research and Evaluation programmes were designed collaboratively with academics from Nelson Mandela and Moi Universities, the Universities of Oldenburg and Dar es Salaam, and the Uganda Management Institute. They aim to equip students with advanced research skills, promote collaboration and expose students to diverse perspectives and research methodologies, in an effort to enhance their research capabilities. The CERM-ESA academic programme has been in operation for the full ten years of the project's funding and beyond and is based at Moi University.

Research schools, co-supervision, cohort supervision support, and peer mentorship

In collaboration with partnering institutions, CERM-ESA offers international research schools that aim at providing students with comprehensive training in research methodologies and academic skills. These schools cover a wide range of topics, including theoretical frameworks, data analysis, and research dissemination strategies. Facilitated by experts from various disciplines and countries, the research schools promote collaboration and provide students with valuable international exposure. These research schools have run annually throughout the life of the CERM-ESA project with venues alternating annually between Kenya and South Africa. They include reciprocal teaching sessions where students, alumni and lecturers take turns to facilitate learning, e.g. through group discussions, presenting their research proposals, methodologies or findings and engaging with each other's work.

The concept of co-supervision, implemented by CERM-ESA, involves assigning multiple supervisors to guide students throughout the research process. This approach fosters international exchange and exposure to diverse research environments, leading to improved research outcomes and reduced completion times for graduate students. Through international collaboration, CERM-ESA aims to move participating academics in Africa towards co-supervision practice, which should result in enhanced research supervision and higher completion rates among students. Co-supervision has been in place since the inception of the project.

CERM-ESA also implements cohort supervision, whereby students work in groups with academics and experts during research schools. This collaborative approach encourages peer learning and knowledge sharing, allowing students to address research challenges collectively. They also have the potential to reduce power dynamics between supervisors and their students, as various perspectives and a range of expertise are included to guide the student in their research journey. By identifying and addressing knowledge gaps, cohort supervision promotes scholarly interaction and research commitment among students.

Finally, CERM-ESA promotes peer mentorship among students, facilitating support and collaboration throughout the graduate research journey and beyond. Peer mentorship activities with active involvement of CERM-ESA's alumni, including mock presentations and peer-to-peer research events, have given students the opportunity to improve their research quality and likelihood of success within the programme. By fostering a supportive academic community, peer mentorship aims at enhancing the overall research experience for CERM-ESA students.

Capacity Building for Lecturers and Supervisors (CABLES) programme

The Capacity Building for Lecturers and Supervisors (CABLES) programme, initiated by CERM-ESA, served as a catalyst for promoting collaborative learning by academics from the DAAD Centres of Excellence in Africa, in other words, key players within sub-Saharan Africa's higher education landscape. The programme focused on strengthening supervision skills, innovative didactics, management of transdisciplinary processes, and research project management, and targeted lecturers and supervisors involved in guiding graduate students, aiming to enhance their capacity in research supervision and management.

The southern African CABLES programme included four African-German Centres of Excellence, namely the Namibian-German Centre of Excellence for Logistics (NUST), the South African-German Centre of Excellence for Development Research (UWC); the South African-German Centre of Excellence for Criminal Justice (UWC); and the East and South African-German Centre of Excellence for Educational Research Methodologies and Management. A total of 21 academics from these Centres of Excellence took part in the programme.

The west African programme run in Accra included 30 participants from the following five African-German Centres of Excellence, namely the West African-German Centre of Excellence for Governance for Sustainable and Integrative Local Development, the West African-German Centre of Excellence for Sustainable Rural Transformation, the Congolese-German Centre of Excellence for Microfinance, the Ghanaian-German Centre of Excellence for Development Studies and included a participant from the Namibian-German Centre of Excellence for Logistics who had missed the southern African workshop. As many of the delegates where from French speaking African countries, on-site interpreters were provided.

The East African programme included 26 academics from all of the East African Centres of Excellence: namely the Tanzanian-German Centre of Excellence for Law in Dar es Salaam, the Kenyan-German Centre of Excellence for Mining, the Centre for Environmental Engineering and Resource Management at Taita Taveta University College in Voi, the Centre of Excellence for ICT in East Africa in Arusha, and East African CERM-ESA partners at Moi University, University of Dar es Salaam (UDSM) and the Uganda Management Institute. This mix aimed at generating a diverse constellation of views which provided a framework for constructive and fruitful engagement over a range of issues that these academics face when supervising and teaching at their home institutions.

The CABLES interventions operated during 2018 and 2019 and were replaced by online cooperation via the DIGI-FACE (digiface.org) platform with the advent of COVID.

Online teaching and learning

The DIGI-FACE project was initiated in late 2019 and it was agreed with the DAAD that the areas covered by the CABLES project be put online as generic modules that can be used by all disciplines in the African Centres of Excellence. These online modules were designed to encourage online cooperation via forums, peer review where applicable, Zoom sessions and shared reflections. The online modules were conceptualised and designed based on the collaborative approach to teaching and learning that had guided the on-site activities. Numerous offerings of these generic online modules by DIGI-FACE and CERM-ESA have furthered the collaboration between members of the Centres of Excellence at African universities.

Design and methods

As this chapter is based on processes that were not specifically designed as research, a bricolage approach is taken. Phillimore et al. (2016) note that bricolage research treats objects of inquiry as part of a historically situated complex system. The bricolage literature highlights the importance of diverse knowledge and practical skills. Bricoleurs rely on their own expertise and social networks due to limited resources. Bricolage is seen as inherently innovative, offering a way to cope with complexity and uncertainty by adapting quickly to changing environments (Phillimore et al., 2016).

As such, data are interpreted in ways that build bridges between individuals' concrete experiences and concepts that draw from larger social, historical, economic and political forces. Phillimore et al. state that "While some see bricolage as an opportunity, others view it more as a second-best option, perhaps the kind of process that individuals or firms adopt in the early stages of addressing a challenge" (Phillimore et al., 2016, p. 1).

Kincheloe (2005) applied this concept in educational research, using it to describe the utilization of multiple research methods from scarce resources. In this framework various methodological approaches are combined within a broader theoretical and critical pedagogical context. As Phillimore et al. (2016) note, it may be seen as a 'second best option'; in the case of the ten-year lifespan, it is the only option.

Academic programme

The master's and PhD programmes, offered collaboratively by CERM-ESA partnering institutions, exposed students to diverse perspectives and research methodologies to enhance their research capabilities. At the heart of the collaborative aspect were the annual international research schools, two-week long intensive learning phases that included a visit to one of the partner institutions. Facilitated by experts from various disciplines and countries, the research schools promoted collaboration and provided students with valuable international exposure. This exposure included a range of methodologies, both qualitative and quantitative.

The cooperative aspect was not specifically evaluated for the CERM-ESA academic programme but can be inferred from overall evaluations and first-hand experiences of the authors, supervisors and students.

At the end of each research school, the students submitted their evaluations consisting of 54 closed and three open-ended questions. The questionnaires covered aspects of the perceived knowledge and skills acquisition, the learning environment and interactions with peers, lecturers and supervisors as well as the topics and methods that were included in the programme. Data were generated from a total of 190 participants over a ten-year period.

During the last months of 2023, CERM-ESA carried out a tracer study to find out where its graduates had been placed in terms of their careers, and how they rated CERM-ESA's academic programme from the position of a professional. Data were generated from 50 alumni.

CERM-ESA co-supervision practice

The co-supervision practice started with the first cohort of CERM-ESA master's students and was implemented for all following master's cohorts. The PhD students generally had their supervisors at the host institutions but participated in the cohort supervision model where they received support and guidance from CERM-ESA faculty of all partner institutions.

Of all the collaborative activities within the CERM-ESA project, the co-supervision of master's students turned out to be the most difficult aspect that needed the project leaders' intervention in some cases and the formalisation of duties and expectations in a 'Co-Supervision Agreement'.

CABLES workshops

There were three week-long face-to-face CABLES workshops held, one in South Africa for the southern African DAAD Centre of Excellence (at the Nelson Mandela University), one in Accra, Ghana for west African Centres and one was held in Zanzibar for east African Centres over 2018/2019. The Centres of Excellence nominated their participants. The programme was evaluated at each workshop quantitatively and qualitatively in two questionnaires. The quantitative questionnaire provided indicators of overall levels of satisfaction (part one), agreement on statements about expectations met (part two) and the participants' perceptions as to the level to which the CABLES programme contributed to the expansion of their skills and cooperation (parts three and four). The qualitative questionnaire consisted of twelve open-ended questions on various academic and organizational aspects, such as the most inspiring learning outcomes of the CABLES programme. These questionnaires were completed on the last day of the CABLES workshop. Data were generated from a total of 77 participants.

Online teaching and learning

With the onset of COVID in 2020, and the opportunity to use the DIGI-FACE platform, many of the teaching and learning resources developed via the academic programme, research schools and CABLES workshops were used to provide online courses and resources. Each of the online generic and mini-module evaluations offered had a question, among many others, related to feeling part of a group and collaboration. These standard and structured online evaluation questionnaires using a four-point scale were filled in anonymously by the participants and analysed at the end of each course. The section that pertains specifically to this chapter is the question about feeling a part of the group and enjoying interacting with their peers and the facilitators. The choices were (i) felt part of a group and enjoyed interacting with the other students, (ii) part of a group even though I didn't communicate directly with anyone, (iii) somewhat isolated from the other course participants or (iv) totally isolated from the other course participants.

Results

Academic programme and research schools

Since its inception, the academic programme has enrolled more than 100 postgraduate students in multiple cohorts, with a significant portion funded by DAAD and CERM-ESA. The programmes produced 73 graduates (59 master's and 14 PhDs) by December 2023, some of whom demonstrated high-quality research outputs, some winning best master's thesis awards across the humanities. Others secured employment in both county and national governmental and non-governmental organizations in east Africa (14%), others have become lecturers in higher education (16%), have continued with a PhD after their master's degree (16%) or taken school leadership positions (11%). The aforementioned figures are based on CERM-ESA's internal tracer study conducted in 2023. These success indicators, although not being able to be causally tied directly to these programmes over a number of cohorts, suggest the importance of international collaboration and innovative teaching approaches in enhancing research capacity in sub-Saharan Africa, something that was at the core of the development of the academic programme.

When asked in an evaluation questionnaire during the CERM-ESA research schools 'How satisfied were you in terms of working with your peers?', 70% of the students were very satisfied and 30% were satisfied. No negative data were given. When asked 'How satisfied were you with the group work in class?', more than 75% recorded 'very satisfied' and the rest said 'satisfied', with no negative responses recorded.

The following are examples of what the participants wrote when asked what they liked most about the research schools:

"The sessions were interactive."

"The activities were very engaging. it was good sharing my proposal and having guidance."

"I really enjoyed the physical interaction with my peers together with advisors."

"Getting feedback on my proposal and getting a clear focus. I also liked the interaction with the facilitators and peers with regard to conducting credible research."

"The interaction with peers and listening to their research journeys was motivational to me."

"The connection between the facilitators and the students while sharing problems and how it was a conducive environment for students to share their research shortcomings and challenges with their supervisors one on one."

"That students were allowed to share their work with very minimal pressure."

"It is the feedback we received from facilitators and students as well as kind of mentorship from our facilitators and all the organizing team."

"I was really touched by the humanizing pedagogy and how we as teachers should be agents of hope and social change. Anchored on Paulo Freire, Pedagogy of the Oppressed, education should be a means to building a "critical consciousness" that would enable people to create change in their lives. This was practised by our professors and supervisors all through the research school. Thank you for passing on the power and the influence whole heartedly to us the young scholars with the pre-requisite 21st century research skills. The humble nature of CERM-ESA makes me feel am at home."

"I liked the level of interaction between facilitators and learners, it was excellent."

"Getting so many different experiences, skills, opinions together."

"Collaborative approaches to capacity development and digitisation."

"The interactions amongst the students including meeting students from different countries and the possibility of "getting advice from well-known academic writers and researchers from all over South and North."

CERM-ESA co-supervision practice

All of the master's and a number of doctoral students were co-supervised by at least two supervisors from different universities within the CERM-ESA programme. The success rate of CERM-ESA scholarship holders was very high in terms of completion rate (nearly 100%), stipulated time frame (80%) and achievements (CERM-ESA students have consistently scored higher on average than other master's graduates at the participating universities).

CABLES programme

Some of the results of the evaluations are presented below. As noted above, three aspects relate to the quantitative questionnaire, namely (1) level of satisfaction, (2) overall fulfilment of expectations and (3) extension of skills. The qualitative results are presented in conjunction with the quantitative results, as they complement each other.

In part three and four of the questionnaire, the participants were given several statements which all referred to their extension of skills in the four main topics of the programme, namely postgraduate supervision, research coherence, curriculum development and interpersonal competencies for excellent teaching. Scores again ranged from 1 (strongly disagree) to 4 (strongly agree).

Four variables were created, which summarize the mean scores of the participants' answers to the individual statements. The mean scores of the participants' answers to the different statements were very close to each other, as were the mean scores of the new variables formed from the statements. All four topics received high indicators for the enhancement of the participants' skills with mean values of 3.5 and 3.6.

Figure 1: *Representation of the Extension of Skills Indicated by the Participants as a Four-point Scale*

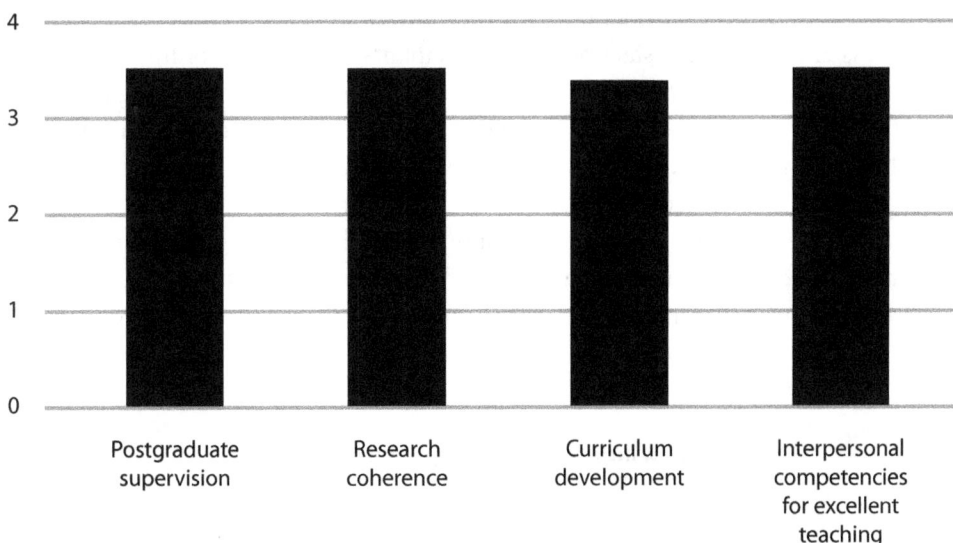

There were many and detailed comments from the participants on the four specific topics that also show the satisfaction with the presentations and contents of the programme. Postgraduate supervision and research coherence were frequently mentioned as topics of particular interest and/or usefulness to participants in the CABLES programme sessions. In the area of postgraduate supervision, the 'supervision models' used for creating cooperation were positively highlighted by the participants.

When it comes to the most inspiring learning outcomes of the participants, comments about interpersonal skills for excellent teaching are especially common. Participants were grateful for the "pedagogical approaches" which are helpful in "*developing emotional relationships with student[s]*" and noted that they had acquired "*[s]kills and knowledge [for] making a difference in the lives of students through interpersonal engagement with them*". One participant wrote: "*You have impacted me to take into account the human aspect of supervision – we are first human and then we are supervising the student.*" Another important aspect noted by the participants in this area was the "*ways of reducing the power imbalance.*"

Individual written comments included, among many others:

"*All sessions were motivating captivating and professional and rigorously prepared*".

"*I find all of the sessions extremely useful to my work*", and

"*It made me reflect on my own way of supervising and being a scholar*".

Online teaching and learning

The evaluations that were part of each course offered online not only revealed that there was high overall satisfaction with the courses in terms of both their general usefulness and general satisfaction. The participants' anonymous online evaluation responses were very positive with over 80% agreeing or strongly agreeing that they found the courses useful and that they were satisfied with the courses and the way that they were presented. A similar pattern was found in terms of the participants feeling a part of the group and enjoying interacting with their peers and the facilitators. The first 100 questionnaire responses are shown in Figure 2. The positive responses to feelings of cooperation and inclusion remained a theme overall in all other evaluations made in terms of online courses.

Figure 2: *Evaluation Responses to Feelings of Inclusion and cooperation (n=100)*

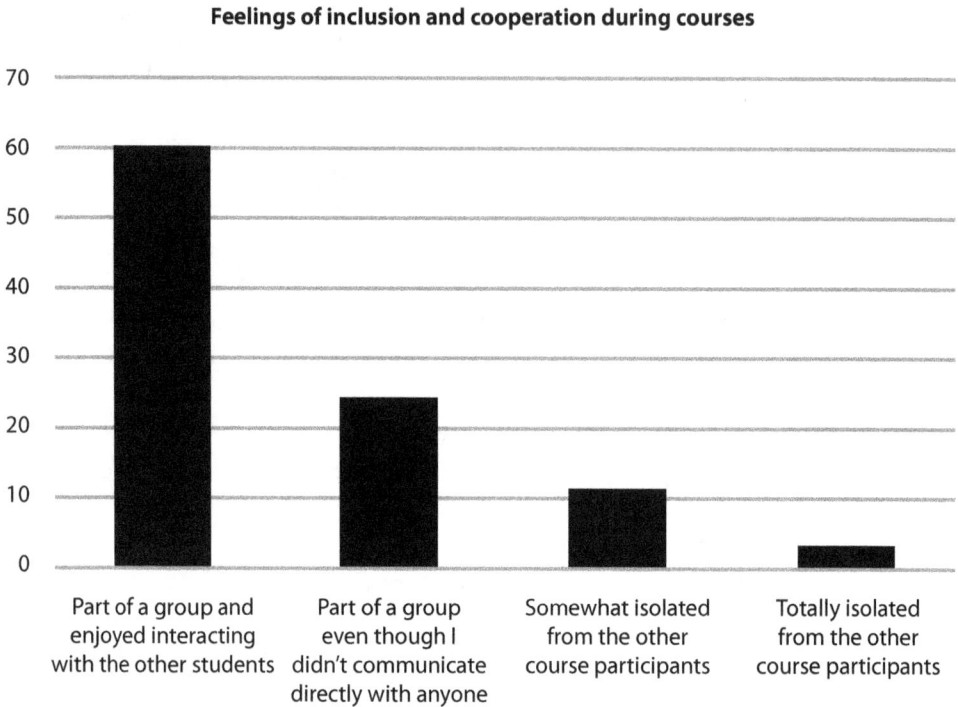

Feelings of inclusion and cooperation during courses

Discussion

The bricolage of results, anecdotes and feelings recorded above suggest that the issue of cooperation was of major importance to the CERM-ESA project. Some may feel that the bricolage approach used in this chapter may be weak, and this criticism is accepted by the authors. Nevertheless, their experience with the project over ten years leads them to believe that the finding is as accurate as it can be under the circumstances and that it is important to note that CERM-ESA's holistic approach does appear to promote collaborative learning theory within sub-Saharan Africa's higher education context.

Similarly, academic programmes like the Master of Education in Research and Doctor of Philosophy in Educational Research and Evaluation, offered in collaboration with Moi University and other institutions, has promoted interdisciplinary collaboration and peer learning (Gaillard, 2010). These programmes have exposed students to diverse research methodologies, enhancing their higher-level thinking and oral communication skills.

The Capacity Building for Lecturers and Supervisors (CABLES) programme, initiated by the Centre of Excellence for Educational Research Methodologies and Management (CERM-ESA), addresses the critical need to enhance research capacity among academic staff in sub-Saharan Africa (Owusu et al., 2014). By providing workshops and training sessions, CABLES equips participants with advanced supervision skills, fostering a collaborative learning environment through peer-to-peer interactions and knowledge exchange (Petrie et al., 2015; Ali et al., 2017; Amde et al., 2014).

Regular seminars, colloquiums, and international research schools organized by CERM-ESA provide platforms for students and faculty members to share research findings and engage in scholarly discussions (Madsen & Adriansen, 2020; Barasa & Omulando, 2018). Leveraging online technologies facilitated peer-to-peer learning and resolution of research challenges, fostering a collaborative learning environment.

Implementation of co-supervision practices and cohort supervision approaches within CERM-ESA programmes also enhanced collaborative learning experiences (Ramadhan et al., 2023; Paul et al., 2014). By assigning multiple supervisors and fostering peer mentorship activities, students benefitted from international exchange and diverse research environments, promoting knowledge sharing and research commitment.

In conclusion, CERM-ESA's holistic approach appears to have promoted collaborative learning theory within sub-Saharan Africa's higher education context, and fostered a culture of collaboration, knowledge exchange and peer support (Singh, 2015; Barrett et al., 2011; Kindiki et al., 2019). By advancing research capacity and academic excellence it can be said that CERM-ESA has contributed to addressing challenges in graduate education and enhanced research outcomes in the region via collaborative teaching and learning.

References
Ali, F., Shet, A., Yan, W., Al-Maniri, A., Atkins, S., & Lucas, H. (2017). Doctoral level research and training capacity in the social determinants of health at universities and higher education institutions in India, China, Oman, and Vietnam: A survey of needs. *Health Research Policy and Systems, 15*(1), 1–11. https://doi.org/10.1186/s12961-017-0225-5

Aliyu, M. M. (2017). Developing oral communication skills through collaborative learning: Implications for Nigerian teachers. *International Journal of English Literature and Social Sciences, 2*(5), 127–130.

Amde, W. K., Sanders, D., & Lehmann, U. (2014). Building capacity to develop an African teaching platform on health workforce development: A collaborative initiative of universities from four sub-Saharan countries. *Human Resources for Health, 12*(31), 1–11.

Barasa, P. L., & Omulando, C. (2018). *Research and PhD capacities in Sub-Saharan Africa: Kenya report.* British Council and DAAD. http://erepository.au.ac.ke/handle/123456789/399

Barrett, A. M., Crossley, M., & Dachi, H. A. (2011). International collaboration and research capacity building: Learning from the EdQual experience. *Comparative Education, 47*(1), 25–43. https://doi.org/10.1080/03050068.2011.541674

Beaudry, C., Mouton, J., & Prozesky, H. (Eds.). (2018). *The next generation of scientists in Africa.* African Minds. https://doi.org/10.47622/978-1-928331-93-3

de Hei, M., Tabacaru, C., Sjoer, E., Rippe, R., & Walenkamp, J. (2020). Developing intercultural competence through collaborative learning in international higher education. *Journal of Studies in International Education, 24*(2), 190–211.

Gaillard, J. C. (2010). Vulnerability, capacity and resilience: Perspectives for climate and development policy. *Journal of International Development, 22*, 218–232. http://dx.doi.org/10.1002/jid.1675

Hmelo-Silver, C. E., & Chinn, C. A. (2015). Collaborative learning. In *Handbook of educational psychology* (pp. 363–377). Routledge.

Johnson, D. W., & Johnson, R. T. (1999). *Learning together and alone: Cooperative, competitive, and individualistic learning* (5th ed.). Allyn & Bacon.

Johnson, D. W., Johnson, R. T., & Stanne, M. B. (2000). Cooperative learning methods: A meta-analysis. University of Minnesota.

Kincheloe, J. L. (2005). On to the next level: Continuing the conceptualization of the bricolage. *Qualitative Inquiry, 11*(3), 323–350. https://doi.org/10.1177/1077800405275056

Kindiki, J., von Möllendorff, M., Speck, K., & Webb, P. (2019). African-German collaboration for decolonising higher education: CERM-ESA approaches and lessons learnt. *Zeitschrift für internationale Bildungsforschung und Entwicklungspädagogik (ZEP)/ Journal for International Educational Research and Development Education), 42*(2), 11–15.

Madsen, L. M., & Adriansen, H. K. (2020). Transnational research capacity building: Whose standards count? *Critical African Studies, 13*(1), 49–55. https://doi.org/10.1080/21681392.2020.1724807

O'Donnell, A. M., & Hmelo-Silver, C. E. (2013). Introduction: What is collaborative learning? An overview. In *The international handbook of collaborative learning* (pp. 1–15). Routledge.

Owusu, F., Kalipeni, E., & Kiiru, J. M. M. (2014). *Capacity building for research leadership: The need, support, and strategies for growing African research leaders.* Partnership for African Social and Governance Research. http://www.pasgr.org/wp-content/uploads/2016/05/PASGR-Research-Leadership-Commissioned-Study_Mar-25.pdf

Paul, P., Olson, J. K., & Gul, R. B. (2014). Co-supervision of doctoral students: Enhancing the learning experience. *International Journal of Nursing Education Scholarship, 11*(1), 31–38. https://doi.org/10.1515/ijnes-2012-0004

Petrie, K., Lemke, G., Williams, A., Mitchell, B. G., Northcote, M., Anderson, M., & de Waal, K. (2015, Nov. 29–Dec. 3). *Professional development of research supervisors: A capacity-building, participatory framework* [Paper presentation]. Australian Association for Research in Education (AARE) Conference, Fremantle, Western Australia.

Phillimore, J., Humphris, R., Klass, F., & Knecht, M. (2016). Bricolage: Potential as a conceptual tool for understanding access to welfare in superdiverse neighbourhoods. *IRiS Working Paper Series* (14). Institute for Research into Superdiversity.

Ramadhan, L., Cassim, T., & Pather, I. (2023). A supervisor-led cohort model of supervising postgraduate students: A reflective account. In J. A. Smit & N. Ndimande-Hlongwa (Eds.), *Transforming postgraduate education in Africa* (pp. 1–32). Alternation African Scholarship Book Series.

Sharan, Y., & Sharan, S. (2021). Design for change: A teacher education project for cooperative learning and group investigation in Israel. In N. Davidson (Ed.), *Pioneering perspectives in cooperative learning: Theory, research, and classroom practice for diverse approaches to CL* (pp. 165–182). Routledge.

Singh, R. J. (2015). Challenges and successes of research capacity building at a rural South African university. *The South African Journal of Higher Education, 29*(3), 183–200.

Skupien, S., & Rüffin, N. (2020). The geography of research funding: Semantics and beyond. *Journal of Studies in International Education, 24*(1), 24–38. https://doi.org/10.1177/1028315319889896

Slavin, R. E. (1995). *Cooperative learning: Theory, research, and practice.* Prentice Hall.

CHAPTER 2

Exploring teacher educator views on place and position of indigenous knowledge in the school curriculum using an indigenous methodology

Janet Ronoh, Paul Webb

Introduction

Indigenous knowledge, with its local focus and cultural attribute-sharing community (Petzold et al., 2020; Wheeler & Root-Bernstein, 2020; Semali & Kincheloe, 1999), forms a comprehensive system influencing beliefs and decision-making (France, 1997). There has been a global paradigm shift towards recognising and incorporating indigenous knowledge into formal education systems. However, despite global interest, integrating indigenous knowledge (IK) into formal education faces challenges, particularly in Africa (Msila, 2016; Higgs, 2016). One of these challenges is attributed to the paucity of dialogic indigenous methodologies to generate authentic responses from indigenous stakeholders (da Silva et al., 2023; Kolawole, 2022).

As such, this chapter describes and interrogates a dialogic indigenous methodology that was used to investigate teacher educators' perceptions of indigenous knowledge that could be incorporated into the school curriculum in Kenya and South Africa. The dialogic indigenous methodology that was used was the *Imbizo/Baraza* method developed for Janet Ronoh's 2017 M.Ed. study.

Kenya and South Africa were chosen as the settings for several reasons, not least that they are hubs for the East and South African Centre of Excellence for Educational Research Methodologies and Management (CERM-ESA), a DAAD funded project of which Janet Ronoh was a scholarship holder.

Imbizo and *Baraza*

Imbizo is a Nguni word for a traditional community gathering called by the chief to solve pertinent community issues. Since the advent of democratic government in South Africa in 1994, the concept of *Imbizo* has been brought into the mainstream (Mabelebele, 2022). It denotes a participatory approach of engagement. It refers to the gathering of people sharing a common nationhood, clan or religion, with a view to discussing issues affecting their development as a group. A *Baraza* is similar to an *Imbizo* and commonly practised in Kenya, which, considering that the Xhosa and

Nandi were part of the Nguni people who migrated from sub-equatorial Central/ East Africa along the eastern part of Africa in their southward migration, is not surprising. Consequently, in both instances the *Imbizo* and *Baraza* sessions in this study were called by a senior member of the community (usually the chief, but in the context of the investigation, the Dean of Education in each case) to discuss the prompt stories offered both in the vernacular and English (see below) as well as issues around incorporating indigenous knowledge in the school curriculum.

Both *Imbizos* and *Barazas*, in South Africa and Kenya respectively, advocate for a dialogic community participatory approach in matters of governmental or cultural importance. The underpinnings of the *Imbizo/Baraza* methodology are to provide a safe, comfortable, and culturally recognisable environment.

Research problem

Authors like Higgs (2016) emphasise the importance of addressing issues related to the inclusion of indigenous knowledge (IK) in the school curriculum, particularly within the African context, with questions such as 'what IK should be learnt?' and 'how should knowledge be organized for teaching?' as well as 'what and how much of the content of indigenous African knowledge systems should be included in the curriculum?' and 'how shall this incorporation take place?' These are pivotal questions in discussions about curriculum reconstruction in Africa which have not been satisfactorily answered (Higgs, 2016).

In this context, arising from the fact that indigenous people are widely recognised as the principal custodians of their culture and knowledge, finding fruitful methodologies that generate authentic information from indigenous teacher educators for shaping the integration of IK into education is important. However, as noted above, a central challenge is the absence of a clearly defined indigenous methodology for eliciting indigenous knowledge from authoritative sources (da Silva et al., 2023; Kolawole, 2022; Higgs, 2016).

Consequently, this chapter, which is part of a larger study on perceptions of the place and position of indigenous knowledge, interrogates an alternative methodology used for investigating teacher educator perceptions concerning indigenous knowledge for inclusion in the school curricula in Kenya and South Africa.

The question focused on in this chapter is 'Do academics perceive the *Imbizo/ Baraza* methodology used in Ronoh's (2017) thesis for data generation as valuable?' In other words, 'do they consider it to be practically pertinent for research and culturally and contextually relevant?' The objective of this chapter is, therefore, to highlight whether teacher educators found the *Imbizo/Baraza* method useful as a research methodology when they used it themselves and whether it generated data that could be considered reliable. The reason for seeking answers to the above objective and research question is that the insights gained should provide information that could assist curriculum developers and teacher educators in making an informed decision as to the value of using an alternative methodology in African contexts when appropriate, namely the *Imbizo/Baraza* method.

Research design

This descriptive case study is underpinned by the view that the dialogic interaction allows the refining of intersubjective knowledge and informed consensus construction (Lopez de Aguileta et al., 2021). In order to stimulate the dialogic opportunity (the *Imbizo* and the *Baraza*), two short local contentious historical stories, written in English and translated to the local languages, were written as stimulus material for discussion during the *Imbizo/Baraza* interaction (which can be considered as culturally modified focus group discussions). As noted earlier, *Imbizo* is a Xhosa term understood by Xhosa people to refer to a meeting held at the chief or traditional leader's homestead when there is an issue to be discussed openly by the community members. The equivalent of an *Imbizo* in Kenya is called a *Baraza*. In this study, the *Baraza* and the *Imbizo* were used as a methodology for data generating as a form of modified focus group discussion in Kenya and South Africa.

The participants of the *Imbizo/Baraza* were given the stories in both paper-based and electronic text form and asked to read the story a week before attending an *Imbizo/Baraza*. The *Imbizo/Baraza* sessions included a discussion of the story and then discussions were held about the type, place and position of IK that could be incorporated in the school curriculum. This design was used to probe deeper understanding of the views and opinions of participants using the *Imbizo/Baraza* methodology as it allows stakeholders to freely engage in dialogue with reflective insights into their identification with the *Imbizo/Baraza* method when discussing IK and its value in relation to their history and the school curriculum. After the time for reading the stories had passed (a week) the dean at each institution called the participants to join in the *Imbizo/Baraza* process.

Methods

As noted above, the data gathering strategies for the study were *Imbizo/ Baraza* focus group dialogues, which were followed by individual interviews of a sample of the *Imbizo/Baraza* participants. The sampling technique used was purposive, with the aim of working with a sample size of 5-10 academics in each of the two universities' Education Faculties/Schools of Education who identify as Xhosa or Nandi. The research employed a descriptive case study research design and relied on qualitative data generated by the *Imbizo/Baraza* discussions that were then transcribed and translated for thematic analysis according to Tesch's method of open coding (Creswell, 2005).

Samples and settings

The study sites were the Nelson Mandela University and Moi University in South Africa and Kenya respectively. The reason for choosing these two universities is that both are part of the DAAD funded CERM-ESA project. Both universities have staff that is generally ethnically/culturally heterogeneous but there is one cultural/language group at each university which is indigenous to that area and also comprises the biggest group at each university. The investigation included 5-10 academics from these cultural/language groups in each of the two Faculties/Schools of Education representing both genders and a range of ages. In other words, the participants were all mother-tongue speakers of isiXhosa (Nelson Mandela University) and Nandi (Moi University). As such, the two universities provided cases of study that have similar institutional structures and situated in areas of each country that has a distinct ethnic majority.

As noted earlier, two short historical stories, written in English and translated to local languages, isiXhosa and Nandi respectively, were provided as stimulus material for the modified focus group discussion. The stories were about culturally sensitive topics and were translated into the local languages to enhance their authenticity and to capture any cultural meaning that might be lost when presented in English. The story items chosen were the historical/political issues of the cattle killing of 1856 by the AmaXhosa in the Eastern Cape of South Africa (for South African respondents) and the Nandi Resistance led by the Nandi warrior Koitalel Arap Samoei against the British in 1905 (for the Kenyan respondents). Both stories have powerful emotional impact and resonance amongst the Xhosa and Nandi people, respectively.

As noted, once the participants had read the story, the Deans of Education in each case called an *Imbizo* or a *Baraza*. The audio recorded discussion was guided by an open-ended protocol provided to the *Imbizo/Baraza* discussion leader (the dean) at the beginning of the sessions that emphasised the importance of everyone in the group contributing equally to the discussion and being included in a culturally 'safe' environment. In other words, being able to contribute within their cultural expectations within a culturally homogenous group (that is, members of the Xhosa or Nandi groupings). The *Imbizo/Baraza* approach was used as an attempt to 'Africanise' what were essentially focus group discussions and the stories were used as stimulus materials to encompass the studies within an indigenous and dialogic context.

Only the vernacular was used for discussions, a meal was served consisting of traditional cuisine, and all present at the *Imbizo/Baraza* were encouraged to participate and share their positions on the story that they had read as well as on issues of the relevance, place and position of indigenous knowledge in the school curriculum. No non-Xhosa or Nandi people were present. The sessions were recorded, then transcribed and translated by Xhosa and Nandi home language speakers.

The stimulus

The Xhosa story, written in English by one of the authors of this chapter, was translated by an isiXhosa native speaker and proofread by an elder isiXhosa speaker (respected and knowledgeable community member) to ensure that meaning was not lost in the process of translation. The English version of the Nandi resistance story, also written by one of the authors, was translated by the other researcher who is a Nandi native and who has full command of the Nandi language. The translation was proofread by a Nandi elder to ensure that meaning had also been preserved in the process of translation.

Conundrum of the cattle killing

The story used, namely the 'Conundrum of the Xhosa cattle killing', is a version of a well-known Xhosa historical event written in English by Jeff Peires, an eminent historian and advisor in Xhosa cultural issues (mostly royal genealogy). The story is about how two strangers appeared to two girls, one named Nongqawuse, in a field near the river. The strangers told the girls to go home and tell the whole Xhosa nation that their ancestors would rise from the dead and healthy, great herds of fat cattle would appear, the grain pits would be filled, and the white man would be driven from Xhosa land into the sea forever, but only if all living cattle were killed and no new crops sown. When Nongqawuse went back home and told this to her uncle, Mkhalaza, whose reputation as a prophet was growing, the word was believed and spread. Xhosa King Sarhili kaHintsa ordered the Xhosa people to kill their cattle with the expectation of a great uprising on 3 January 1857, when the sun would rise in the west.

On the expected day, nothing happened. The sun rose in the east. Thousands starved to death; survivors set off for the white towns where they signed contracts with Sir George Grey's administration for farm labour in exchange of food. The Xhosa people lost much of their land to the colonial government.

This cultural story has deep resonance with the Xhosa people and that is why it was used as a stimulus to encourage the participants to reflect on their indigenous experiences and focus on valued isiXhosa IK, talk about where in the curriculum IK should be positioned in the recognised subjects and grades, and suggest principles that should guide its integration in the curriculum.

The Nandi resistance

The Nandi resistance is a story that is told by Nandi elders about how the Nandi community resisted colonial rule in the late 19th and early 20th centuries. This was a military conflict between the British army and the Nandi community warriors that took place between 1890 and 1906. The Nandi were a dominant community that resisted the British efforts to build the Uganda railway through their land in

1899. The Nandi community used guerrilla warfare to attack and raid the Europeans through the leadership of the Nandi prophet Koitalel Arap Samoei.

Koitalel became a powerful Nandi leader who led an eleven-year resistance movement against the railway construction. The British Colonel Richard Meinertzhagen believed that the death of Samoei would lead to the death of the Nandi resistance and, on 19 October 1905, Koitalel was asked to meet Colonel Richard Meinertzhagen under the guise of negotiating a truce. However, when the Nandi arrived to meet, he was assassinated in cold blood together with his 22 chief advisors.

The Nandi became disorganized after the death of their prophet, they were overpowered by the whites and relocated. It is believed that this led to the unjust eviction of the Nandi people from their original lands to the reserves and finally they lost their land to European settlement. As with the Xhosa participants, this story was used to get participants to think and reflect on valued IK experiences in the Nandi community and their place and position in the school curriculum.

Data analysis

As noted earlier, the research employed a descriptive case study research design and the data generated from the *Imbizo* and the *Baraza* and the individual interviews were categorised, coded and thematically analysed using the Tesch method (Creswell, 2005). Biographic, close-ended and Likert scale questions used in the larger study by Ronoh (2017) provided descriptive statistics but are not commented on in this chapter.

Findings

The data suggest that the two cultural stories captured the participants' attention and stimulated discussion on IK and the school curriculum during the *Imbizo* and *Baraza*, and that the *Imbizo/Baraza* processes were a useful methodology in terms of generating dialogic interaction towards indigenous knowledge. As one *Imbizo* participant said:

"It brought back old memories … what the Imbizo did was to get us think about it again and look at it from different angles and get to hear what the other people think about the story because that is what is being lacking everybody else has his own ways of interpreting the story." (The conundrum of the cattle killing)

Another participant expressed how the *Imbizo* allowed free sharing of ideas about and perceptions of indigenous knowledge. He said:

"Okay starting with the Imbizo itself, Imbizo … [silence] as an indigenous way of meeting and gathering information and ideas was very much meaningful to me. It sets … a tone where people can express themselves freely and … it allows for example for the outflow of ideas from one's mind and in the process, it affords one an opportunity to get

to know how do other people that are part of Imbizo perceive what you understand as an individual. So, it … it allows for some kind of sharing of ideas. Yaah."

A majority of the participants agreed that as one can best express experiences in the way they were learnt, and because most people learn IK and culture in indigenous languages, it was good that they were able to express themselves in their mother tongues. An *Imbizo* respondent affirmed that by saying:

"Obviously it is clear that if we were talking about our African experiences [during Imbizo], and those experiences cannot be carried on or expressed in English language. Because what happens is … the terminology you know, and the way you remember or the way you experienced that. You know you would still need to find a way of explaining it in English which is not really what you wanted to say."

In terms of the *Baraza*, one Nandi participant said:

"I think we were able to discuss better our cultural experiences and indigenous knowledge that eeh that we went through while we were young on the same level."

Another Kenyan said:

"I remember asking my colleague the English name for 'teliat' [traditionally dried meat] and 'irokwet' [a medicinal herb] and he said that you can't find an exact substitute word in English. Language was not a barrier to our discussion and so for me I think the Nandi part of the discussion helped us to share our understanding of … okay …Nandi values yaah and cultural knowledge deeply."

A Nandi academic argued that such forums can be used to come up with knowledge that can be proposed to the Kenya Institute of Curriculum Development (KICD) for integration.

"Actually … Baraza like the one we had can be used by the senior faculty members to propose to KICD the common IK content and knowledge that can be integrated in the curriculum … syllabus, otherwise the coming generation will have lost that knowledge as you can see. You can see even some lecturers are finding a problem with indigenous eeeh language."

All of the South African participants attested that when they used their indigenous language in the *Imbizo* it inspired them to trace their cultural roots and IK, as noted by Msila (2016). They also proposed that a follow-up *Imbizo* and a joint book and newsletter publications of indigenous knowledge that arose from their discussions be considered.

"There are important views that have been raised here [in the Imbizo]. If we just leave them, they will disappear into thin air."

"Beyond this Imbizo we can sit and plan how we can capture all these and make it a project."

"We must meet and have our own Imbizo and extend this discussion. I propose a book. We can have solid chapters."

"We can have a book with stories aiming at little children. And we can have an academic book."

"It's our history [Nongqawuse and the cattle killing story]*. The only problem is that it was not written by and owned by isiXhosa speakers."*

The following is a response from a participant in the research process and it highlights the forum that the *Imbizo/Baraza* process affords:

"Old folks no longer tell these stories to children. Not much has been written clearly about such stories of the Nandi community. What is available is in a few books available to scholars only. No forum for internalizing those [sic] kind of knowledge."

Another participant commented on the lack of documentation of indigenous knowledge:

"I remember our parents telling us tongoch? cho!! [an introduction part of a Nandi riddle] *and sometimes I would like to remember some of those Nandi riddles but there is no document that you can reference such important knowledge in school."*

In terms of the reliability (or authenticity) of the findings on the types of indigenous knowledge that could/should be incorporated in the school curriculum, the concordance with the findings of other research in this area (e.g. da Silva et al., 2023; Webb, 2013) reflects the efficacy of the *Imbizo/Baraza* methodology. Similar themes were brought up as documented in the literature.

Interrogation of data from both cases (South Africa and Kenya) revealed that participants generally understood IK as local knowledge unique to a culture, a way of knowing, experiential knowledge and 'special' knowledge embedded in local languages, and that the participants valued local languages, history and culture, agricultural and environmental skills, herbal medicine and science and technological skills. Themes such as arts, language and science also emerged. Suggested principles that could guide integration of IK into school curriculum were also presented. Principles noted included political influence, knowledge demarginalisation, knowledge relevance and developmental appropriateness. Lastly, as noted earlier, the value of the *Imbizo/Baraza* as African methodologies emerged. Generally, there was a call by the respondents for inclusion and appropriation of various IK items in the school curriculum content, all of which appear in literature on indigenous knowledge (da Silva et al., 2023), including emphasis on the need to establish intercultural dialogue between traditional community leaders and educators and the need for an indigenous dialogic methodology (e.g. Cortesão & Cuale, 2011).

A participant said, "*language was not a barrier to our discussion and so … the Nandi part of the discussion helped us to share our understanding of … okay … Nandi values yaah and cultural knowledge deeply*". All of the Kenyan participants commented positively on the *Baraza* approach to IK research, stating that it upholds the heritage of the community in the academic field. They proposed that the Kenya Institute of Curriculum Development (KICD) should take advantage and use such forums to select common relevant IK content for integration into the school curriculum.

Generally, participants from both cases revealed that it is difficult to share IK experiences and culture purely in a second language like English because culture is symbolic (Shava, 2016), and said that even if it can be done, '*you find that the context of the knowledge like the proverbs, folktales, riddles etc. gets distorted*". All of the participants called for the use of the African methodologies to enhance and contextualize African research. These findings concur with Higgs (2016), who points out that an African philosophy of education needs to empower communities to participate in their educational development by enhancing the experiences of the learners and teachers. The participants' conception of the *Imbizo/Baraza* as an African methodology conforms with Shizha's (2013) notion that pedagogical practices that integrate history are conducive to a reconstructed curriculum that incorporates reality as perceived from different culturally historical moments.

Discussion

The findings of this study underscore the value of utilizing indigenous methodologies, such as the *Imbizo* in South Africa and the *Baraza* in Kenya, to gather insights on indigenous knowledge (IK) in the context of the school curriculum. The South African participants unanimously regarded the *Imbizo* as a novel and appropriate means of collecting information on IK, emphasising its contextual relevance and effectiveness compared to standard focus-group interviews. They appreciated how the *Imbizo* facilitated a dynamic exchange of IK ideas among participants, fostering a deeper understanding of common IK issues. As one participant reflected, the *Imbizo* reignited memories and offered diverse perspectives on shared stories, enriching their interpretations.

Moreover, participants highlighted the significance of using their indigenous languages during the *Imbizo*, as it facilitated a connection with their cultural heritage and stimulated discussions on IK. This aligns with Msila's (2016) assertion regarding the importance of language in tracing cultural roots and preserving IK. Additionally, participants proposed follow-up *Imbizos* and collaborative publications to document the IK discussed, recognising the need to safeguard and disseminate this knowledge.

Similarly, in the Kenyan context, the *Baraza* emerged as a fitting method for exploring participants' attitudes and experiences related to IK in the school curriculum. Like their South African counterparts, Kenyan participants emphasised the importance of using their local language, Nandi, during discussions to authentically convey traditional cultural concepts and experiences. They viewed the *Baraza* as a means of upholding community heritage within the academic realm and suggested its integration into curriculum development processes by institutions like the Kenya Institute of Curriculum Development (KICD).

The findings from both cases underscored the limitations of conveying IK solely in a second language like English, as it may lead to the distortion of cultural nuances and expressions. Participants advocated for the utilization of African methodologies to enhance and contextualize educational research, aligning with the principles of an African philosophy of education outlined by Higgs (2016). This resonates with Shizha's (2013) perspective on pedagogical practices that integrate historical and cultural realities into curriculum development, emphasising the importance of acknowledging diverse cultural perspectives.

In conclusion, the utilization of indigenous methodologies such as the *Imbizo* and *Baraza* offers valuable insights into IK and its integration into the school curriculum. These approaches not only facilitate meaningful dialogue and knowledge exchange but also contribute to the preservation and promotion of cultural heritage within educational contexts. Moving forward, there is a need for continued exploration and adoption of African methodologies to enrich educational practice and empower communities in shaping their educational development.

References

Cortesão, L., & Cuale, J. (2011). "School does not teach burying the dead": The complexity of cultural dialogue. *Pedagogy, Culture & Society, 19*(1), 119–131.

Creswell, J. W. (2005). *Educational research: Planning, conducting and evaluating quantitative and qualitative research* (2nd ed.). Pearson Education.

da Silva, C., Pereira, F., & Amorim, P. (2023). The integration of indigenous knowledge in school: A systematic review. *Compare: A Journal of Comparative and International Education.* https://doi.org/10.1080/03057925.2023.2184200

Higgs, P. (2016). The African Renaissance and the decolonization of the curriculum. In V. Msila & M. T. Gumbo (Eds.), *Africanising the curriculum: Indigenous perspectives and theories* (pp. 1–15). African Sun Media.

Kolawole, O. (2021). Is local knowledge peripheral? The future of indigenous knowledge in research and development? *AlterNative: An International Journal of Indigenous Peoples, 18*(1). https://doi.org/10.1177/11771801221088667

De Auguileta, G., Torres-Gomez, E., Padros, M., & Oliver, E. (2021). Dialogic reconstruction of memory: A methodological contribution aimed at social impact on youth's sexual-affective relationships. *International Journal of Qualitative Methods, 20*(1). https://doi.org/10.1177/16094069211034596

Mabelebele, J. (2022). Ideological objectives underpinning imbizo as a model of communication and governance. *Communicare: Journal for Communication Studies in Africa, 25*(2), 103–125. https://doi.org/10.36615/jcsa.v25i2.1749

Msila, V. (2016). Africanisation of education and the search for relevance and context. In V. Msila & M. T. Gumbo (Eds.), *Africanising the curriculum: Indigenous perspectives and theories* (pp. 57–69). African Sun Media.

Petzold, J., Andrews, N., Ford, J., Hedemann, C., & Postigo, J. (2020). Indigenous knowledge on climate change adaptation: A global evidence map of academic literature. *Environmental Research Letters, 15*(113007). https://doi.org/10.1088/1748-9326/abb330

Ronoh, J. (2017). *Indigenous knowledge in the school curriculum: Teacher educator perceptions of place and position* [Unpublished MEd thesis]. Nelson Mandela Metropolitan University.

Semali, L. M., & Kincheloe, J. L. (1999). *What is indigenous knowledge? Voices from the academy.* Falmer Press.

Shava, S. (2016). The application/role of indigenous knowledge in transforming the formal education curriculum: Cases from Southern Africa. In V. Msila & M. T. Gumbo (Eds.), *Africanising the curriculum: Indigenous perspectives and theories* (pp. 121–139). African Sun Media.

Shizha, E. (2013). Reclaiming our indigenous voices: The problem with postcolonial sub-Saharan African school curriculum. *Journal of Indigenous Social Development, 2*(1), 1–18.

Webb, P. (2013). Xhosa indigenous knowledge: Stakeholder awareness, value, and choice. *International Journal of Science and Mathematics Education, 11*(1), 89–110.

Wheeler, H., & Root-Bernstein, M. (2020). Informing decision-making with indigenous and local knowledge and science. *Journal of Applied Ecology, 57*(9), 1634–1643. https://doi.org/10.1111/1365-2664.13734

CHAPTER 3
A quantitative study on academic resilience among engineering students at a South African university

Curwyn Mapaling, Paul Webb, Belinda du Plooy

Background

Existing literature acknowledges the concept of academic resilience as critical to student success, particularly in challenging fields such as engineering, where some of the highest drop-out and lowest through-put rates have been observed. However, empirical research on resilience remains scarce, particularly in African contexts and specifically within South Africa. Furthermore, the majority of these studies have relied predominantly on qualitative methodologies. The use of quantitative methods in exploring academic resilience, especially within the South African engineering education environment, is not well-documented.

Theoretical perspectives on student academic resilience

In the pursuit of a comprehensive understanding of academic resilience, this literature review will delve into both established metrics and student perceptions. While the use of specific measures offers rigorous, data-driven insights, it is equally crucial to examine how students themselves conceptualise resilience. Thus, this literature review provides a nuanced perspective that complements the quantitative data presented later in this chapter, thereby enriching our overall understanding of academic resilience. Including literature on student perspectives serves to contextualize the subsequent quantitative results.

In an insightful exploration by Carnell et al. (2020), the intricate relationship between academic performance, the independent variable measured through improved grades, and students' perceived satisfaction, the dependent variable, was investigated amongst engineering students. The examination unfolded by administering detailed questionnaires following the first mid-term in a sophomore engineering statics course, aiming to reveal any inherent correlations between the independent and dependent variables. To obtain a well-rounded perspective, a Likert scale survey was implemented, alongside open-ended questions. This methodological approach garnered quantitative data and qualitative insights regarding the students' satisfaction levels, allowing for a detailed interpretation of students' subjective feelings and perceptions related to their academic results.

A cohort of 95 engineering undergraduates was engaged in a reflective analysis of their academic performance for a duration of four weeks prior to participating in the survey. To synthesise the findings effectively, levels of satisfaction were classified into low, moderate, and high categories. Instances revealing a discrepancy between satisfaction and performance, coined as 'off diagonals', were subjected to meticulous analysis. This examination uncovered a range of attributions to underperformance, from external contributors like time constraints and course structure to internal ones. It was observed that students who related their underperformance to external factors experienced heightened stress levels. Conversely, students whose grades improved more than their indicated levels of satisfaction usually accentuated internal elements and harboured positive perspectives towards self-betterment. This mixed-method approach, scrutinising academic accomplishments through improved grades and assembling qualitative perceptions of satisfaction, clarified the complex interplay between objective academic achievements and subjective student experiences, offering profound insights into the dimensions of academic resilience and adaptability within educational settings.

A South African study by Campbell et al. (2021) underscored the role of mindset in engineering students' resilience. Those who dropped out were found to possess a 'fixed mindset,' believing their intelligence was immutable. This mindset increased their vulnerability to academic challenges (Campbell et al., 2021). On the other hand, those with a 'growth mindset'—believing that effort could improve their intelligence—were more resilient (Campbell et al., 2021).

The highly competitive nature of engineering studies can also generate stress, as pointed out by Downs and Eisenberg (2012). The prevailing culture in engineering academia often equates stress with normalcy, which can dissuade students from seeking mental health treatment (Downs & Eisenberg, 2012). This portrayal of stress as an inherent trait of engineering students can harm both existing and future students. Newcomers may feel compelled to adopt this stress culture, perpetuating a misleading academic environment (Downs & Eisenberg, 2012). Other studies have found that students with preexisting high stress, anxiety, or lack of support were more vulnerable to developing anxiety disorders (Bantjes et al., 2020; Macgeorge et al., 2005).

Cross (2018) examined the Engineering Stress Culture (ESC) by employing self-administered surveys focusing on stress and anxiety metrics. The study revealed that a substantial proportion of students suffered from mental health issues: 22.4% experienced moderate to severe stress, 29.9% endured moderate to severe anxiety, and an equal percentage showed signs of moderate to severe depression (Cross, 2018). Gaining insights into how students interpret stress can inform the creation of targeted interventions to alleviate stress, thereby contributing to student recruitment, retention, and overall success (Cross, 2018).

Bennett et al. (2014) explored a somewhat neglected area of research concerning how engineering students, both domestic and international, perceive their career prospects and personal attributes. Surveying over a thousand first-year engineering students in Australia, the study found that both groups valued qualities like ethical conduct, communication skills, creativity, professionalism, and teamwork in engineers. Interestingly, 'orderly management' was highly valued among Australian students, whereas 'intelligence' topped the list for international students (Bennett et al., 2014). When asked to self-assess based on these qualities, international students rated themselves lower in eight of the nine identified traits (Bennett et al., 2014). While this might suggest lower self-esteem among international students, it could also be reflective of cultural and educational differences (Bennett et al., 2014). For example, 49% of the sample comprised international students who were non-native English speakers, underlining the necessity for engineering curricula to incorporate English language proficiency modules (Bennett et al., 2014). The one area where international students felt confident was in intelligence, a trait that Willingham (2021) notes is generally considered fixed in Western cultures but more flexible in Eastern perspectives.

In addition to academic pressures, engineering students face a range of external challenges that further complicate their educational journey, including language barriers, faculty shortages, financial constraints, limited industry exposure, and employability concerns (Danta, 2023).

Language barriers: Language proficiency can present significant obstacles in engineering education, which is predominantly taught in English. This can adversely impact students who are not native English speakers, affecting not just their academic performance but also their self-confidence and societal integration (Gerwel Proches et al., 2018; Peled, 2017; Feinberg et al., 2021). A United States-based study revealed that over 75% of respondents identified English as their first language, a sharp contrast to South Africa where only a small minority speak either of the two primary languages of instruction—English and Afrikaans—as their first language (Cross, 2018).

Staff shortages: A dearth of qualified faculty plagues engineering programmes, especially in India. Both public and private institutions are impacted, leading to compromised education quality (Alva, 2018; Danta, 2023). The issue is also prevalent in South Africa, losing skilled engineers to emigration at an alarming rate (Staff Writer, 2019).

Financial constraints: High tuition and additional expenses form a significant barrier to engineering education. Financial hardships disproportionately affect students from lower socio-economic backgrounds, making engineering degrees particularly elusive for this demographic (Danta, 2023; Goodier, 2019; Cross, 2018). Although student loans offer a temporary respite, they lead to a burgeoning crisis of student debt, particularly affecting minority communities in the United States (Hanson, 2021).

Limited industry interaction: Many engineering curricula emphasise theoretical aspects over practical, industry-relevant skills. This lack of real-world exposure creates a skills gap in engineering graduates, leaving them less prepared for employment (Danta, 2023; Gero et al., 2017).

Employability concerns: The competitive job market in engineering poses its own set of challenges. Foreign engineers willing to accept lower salaries exacerbate employment difficulties for local graduates. In the U.S., the manufacturing sector is the largest employer of engineers, highlighting the field's competitiveness (Leibbrandt, 2010; Torpey, 2018). In South Africa, the lack of skilled engineers makes these positions especially hard to fill (Bengesai & Pocock, 2021).

The transition to online distance learning (ODL) has added another layer of complexity to engineering students' perceptions of their academic resilience and challenges. The shift to online learning due to the COVID-19 pandemic has been met with mixed reviews (Wang, 2014; Saidalvi et al., 2021). For instance, Mathew and Chung (2020) sampled 608 university students in Malaysia and found diverging opinions on ODL, attributed primarily to resource limitations and poor internet connectivity. Another Malaysian study echoed a generally positive reception of online learning, citing factors like enthusiasm, self-efficacy, and satisfaction (Sim et al., 2021).

Similarly, in a study conducted among 360 Ghanaian international students, the majority found online learning beneficial and effective (Demuyakor, 2020). Indian students in Delhi also reported benefits such as a greater sense of freedom and increased connection with teachers (Khan et al., 2020). On the flip side, some students have found the transition to online learning frustrating, challenging to adapt to, and potentially a reason to withdraw from their academic programmes (Saidalvi et al., 2021; Song et al., 2004). Factors influencing these drop-out risks include poor home learning environments, technical issues, and lack of resources.

The conflicting findings from various studies point to the complicated nature of ODL readiness across different contexts. For instance, while one study claimed that Malaysia was prepared for the online shift due to the availability of necessary gadgets among students, another study argued the opposite, especially for students in rural areas (Saidalvi et al., 2021; Yeoh, 2020).

Although research has extensively examined resilience and challenges faced by engineering students, there has been a notable gap in capturing students' own perceptions of their academic experiences (Bennett et al., 2014). By exploring these perceptions across various academic domains, this review aims to shed light on influential factors like mindset, academic performance, satisfaction, and challenges, thereby contributing to a deeper understanding of engineering students' experiences. The next section will outline the aim of the study.

Aim of the study

Recognising a gap in the existing literature on academic resilience among engineering students in Africa, and more specifically within the South African higher education context, this research was designed to describe and correlate the resilience characteristics of final-year students in the Bachelor of Engineering Technology (BET) programme at Nelson Mandela University. While this chapter is a subset of a broader mixed-method investigation into resilience (Mapaling, 2023), it emphasises the quantitative aspects of the research, offering a distinct contribution to the current understanding of resilience in engineering education. In particular, the objective of the quantitative phase of the broader study was to contextualize the academic resilience of engineering students in South African higher education.

Methodology

Research design

In alignment with the criteria of an exploratory case study (Yin, 2018), this study employed a mixed-method approach involving both quantitative and qualitative data generation techniques, executed in two consecutive phases. It should be noted, however, that this chapter focuses solely on the quantitative results; the qualitative insights have been comprehensively explored in previous publications (Mapaling et al., 2021, Mapaling et al., 2022, Mapaling et al., 2024).

Participants and setting

The study utilized a purposive sampling method, enrolling 66 final-year students from the BET programme. Out of these participants, 47 successfully completed the full set of four measuring instruments that were administered in the study. This sample accounted for approximately 74.6% of the graduating BET class of 2020, which originated from the first admission cycle in 2018. The research took place at Nelson Mandela University, an institution with a dual focus on academic and vocational training, located in South Africa's Eastern Cape region.

Measuring academic resilience: Instruments for risk and resilience

Risk

Diagnostic and Statistical Manual of Mental Disorders Fifth Edition Self-Rated Level 1 Cross-Cutting Symptom Measure-Adult (DSM-5 CCSM-A; American Psychological Association, 2013)

The DSM-5 CCSM-A is a self-report scale developed by the American Psychiatric Association for trans-diagnostic mental health assessment. Employed in the current case study, the adult version includes 23 questions across 13 domains such as depression, anxiety, and substance use. Respondents use a 5-point Likert scale to indicate symptom experience over the past two weeks, with scores of 2 or higher in most domains indicating clinical relevance.

This tool has primarily been validated in clinical settings. However, Bravo (2018) extended its application to a non-clinical population of 7,217 university students across the U.S., using matrix sampling. The study supported the DSM-5 CCSM-A's internal, convergent, and criterion-related validity for assessing psychopathology among university students.

The Kessler Psychological Distress Scale (K10; Kessler et al., 2002)

The K10, a 10-question Likert scale instrument, screens for psychological distress, particularly anxiety and depression. Scores range from 10 to 50, and the tool is commonly used both clinically and in general populations.

In an Australian national survey by Andrews et al. (2001), 10,641 adults participated, revealing a mean K10 score of 14.2. The study showed a strong correlation between K10 scores and clinical diagnoses of anxiety and affective disorders, suggesting the tool's clinical utility. Yet, appropriate cut-off scores for clinical decision-making remain to be clarified.

Chiara et al. (2021) employed the K10 among 261 foreign students in South Korea. The study found that high K10 scores were linked to elevated psychological distress levels, with a satisfactory internal reliability score of 0.89. Nearly 30% of these students reported high distress, and the study identified certain sociodemographic factors linked to elevated distress.

In Pakistan, Qamar et al. (2014) used the K10 to assess 405 medical students. The study classified stress levels into mild, moderate, and severe categories, with an average stress score of 19.61. About 42% of the sample reported some level of stress, but the data did not show a significant association between stress and academic year. Both studies contribute to the broader application of the K10 as an effective tool for evaluating psychological distress in educational settings.

Resilience

The Adult Resilience Measure (ARM-28; Resilience Research Centre, 2018)

The ARM-28 is an adaptation of the CYRM-R-28 (Resilience Research Centre, 2018), designed to assess resilience in adults. It operates on the premise that resilience is built on contextually relevant resources like physical assets, relational supports, and services, and that resilience is dynamic over time. The ARM-28 targets three key areas: relational, individual, and contextual resilience processes. It aims to identify the socio-ecological resilience resources available to adults exposed to environmental risks.

Clark et al. (2022) used the ARM-28 to explore resilience in victims of conflict-related sexual violence from three different countries: Bosnia and Herzegovina, Colombia, and Uganda. The study posited that the ARM-28 is a 28-item scale focusing on measuring protective resources across individual, relational, and contextual domains. Findings revealed that while there were common elements of resilience across these countries, significant differences also existed, reflective of each country's unique cultural and situational context. Therefore, the study concluded that a one-size-fits-all factor structure for the ARM-28 is inadequate for capturing the nuanced protective factors linked to each nation's specific circumstances.

The Academic Resilience Scale (ARS-30; Cassidy, 2016)

The ARS-30 is a specialised tool designed to measure resilience in academic settings, capturing more than just outcomes by emphasising the processes that underlie resilience. Created by Cassidy in 2016, this scale operates on a Likert scale ranging from 1, which signifies "likely," to 5, for "unlikely." It includes vignettes to simulate adverse academic situations, making it particularly relatable for students. The scale examines three primary factors: perseverance, reflective and adaptive help-seeking, and negative emotional responses. High scores in the first two factors coupled with low scores in the third factor indicate higher resilience.

In Cassidy's initial study, the ARS-30 was administered to a sample of 532 British undergraduate students. The study revealed acceptable levels of internal consistency with a Cronbach's alpha of 0.90 and accounted for a significant 42.4% variance in academic resilience scores. The study also segmented its sample into two groups to test both the original and an alternative version of the questionnaire, aiming to assess its discriminant validity.

However, the scale has a few limitations. The study had a notable gender imbalance, which might affect the generalisability of its findings. In addition, while the ARS-30 aims to capture the ability to 'bounce back' from academic setbacks, this particular aspect needs further empirical validation. Future research should aim to confirm these findings and examine the scale's applicability to a more diverse student population, particularly focusing on the underrepresented male demographic. Despite these limitations, the ARS-30 stands as an innovative tool for capturing the complexities of academic resilience.

Procedure and ethical aspects

The study obtained ethical clearance from Nelson Mandela University's Research Ethics Committee: Human (REC-H) under the approval reference number: H20-EDU-ERE-026. Following this approval, additional institutional permissions were acquired from the appropriate university managerial gatekeepers to facilitate research involving students. Recruitment and orientation of participants were conducted through digital channels; this included sending informational emails and hosting an online session to outline the study's objectives and protocols. Participation was entirely elective, and all individuals were informed that they could opt out at any stage of the study without offering a justification or incurring any penalties. To guarantee confidentiality, each participant's responses were numerically coded to safeguard anonymity.

Data analysis

The study employed both descriptive (Fisher et al., 2009) and inferential statistical techniques (Allua & Thompson, 2009) to analyse the quantitative data collected. Descriptive statistics were computed based on the administered measuring instruments to provide a detailed overview. For inferential analysis, statistical tests were conducted to ascertain if significant relationships existed among variables such as perseverance, negative affect, reflective help-seeking, academic resilience, personal resilience, relational resilience, resilience, and distress scores generated by the participants.

Results

The quantitative data collected in this study offered several crucial insights into the academic resilience of the final-year BET students at Nelson Mandela University. In this phase, 66 students from industrial, civil, electrical, marine, and mechanical engineering courses participated by completing a series of the above-mentioned standardised psychometric measurement tools. The study participants demonstrated high levels of resilience, a finding that was to be expected considering their stage of study (final-year) and the perseverance required to complete their BET courses. These results offer a quantitative perspective on academic resilience among South African engineering students, highlighting the multifaceted nature of resilience and the myriad factors that contribute to it.

Differences were noted between branches of engineering, but across the board, those students who could self-identify their psychological distress symptoms and challenges proactively sought out resources such as orientation, peer support, and academic success strategy workshops provided by the University. Students entering university with higher scores in mathematics and physical sciences displayed greater academic resilience in their engineering studies, a promising indicator for academic admission processes.

Overall, our study reveals that the majority of the student sample demonstrated minimal symptoms related to mental health, with anxiety and mania being the only conditions where over 30% reported moderate or severe symptoms. Our sample generally reported high levels of personal, relational, and academic resilience, supported by strong family bonds and a sense of community.

With regards to risk, the DSM-5 CCSM-A and other scales employed in the study indicated a range of mental health experiences, from mild to severe, across domains like depression, anxiety, and mania. Table 1 presents frequency distributions for the DSM-5 CCSM-A domains.

Table 1: *Frequency Distributions: DSM-5 CCSM-A Domain Categories (n = 59)*

	None/Slight		Mild/Moderate/Severe	
Depression	26	44%	33	56%
Anger	43	73%	16	27%
Mania	21	36%	38	64%
Anxiety	25	42%	34	58%
Somatic symptoms	44	75%	15	25%
Suicidal ideation	51	86%	8	14%
Psychosis	55	93%	4	7%
Sleep problems	41	69%	18	31%
Memory	47	80%	12	20%
Repetitive thoughts and behaviours	39	66%	20	34%
Dissociation	45	76%	14	24%
Personality functioning	38	64%	21	36%
Substance use	48	81%	11	19%

According to Table 1, the majority of the participants in the sample reported to have experienced none or slight distress in relation to all the domains, with the exception of depression, mania and anxiety.

Similarly, with regards to resilience, the resilience measures indicated a spread from low to very high levels. Table 2 presents the frequency distribution for the Adult and Academic Resilience scales.

According to Table 2, the majority of the participants in the sample reported to have experienced high to very high resilience with regards to Relational Resilience (88%), Personal Resilience (77%), Adult Resilience (85%), Perseverance (77%) and Reflection Help Seeking (85%). Most participants (95%) indicated to have experienced middle to high resilience in relation to Academic Resilience. The majority (58%) of the sample reported to have experienced very low to low resilience with regards to Negative Affect.

The volume of data gathered in this study is extensive, and for the sake of brevity and readability, only a summary of the descriptive and inferential statistics is provided next.

Table 2: *Frequency Distributions: Adult and Academic Resilience Scales*

	Very Low 0.00 to 19.99		Low 20.00 to 39.99		Middle 40.00 to 60.00		High 60.01 to 80.00		Very High 80.01 to 100.00		Total	
Personal Resilience:												
Relational resilience	2	4%	2	4%	2	4%	14	26%	33	62%	53	100%
Personal resilience	0	0%	3	6%	9	17%	18	34%	23	43%	53	100%
Adult resilience	0	0%	3	6%	5	9%	20	38%	25	47%	53	100%
Academic Resilience:												
Perseverance	0	0%	2	4%	9	19%	29	62%	7	15%	47	100%
Reflection help seeking	1	2%	1	2%	5	11%	18	38%	22	47%	47	100%
Negative affect	12	26%	15	32%	14	30%	6	13%	0	0%	47	100%
Academic resilience	0	0%	2	4%	10	21%	35	74%	0	0%	47	100%

Summary of descriptive statistics

The sample encompassed 66 BET students in their final year (average age 23.3 years, SD = 3.02). All participants provided demographic information and completed the K10 (Kessler et al., 2002). Subsequently, a subset of 59 students from the final year completed the DSM Self-Rated Level 1 CCSM-A (American Psychiatric Association, APA, 2013); 53 engaged with the ARM-R (Resilience Research Centre, 2018); and 47 responded to the ARS-30 (Cassidy, 2016).

Ninety-two per cent of the participants identified as citizens of South Africa, with the remaining 8% being international students. In terms of racial composition, 61% identified as 'black', 24% as 'white', and 15% as 'coloured'. The predominant home language spoken among the respondents was isiXhosa, represented by 43%, with Afrikaans and English both at 29%. Only a single participant disclosed living with a diagnosable mental disorder when completing the survey. No participants indicated living with a disability.

The majority of the sample consisted of students studying mechanical engineering (35%), with civil engineering students comprising 32%, electrical engineering students making up 26%, industrial engineering at 6%, and marine engineering at 2%. A significant majority, 65%, stated they participated in the How2@Mandela orientation programme (aimed at first-year transition) at the onset of their academic pursuits. However, less than half, 44%, reported attending sessions for subject-specific tutoring (offered for high-risk modules such as mathematics, physics, and engineering drawings), and fewer, only 24%, mentioned their attendance at the academic success strategy workshops (focused on time management, study skills, etc.) during their academic years.

The majority of participants specified that Nelson Mandela University was their preferred tertiary institution, with 71% stating it was their first choice. Additionally, 86% were accepted into their primary choice of academic programme, and 82% mentioned they didn't have to undertake an admission test. Such tests are necessitated when prospective students don't fulfill the direct admission prerequisites for a specific academic programme. South African universities employ an Admission Point Score (APS) system, whereby each subject undertaken in the final high school year is allocated an APS. The total APS acquired determines eligibility for different courses or degrees based on their respective requirements. The predominant score range for mathematics was 70-79%, as reported by 38% of the participants, and for physical science, 33% of the participants achieved scores within the 60-69% range during their Grade 12 year (the concluding year of South African secondary education).

Fifty per cent of the participants were first-generation university students, signifying they were the inaugural members of their families to attend university. Concerning financial aid, a substantial number of students, 41%, received support from the National Student Financial Aid Scheme (NSFAS) provided by the South African government. An equivalent proportion, 17%, indicated receiving financial support either from parents or family or through a bursary from a public organization, while a smaller segment, 11%, stated they were self-funded. Additionally, 21% of the participants benefitted from the School of Engineering's Meal-A-Day project, a programme aimed at offering one meal per day to students in financial need.

Summary of inferential statistics

Turning to our inferential statistics, we used the Chi-square (Chi^2) tests of independence to explore the relationships between categorical variables. Among these, we found nuanced differences in mental health symptoms and resilience markers across language, gender, and age groups.

The ability to study and learn in their home language seemed to contribute positively to students' academic resilience and their ultimate success in course completion. For instance, English-speaking students reported higher levels of personal resilience compared to their Afrikaans and Xhosa counterparts. Table 3 presents the relationship between home language and Personal Resilience.

Table 3 indicates that a significantly larger proportion of Xhosa-speaking students (42%) experience lower (<=60) levels of Personal Resilience compared to English and Afrikaans-speaking students (8%).

Table 3: *Contingency Table – Home Language and Personal Resilience*

Home Language	Personal Resilience					
	<=60		>60		Total	
Afrikaans or English	2	8%	24	92%	26	100%
Xhosa	5	42%	7	58%	12	100%
Total	7	18%	31	82%	38	100%

Chi² (d.f. = 1, n = 38) = 4.70; p = .030; V = 0.35 Medium. Constant 4 added to observed frequencies to meet the requirements for minimum expected frequencies.

Female students, outnumbered in the engineering field, tended to somatise psychological distress more than their male counterparts. Table 4 presents statistics for the relationship between gender and somatic symptoms.

Table 4: *Contingency Table – Gender and Somatic Symptoms*

Gender	Somatic Symptoms					
	None/Slight		Mild/Moderate/ Severe		Total	
Male	37	84%	7	16%	44	100%
Female	7	50%	7	50%	14	100%
Total	44	76%	14	24%	58	100%

Chi² (d.f. = 1, n = 58) = 6.74; p = .009; V = 0.34 Medium

Table 4 indicates that a significantly larger proportion (50%) of female students experience mild/moderate/severe problems related to somatic symptoms compared to the male students (16%). This is consistent with the widespread phenomenon of women's tendency to somatise problems (Delisle et al., 2012).

Younger students (20-24 age group) showed higher resilience levels than those aged 25 and above. Table 5 presents statistics for the relationship between age category and Personal Resilience.

Table 5: *Contingency Table – Age Category and Personal Resilience*

Age Category	Personal Resilience					
	<=60		>60		Total	
20-24	7	17%	35	83%	42	100%
25+	5	45%	6	55%	11	100%
Total	12	23%	41	77%	53	100%

Chi² (d.f. = 1, n = 53) = 4.12; p = .042; V = 0.28 Small

Table 5 reveals that a significantly larger proportion of students in the 25+ age category (45%) experience lower (<=60) levels of Personal Resilience compared to students in the 20-24 age category (17%). This discrepancy highlights the need for targeted support and interventions for older students who seem to be struggling more with Personal Resilience. Table 6 presents statistics for the relationship between age category and Adult Resilience.

Table 6: *Contingency Table – Age Category and Adult Resilience*

| Age Category | Adult Resilience | | | | | |
	<=60		>60		Total	
20-24	4	10%	38	90%	42	100%
25+	4	36%	7	64%	11	100%
Total	8	15%	45	85%	53	100%

Chi^2 (d.f. = 1, n = 53) = 4.90; p = .027; V = 0.30 Medium

Table 6 illuminates that a significantly larger proportion of students in the 25+ age category (36%) experience lower (<=60) levels of Adult Resilience compared to their younger counterparts in the 20-24 age category (10%). This divergence underscores the heightened struggles faced by the older students in building Adult Resilience.

The divergences observed in Tables 5 and 6 underscore the pronounced struggles of students in the 25+ age category, both with Personal and Adult Resilience. These results highlight the imperative for exploring and implementing targeted interventions and supportive measures specifically tailored to address the resilience needs of this older demographic, thereby aiming to mitigate the identified resilience gaps.

Furthermore, attending orientation programmes and academic success workshops appeared to positively influence resilience and reduce symptoms of depression and anger as well as sleep problems. Tables 7 to 9 present statistics for the relationship between whether the students attended any academic success strategy workshops and DSM-5 CCSM-A variables, specifically depression, anger, and sleep problems.

Table 7: *Contingency Table – Academic Success Strategy Workshop Attendance and Depression*

| Attend any Academic Success Strategy Workshops | Depression | | | | | |
	None/Slight		Mild/Moderate/ Severe		Total	
Yes	10	67%	5	33%	15	100%
No	16	36%	28	64%	44	100%
Total	26	44%	33	56%	59	100%

Chi^2 (d.f. = 1, n = 59) = 4.17; p = .041; V = 0.27 Small

Table 7 indicates that a significantly larger proportion of students who did not attend any Academic Success Strategy Workshops experienced mild/moderate/severe depression (64%) compared to those who attended such workshops (33%).

Table 8: *Contingency Table – Academic Success Strategy Workshop Attendance and Anger*

Attend any Academic Success Strategy Workshops	Anger					
	None/Slight		Mild/Moderate/ Severe		Total	
Yes	14	93%	1	7%	15	100%
No	29	66%	15	34%	44	100%
Total	43	73%	16	27%	59	100%

Chi^2 (d.f. = 1, n = 59) = 4.26; p = .039; V = 0.27 Small

Table 8 reveals that a significantly larger proportion of students who did not attend any Academic Success Strategy Workshops experienced more than slight anger (34%) compared to those who attended such workshops (7%).

Table 9: *Contingency Table – Academic Success Strategy Workshop Attendance and Sleep Problems*

Attend any Academic Success Strategy Workshops	Sleep Problems					
	None/Slight		Mild/Moderate/ Severe		Total	
Yes	14	93%	1	7%	15	100%
No	27	61%	17	39%	44	100%
Total	41	69%	18	31%	59	100%

Chi^2 (d.f. = 1, n = 59) = 5.39; p = .020; V = 0.30 Medium

Table 9 unveils that a significantly larger proportion of students who did not attend any Academic Success Strategy Workshops experienced more than slight sleep problems (39%) compared to those who attended such workshops (7%).

The insights derived from Tables 7, 8, and 9 collectively illustrate the substantial implications of non-attendance at Academic Success Strategy Workshops on students' well-being. The data underscores a discernible correlation between non-attendance and elevated levels of depression, heightened expressions of anger, and increased prevalence of sleep problems among students. These interlinked results emphasise the critical need for reinforced strategies, perhaps in the form of enhanced encouragement or mandates for workshop attendance, aimed at alleviating the myriad of adverse effects observed. Further exploration is warranted to ascertain the optimal approaches and interventions necessary to mitigate these prevalent issues and foster an environment conducive to both academic success and holistic well-being of the students.

Relationships between the scales

Table 10 presents the Pearson correlation coefficients that were used to recognise and analyse the strength and direction of the relationships between the scales. Correlations with absolute value greater than or equal to 0.30 are deemed significant according to the recognised guidelines and are in bold in Table 10.

Table 10: *Pearson Product Moment Correlations for the Scales*

		Academic Resilience				Adult Resilience			Kessler
		Perseverance	Negative affect	Reflection	Academic resilience	Personal resilience	Relational resilience	Adult resilience	Psychological distress
Academic Resilience	Perseverance	–	-.225	.749	.845	.096	.139	.128	-.341
	Negative affect	-.225	–	-.229	.133	-.299	-.071	-.218	.481
	Reflection	.749	-.229	–	.878	.118	.233	.188	-.265
	Academic resilience	.845	.133	.878	–	.017	.198	.109	-.154
Adult Resilience	Personal resilience	.096	-.299	.118	.017	–	.632	.925	-.472
	Relational resilience	.139	-.071	.233	.198	.632	–	.879	-.295
	Adult resilience	.128	-.218	.188	.109	.925	.879	–	-.435
Kessler	Psychological distress	-.341	.481	-.265	-.154	-.472	-.295	-.435	–

The results in Table 10 summarized according to the scales are (values in parentheses are correlations):

Academic Resilience

o Perseverance:
  • Positively correlated with Reflection (.749) and Academic Resilience (.845).
  • Negatively correlated with Kessler Psychological Distress (-.341).
o Negative affect:
  • Positively correlated with Kessler Psychological Distress (-.481).
o Reflection:
  • Positively correlated with Perseverance (.749) and Academic resilience (.878).

o Academic resilience:
- Positively correlated with Academic Resilience (.845) and Reflection (.878).

Adult Resilience

o Personal resilience:
- Negatively correlated with Kessler Psychological Distress scale (-.472).
o Adult resilience:
- Negatively correlated with Kessler Psychological Distress scale (-.435).

Kessler Psychological Distress

- Positively correlated with Negative Affect (.481).
- Negatively correlated with Perseverance (-.341) and Personal Resilience (-.472).

As observed in Table 10, the data elucidates the paramount importance of bolstering both perseverance and personal resilience as crucial strategies for mitigating distress. Interestingly, both the symptoms and domains from the DSM-5 exhibit a positive correlation with negative affect and the Kessler Distress Scale, aligning with conventional expectations. However, they do not correlate with perseverance or reflection under the academic resilience measure. This absence of correlation is somewhat surprising, particularly considering the observed negative correlation with adult resilience, indicating a potential differentiation in the roles and impacts of academic and adult resilience in relation to distress. These intricacies point toward a nuanced and multifaceted interplay between different aspects of resilience and mental health, setting the stage for a more comprehensive understanding of students' mental states and resilience capacities. Overall, the results offer a nuanced view of the students' mental health and resilience statuses, enriched by statistical testing, as seen above, to highlight relationships between variables. The insights gleaned from this examination serve as a precursor to the concluding reflections, aiming to synthesise the results into coherent insights and implications.

Conclusion

The quantitative data from this study revealed generally strong levels of academic resilience among the final-year BET students. The measures of risk and resilience, as assessed by the measurement items, revealed statistically significant levels of perseverance and resilience in the face of academic challenges. The diversity of the results suggests that categorical variables do indeed have an impact, affecting the likelihood of a student belonging to a particular group for a given measure.

The qualitative findings, particularly from the lecturer and support staff sub-samples which have been explored extensively in prior published work (Mapaling et al., 2021, Mapaling et al., 2022, Mapaling et al., 2024), depict a contrasting, more challenging picture of the students' lives. During the interviews with the different sample groups, it was observed that students, answering based on their experiences, were likely more engaged, while the staff, overwhelmed by numerous responsibilities during the COVID-19 pandemic, were more observational in their responses. Another explanation for the discrepancy observed is the potential inclination of individuals towards impression management when responding to psychometric instruments (Riemer & Shavitt, 2011), leading to more favourable responses. This variance between the qualitative and quantitative findings underscores the complexities of academic resilience. This chapter emphasises the importance of quantitative research in revealing aspects of resilience that qualitative data might overlook and has significant implications for improving student support interventions in challenging academic environments like engineering.

In addition, according to lecturers (as part of the broader study) (Mapaling, 2023), there has been a change in the practical training received by students, with those enrolled in the diploma programme receiving a year of practical training in preparation for their future careers, unlike the current BET degree students. This brings forth the necessity for further research to refine interventions and to delve deeper into the under-researched areas related to students' perceptions of their university training in relation to their future careers.

Strengths and limitations of the study

The study is underpinned by several noteworthy strengths that lend it both depth and breadth. It features a comprehensive review of existing literature, incorporating global perspectives that span from South Africa to India and beyond. The inclusion of recent phenomena such as the impact of COVID-19 and online distance learning adds a layer of timeliness and relevance to the research. Furthermore, the focus on students' self-reported experiences provides invaluable qualitative insights, enriched by an awareness of cultural and linguistic differences.

While the study provides valuable insights, it also has certain limitations. The dependence on self-reported data could introduce subjective biases, potentially affecting the study's broader applicability. Additionally, the focus on engineering students may limit the relevance of the findings to other academic disciplines. The study mainly offers a snapshot of student perceptions, which could be influenced by other external variables not examined, such as prevailing economic or educational policies. Moreover, the research is confined to a relatively small geographic area and setting, specifically the Nelson Mandela University, which may not capture the diverse experiences and challenges faced by students in other parts of South Africa.

Furthermore, the study is not without its methodological limitations. For example, the use of the DSM-5 CCSM-A as a screener for mental health issues in higher education introduces several gaps. The current study failed to collect clinical diagnostic data and did not compare the DSM-5 CCSM-A to more comprehensive psychopathology scales. Furthermore, the instrument has not been assessed according to recognised standards like the Standards for Educational and Psychological Testing and lacks normative data, calling into question its specificity and suitability for this particular setting. As for the K-10 scale, the lack of established cut-off scores and normative data for the specific populations in the study necessitates further research for its effective application. The study also utilized the ARM-R and ARS-30 instruments to measure resilience. These instruments, originating from Canada and Britain respectively, were administered without prior usage in a South African context (Laher & Cockcroft, 2013), although they have been found to be reliable in international contexts. Some of the items on the ARS-30 were reverse scored, adding another layer of complexity. Despite their international validity, questions remain about their applicability within South Africa, particularly considering the nation's unique cultural and linguistic landscape. Therefore, more research is warranted to validate these measures for local usage. Overall, these limitations related to measurement tools point to the need for further research to establish their validity and reliability in diverse academic settings.

Acknowledgements

We express our profound gratitude to Kirstie Eastwood and Dr Danie Venter for their meticulous assistance with the statistical analysis. A special acknowledgement to Dr Venter for his critical reading and insightful scrutiny of the statistics presented in this chapter, which immensely contributed to the precision and reliability of our results.

References

Allua, S., & Thompson, C. B. (2009). Inferential statistics. *Air Medical Journal, 28*(4), 168–171. https://doi.org/10.1016/j.amj.2009.04.013

Alva, N. (2018, March 31). 34% faculty shortage hits IITs across India. *The Times of India*. https://timesofindia.indiatimes.com/city/bengaluru/34-faculty-shortage-hits-iits-across-india/articleshow/63552686.cms

American Psychiatric Association (APA). (2013). *Diagnostic and statistical manual of mental disorders* (5th ed.). https://doi.org/10.1176/appi.books.9780890425596

Andrews, G., Henderson, S., & Hall, W. (2001). Prevalence, comorbidity, disability, and service utilisation: An overview of the Australian National Mental Health Survey. *British Journal of Psychiatry, 178*(2), 145–153.

Bantjes, J., Saal, W., Lochner, C., Roos, J., Auerbach, R. P., Mortier, P., Bruffaerts, R., Kessler, R. C., & Stein, D. J. (2020). Inequality and mental healthcare utilisation among first-year university students in South Africa. *International Journal of Mental Health Systems, 14*(5), 1–11. https://doi.org/10.1186/s13033-020-0339-y

Bengesai, A. V., & Pocock, J. (2021). Patterns of persistence among engineering students at a South African university: A decision tree analysis. *South African Journal of Science, 117*(3/4), 1–9. https://doi.org/10.17159/sajs.2021/7712

Bennett, D., Maynard, N., Kapoor, R., & Kaur, R. (2014). Engineering students' perceptions for engineers and engineering work. In *Proceedings of the Australasian association of engineering education conference 2014* (pp. 894–901). School of Engineering & Advanced Technology, Massey University.

Bravo, A. J., Villarosa-Hurlocker, M. C., & Pearson, M. R. (2018). College student mental health: An evaluation of the DSM-5 Self-rated Level 1 Cross-cutting Symptom Measure. *Psychological Assessments, 30*(10), 1382–1389.

Campbell, A. L., Direito, I., & Mokhithi, M. (2021). Developing growth mindsets in engineering students: A systematic literature review of interventions. *European Journal of Engineering Education, 46*(4), 503–527.

Carnell, P. H., Schwab, M. C., Sochacka, N. W., & Hunsu, N. J. (2020, October). Performance and perception: A preliminary examination of factors that may motivate students to bounce back. In *2020 IEEE Frontiers in Education Conference* (FIE) (pp. 1–4).

Cassidy, S. (2016). The Academic Resilience Scale (ARS-30): A new multidimensional construct measure. *Frontiers in Psychology, 7*(1787), 1–11. https://doi.org/10.3389/fpsyg.2016.01787

Chiara, A., Lee, T. J., & Lee, M. S. (2021). Psychological well-being of foreign university students during the COVID-19 pandemic: A cross-sectional study in South Korea using the Kessler Psychological Distress Scale (K10). *Journal of Global Health Science, 3*(2), e15. https://doi.org/10.35500/jghs.2021.3.e15

Clark, J. N., Jefferies, P., Foley, S., & Ungar, M. (2022). Measuring resilience in the context of conflict-related sexual violence: A novel application of the Adult Resilience Measure (ARM). *Journal of Interpersonal Violence, 37*(19–20), NP17570–NP17615. https://doi.org/10.1177/08862605211028323

Cross, K. J., & Jensen, K. J. (2018, January 24–27). *Work in progress: Understanding student perceptions of stress as part of engineering culture* [Conference paper]. American Society of Engineering Education annual conference and exposition, Salt Lake City, UT, United States.

Danta, N. (2023, January 12). *Challenges engineering students face today in the education system* [Post]. LinkedIn. https://www.linkedin.com/pulse/challenges-engineering-students-face-today-education-system-danta/

Delisle, V. C., Beck, A. T., Dobson, K. S., Dozois, D. J. A., & Thombs, B. D. (2012). Revisiting gender differences in somatic symptoms of depression: Much ado about nothing? *PLoS ONE, 7*(2), e32490.

Demuyakor, J. (2020). Coronavirus (COVID-19) and online learning in higher institutions of education: A survey of the perceptions of Ghanaian international students in China. *Online Journal of Communication and Media Technologies, 10*(3), e202018.

Downs, M. F., & Eisenberg, D. (2012). Help seeking and treatment use among suicidal college students. *Journal of American College Health, 60*(2), 104–114.

Feinberg, I., O'Connor, M. H., Owen-Smith, A., & Dube, S. R. (2021). Public health crisis in the refugee community: Little change in social determinants of health preserve health disparities. *Health Education Research, 36*(2), 170–177.

Fisher, M. J., & Marshall, A. P. (2009). Understanding descriptive statistics. *Australian Critical Care, 22*(2), 93–97.

Gero, A., Stav, Y., & Yamin, N. (2017). Use of real-world examples in engineering education: The case of the course electric circuit theory. *World Transactions on Engineering and Technology Education, 15*(2), 120–125.

Gerwel Proches, C. N., Chelin, N., & Rouvrais, S. (2018). Think first job! Preferences and expectations of engineering students in a French 'Grande Ecole'. *European Journal of Engineering Education, 43*(2), 309–325.

Goodier, R. (2019, December 19). Engineers are not ending poverty. Time for a change? *Engineering for Change.* https://www.engineeringforchange.org/news/engineers-not-ending-poverty-time-change/

Hanson, M. (2021, December 12). Student loan debt by race. *Education Data Initiative.* https://educationdata.org/student-loan-debt-by-race

Kessler, R. C., Andrews, G., Colpe, L. J., Hiripi, E., Mroczek, D. K., Normand, S. L., Walters, E. E., & Zaslavsky, A. M. (2002). Short screening scales to monitor population prevalences and trends in non-specific psychological distress. *Psychological Medicine, 32*(6), 959–976. https://doi.org/10.1017/s0033291702006074

Khan, M. A., Nabi, M. K., Khojah, M., & Tahir, M. (2020). Students' perception towards e-learning during COVID-19 pandemic in India: An empirical study. *Sustainability, 13*(1), 57.

Laher, S., & Cockcroft, K. (2013). Current and future trends in psychological assessment in South Africa: Challenges and opportunities. In S. Laher & K. Cockcroft (Eds.), *Psychological assessment in South Africa: Research and applications* (pp. 535–552). Wits University Press.

Leibbrandt, M., Woolard, I., McEwen, H., & Koep, C. (2010). *Employment and inequality outcomes in South Africa.* Southern Africa Labour and Development Research Unit and School of Economics, University of Cape Town.

Liebenberg, L., & Moore, J. C. (2018). A social ecological measure of resilience for adults: The RRC-ARM. *Social Indicators Research, 136*(1), 1–19. https://doi.org/10.1007/s11205-016-1523-y

Macgeorge, E. L., Samter, W., & Gillihan, S. J. (2005). Academic stress, supportive communication, and health. *Communication Education, 54*(4), 365–372.

Mapaling, C. (2023). *Academic resilience of engineering students: A case study* [Unpublished doctoral thesis]. Nelson Mandela University. https://vital.seals.ac.za/vital/access/manager/Repository/vital:67337?site_name=GlobalView&f0=sm_mimeType%3A"application%2Fpdf"

Mapaling, C., du Plooy, B., & Webb, P. (2024). Diverse perceptions among engineering students and staff of the enablers and constraints of academic resilience. *South African Journal of Higher Education, 38*(4), 171–189. https://doi.org/10.20853/38-4-5764.

Mapaling, C., Webb, P., & du Plooy, B. (2021). "Everyone plays a key role": Students, lecturers and support staff in South Africa talk about the academic resilience of engineering students. In *Proceedings of the 14th annual international conference of education, research and innovation* (pp. 7201–7207). https://doi.org/10.21125/iceri.2021.1615

Mapaling, C., Webb, P., & du Plooy, B. (2022). "I would help the lecturer with marking": Entrepreneurial education insights on academic resilience from the perspectives of engineering students in South Africa. In J. Halberstadt, J. Greyling, A. A. de Bronstein & S. Bisset (Eds.), *Transforming entrepreneurship education: Interdisciplinary insights on innovative methods and formats* (pp. 177–196). Springer Nature. https://link.springer.com/chapter/10.1007/978-3-031-11578-3_10

Mathew, V. N., & Chung, E. (2020). University students' perspectives on open and distance learning (ODL) implementation amidst COVID-19. *Asian Journal of University Education, 16*(4), 152–160.

Peled, Y. (2017). Language and the limits of justice. *Journal of Multilingual and Multicultural Development, 38*(7), 645–657.

Qamar, K., Kiani, M. R., Ayyub, A., Khan, A. A., & Osama, M. (2014). Higher stress scores for female medical students measured by the Kessler Psychological Distress Scale (K10) in Pakistan. *Journal of Educational Evaluation for Health Professions, 11*, 27. https://doi.org/10.3352/jeehp.2014.11.27

Resilience Research Centre. (2018). *CYRM and ARM user manual*. Resilience Research Centre. https://resilienceresearch.org/home-cyrm/

Riemer, H., & Shavitt, S. (2011). Impression management in survey responding: Easier for collectivists or individualists? *Journal of Consumer Psychology: The Official Journal of the Society for Consumer Psychology, 21*(2), 157–168. https://doi.org/10.1016/j.jcps.2010.10.001

Saidalvi, A., Noorezam, M., Zakaria, N., Sa'adan, N., Wan, W. F. W., Fakhruddin, N. N. R., & Rahman, S. A. S. A. (2021). Diploma engineering students' perceptions of online distance learning. *International Journal of Recent Technology and Engineering, 10*(2), 119–128.

Sim, S. P. L., Sim, H. P. K., & Quah, C. S. (2021). Online learning: A post COVID-19 alternative pedagogy for university students. *Asian Journal of University Education, 16*(4), 137–151.

Song, L., Singleton, E. S., Hill, J. R., & Koh, M. H. (2004). Improving online learning: Student perceptions of useful and challenging characteristics. *The Internet and Higher Education, 7*(1), 59–70.

Staff Writer. (2019, July 10). Why South African engineers are leaving the country – despite huge demand and R1 million salaries. *Business Tech*. https://businesstech.co.za/news/business/328447/why-south-african-engineers-are-leaving-the-country-despite-huge-demand-and-r1-million-salaries/

Torpey, E. (2018, February). Engineers: Employment, pay, and outlook. *Bureau of Labor Statistics*. https://www.bls.gov/careeroutlook/2018/article/engineers.htm

Wang, H. (2014). Learner autonomy based on constructivism learning theory. *International Journal of Cognitive and Language Sciences, 8*(5), 1552–1554.

Willingham, D. T. (2021). *Why don't students like school? A cognitive scientist answers questions about how the mind works and what it means for the classroom* (2nd ed.). Jossey-Bass.

Yeoh, A. (2020, April 27). MCO: As lessons move online, local teachers and students struggle with uneven internet access. *The Star*. https://www.thestar.com.my/tech/tech-news/2020/04/27/mco-as-lessons-move-online-local-teachers-and-students-struggle-with-uneven-internet-access

Yin, R. K. (2018). *Case study research and applications: Design and methods* (6th ed.). Sage.

CHAPTER 4
Exploring faculty and student perspectives regarding training and research interventions on climate change and sustainability at Makerere University in Uganda

David Ssekamatte, Karsten Speck, Bernd Siebenhüner

Introduction

Climate change concerns continue to exert significant impacts across various sectors globally (IPCC, 2022), posing challenges to the attainment of the UN Sustainable Development Goals (SDGs), particularly in developing countries (Akinbami & Akinbami, 2017). These challenges extend beyond environmental concerns, affecting leaders and stakeholders worldwide (Morgan et al., 2017). Given the multifaceted nature of climate change, addressing it necessitates innovative strategies tailored to specific contexts and collaborative efforts among stakeholders (Calzadilla et al., 2013). Human behaviour plays a central role in responding to climate change, underscoring the importance of fostering knowledge, skills, and attitude changes (Celik, 2020). Recognising education as a key response to climate change, efforts have been made to integrate climate change education at all levels (Duenas & Ochoa, 2016).

The UN Framework Convention on Climate Change (UNFCCC) Article 6(a) (i) mandates parties to initiate and promote education and public awareness interventions on climate change, emphasising training, research, and community sensitization at all levels (UN, 1992). This obligation was reaffirmed by the Paris Agreement in 2015, wherein parties committed to promoting education responses to climate change, ensuring quality training, public awareness, and participation (UN, 2015). Consequently, education systems are positioned to support national and local efforts to mitigate and adapt to climate change (UNESCO, 2015).

Numerous scholars advocate for mainstreaming climate change issues into education systems, encompassing both formal and informal curricula (O'Keeffe, 2016; Ssekamatte et al., 2021; Locke et al., 2013; Tosam & Mbih, 2014; Uitto & Saloranta, 2017). Higher education institutions play a critical role in climate change mitigation and adaptation, conducting scientific research and engaging policymakers and communities based on evidence (Abazeed, 2018; Akinbami & Akinbami, 2017; Alghamdi, 2018). Through training functions, universities can integrate climate change aspects into academic programmes, raising awareness and producing specialised professionals (Bentz, 2020; Boateng & Boateng, 2015). Additionally, universities, through community engagement, can support evidence-based solutions and interventions by collaborating with decision-makers across sectors (Buckland et al., 2018).

Despite the potential, literature suggests that many universities, especially in developing countries, have not fully integrated climate change into academic programmes and research agendas (Boyde & Hume, 2015; Buckland et al., 2018; Calzadilla et al., 2018). Limited research on climate change and inadequately trained staff further constrain universities' capacity to address climate change (Cordero et al., 2008; Fahey et al., 2014). Therefore, this study aims to explore faculty and student perspectives on training and research interventions on climate change and sustainability at Makerere University in Uganda. The research questions guiding this study are:

What are the perspectives and views of faculty and students regarding training interventions on climate change at Makerere University in Uganda?

How do faculty and students perceive research interventions on climate change and sustainability at Makerere University?

This chapter seeks to provide insights into training and research initiatives supporting climate change mitigation, adaptation, and sustainability, drawing from the experiences of the relevant faculty and student bodies at Makerere University. It begins with a contextual background, followed by a methodology overview, key findings, conclusions, and recommendations.

Contextual background

This study was conducted in Uganda at Makerere University, Kampala (MAK). Makerere University is the oldest and biggest public university in Uganda. The university has its main campus on Makerere Hill in Kampala, Uganda, and other campuses across the country. The university runs undergraduate and postgraduate programmes delivered across the various colleges and schools at the main campus, upcountry branches as well as affiliated institutions across the country. At the time the study was conducted the university had 275 academic programmes (16 ordinary diploma, 134 bachelor's degree, 14 postgraduate diploma, 103 master's degree and 8 PhD degree programmes); and 39,546 students (36,947 in undergraduate programmes and 2,599 in postgraduate programmes) were enrolled at the main campus. Makerere University Business School had an enrolment of 10,494 students at postgraduate and undergraduate levels. The total enrolment for the university was 50,040 students at the time of the study (MAK, 2017).

The College of Agriculture and Environmental Sciences (CAES), the academic unit of interest in this study, runs various training and research programmes at undergraduate and postgraduate levels in the areas of agriculture and environment.

The college houses the School of Agricultural Sciences; School of Forestry, Environmental and Geographical Sciences, and the School of Food Technology, Nutrition, and Bioengineering. The researchers purposively sampled the two schools (School of Agricultural Sciences and the School of Forestry, Environmental and Geographical Sciences) because they run courses and programmes related to climate change and sustainability at both undergraduate and postgraduate levels. The college runs 18 graduate programmes and employs 410 administrative and faculty staff.

The college is engaged in various research areas including those on climate change and sustainability and these include:

- Agricultural value chains;
- food product development and value addition;
- crop improvement;
- forestry and biodiversity;
- waste management and pollution assessment;
- natural resource management and climate change; and
- hazard and disaster science.

The university has been ranked 5th best on the African continent according to the 2020 World University Rankings by Times Higher Education and the 8th best on the continent according to the 2023 Sub-Saharan Africa University Rankings.

Approach and methods

From a social constructivist perspective, the researchers adopted a qualitative research approach and a holistic descriptive case study research design (Yin, 2016). After acquiring ethical clearance from the Uganda National Council for Science and Technology (UNCST), the researchers generated data from faculty and students using semi-structured interviews and focus group discussions (FGDs). The study participants were purposively selected from academic units that offer programmes on climate change and sustainability within the college of agriculture and environmental sciences. The nine (9) interviews with faculty were conducted in their offices lasting between 40–60 minutes while the two (2) focus group discussions with undergraduate and postgraduate students were conducted in a safe and convenient room at the university campus. Data were generated from 25 participants including 9 lecturers, 8 undergraduate students and 8 postgraduate students on climate change and sustainability related programmes. Data from lecturers were generated using semi-structured in-depth interviews, while data from students were generated using FGDs.

The interviews with the faculty focused on the existing training and research engagements and programmes on climate change and sustainability and how they are involved in the design and delivery of these programmes. An interview guide with open-ended questions guided the interviews and capturing of the data was done using a voice recorder to allow transcription and further analysis. The focus group discussions with students were centred on the various courses and programmes they were involved in related to climate change and sustainability, and how they found them relevant to their study needs. The conversations explored students' experiences in these programmes and how these have enabled them to effectively learn issues of climate change and sustainability. A focus group discussion guide was used to direct the course of the conversation and a voice recorder was used to capture the discussion after seeking consent of the participants.

The data analysis commenced with the transcription of recorded interviews (Kowal & O'Connell, 2014). Subsequently, the transcripts were meticulously reviewed to ensure accuracy and fidelity. Following this, a thematic analysis approach, as outlined by Braun and Clarke (2006), was employed with the assistance of MAXQDA software. Initial coding was conducted to generate codes, which were then organized into categories to facilitate data comprehension (Saldana, 2009). These categories, emerging from the data itself, were scrutinised to identify patterns, culminating in the identification of overarching themes for coherent data interpretation. This systematic process facilitated the condensation of voluminous data into analytical units, aiding in the extraction of meaningful insights from the perspectives of faculty and students (Willig, 2013).

The identified themes were meticulously documented and substantiated with pertinent quotations from the study participants. To ensure the integrity and rigour of the entire process the researchers attempted to maintain credibility and quality at every stage, beginning with thorough fieldwork planning and ethical review of data generation tools. This commitment to quality was sustained throughout the data analysis phase and the composition of the findings (Patton, 2015).

Key findings

The main themes that were identified are presented in Table 1.

Table 1: *Themes and Categories of Training and Research Interventions on Climate Change and Sustainability at Makerere University*

Themes	Categories
Theme 1: Training interventions on climate change and sustainability	• Short courses • Long courses • Undergraduate programmes • Postgraduate programmes
Theme 2: Research interventions on climate change and sustainability	• Climate change science research • Climate change mitigation research • Climate change adaptation research • Climate change policy research

Theme 1: Training interventions on climate change and sustainability

Universities the world over engage in short-term and long-term training. Teaching and training are key functions of any university. It was reported that the university offers various courses and programmes on climate change and sustainability. These are categorised into short courses, long courses, undergraduate and postgraduate programmes. The findings on each are presented below.

Short courses on climate change and sustainability

These courses are delivered targeting specific audiences to create awareness and provide basic knowledge and skills on climate change and sustainability. They are usually delivered for 1-2 weeks depending on the target participants. The Makerere University Centre for Climate Change and Innovation (MUCCRI) in collaboration with various departments within the selected schools run these courses targeting policymakers, farmer groups, practitioners from the NGO sector and students who are interested in learning basic aspects of climate change and sustainability. Findings revealed that many of these short courses are demand-driven and therefore they are designed to meet the needs of the target audiences. The intention of these courses has been sensitizing policymakers, practitioners, students, and government technocrats on climate change and sustainability and introducing them to mitigation and adaptation interventions they can adopt across their sectors and kinds of work in which they are engaged. The idea behind such trainings is to empower the participants and call for climate action. The short courses also targeted academia and administrators from other universities who need such knowledge and skills.

Long courses on climate change and sustainability

The university also offered long-term training courses that are taught within selected undergraduate and postgraduate programmes within the college of agriculture and environmental sciences as well as other colleges. A review of documents and interaction with faculty and students revealed that many of the undergraduate and postgraduate programmes included semester-long courses on these aspects. Such programmes included; BSc Forestry, BSc Agriculture, MA in Geography and MSc Environmental Management. Study participants indicated that these courses introduce students to climate, weather, and atmospheric processes; climate change science; energy, environment, and climate change as well as climate change and forestry. The semester courses are integrated in the programmes and are examinable at the end of the semester. The MUCCRI was also working on a university-wide course on climate change and sustainability that would run across all university programmes ensuring that all students that enrol for any university programme acquire knowledge, skills, and attitudes on these aspects. This is a good idea because it promotes climate action at all levels across various disciplines and sectors. It would create a critical mass of climate change and sustainability actors and therefore contribute to the promotion of sustainability and implementation of SDGs at various levels. One of the participants said:

> "We had a project that was looking at mainstreaming climate change in all college programmes. So we did that, we looked at the different college programmes, and we developed 2 course units which are common, which are taught across the college, addressing basic issues of climate change, climate and weather, and all those things."

The participant called for curriculum review of all programmes to mainstream aspects of climate change and sustainability across disciplines as well as retooling faculty on these programmes to deliver on these aspects.

Undergraduate programmes related to climate change and sustainability

The findings revealed various undergraduate programmes that are offered at the case university focusing on climate change and sustainability. These are 3-year programmes that culminate in the awarding of a bachelor's degree. The programmes have a course work component where students cover a series of courses on a semester basis. The students also have an attachment for fieldwork experience and a research project that translates into a thesis submitted as a requirement for the award of the degree. A review of grey literature and interactions with faculty and students revealed that the college and selected schools run several undergraduate courses focusing on climate change and sustainability. These included: the BSc in Geography, the BSc in Meteorology and the BSc in Forestry. These programmes are offered mostly to students who have recently completed secondary school and a few who enrol with prior training at diploma level. The programmes focus on equipping the students with a significant amount of knowledge, skills, and attitudes to enable them to offer professional expertise as climatologists, climate mitigation and adaptation professionals, environmental specialists, and technical officers in the areas of climate change and sustainability across various sectors.

Postgraduate programmes on climate change and sustainability

This category of training interventions includes programmes offered to students at postgraduate levels. Findings revealed that the university offered the postgraduate diploma in Meteorology, MA in Geography, MSc in Land Use and Regional Development and the PhD in Geographical Sciences. The postgraduate diploma was a 1-year programme while the Master of Science degree programmes were 2 years containing course work and research components. The PhD programme was a 3–5-year programme with both course work and research components. While interacting with study participants, they reported various programmes that were already developed and undergoing accreditation processes. These were an MSc in Disaster Risk Management, an MSc in Climate Change and Sustainability, and an MSc in Meteorology. At the time of the study, these had been approved by the respective departments and schools within the college and were awaiting approval by the senate and accreditation by the National Council for Higher Education (NCHE). A participant reported that:

> "There is a PhD programme being worked on in climate risk management, and in the department of geography there are several courses on climate change."

The case university was seen as moving in the right direction in terms of developing postgraduate programmes in the area of climate change and sustainability. This is because having several and diverse programmes on these aspects builds a critical mass of professionals that are able to support various sectors in addressing issues of climate change and sustainability. This is critical for the achievement of SDGs and contributes to mitigation and adaptation efforts. The PhD programme has the potential of growing a pool of academics who would strengthen training and research in these areas at this case university and other universities.

Theme 2: Research interventions on climate change and sustainability

This theme presents the findings from the study on research interventions related to climate change and sustainability. Undertaking research is yet another key function of any university. Makerere University is a research university and has been highly ranked over the years within the African continent and at global level. At the time of the study, the university research agenda included research on climate change and sustainability. This was a strategic area and therefore fully supported by the university leadership and management. Findings reveal that the faculty and students undertake several research projects on climate change and sustainability. The research projects are mainly categorised into climate change science, climate change mitigation, climate change adaptation and climate change policy research areas. Each of these is explored below.

Climate change science research

Findings revealed that the faculty and students at the case university have several research projects that are focused on climate science. The participants reported that they conduct research to understand processes and impacts of climate change on various sectors as well as ecosystems. They reported doing studies on weather-related predictions and modelling for various sectors within the country. One of them said:

> "[A] big chunk of what we have to do, and science means we have to conduct research in these fields to understand the processes, to down scale or understand climate change at the lowest level possible. We have to look at impact across different sectors, but also look at maybe innovations. ... [W]e have been doing weather-related prediction studies across Uganda."

They reported undertaking research on the various local innovations aimed at advancing the understanding of climate science, with a focus on generating information to guide mitigation and adaptation efforts at multiple levels. The weather predictions and climate information generated are used by local farmer groups, researchers in academic institutions and policymakers in government ministries, departments, and agencies. It was revealed that the faculty and students did contribute to monthly weather bulletins especially in the dry pastoral regionals like Karamoja and were exploring doing studies on indigenous knowledge and how it can inform weather forecasting in various regions. The monthly forecasts are very key for farmers because it helps them make evidence-based decisions on when to plant and possible irrigation in case of a change in rain patterns. It was reported that the university has a weather station and a meteorological unit with the required facilities and equipment. The station and unit have been key in generating weather and climate information and are now working with the Uganda National Meteorological Authority (UNMA) to support in packaging and disseminating this information for users. This is expected to support adaptation efforts at individual and community levels.

Climate change mitigation research

It emerged that the faculty and students do engage in research focused on climate change mitigation. Study participants noted that only a few studies focus on measuring the contributions of various sectors and human activities to the country's greenhouse gas emissions. Some studies focused on exploring behavioural and technological strategies that can be adopted in mitigation efforts. Research studies under this category explored how human behaviour and mindset contribute to sustainability and environmental protection. They also explored the local technologies that can be advanced to mitigate climate change in agriculture and other production systems. However, some of the participants reported that climate change mitigation research is not funded well like adaptation research. One of them noted:

> "Hmm, mitigation is always a challenge and it is not just on our own, I think it is also related to the global setting that in Africa here, even the funding for mitigation is quite less compared to the funding for adaptation."

According to her, most of the available funding is for adaptation and therefore less research is done on mitigation. She noted that in Africa, mitigation research funding is so limited which explains the limited studies on mitigation. This challenge has greatly affected student researchers in universities who cannot afford equipment and other facilities they require to conduct high quality research on climate change mitigation and sustainability.

Climate change adaptation research

This kind of research relates to studies undertaken by the faculty and students on various aspects of adaptation to climate change especially in the local communities in Uganda, like the pastoral communities and those in semi-arid areas like Karamoja at Makerere University. It was reported that most of the adaptation research conducted focused on agriculture (crop and animal livestock), farming in dry areas in Uganda. Many of the projects focused on climate resilience in the cattle corridor, mainly Karamoja areas, where climate change has severely impacted pastoral farming. Study participants reported that the research studies in this area were mainly focusing on supporting livestock farmers to find effective ways of adapting to the effects of climate change amidst scarcity of water and pasture during dry spells.

The research interventions on perceptions and adaptations were mainly to support communities to be resilient but also to find alternative ways of dealing with effects of climate change in their areas. It also emerged that the faculty and students were also engaged in research that is focused on developing resilient and climate smart crop varieties for farmers especially in dry areas but also in mountainous and highland regions that experience landslides. Many of these studies have been very useful for such communities, as evidenced by high adoption levels. Studies related to safety in areas characterised by landslides have been conducted and disseminated widely. Many policymakers and NGOs in those areas have adopted some of the recommendations and innovative strategies from the studies conducted by the faculty and students at the university.

Climate change policy research

It emerged that the faculty and students are engaged in several research projects on climate policy related issues. The research studies are focused on informing policymakers on various issues that relate and have serious implications on climate change and sustainability within the country and community contexts. Most of the research on climate change that faculty and students have conducted resulted in developing policy briefs. One of the participants reported:

> "[W]hat I know is that there are hundreds of policy briefs. This is one of the common things that people are doing from their research pieces. All the research pieces I have mentioned; ... one research project comes out with more than one policy brief. So, there are quite a number of policy briefs that have been written targeting different sectors, ranging from road sector, those linked to Kampala [Capital] City Council especially linked to climate change policy, strategy, all these have been informed by our research."

The policy briefs developed from the research findings are used to engage policymakers in making them aware of the climate change situation but also motivating them to think about the possible mitigation or adaptation interventions and the related policy options. Many of these policy briefs from Makerere University have been handy in informing policy and other relevant decisions by government related to climate change across various sectors.

Discussion and conclusion

The findings from this study shed light on the range of training interventions and research initiatives related to climate change and sustainability at Makerere University. Through its various educational programmes, it appears that Makerere University plays an appropriate role in equipping students and practitioners with the necessary knowledge and skills to address climate change challenges.

Training interventions at Makerere University encompass a spectrum of short-term and long-term courses tailored to different audiences. Short courses target specific groups, such as policymakers, farmer groups, and practitioners, aiming to raise awareness and provide foundational knowledge on climate change and sustainability. These courses are demand-driven and designed to meet the needs of diverse stakeholders, empowering participants to take climate action within their respective sectors. Conversely, long-term courses embedded within undergraduate and postgraduate programmes offer more comprehensive training, integrating climate change and sustainability themes into academic curricula. The university's efforts to develop a university-wide course on climate change and sustainability reflect a proactive approach to mainstreaming these topics across disciplines, fostering a multidisciplinary approach to addressing climate challenges.

In addition to training, Makerere University is actively engaged in research initiatives focused on climate change and sustainability. The university's research agenda encompasses various aspects, including climate change science, mitigation, adaptation, and policy research. Faculty and students undertake studies to deepen understanding of climate processes, assess impacts on different sectors, and develop innovative solutions for mitigation and adaptation. Notably, research outputs, such as policy briefs, play a role in informing policymakers and shaping climate-related policies and strategies at both local and national levels.

However, challenges exist, particularly regarding funding for research on climate change mitigation. Limited funding in this area inhibits the exploration of behavioural and technological strategies for mitigation, potentially hindering progress towards sustainability goals. Moreover, while Makerere University demonstrates commitment to addressing climate change through its training and research initiatives, there appears to be a need for greater investment in infrastructure and resources to support high-quality research, especially in areas such as climate resilience and adaptation. Additionally, there is a need for ongoing collaboration between academia, government, and civil society to translate research findings into actionable policies and interventions that promote sustainability and resilience in the face of climate change.

References

Abazeed, R. A. M. (2018). Impact of transformational leadership style on organizational learning in the Ministry of Communication and Information Technology in Jordan. *International Journal of Business and Social Science, 9*(1), 118–129.

Akinbami, J. F. K., & Akinbami, C. A. O. (2017). Climate change mitigation and adaptation studies in Nigerian universities: Achievements, challenges and prospects. In W. L. Filho (Ed.), *Climate change research at universities* (pp. 139–152). Springer International Publishing AG.

Alghamdi, N. (2018). Knowledge and awareness of sustainability in Saudi Arabian public universities. In W. L. Filho (Ed.), *Handbook of sustainability science and research* (pp. 103–127). Springer International Publishing AG.

Bentz, J. (2020). Learning about climate change in, with and through art. *Climate Change, 162,* 1595–1612.

Boateng, C. A., & Boateng, S. D. (2015). Tertiary institutions in Ghana curriculum coverage on climate change: Implications for climate change awareness. *Journal of Education and Practice, 6*(12), 99–106.

Boyd, M. C., & Hume, T. (2015). Addressing the challenges of climate change: The potential role of development education in the tertiary sector. *Policy & Practice: A Development Education Review,* (21), 63–86.

Braun, V., & Clarke, V. (2006). Using thematic analysis in psychology. *Qualitative Research in Psychology, 3*(2), 1–41.

Buckland, P., Goodstein, E., Alexander, R., Muchnick, B., Mallia, M. E., Leary, N., Andrejewski, R., & Barsom, S. (2018). The challenge of coordinated civic climate change education. *Journal of Environmental Studies and Sciences, 8,* 169–178.

Calzadilla, P. V., Mauger, R., & Plessis, A. D. (2018). Climate change communication in higher education institutions: The case of the North-West University in South Africa. In W. L. Filho (Ed.), *Handbook of climate change communication* (Vol. 3, pp. 241–255). Springer International Publishing AG.

Calzadilla, A., Zhu, T., Rehdanz, K., Tol, R. S. J., & Ringler, C. (2013). Economy-wide impacts of climate change on agriculture in sub-Saharan Africa. *Ecological Economics, 93,* 150–165.

Celik, S. (Ed.). (2020). *The effects of climate change on human behaviors.* Springer.

Cordero, E. C., Todd, A. M., & Abellera, D. (2008). Climate change education and ecological footprint. *American Meteorological Society,* 865–872.

Duenas, D. I. C., & Ochoa, L. I. C. (2016). Climate change and health-related challenges as a trigger for educational opportunities to foster social knowledge and action. In W. L. Filho, U. M. Azeiteiro & F. Alves (Eds.), *Climate change and health, climate change management* (pp. 297–312). Springer International Publishing Switzerland.

Fahey, S. J., Labadie, J. R., & Meyers, N. (2014). Turning the Titanic: Inertia and the drivers of climate change education. *Journal of Applied Research in Higher Education, 6*(1), 44–62.

IPCC. (2022). *IPCC sixth assessment report (AR6): Climate change 2022-impacts, adaptation, and vulnerability.* Cambridge University Press.

Kowal, S., & O'Connell, D. C. (2014). Transcription as a crucial step in data analysis. In F. Uwe (Ed.), *The Sage handbook of qualitative data analysis* (pp. 65–78). Sage Publications Inc.

Locke, S., Russo, R. O., & Montoya, C. (2013). Environmental education and eco-literacy as tools of education for sustainable development. *The Journal of Sustainability Education, 4.* https://www.researchgate.net/publication/240712578_Environmental_education_and_eco-literacy_as_tools_of_education_for_sustainable_development

MAK. (2017). *Makerere University strategic plan review report 2017.* Makerere University Press.

Morgan, E. A., Hallgren, W., Helfer, F., Sahin, O., Nalau, J., Onyango, E., Hadwen, W., & Mackey, B. (2017). Implications of the Paris Agreement for adaptation research and universities. In W. L. Filho (Ed.), *Climate change research at universities* (pp. 251–262). Springer International Publishing AG.

O'Keeffe, P. (2016). The role of Ethiopia's public universities in achieving the United Nations sustainable development goals. *International Review of Education, 62*, 791–813.

Patton, M. Q. (2015). *Qualitative research & evaluation methods* (4th ed.). Sage Publications Inc.

Saldana, J. (2009). *The coding manual for qualitative researchers*. Sage Publications Inc.

Ssekamatte, D., Speck, K., & Siebenhüner, B. (2021). The challenges and opportunities for climate change education at Makerere University in Kampala, Uganda. In W. Leal, R. Pretorius & L. O. de Sousa (Eds.), *Sustainable development in Africa: Fostering sustainability in one of the world's most promising continents* (pp. 201–219). Springer Nature Switzerland AG.

Tosam, M. J., & Mbih, R. A. (2014). Climate change, health and sustainable development in Africa. *Environment, Development and Sustainability, 17*, 787–800.

Uitto, A., & Saloranta, S. (2017). Subject teachers as educators for sustainability: A survey study. *Education Sciences, 7*(8), 1–19.

UNESCO. (2015). *The UNESCO climate change initiative*. https://www.unesco.org/en/climate-change/education

United Nations. (1992). *United Nations framework convention on climate change*. https://unfccc.int/resource/docs/convkp/conveng.pdf

United Nations. (2015). *Paris Agreement to the United Nations framework convention on climate change*, No. 16-1104.

Willig, C. (2013). Interpretation and analysis. In F. Uwe (Ed.), *The Sage handbook of qualitative data analysis* (pp. 341–353). Sage Publications Inc.

Yin, R. K. (2016). *Qualitative research from start to finish* (2nd ed.). The Guilford Press.

CHAPTER 5

University-community engagement opportunities to address climate change issues in an African context. The case of Makerere University, Uganda

Nelson Mandela, David Ssekamatte, Benjamin Kyalo Wambua

Introduction and background

University-community partnerships have the potential to respond to society's most pressing needs through engaged scholarship (Pundt & Heilmann, 2020). Because of their independent and science-driven perspective, universities can mediate between different actors such as NGOs and community members. Collaborative approaches in which a university not only coordinates, but mediates, third mission activities by reaching out to local communities, organizations, enterprises, underpinned by an *Ubuntu* philosophy of interdependence and reciprocity within an African society, can contribute to addressing societal, environmental and political issues as long as institutions of higher education see themselves as co-belonging to a community of humans on the basis that there is no precondition for belonging (Waghid, 2020).

Despite a plethora of third mission (community service) potentials, universities continue to be mistakenly viewed as 'ivory towers' that are isolated entities and are elitist in nature and disconnected from the places in which they are situated. Treating research and teaching and community service as separate entities from communities and societal problems may account for the gap between teaching, research, and community engagement.

Universities are particularly well-positioned to solve problems related to climate change by virtue of being generators of knowledge. This is core for transdisciplinary research where higher institutions of learning engage stakeholders in significant ways throughout the research process, rather than collecting data, informing stakeholders or valorizing knowledge afterwards. For instance, such synergies between universities and communities can raise awareness about issues of public concern like climate change mitigation and adaptation and working more systematically to create positive change.

Among the targets is improving education, awareness-raising and human and institutional capacity on climate change mitigation, adaptation, impact reduction and early warning in an African context. This is because African countries are said to be more at risk from climate change effects because of several factors including limited skills and equipment for disaster management, limited financial resources, weak institutional capacity and heavy dependence on rain-fed agriculture (Schilling et al., 2020; Welborn, 2018).

Disasters induced by climate change damage educational facilities and systems, threatening the physical safety and psychological well-being of communities and interrupting agricultural sustainability, which 70% of Africans depend on for livelihoods. For instance, Uganda has in past decades experienced more erratic rainfalls leading to frequent bursting of rivers, mudslides and landslides in areas like Bududa, changing weather patterns, drops in water levels. Relatedly, Uganda has also experienced increased frequency of extreme droughts that continue to lead to loss of lives and property of communities. Those living in the mountainous areas of Kasese, particularly the Rwenzori Mountains, have especially been affected by, for example, glacier melting which increases water levels in the Nyamwamba, Mubuku, and Ruimi Rivers (Mertens et al., 2016; Taylor et al., 2009).

While the motivation and need to address climate change are real and present, its translation into action lacks immediacy and severity. USAID (2022) has noted that while climate action is included as one of the 17 SDGs, climate impacts will affect and undermine global efforts to achieve virtually all of these goals. Whereas there are a number of existing solutions, there has been an over-reliance on technological responses with minimal attention paid to the role of social solutions. While several studies have been done on third mission activities of universities (Nabaho et al., 2022; Papadimitriou, 2020; Schnurbus, & Edvardsson, 2022; Nicotra et al., 2021; Axon 2015), there is insufficient literature on university-community engagement activities and programmes on climate change action, particularly in an African context. Most extant studies focus on technological solutions towards addressing climate change and are largely skewed towards the European and American higher education contexts. This provides an opportunity for the third mission by the universities to demonstrate their potential as effective approaches for addressing climate change and the multitude of benefits that can result from engagement programmes at universities in the African context. University community engagements towards community-based carbon reduction strategies are but one example of collaborative actions towards achieving sustainability and addressing climate change.

This study explored the views and perspectives of university staff and students regarding opportunities for university-community engagement (U-CE) towards climate change action in an African context at the case university. This was done to better understand the role of the third mission of higher institutions of learning in addressing the challenges of climate change and achieving a sustainable world. The key research question that guided the study was 'What are the opportunities that might be able to support policy making and enhance the third mission programmes towards climate change issues at the case university?'

Literature review

Climate change is defined as the shift in climate patterns mainly caused by greenhouse gas emissions from natural systems and human activities (Fawzy et al., 2020). There is scientific consensus that climate change is real, manifested through increasing temperatures, changing rainfall patterns, and increasing frequency and severity of extreme weather events, including drought, flooding, and cyclones.

There is a strong and growing impetus for universities and colleges to ensure that their presence within various communities is productive and transformative (Bowers, 2017). Similarly, there have recently been calls to use the SDGs as guidelines for socially responsive universities as key players in the race for sustainable development (Kestin et al., 2017). Alongside this positioning, there has been an increasing emphasis on the role of communities to facilitate and sustain carbon reduction practices. UNESCO (2015, p. 67) has argued that to promote climate change actions, players need to form or strengthen "partnerships and collaborations". These could be formed between "education institutions, communities, public organizations, NGOs, local communities, entrepreneurs etc" (Virtanen, 2010).

There are numerous success stories of university-community engagement programmes across the globe and their efforts to achieve the SDGs, particularly climate change action. In the United States of America, universities started implementing the third mission of universities to have a positive impact on communities for sustainable development. The objective of driving sustainable transformation in particular regions and cities has even been elevated to an institutional priority. For example, the Berkley and San Diego campuses of the University of California have made tremendous efforts to accelerate a regional transition to a high-tech green economy and hasten the uptake of smart grid technologies and renewable energy (Trencher et al., 2014).

Raditloaneng (2013) highlighted a key opportunity for African universities to collaborate on projects that showcase their community service efforts addressing climate change within their regions. This is based on the 'Impact of "Implementing the Third Mission of Universities in Africa (ITMUA) collaborative research project, 2010-2011'". At the University of Botswana, it was felt that the SDGs serve as a benchmark and tool for a number of cross-cutting issues that are addressed in the university curricula such as community development, environmental awareness, global warming and climate change as part of university-community collaborations.

In Tanzania, at the University of Dar es Salaam, Ssekamate (2022) noted that the university is a leader in action on climate change in communities. This is done through outreaches and engaging local communities in adaptation initiatives that are simple and friendly or easy to implement, supported by the research conducted on climate change. However, Ssekamate observed that there is a need to have these local-based adaptation initiatives supported or rooted in communities themselves, rather than imposing unsolicited science-based information onto our local communities.

In Uganda, Ssekamatte (2022) has noted that some universities like Makerere have been implementing several training, research, and community engagement programmes with regard to climate change education. Ssekamatte indicated that the training programmes were short courses, seminars, undergraduate and postgraduate programmes on climate change. The universities conduct various research programmes mainly on climate change adaptation. Findings from Ssekamatte's study showed that implementing units at these universities conducted sensitization events, local adaptation community initiatives, policy engagement events, climate change festivals, and identification as well as empowerment of climate change champions in various communities across the sampled group.

Theoretical framework

With recent calls to Africanise African Studies and a wave of deep knowledge work excavating African intellectual traditions within African universities, the key findings on university community engagement opportunities to address climate change issues were generated based on the *Ubuntu* theory. This is a deeply held African philosophy with ideals of a community rooted in interconnectedness with others (Tutu, 1999). It is regarded as a key cultural strength of communities (Nkosi & Daniels, 2007), and can be used as a theory of higher education in Africa (Waghid. 2020). Educators and researchers, especially in African contexts, have the twin responsibilities of embracing *Ubuntu* and using the values of *Ubuntu* and other African philosophies to arrive at solutions to African societal problems and achieve sustainable development (Rajah, 2019; Boogaard, 2019; Mosia, 2023).

With the overwhelming consensus that global climate is changing, largely due to human activities, with heightened risk levels for social and ecological systems, *Ubuntu* provides an epistemic framework to arrive at solutions to such community problems (Okoliko & David, 2021). Thus, using this theoretical lens, the researcher asked study participants across the case university to share their views, perspectives and opinions regarding the practical university-community engagement opportunities that can be tapped into/explored to address issues of climate change in the African context. The study of these opportunities was based on the key interrelated tenets of *Ubuntu* as a theoretical framework of interdependence/human interconnectedness, reciprocity (mutually beneficial relationship) and communalism/collectivism/solidarity.

To better understand practical university-community engagement (U-CE) opportunities to address issues of climate change, *Ubuntu* principles assert that social responsibility, interdependence with and social concern for others, society and the environment and civic engagement ought to become a central part of the mission of African universities. More specifically, a philosophy of higher education in Africa is intertwined with a notion of *Ubuntu*, an African dictum for human interdependence and its associated link with actions such as social responsibility, citizenship, and an attentiveness to otherness. Of course, it is important to note that the researcher is not denying that Western forms of inquiry can contribute significantly to enhancing relations among individuals, institutions and community, most notably the practice of deliberation that emanated from Western forms of human engagement. However, the contention is that African moral theory has the potential to rupture those Western practices that seem to be remiss of advancing communal humility, interdependence, social justice, and reciprocity of actions towards sustainable development. The *Ubuntu* framework thus gives an opportunity to recover, present and enable valorization of African epistemologies from early African thinkers to explore African-context based university-community engagement opportunities to address issues of climate change. Climate change impacts affect continents differently and thus U-CE in Africa ought to be addressed in relation to a defensible rationale or plausible philosophy.

Notably, national development and achieving SDGs in the twenty-first century is dependent on a particular understanding of higher education, which cannot simply be aggregated to a dearth of appropriate ontology, epistemology, expertise, African value-laden social responsibility and catching up numerically with the rest of the world. According to Nyerere, higher education needs to address the realities of African societies and foster the social goals of living together and working together for the common good (Nyerere, 1968). Thus, the study appropriated concepts from the theory such as interconnectedness, indigenous knowledge, corporations, interdependence, and collaborative practices. These concepts helped in investigating the U-CE activities and programmes that the case university engages in to address climate change issues, and the ways in which these different activities and programmes are developed and coordinated between the university and the community. The theoretical framework provided a better way of collecting relevant contextual information and understanding the challenges, drivers, and opportunities available for U-CE towards climate change action at the case university.

Approach and methodology

Based on an interpretivist paradigm, this study adopted a qualitative approach and a multiple case study design according to Yin (2012). Drawing on this approach, and as recommended by Creswell and Clark (2018), qualitative research investigates the understanding and interpretation of individuals regarding their social worlds which leads to the epistemological position of interpretivism (Alharahsheh & Pius, 2020). In line with this multiple case study, the interpretivist paradigm locates this study through recognising negotiation between the researchers and the researched to produce an account of the insider's perspective, so both the researcher and the researched are 'present'. The data are accounts, which researchers then code for emergent themes, look for connections, and construct higher-order themes (Hancock et al., 2001). Notably, Yin (2012) opines that a multiple case study design enhances literal replication which may help to yield theoretical constructions that can be replicated across cases of the same contexts. Using this design, the researcher considered data generated from Makerere University in Uganda. Makerere University is Uganda's oldest public university, situated at the centre of the capital city Kampala. The university acknowledges knowledge extension and outreach services as its third mission (community engagement) programmes.

Makerere University being the oldest institution of higher learning in Uganda (and East Africa) plays an exemplary role to other public and private universities in Uganda. First established as a technical school in 1922, Makerere University is not only Uganda's oldest institution of higher learning, it is also its largest. Today, Makerere University is composed of nine colleges and one school offering programmes for about 36,000 undergraduates and 4,000 postgraduates. Sustainable development is embedded in the university's core ideology. Its centre for climate change and Sustainability Research Unit (SRU) are the dedicated interdisciplinary research group focusing on the sustainability of complex social-ecological systems in the communities through improved collaboration toward the SDGs. This chapter presents findings from a larger study conducted in 2023 to explore views and perspectives of staff and students regarding opportunities that Makerere University in Uganda can utilize to address issues of climate change. The selection of the case university was therefore purposive.

Data were generated using semi-structured in-depth interviews of 5 university staff and 5 community leaders and focus group discussions with 10 students undertaking programmes and courses related to climate change and sustainability at the case university. For both interviews and focus groups, an audio recorder was used during data generation which later enabled the researchers to transcribe the data for analysis. Data were analysed using Braun and Clarke (2006)'s six-phase thematic analysis model. The analysis began with a thorough reading of the transcripts to familiarize the researcher(s) with the data. The researchers then generated initial codes with the help of MAXQDA software. The codes were then categorised to help in searching for themes that were later reviewed and a final list of themes that answer the research questions was reached. The final themes were then written up into this chapter.

Key findings and discussion

Talking about what they think of the opportunities, the university staff, students, and community leaders from Makerere University noted the following opportunities for effective university community engagements and climate change action in the context of Africa. The analysis revealed several opportunities, which are organized in five categories as presented in Table 1.

Table 1: *Views and Perspectives of University Staff, Students, and Community Leaders Regarding Opportunities for the University to Contribute to Climate Change (CC) Mitigation and Adaptation through University-Community Engagement (U-CE)*

Theme	Categories
Opportunities for using the third mission of the university to contribute to climate change mitigation and adaptation	Institutional commitment to community engagement towards climate change mitigation and adaptation.
	Leveraging traditional conversation spaces (*Barazas*) for U-CE and pathways for sensitization.
	Incorporating CC indigenous knowledge in mainstream academic and engagement programmes.
	Harnessing women's knowledge, experiences and contribution towards CC mitigation and adaptation practices.
	Community empowerment and income diversification as key to building climate resilient communities.

Institutional commitment to community engagement (CE) towards climate change (CC) mitigation and adaptation

The university staff and students viewed institutional commitment to community engagement programmes as a core opportunity for any African university (like Makerere) to reach out to its indigenous communities about problems that they face. Participants felt that for effective university community engagement and climate change action, there needs to be explicit commitment from the university management and administration in terms of unending actualization of community engagement policies, budget allocations, broad staff understanding of and support for CE, infrastructure, faculty roles and rewards, and integration of engagement activities into other aspects of institutional work and academics.

Despite the review of documents showing that Makerere University acknowledges CE as one of its core functions and with some aspects of CE integrated into its curriculum and policies, some of these CE programmes remain largely unsupported and the contributions to CE are inadequately rewarded. The university staff, community leaders and students in this study believe that for any community engagement programmes regarding climate change to be effective and meaningful, university management ought to establish a more explicit leadership structure for engagement, set aside a specific budget for engagement programmes on climate change action, regulate the sensitization/dissemination of climate change information to communities, review institutional policies to accommodate mandatory student engagement, advocate for changing the incentive regimes of African universities and set aside a specific budget for engagement programmes on CC action, among others. These sentiments are expressed in the following statements:

> "In my experience and interest in community engagement, I think that one of the things that need to change is the incentives in universities, incentive regimes in universities need to change. Now, whereas universities are expected to do community outreach, in essence, the incentive regimes do not promote that. In universities, you hardly have any incentive, for example, promotion, because you've been doing community engagement, at least for Makerere University."

> "Research should be separated from extension because currently, we receive funding which is for both. But usually whenever you're planning for both, as a researcher, the experience I got is that researchers do a lot of desktop work, which is less (financially) compared to community work. Community engagement can have an established budget on its own."

Undoubtedly, it is the university staff members' belief that the university's commitment to have explicit structures, funding and support for community engagement programmes on climate change action could enhance a range of possibilities of engaging members of the public with the design, conduct and dissemination of research – all with the goal of generating mutual benefits by enhancing the quality and socio-economic impact of research. Mugabi (2015) notes that, if effectively actualized, it also facilitates the exchange of knowledge between universities and external communities, enables universities to mobilize external funding and enriches the learning experiences of students. Accordingly, it is unsurprising that Makerere University recognises the importance of the involvement of external communities in its academic activities and decision-making processes. The university needs to show serious commitment and actualization of this recognition (of community engagement) through holding consultative conferences within communities (especially local) during which it shares information with, and involves, other external stakeholders in its decision-making processes. Underscored and guided by *Ubuntu* values, more attention needs to be given to strategies that build on the social responsibility and civic engagement role of higher education.

Leveraging traditional conversation spaces (*Barazas*) for U-CE and pathways for sensitization

The second category that emerged from the data relates to creating traditional conversational spaces commonly known (in African contexts) as *Barazas* not only to enhance university community engagement programmes on climate change action but also to create opportunities for shared awareness between the universities and communities. The *Barazas* is a semi-formal public gathering held in communities in African contexts at the behest of local administrators (Omanga, 2015). The aims of the *Barazas* are to pass on critical information, to deal with emerging information in a locality and to collect the views of the local community on certain issues. In this regard, participants indicated that this could give universities and communities a common ground and be able to position such institutions as being close and relevant to the communities, partners and action-oriented in their efforts to change the mindset and perceptions of communities about universities and engagement programmes. In similar sentiments, participants opined that such African traditional spaces would be fertile for universities to express commitment with different external stakeholders like national policymakers, scientists, local knowledge holders and local community members to deliberate on how to address climate change issues (knowledge, adaptation and mitigation). Some of the participants noted:

> "That's what I called co-production of these frameworks. So, for instance, when you look at a community like Karamoja, Buganda which is now so congested with different tribes, and other communities of this country like Northern Uganda, Eastern Uganda, Western Uganda, where we've had their cultural and local knowledges still existing and is still in play. You cannot sit here in Makerere and come up with a community engagement project before reaching [out] to those people because they understand the local context very well. You have to look at what has been happening in their area that you can say, okay, if we need to change this, it should be in line with their local context such that people embrace it."

> "We can explore any local community spaces for conversations and sensitizations. For example, our local council meetings, local community meetings etc. this could create a platform where we can engage, share knowledge, and work together ... if there is this engagement opportunity, then we could be sharing with them the challenges that communities are facing, actually includes what students are facing, and the issues that we have with them especially to do with the environment. Thus, a common local platform is very, very, very necessary."

Such traditional spaces can also provide another alternative room for awareness creating. According to the university staff and community leaders, this opportunity can provide a dialogue space among local communities, universities and other relevant stakeholders to identify climate change themes, challenges, and policy questions to be addressed by relevant bodies like the National Environment Management Authority (NEMA), the National Forestry Authority (NFA), and relevant government ministries among others. These participants noted that preparing for these workshops should involve a variety of integrated activities aimed at building trust among the involved entities, such as local organizations and universities participating in forest-planting initiatives. Thus, during these workshops, the university can implement its third mission but also provide an opportunity for community members and university members to learn from each other, exchange knowledge, culture and experiences through showcasing the application of local knowledge in the use and management of climate change actions.

As indicated by the university staff and community leaders, the *Baraza*, in the form of an open-air meeting, needs to be convened by a local leader in collaboration with institutional leadership for the purposes of addressing climate change issues and to ensure that the government agenda and policy reaches the grassroots (Omanga, 2015). This traditional formal gathering is used for the purpose of interaction among different stakeholders. A *Baraza* is a forum arranged by the public administration aimed at consensus rather than debate. Actually, currently all Kenyan chiefs are required by law to convene at least two *Barazas* every month (Omanga, 2015). Underpinned by the *Ubuntu* values of collectivism and reciprocity, Makerere University can thus ensure a well-established relationship with local area chiefs, their assistants and village elders within communities in Uganda. This could be critical for disseminating information or enforcing relevant rules or conduct regarding climate change mitigation and adaptation and sensitization on climate change policies within their localities.

Incorporating climate change and indigenous knowledge in mainstream academic and engagement programmes

Indigenous knowledge or African knowledge (used interchangeably) is experiential knowledge based on a worldview and a culture. This knowledge is passed from generation to generation usually by word of mouth and cultural rituals, and has been the basis for agriculture, food preparation and conservation, health care, education, and a wide range of other activities that sustain a society and its environment in many parts of Africa. It was clear from the university staff, students and community leaders in this study suggesting a bottom-up approach that they value African knowledge systems. It was clear that universities only seeing themselves as experts and sole knowledge creators creates unfair and unrealistic engagement with communities. Thus, exploring indigenous knowledge as a crucial element is part of the broader effort to move beyond the prevailing paradigm where universities merely extract information from communities. Instead, they should work with communities as collaborators, recognising and valuing their knowledge systems. Moreover, this experiential knowledge is highly regarded and trusted by community members and its potential for addressing climate change would be fully valued and acknowledged were it to be incorporated in mainstream academic and engagement programmes. Regarding valuing traditional knowledge regarding climate change action, some participants noted that:

> "I talked about experiences, and especially the context of climate change, valuing experiential knowledge, tacit knowledge, rather than focusing on explicit knowledge, so, it's part of that broader equation, that it's one of the missing links, where communities have capacities, they have capabilities that are never valued in knowledge creation, knowledge use and practice."

> "Indigenous knowledge is very important and is becoming very critical and popular, because you cannot come up with innovations about climate change that are quite disoriented from the traditional knowledge. We can start from there, what is it that people can contribute, what is it that they already know, let us not assume that they do not know and avoid overdependence on the knowledge created at the university. Once people begin with what they know, they can integrate with what they do not know that can be accommodated with in their knowledge and resources."

Acknowledgement of and valuing indigenous knowledge systems in the African context are core for meaningful and constructive engagement opportunities to address issues of climate change. Building on what people know. As the saying goes, 'the best scientists are the practitioners', because they have field experience. It should never be assumed that practitioners have knowledge about a phenomenon they experience on a daily basis. This implies that what universities can do is to take what is already possible in nature, or with people, and put it in a scientific way. So, the existence of indigenous knowledge on climate change mitigation and climate change adaptation strategies presents a valuable opportunity for cross pollination, as some communities may be more advanced in how they are addressing climate change issues. That presents an opportunity that this information can be disseminated or can be even modelled to predict what is likely to be because of the dynamic nature of indigenous knowledge. thus, in that way, universities can model and know how that is likely to change, maybe over the next 50 or 100 years, given the impacts of development on community in the Global South.

This opportunity provides an intersection of diverse worldviews and knowledge to develop contextualized programmes and activities and ultimately collaborate to create solutions for the natural environment. A representative of different communities can be engaged and knowledge exchange can occur across and between local communities together with the university knowledge experts. It would also expand the knowledge base and broaden contextualized policy options for informed and locally appropriate decision-making. Indeed, universities should consider indigenous and local communities, whose traditional knowledge could significantly enrich global efforts towards climate change action. Relatedly, an *Ubuntu*-informed philosophy of higher education engagement in Africa has the potential to cultivate numerous programmes of reciprocated U-CE activities that can potentially enhance CC awareness, contextualized CC adaptation and mitigation practices within African universities and communities.

Harnessing women's knowledge, experiences and contribution towards CC mitigation and adaptation practices

Despite wide acknowledgement of women's role and enormous potential leadership for sustainable development, there were clear concerns from participants that such women's capacity is not effectively integrated/activated especially in the African context where there are several constructions on the role of a women in society. Thus, there is still a need and an opportunity to mainstream gender knowledge, experiences and contribution towards climate change knowledge, mitigation and adaptation. Some university staff and community leaders suggested that universities need to work hand in hand with local communities and appreciate potentially integrated approaches suited to gendered equal contributions to climate change action, triggering new dynamic social spaces for women to engage for instance in policy formulation and decision-making.

> *"All those constraints are what we can try to mitigate alongside climate change, so that a man and a woman are able to work better for the well-being of the family in the face of climate change. So that even the new interventions that are coming up target both, so that and primarily the woman, the woman, you know, because women are the ones who are always in the garden longer compared to the men, especially in northern Uganda, women are they like, they do a lot of work, they are the ones in the garden, men are just served food, they lie in the trading centres drinking."*

> *"Women knowledge and experience must be used. They face a lot of disadvantages, as we might, we might also know in terms of underlying social cultural construct, they don't own land, they don't own resources, in terms of income, rarely, they are harassed by the communities in terms of opportunity, the control of income, sometimes in the hands of a husband, if the woman makes the money. But in African setup, largely, women interact with land and the environment at largely, more than men, if both university and communities can work together to mitigate these gender-based exclusion and then utilize the opportunity, we could move faster in stabilizing the climate."*

In order to mitigate social-cultural constraints that limit women's full participation in engagement programmes towards climate change action, participants feel that there is a need to effectively utilize women's experiences with the environment, their knowledge with agriculture and climate change to efficiently implement mitigation measures that are gender sensitive. This means that a feminist approach to climate change action not only addresses injustices and barriers that keep people from participating in sustainable change but encourages all people to work together toward climate-resilient and sustainable development. In an African setup where women have no say on environmental issues, as in most communities, land ownership and decision-making, universities and community leaders ought to initiate engagement programmes on climate change action that are explicitly geared towards inclusion.

As noted by the participants, gender justice is key to an effective climate action especially policy. In fact, if universities and communities effectively explore gender equitable structures, it could prove to be a crucial factor in reducing Uganda's greenhouse gas emissions and building resilience among community members. Due to the widespread, gender-specific distribution of everyday tasks and care work in different African contexts, women have specific knowledge and skills as providers, educators, energy users, and land managers while they work in agriculture in most rural setups. Therefore, they have important knowledge to deal with the climate-related risks to water and food security. Relatedly, indigenous peoples, especially indigenous women, are crucial knowledge carriers for biodiversity conservation and climate action. Their transformative potential can only unfold if their rights are respected and they are participating in political processes. Actually, the Paris Agreement declares gender equality as a principle in addressing climate change. The implementation of the Paris Agreement and the 2030 Agenda for sustainable development requires a just transition of our societies. In the process, discriminatory structures must be removed and an empowering environment for women and disadvantaged groups must be created to ensure values of collectivism and unity in approaching societal problems.

Community empowerment and income diversification as key to building climate resilient communities

University students and community leaders thought that both universities and communities can collaborate to empower community leadership, resilience to climate change impacts and at the same time strengthen their sources of livelihood to restrain them from tampering with the environment and other carbon sinks. Participants noted that building strong capabilities and capacities at the local level could be crucial in sustaining climate change action and engagement efforts between universities and communities. Some university staff, students and community leaders argued that there is a need to fundamentally shift the current paradigm of thinking and action within the universities. This shift should start by strengthening institutional arrangements and capabilities at the local level, enabling people to adapt their skills as changes occur and anticipate future challenges. It was further noted that a chance should be given to community-based research arrangements through community-based information exchange to stimulate community-based adaptation and mitigation measures. To this, a participant added that:

"We need to ask ourselves what is driving the community members to destroy the environment. Our biggest hurdle is poverty and hunger, that is why you have all this charcoal burning, swamp destruction and other causes of climate change. Once we understand this, can we look for avenues to empower these community members. I believe if civil society, university management and us community leaders combine our efforts, we can improve the livelihoods of these community members."

"We should develop small group or neighbourhood models or household models where people come up with ideas of how they would want their neighbourhood to look like or what they would want to have or the policies they want or the things that they would want to follow and how they would conserve and protect their environment. So, in those small groups, I can say about 10 homes, they will have a leader who effectively checks on the progress of these ideas they come up with to effectively involve the communities."

Continuing support for income diversification is required to ensure that effective capacity is maintained and strengthened. Universities engaging closely with a range of different community groups and associations in developing and implementing project activities can assist communities to more effectively build their capacity to provide ongoing support for local adaptation actions in a collaborative and holistic manner and reduced destruction of the environment. Across many rural communities in African contexts, rising temperatures and unpredictable rains are upending food security and diminishing already low structured household income. A collaboration of universities and communities can come up with a comprehensive plan for climate risks, take up or have trainings on climate resilient agribusiness practices to strengthen their livelihoods through diversification, knowledge about climate resilient agricultural commodities like cowpeas, sunflower, and peanuts.

Conclusion and discussion

It was clear from the perspectives of community leaders, university staff and students that with a rapidly closing window of opportunity to secure a liveable and sustainable future for all, university-community engagement offers African universities contextualized opportunities that are necessary and can accelerate climate action. The choices and actions implemented might be able to support policy making and enhance the third mission programmes towards addressing climate change issues and sustainability at African universities and communities. University-community engagement that involves all partners is the glue that creates trust, generates new lines of work, funding, inclusion, income diversification and keeps shared goals as well as expectations visible to both universities and communities. The actual core work of the engagement is building reciprocal relationships between communities and universities (as per *Ubuntu* theory) that endure beyond individual projects or grants to programmes that enhance climate action and scales the impact to entire communities. In this way, engagement opportunities can build sustained relationships that respect the needs and interests of all partners, and assessment as a constant tool for reflecting on our contributions and benefits should often be used, thus building deeper and more authentic reciprocity.

Ultimately, careful implementation of these context-specific opportunities can help reduce the worsening impacts of climate change caused by human activity. Findings suggest that observed widespread and substantial impacts and related losses and damages attributed to climate change can decelerate through synergies between universities and communities. Impacts are driven by changes in multiple physical climate conditions, which are increasingly attributed to human influence. To effectively utilize these opportunities, CE at African universities requires each university to pay attention to its institutional context, such as history, disciplinary focus, location, ownership, mission, culture, values and community engagement priorities, and national policy agendas. As postulated by Rajah (2019), the conceptualisation, implementation and sustainability of CE programmes in African contextualized higher education institutions (especially universities) should reflect indigenous epistemologies that build on African philosophies as its core foundations. This can be possible through synergy to advance policy development and target-setting at university and community levels, particularly in relation to climate change knowledge, mitigation, adaptation as well as enhanced transparency of engagement programmes on climate action and support.

Deep, rapid, and sustained engagement programmes on mitigation and accelerated implementation of adaptation actions would reduce projected losses and damages for humans and ecosystems and deliver many co-benefits, especially for universities and communities. Climate resilient development benefits from drawing on diverse knowledge Diverse knowledge and values include cultural values, indigenous knowledge, local knowledge, and scientific knowledge. The U-CE opportunities towards climate change action itself can be the game changer: its holistic view makes adaptation everyone's responsibility and shows that the two entities ought to infuse engagement programmes with climate considerations to successfully adapt. At their core, these engagement opportunities are about biodiversity and about protecting the most vulnerable.

Recommendations

The universities ought to prioritize inclusive, transparent, and equitable decision-making, and improve access to finance and technology by community members. To actualize such opportunities, universities and community leaders should ensure that all voices are involved in planning and decision-making and that communication channels remain open on both sides. Universities should emphasise the need for intentional processes that ensure all have a voice in planning, problem-solving, and management of the engagement programmes. Shared control can also help keep the entire partnership alert to the need to bring in community members on board as engagement programmes evolve.

Universities and their partners should embark on a re-imagining process to understand the intellectual, scholarly, and demonstrable work needed to support the university's transformative engagement agenda towards climate change issues. The process of this re-imagination can involve developing an understanding *of*, and continual support *for*, engagement programmes, as well as providing strategic direction to the hybrid engagement praxes across the university through well laid university community engagement structures.

African universities need to develop a community of practice to guide the Africanisation and decolonisation of engagement programmes on climate change action to foster a diverse, inclusive, and representative engagement rooted in knowledge democracy. HEIs should endeavour to seek feedback from and interaction with communities in order to investigate and co-create processes that will guide engagement programmes. Local traditional platforms should be consistently utilized as collaborative multi-stakeholder spaces of exploration for the positioning and re-positioning of the engagement and transformation interface of African universities. It is both a feasible and doable option for re-imagining the engagement programmes as a university in service to society.

Government, civil society and other university and community partners ought to create and avail incentives and funding opportunities to both the universities and community-based organizations and associations that aim to support and achieve income diversification. For instance, this can be through availing fairly competitive grants for universities, wealth creation programmes for community members that can ably enhance university-community engagement activities and also scale up community resilience to effects of climate change like poverty and food insecurity.

References

Alharahsheh, H. H., & Pius, A. (2020). A review of key paradigms: Positivism vs interpretivism. *Global Academic Journal of Humanities and Social Sciences, 2*(3), 39–43.

Axon, S. (2016). "The good life": Engaging the public with community-based carbon reduction strategies. *Environmental Science & Policy, 66*, 82–92.

Boogaard, B. K. (2019). The relevance of connecting sustainable agricultural development with African philosophy. *South African Journal of Philosophy = Suid-Afrikaanse Tydskrif vir Wysbegeerte, 38*(3), 273–286.

Bowers, A. M. (2017). University-community partnership models: Employing organizational management theories of paradox and strategic contradiction. *Journal of Higher Education Outreach and Engagement, 21*(2), 37–64.

Braun, V., & Clarke, V. (2006). Using thematic analysis in psychology. *Qualitative Research in Psychology, 3,* 77–101.

Creswell, J. W., & Plano Clark, V. L. (2018). *Designing and conducting mixed methods research* (3rd ed.). SAGE.

Fawzy, S., Osman, A. I., Doran, J., & Rooney, D. W. (2020). Strategies for mitigation of climate change: A review. *Environmental Chemistry Letters, 18,* 2069–2094.

Hancock, B., Ockleford, E., & Windridge, K. (2001). *An introduction to qualitative research.* Trent Focus Group.

Kestin, T., van den Belt, M., Denby, L., Ross, K., Thwaites, J., & Hawkes, M. (2017). *Getting started with the SDGs in universities: A guide for universities, higher education institutions, and the academic sector.* Sustainable Development Solutions Network.

Mertens, K., Jacobs, L., Maes, J., Kabaseke, C., Maertens, M., Poesen, J., Mervyn, M., & Vranken, L. (2016). The direct impact of landslides on household income in tropical regions: A case study from the Rwenzori Mountains in Uganda. *Science of the Total Environment, 550,* 1032–1043.

Mikhaylov, A., Moiseev, N., Aleshin, K., & Burkhardt, T. (2020). Global climate change and greenhouse effect. *Entrepreneurship and Sustainability Issues, 7*(4), 2897–2913.

Mosia, P. A. (2023). Using African philosophies in the alignment of inclusive education programmes with sustainable development goals. In *Using African epistemologies in shaping inclusive education knowledge* (pp. 203–218). Springer Nature Switzerland.

Mugabi, H. (2015). Institutional commitment to community engagement: A case study of Makerere University. *International Journal of Higher Education, 4*(1), 187–199. https://www.sciedu.ca/journal/index.php/ijhe/article/view/6367/3821

Mugumbate, J. R., & Chereni, A. (2020). Now, the theory of Ubuntu has its space in social work. *African Journal of Social Work, 10*(1), v–xv.

Nabaho, L., Turyasingura, W., Twinomuhwezi, I., & Nabukenya, M. (2022). The third mission of universities on the African continent: Conceptualisation and operationalisation. *Higher Learning Research Communications, 12*(1), 81–98.

Nicotra, M., Del Giudice, M., & Romano, M. (2021). Fulfilling university third mission: Towards an ecosystemic strategy of entrepreneurship education. *Studies in Higher Education, 46*(5), 1000–1010.

Nkosi, B., & Daniels, P. (2007). Family strengths: South Africa. *Marriage & Family Review, 41*(1-2), 11–26.

Nyerere, J. K. (1968). *Freedom and socialism – Uhuru na ujamaa: A selection from writings and speeches, 1965-1967.* Oxford University Press.

Okoliko, D. A., & David, J. O. (2021). Ubuntu and climate change governance: Moving beyond conceptual conundrum. *Journal of Public Affairs, 21*(3), e2232.

Omanga, D. (2015). 'Chieftaincy' in the social media space: Community policing in a Twitter-convened Baraza. *Stability: International Journal of Security & Development, 4*(1), 1–16.

Papadimitriou, A. (2020). Beyond rhetoric: Reinventing the public mission of higher education. *Tertiary Education and Management, 26*(1), 1–4.

Pundt, H., & Heilmann, A. (2020). Building collaborative partnerships: An example of a 3rd mission activity in the field of local climate change adaptation. In *Universities as living labs for sustainable development* (pp. 621–636). Springer.

Raditloaneng, W. N. (2013). Impact of "Implementing the Third Mission of Universities in Africa (ITMUA) collaborative research project, 2010-2011". *International Journal of Peace, 4*(5), 90–99.

Rajah, S. S. (2019). Conceptualising community engagement through the lens of African indigenous education. *Perspectives in Education, 37*(1), 1–14.

Schilling, J., Hertig, E., Tramblay, Y., & Scheffran, J. (2020). Climate change vulnerability, water resources and social implications in North Africa. *Regional Environmental Change, 20*(1), 1–12.

Schnurbus, V., & Edvardsson, I. R. (2022). The third mission among Nordic universities: A systematic literature review. *Scandinavian Journal of Educational Research, 66*(2), 238–260.

Ssekamatte, D. (2021). Participants' perspectives regarding the role of university governance in promoting climate change and sustainability interventions at University of Dar es Salaam in Tanzania. *Developments in Administration, 3(1)*, 31–41.

Ssekamatte, D. (2022). The role of the university and institutional support for climate change education interventions at two African universities. *Higher Education, 1*(1), 1–15.

Taylor, R. G., Mileham, L., Tindimugaya, C., & Mwebembezi, L. (2009). Recent glacial recession and its impact on alpine river flow in the Rwenzori Mountains of Uganda. *Journal of African Earth Sciences, 55*(3–4), 205–213.

Trencher, G., Yarime, M., McCormick, K. B., Doll, C. N., & Kraines, S. B. (2014). Beyond the third mission: Exploring the emerging university function of co-creation for sustainability. *Science and Public Policy, 41*(2), 151–179.

Tutu, D. (1999). *No future without forgiveness*. Image.

UNESCO. (2015). *Putting climate change education into practice*. United Nations Educational Scientific and Cultural Organization.

USAID. (2022). *USAID climate strategy 2022-2030*. https://www.usaid.gov/policy/climate-strategy

Virtanen, A. (2010). Learning for climate responsibility: Via consciousness to action. In W. L. Filho (Ed.), *Universities and climate change* (pp. 231–240). Springer.

Welborn, L. (2018). Africa and climate change—Projecting vulnerability and adaptive capacity. *ISS Africa Report, 14*(1), 1–24.

Waghid, Y. (2020). Towards an Ubuntu philosophy of higher education in Africa. *Studies in Philosophy and Education, 39*(3), 299–308.

Yin, R. K. (2012). *Application of case study research* (3rd ed.). Sage Publications Inc.

CHAPTER 6
Picturing the experiences of the student–supervisor relationship towards completion of doctoral studies in African universities

Cornelius Kipleting Rugut

Introduction

Nations around the globe need scholars and lifelong researchers who can be involved in knowledge creation to meet national and global challenges. Governments are recognising that the foundation of a productive and prosperous country is a well-educated population, especially doctoral graduates who can be involved in research and take the lead in coming up with new and better ways of dealing with various aspects of the development of a country. However, statistics show that the completion rate of doctoral studies in Africa is still very low (Bacwayo et al., 2017). In order to increase the number of doctoral graduates, there must be quality postgraduate supervision which is one of the invaluable areas of higher education.

This study, therefore, focused on the experiences of the student–supervisor relationship in postgraduate supervision and the completion of doctoral studies in African universities. The relationship between the supervisor and the doctoral student is paramount to the completion of doctoral studies. Research indicates that the most important factor in students' decisions to continue and complete their doctoral studies or to withdraw is their relationship with their supervisors (Jones, 2013; Kiley, 2011). Several studies have also revealed that successful supervision is anchored in a quality student–supervisor relationship (Abiddin, 2009; Hodza, 2007) and yet there is no established procedure for effective supervision nor student–supervisor relationship. Individual supervisors seem to approach the student–supervisor relationship differently.

Research objective

As already stated, the focus of this study was to explore the experiences of the student–supervisor relationship in postgraduate supervision and the completion of doctoral studies in African universities. The study participants were doctoral graduates who recently completed their educational doctoral studies in two African universities.

The research question was framed as 'What are the experiences of the student–supervisor relationship in a doctoral study?'

Theoretical perspective on experiences of the student–supervisor relationship

Doctoral students have varied experiences of their doctoral studies depending on the nature of the student–supervisor relationship. Most researchers agree that a close working relationship between the student and the supervisor is central to the completion of the study (Bacwayo et al., 2017; Matheka, 2020b). Compared to other educational relationships, the student–supervisor relationship can make or break students' success and career for life if it is not properly managed (Grevholm et al., 2005). This literature refers to pleasant and unpleasant experiences encountered by doctoral students.

Sverdlik et al. (2018) noted that students sometimes experience discontent in their relationship with their supervisors. This happens mostly when students have a poor relationship with their supervisors. These authors identified three main causes of student discontent in the student–supervisor relationship, namely, personality factors, professional factors and organizational factors. Personality factors may include interpersonal differences or a personality clash between the student and the supervisor. Professional factors that may cause discontent could be a supervisor who is misinformed or who has different research interests to that of the student. Lastly, organizational factors such as the supervisor having too many competing responsibilities or too many students may lead to less attention to the student and as such, the student may feel neglected (Krauss & Ismi, 2010). Such experiences of discontent may lead to failure in completing the PhD (Sverdlik et al., 2018). Students with feelings of discontent in the relationship may choose to drop out or discontinue their studies (Grevholm et al., 2005; Zainal, 2007).

Some students described their relationship with their supervisors as a frustrating experience (Sayed et al., 2006). In the study by Krauss and Ismi (2010), which explored student experiences in the student–supervisor relationship, some doctoral students pointed out frustrating experiences where their supervisors suppressed their opinions, or rejected their work with unpleasant comments, even when such arose from supervisors' suggestions. There are also instances in some relationships where students have been compelled to change their supervisors due to frequent disagreements with their supervisors (Sverdlik et al., 2018). In spite of the difficulties, many doctoral students do their best to produce a good piece of work that would impress their supervisor (Sayed et al., 2006).

Kosgei et al. (2019) outline the negative critiques received by doctoral students in their relationship with their supervisors. According to Morris (2011), some supervisors treat their students with a dictatorial and commanding attitude. Participants in Morris' study narrated how their supervisors talked to them in a demeaning way, dismissing their ideas and rarely acknowledging the good work they were doing (Kosgei et al., 2019). Some students have reported how their supervisors expressed anger towards them by condemning or shouting at them or even yelling at them in front of others to publicly humiliate them (Morris, 2011; Kosgei et al., 2019; Zainal, 2007). While referring to the humiliating critiques, one of the students in Morris' study said, "I had my PhD from hell" (Morris, 2011, p. 551).

The power dynamic in the student–supervisor relationship is perceived to be unequal (Ahmadi et al., 2020). Several scholars (Dimitrova, 2016; Grant, 2003; Morris, 2011) have highlighted experiences of power-struggles between the PhD students and their supervisors. Students have reported bitter feelings of powerlessness in the student–supervisor relationship (Ahmadi et al., 2020). The power dynamics play a key role in the success of the doctoral student, as well as the satisfaction of the student in the relationship (Grant, 2005). While the relationship between two professionals can occur on an equal basis, the relationship between the student and the supervisor is seen to be a teacher–student relationship and therefore being unequal (Wubbels & Mieke, 2006). Negative experiences in the relationship can have a profound impact on the student's research productivity (Dimitrova, 2016). If the power dynamic in the relationship is not properly managed, it may lead to delay or non-completion of the PhD (Grant, 2005).

Doctoral students have also expressed their experiences of confusion and unrealistic workload demands from their supervisors (Sverdlik et al., 2018; Philips & Jonson, 2022). Some students are left by their supervisors to work on their own, while others do not receive the advice they expect from their supervisors and as such students feel abandoned and confused (Sverdlik et al., 2018; Smallwood, 2004). Other students have expressed how their supervisors placed unrealistic deadlines for submission of their written chapters during their candidature. They described working long hours, even spending sleepless nights, and working during weekends to meet their supervisors' demands (Kosgei et al., 2019).

Bullying is a bad experience that PhD students have complained about in their studies (Lewis, 2004; Morris, 2011). Students have reported situations where their supervisors project their workload pressures onto them in the form of insults, intimidations, and other forms of bullying (Philips & Johnson, 2022). Unlike the university staff who are protected from staff bullying, research students are not protected by any law in the university and as such, they are vulnerable to any kind of supervisory bullying (Lewis, 2004). Some scholars have grouped doctoral supervisory bullying behaviours into five categories, namely, "threat to professional status, threat to personal standing, isolation, overworking and destabilization" (Morris, 2011, pp. 547–548). Threat to professional status involves humiliations like accusations regarding lack of effort, while threat to personal standing can be insults, intimidation and name-calling. Isolation may come in the form of withholding of information or preventing access to opportunities; overworking involves undue pressure and impossible deadlines, while destabilisation refers to failing to give credit when due and repeated reminders of blunders (Morris, 2011). Students experiencing supervisory bullying may take longer to complete their studies, while others may drop out due to humiliations (Dimitrova, 2016).

Even though many PhD graduates have described going through unpleasant experiences in their studies, many others hold a different view. Some graduates have expressed positive experiences in student–supervisor relationships (Cadman, 2010; Grevholm et al., 2005; Halse, 2011). They reported that their supervisors offered different comments which gave them direction in their work and enabled them to do their best. Others noted that, even though their supervisors were too busy, they created time to meet with them and discuss their work (Ali et al., 2016; Malfroy, 2005). A study in an Australian university by Cadman (2010) found that students have varied views on their experiences with their supervisors. Some students paid tribute to the commitment of their supervisors, acknowledging their supervisors as guides and mentors. They appreciated having learned many things they had not been aware of through their interaction with the supervisors (Cadman, 2010). These students showed strong attachment to their supervisors by using words like "especially my supervisor", "I am grateful of my supervisor", "I got this from my supervisor" (Cadman, 2010, p. 483).

Different cultural backgrounds are another aspect within supervision that supervisors have to acknowledge. This was evident from a study by McClure (2005) when he interviewed postgraduate students of Chinese origin who had newly enrolled for their studies in Singapore. The study found that culture-based differences brought a unique challenge in supervising international students or students of different races and cultures within a nation. The students go through an experience of adjustment and are challenged to fit into the new system (Son & Park, 2014). According to Son and Park (2014) it is advisable to appoint a local mentor or supervisors with intercultural competence who can work well with students of different cultural origin. There is a need for supervisors to be intellectually and culturally flexible in order to accommodate the expectations of different students with different cultural backgrounds (Son & Park, 2014).

A study by Backhouse et al. (2015) also gives some insight into the student experiences with their supervisors. In this study, students told stories of experiences with their supervisors who were in the same discipline and the same department, but had widely differing opinions of what the PhD students had to do, how they had to do it and what the supervisor's role was in the process. Even though there is no set formula for successful supervision, supervisors need to be aware of students' concerns (Philips & Johnson, 2022; Backhouse et al., 2015), as this enables them to become more mindful of their interaction with the students and hence work towards improving the student–supervisor relationship.

Materials and methods

This was a qualitative study located in the interpretivist paradigm in which reality is socially constructed. The participants for this case study were purposively selected. They had a doctoral degree in education and were within a bracket of five years after graduation. The ten participants, seven women and three men, were graduates from Moi University (five) and Nelson Mandela University (five) and were willing to share their experiences of their student–supervisor relationships, making the voices of postgraduate students heard. Contacts were obtained through administrators in postgraduate offices in each university. Emails were sent calling for their participation. The first ten positive responses, five from each university, participated in the study.

The data were generated by use of drawing as a data collection method. Drawing is a technique which is used to explore conscious and unconscious issues and experiences (Theron et al., 2011). It has the potential of bringing out hidden or repressed perceptions or views not previously known or expressed (De Lange, 2011). Hence, utilizing drawing is an important method that has the possibility of prompting discussion around a topic of concern, and it helps a researcher to get access to the aspects of knowledge which could be very hard to express in words and might be ignored or remain hidden (Theron et al., 2011). When drawing is used as a research method the participant is given time to draw and write a caption (De Lange, 2011). A caption is a brief explanation provided by the participant in writing to describe the meaning embedded in the drawing (De Lange, 2011). The participants in this study were engaged in drawing their experiences of the student–supervisor relationship during their study. The participants were assured that there is no such thing as a wrong or poor drawing, the rationale being to encourage them not to worry about the aesthetics of their drawings. Thematic analysis was used to analyse the captions of the ten drawings.

The following prompt was provided to them:

- Draw how you experienced your student–supervisor relationship.

Every participant was given a plain piece of A4 paper and a pencil and had ten minutes to draw and to write a caption.. The participants had to explain the meaning embedded in the drawing by writing a caption of what the drawing meant. Each of the drawings made was scanned and the accompanying captions typed in Microsoft Word below the drawing. Ten drawings were made. Figures 1 to 5 are examples of the drawings made by the participants. Where supporting quotations come from these five drawings and their captions, the figure number is inserted. Where the supporting quotations come from drawings which are not included in this chapter, only the pseudonym of the participant is inserted. It is important to take note that the captions as written by the participants have been typed without any alteration or correction of punctuation, spelling, or tense. The names given to the participants are pseudonyms.

Figure 1: *Drawing by Dr Nelly. A Flag to Represent My PhD Experience*

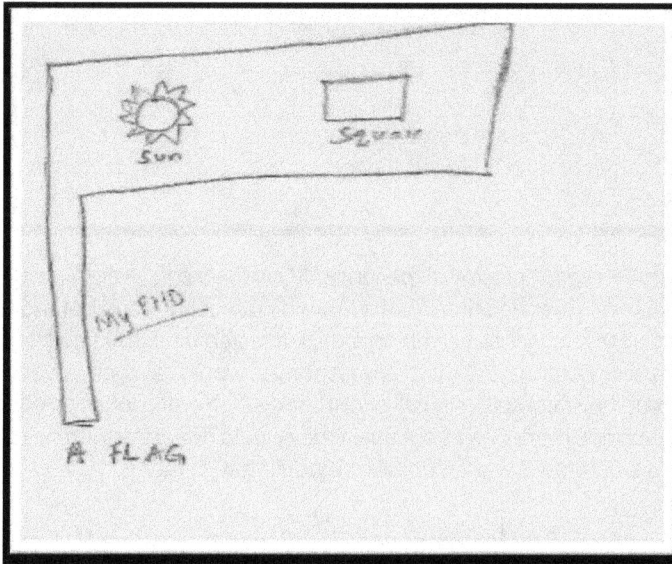

I have drawn a flag which represents my PhD. I believe that a doctoral relationship encompasses the PhD, the student and the promoter. As you might know, a flag symbolises unity of a nation, it is sovereignty and the values it encompasses. In my case, the flag represents my PhD which brought us together in unity with my promoter. We had a relationship in the study itself. I drew a sun because it is a source of energy, whenever I was discouraged in my study I would get an encouragement from my promoter and be energised again. The sun also represents the light. With the support of my supervisor I would see where I was going because there was light in terms of guidance I was getting from my promoter. I have also drawn a square. A square has four equal sides with opposite angles. This is to represent that I was bring knowledge into the study as much as my supervisor. We had different lenses to look at some aspects of the research. In a nutshell my experience was enjoying though we did not always agree.

Figure 2: *Drawing by Dr Winny. A Hill Representing My Experience*

This is a hill which represents my experience. My supervisors were knowledgeable and experienced, but they never had time for me. Arranging meetings and getting feedback from them was an uphill task, it was like climbing a thick-forested hill. Sometimes I would send my work but it takes over six months without any response. I would call them several times or send text messages, but they rarely pick my call or call back. Whenever I got an opportunity to meet them, they would guide me very well but again they would disappear with no communication or response for a long time. It was an uphill task working with them.

Figure 3: *Drawing by Dr Beatrice. Forest and Clear Road Representing My Experience*

The drawing shows a forest, at the edge of the forest is a clear road but with some stones. My experience with my supervisors at the beginning of my PhD was difficult, they did not give me the assistance I needed and they always disagreed, I have drawn a forest to represent this difficult experience with them, they are the dark moments in a forest without direction and guidance from the supervisors, I was just confused. Later the supervisors were changed and my new supervisors gave me direction and guidance, I see this as coming of the forest and following a clear route. We worked together with the new supervisors, and they always encourage me to complete my PhD.

Figure 4: *Drawing by Dr Dan. Two Hills Representing My Student–Supervisor Relationship*

I represent my student-supervisor relationship with the two hills above that are linked by a bridge. The two hills represent me and my supervisor. I saw my supervisor as a knowledgeable person experienced in research, my study was a link (the bridge). The bridge enabled me to tap the knowledge from him. Our relationship was bright and warm as you can see the sun in the drawing which represents the warmness of our relationship, my supervisor was supportive and he motivated me throughout my study. I have also drawn clouds to represent the challenges in my relationship with my supervisor, it was not always bright and warm but sometimes gloomy when I felt my supervisor was criticising my work even when I thought I had done my best. I had to do it several times until he was satisfied. There was also a time when my supervisor was busy and would not be available for me, these where dark moments for me.

Figure 5: *Drawing by Dr Careen. A Dove Representing My Student–Supervisor Relationship*

The drawing shows a dove. A dove is mostly used to represent peace. In my experience, this dove represents the peaceful working relationship with my supervisors. My supervisors were humble and peaceful, they were not arrogant, and they did not create barriers in our relationship. It was easy to work with them because there was respect for one another. They were busy people and sometimes feedback would delay but I understood them. They created time for me and we worked with understanding.

Findings and discussion

A summary of the findings is presented in the figure below.

Figure 6: *Diagrammatic Representation of the Findings; Experiences of the Student–Supervisor Relationship*

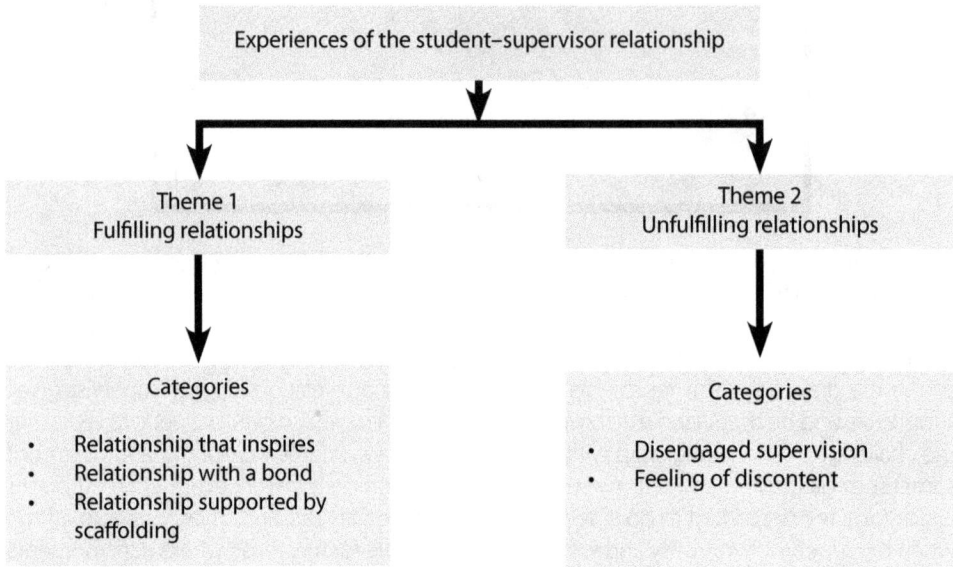

The findings presented in Figure 6 highlight two themes which are discussed in this section, *fulfilling relationships* and *unfulfilling relationships*.

Fulfilling relationships

Experiences of doctoral studies can be fulfilling and satisfying to the doctoral student. A fulfilling relationship is a supportive relationship that enhances learning and enables the research student to work in the best way possible. It is a relationship that promotes the completion of the research project and the production of quality work. The participants highlighted three aspects that related to fulfilling relationships namely, (i) a relationship that inspires (ii) a relationship in which there is a bond and (iii) a relationship supported by scaffolding.

A relationship that inspires

In this context an inspiring relationship refers to how the supervisor manages the relationship in order to enable the doctoral student to work confidently and creatively during the research process. In describing their experiences, the participants expressed their views on how their supervisors inspired them to progress and complete their studies. They recalled the encouragement, energy, and motivation from their supervisors, as can be seen from their captions:

> *"My supervisor was supportive, and he motivated me throughout my study."* (Drawing caption, Dan, Figure 4)

> *"I drew a sun, because it is a source of energy, whenever I was discouraged in my study; I would get an encouragement from my promoter and be energised again."* (Drawing caption, Nelly, Figure 1)

> *"We worked together with the new supervisors and they always encourage me to complete my PhD."* (Drawing caption, Beatrice, Figure 3)

> *"I am at my own, but I know that my supervisor is there for me and I am safe."* (Drawing caption, Alice)

The quotations above suggest an inspiring relationship that promoted the student's doctoral learning. It seems that supervisors played an important role in encouraging and motivating the candidates to persevere and complete their studies. According to Matheka (2020b), research students flourish when their supervisors give them the energy to work smarter and produce quality work within the expected time. Schulze (2012) argues that it is important for the supervisor to acknowledge the candidate as a person first, in addition to being a learner and as such motivate them to continue the research process. However, it is important to note that some doctoral students also experience harshness and discouragement from their supervisors, which make them feel demotivated and insecure in the relationship and may opt to discontinue their studies (Morris, 2011). It is therefore necessary for the supervisor to provide support through encouragement and motivation (Schulze, 2012). This could create a bond in the relationship, as discussed in the next category.

A relationship with a bond

A relationship with a bond refers to the kind of relationship where there is a strong affiliation between the student and the supervisor. The participants expressed their experiences of a bonding relationship which involved working with the supervisor as a friend, being in a warm relationship and a relationship of understanding and peace. This became evident from the following quotations:

> *"They became great friends to me. It was an interesting and nurturing experience with them."* (Drawing caption, Mike)

> *"Our relationship was bright and warm as you can see the sun in the drawing which represents the warmness of our relationship."* (Drawing caption, Dan, Figure 4)

> *"They created time for me and we worked with understanding."* (Drawing caption, Careen, Figure 5)

> *"In my experience, this dove represents the peaceful working relationship with my supervisors … it was easy to work with them because there was respect for one another."* (Drawing caption, Careen, Figure 5)

The quotations above suggest that a bond between the student and the supervisor seems to promote the doctoral learning process, as it opens the possibility for engagement. Most researchers agree that completing the PhD is a process that depends on a close working relationship between the student and supervisor (Abiddin et al., 2009; Dimitrova, 2016). A bond between the doctoral student and the supervisor offers strong support which enables the student to progress steadily in the research process (Radloff, 2010). Many supervisors work closely with students to nurture them in the research field (Bacwayo et al., 2017). A supervisor who is friendly creates opportunities for a peaceful working relationship with the student, which enhances the learning process, hence promoting the completion of doctoral studies (Mainhard et al., 2009). A relationship guided by respect and understanding not only promotes faster completion of the doctoral studies, but also enables the student to produce quality work (Bacwayo et al., 2017). The production of quality work requires the supervisor's support through scaffolding, which is the focus of the next category.

A relationship supported by scaffolding

Scaffolding is a supportive learning process that aims at promoting a deeper level of learning for the doctoral student. It involves a variety of techniques applied by the supervisor to enable the doctoral student to progress towards a stronger understanding of the doctoral work. The participants explained how they had supportive and satisfying experiences with their supervisors. They described their supervisors as people who nurtured them in the research process by providing thorough guidance and training. This was evident from the following responses:

> *"With the support of my supervisor I would see where I was going because there was light in terms of guidance I was getting."* (Drawing caption, Nelly, Figure 1)

> *"They gave me thorough training in how to do my work just like a leopard trains its young one to hunt perfectly."* (Drawing caption, Mike)

> *"She will also show me the interesting things in her book which I also need to go and learn. When I am nourished and ready to continue playing and exploring, I go back across the river to my own place where I continue."* (Drawing caption, Alice)

> *"I enjoyed my relationship with my supervisor, and I was happy and satisfied with the guidance she gave me."* (Drawing caption, Mary)

The quotations above provide evidence of the efforts made by the supervisors to scaffold the students' doctoral learning. Mainhard et al. (2009) describe a helpful working relationship where the supervisor balances between controlling the student's research process and ensuring that the required guidance is provided to support the progress of the student. The supervisor should take the responsibility of guiding and training the research student to produce quality theses and complete their studies on time (Vladimir, 2010). The supervisor's guidance is the light that illuminates the way for the research student to progress. Sayed et al. (2006) argue that students like to work with supervisors who read their drafts and provide thorough guidance on their work, as it gives direction to the student on what is required of a PhD.

Even though the student–supervisor relationship can be fulfilling as described in this section, some relationships can be disappointing to the doctoral students. The next theme refers to experiences which caused dissatisfaction in the student–supervisor relationship.

Unfulfilling relationships

While the student–supervisor relationship can work to the benefit of the student and be fulfilling, it can also be unfulfilling. An unfulfilling relationship refers to a less supportive working relationship between the student and the supervisor. In this theme, the participants pointed to their dissatisfaction with and within the relationship, referring to two issues, namely, (i) disengaged supervision and (ii) feelings of discontent.

Disengaged supervision

Disengaged supervision refers to a relationship of little contact and little communication between the student and the supervisor. The research process is an arduous task that requires frequent communication and contact in the student–supervisor relationship, enabling engagement with the study. However, minimal engagement between the student and the supervisor during the study or during some phases of the study, places strain on the student, who then might not know how to proceed. Participants spoke of their experiences of being lonely in the relationship when their supervisors are unavailable to attend to them. Some talked of delayed feedback and insufficient communication. The above is evident from the following quotations:

> "Sometimes I felt that my supervisor was too busy to attend to my work or meet with me, I felt I was lonely." (Drawing caption, Mary)

> "My supervisor was busy and would not be available for me, these were dark moments for me." (Drawing caption, Dan, Figure 4)

"My supervisors were knowledgeable and experienced, but they never had time for me." (Drawing caption, Winny, Figure 2)

"Sometimes I would send my work, but it takes over six months without any response." (Drawing caption, Winny, Figure 2)

These quotations provide evidence of a dissatisfying relationship where the engagement between the student and the supervisor is not adequate. Grossman and Crowther (2015) concur with the stated quotes that research students can sometimes find themselves lonely in a relationship where their supervisors are busy and unavailable for consultation. The issues raised above were due to the supervisors being busy with administration, teaching responsibilities, having too many students to supervise or sometimes being away from the university (Philps & Johnson, 2022). A supervisor's workload may cause less contact with the student and delayed feedback (McClure, 2005). Students feel abandoned when they work on their own without the supervisor's guidance (McClure, 2005). It is therefore important for the student and the supervisor, at the outset of the study, to negotiate the frequency of meetings and the way consultations are to be done in the relationship (Detsky & Baerlocher, 2007). This should include arrangements for supervision when the supervisor is busy or away for an extended period of time (Kosgei et al., 2019). Disengaged supervision may cause discontent in the relationship, as outlined in the next category.

Feelings of discontent

Discontent, in the context of the student–supervisor relationship, refers to the student feeling dissatisfied with the supervisor's guidance. The relationship between the student and the supervisor can be characterised by discontent if not well managed and if it lacks transparency. Participants expressed their experiences which led to discontent, as the lack of robust guidance and direction, the lack of regular and clear communication from their supervisors, being discouraged by supervisor critique and the demanding nature of the research work. These aspects became evident when the participants articulated their experiences as follows:

"My experience with my supervisors at the beginning of my PhD was difficult, they did not give me the assistance I needed and they always disagreed, I have drawn a forest to represent this difficult experience with them, they are the dark moments in a forest without direction and guidance from the supervisors, I was just confused." (Drawing caption, Beatrice, Figure 3)

"I would call them several times or send text messages, but they rarely pick my call or call back." (Drawing caption, Winny, Figure 2)

"It was not always bright and warm but sometimes gloomy when I felt my supervisor was criticising my work even when I thought I had done my best." (Drawing caption, Dan, Figure 4)

"My relationship with my supervisors was an overburdened relationship which I can compare to a donkey's work." (Drawing caption, Newton)

From the quotations above it seems that the participants experienced discontent in their relationships. Doctoral students expect their supervisors to guide them during the research process and when this does not happen, it creates feelings of discontent. A study on student experiences by Krauss and Ismi (2010) concurs that research students tend to experience discontent when they fail to receive the necessary guidance from their supervisors. Furthermore, it is frustrating to the student when the supervisor fails to communicate and to provide direction related to the research process (Ahmadi et al., 2020). Communication is the key to establish and sustain a productive student–supervisor relationship (Ahmadi et al., 2020; Dimitrova, 2016).

Supervisor critique is an important factor that provides a blend of ideas to strengthen and support the research project (Grossman & Crowther, 2015) and to enable the doctoral student to think critically about his or her own work. However, the critique may not always go down well with the student and can be a source of discontent, especially when the student feels unfairly criticised (Sayed et al., 2006). The student workload can also be very demanding and as such this could also cause student discontent as indicated by McClure (2005) who refers to the doctoral studies as a demanding research process. Many research students work long hours, spend sleepless nights and work during weekends to meet PhD demands (Sverdlik et al., 2018). When this does not yield satisfactory results and positive feedback from the supervisor, the student may feel discontent and reluctant to continue with their studies.

Conclusion

It is clear from the findings that student–supervisor relationships have a significant impact on doctoral students' success. African universities struggling with the through-put rate of doctoral students could learn from this research. Establishing effective student–supervisor relationships is central in promoting the success rate of doctoral students. It is therefore necessary for universities to develop a culture of continuous negotiation and constant communication between the student and the supervisor to promote a positive relationship. There should also be mechanisms within faculties and departments for amicable conflict resolution in case conflict occurs in the supervision process. This could prevent a dissatisfying supervision relationship that may delay doctoral completion or lead to students' discontinuing their studies.

References

Abiddin, Z., Hassan, A., & Ahmad, R. (2009). Research student supervision: An approach to good supervisory practice. *The Open Education Journal, 2*(1), 11–16.

Ahmadi, F., Shamsi, A., & Mohammadi, N. (2020). Using intelligent interaction to manage student–supervisor conflict: A qualitative study. *Journal of Education and Health Promotion, 9.*

Ali, P., Watson, R., & Dhingra, K. (2016). Postgraduate research students' and their supervisors' attitudes towards supervision. *International Journal of Doctoral Studies, 11*, 227–241.

Backhouse, J., Cross, M., & Ungadi, B. (2015). They can't even agree: Student conversations about their supervisors in constructing understanding of the doctorate studies. *South African Journal of Higher Education, 29*(4), 14–34.

Bacwayo, K. E., Nampala, P., & Oteyo, I. N. (2017). Challenges and opportunities associated with supervising graduate students enrolled in African universities. *International Journal of Education and Practice, 5*(3), 29–39.

Cadman, K. (2010). Voices in the air, an evaluation of learning experiences of international postgraduate students and their supervisors. *Teaching in Higher Education, 5*(4), 475–491.

Creswell, J. (2014). *Research design: Qualitative, quantitative and mixed methods approaches.* SAGE.

De Lange, N. (2011). Learning together: Teachers and community healthcare workers draw each other. In L. Theron, C. Mitchell, A. Smith & J. Stuart (Eds.), *Picturing research: Drawing as visual methodology* (pp. 177–190). Sense Publishers.

Detsky, A., & Baerlocher, M. (2007). Academic mentoring: How to give it and how to get it. *Journal of the American Medical Association, 297*(19), 2134–2136.

Dimitrova, R. (2016). Ingredients of good PhD supervision – Evidence from a student survey at Stockholm University. *Utbildning & Lärande, 10*(14), 40–52.

Grant, B. (2003). Mapping the pleasures and risks of supervision discourse. *Studies in the Cultural Politics of Education, 24*(2), 175–190.

Grant, B. (2005). Fighting for space in supervision: Fantasies, fairy tales, fictions, and fallacies. *International Journal of Qualitative Studies in Education, 18*(3), 337–354.

Grevholm, B., Pearson, L., & Wall, P. (2005). A dynamic model for education of doctoral students and guidance of supervisors in research groups. *Educational Studies in Mathematics, 60*(2), 173–197.

Grossman, E., & Crowther, J. (2015). Co-supervision in postgraduate training: Ensuring the right hand knows what the left hand is doing. *South African Journal of Science, 111*(11/12), 1–8.

Halse, C. (2011). Becoming a supervisor: The impact of doctoral supervision on supervisors' learning. *Studies in Higher Education, 36*(5), 557–570.

Hodza, F. (2007). Managing the student-supervisor relationship for successful postgraduate supervision. *South African Journal of Higher Education, 21*(8), 1155–1165.

James, R., & Baldwin, G. (1999). *Eleven practices of effective postgraduate supervision.* University of Melbourne Centre for the Study of Higher Education and The School of Graduate Studies.

Jones, M. (2013). Issues in doctoral studies: Forty years of journal discussion: Where have we been and where are we going? *International Journal of Doctoral Studies, 8*, 83–104.

Kiley, M. (2011). Development in research supervisor training: Causes and responses. *Studies in Higher Education, 36*(5), 585–589.

Kosgei, P., Githinji, F., & Simwa, K. (2019). Experiences of student-supervisor interaction in public universities in Kenya. *International Journal of Research in Education and Social Sciences, 2*(4), 34–53.

Krauss, S., & Ismi, A. (2010). PhD students' experiences of thesis supervision in Malaysia: Managing relationships in the midst of institutional change. *The Qualitative Report, 15*(4), 802–822.

Lewis, D. (2004). Bullying at work: The impacts of shame among university and college lecturers. *British Journal of Guidance and Counselling, 32*(3), 281–299.

Lovitts, B. (2001). *Leaving the ivory tower: The causes and consequences of departure from doctoral study.* Rowman and Littlefield Publishers.

Mainhard, M., Roeland, R., Tarkwijjjk, J., & Wubbels, T. (2009). A model for the supervisor-doctoral student relationship. *Higher Education, 58*(3), 359–373.

Malfroy, J. (2005). Doctoral supervision, workplace research, and changing pedagogic practices. *Higher Education Research and Development, 24*(2), 165–178.

Matheka, H. M., Jansen, E. P., & Hofman, W. A. (2020). Kenyan postgraduate students' success: Roles of motivation and self-efficacy. *Perspectives in Education, 38*(1), 115–129.

McClure, J. (2005). Preparing a laboratory-based thesis: Chinese international research students' experiences of supervision. *Teaching in Higher Education, 10*(1), 3–16.

Morris, S. (2011). Doctoral students' experiences of supervisory bullying. *Journal of Social Sciences and Humanities, 19*(2), 547–555.

Nieuwenhuis, J. (2007). Introducing qualitative research. In K. Maree (Ed.), *First steps in research* (pp. 47–66). Van Schaik.

Phillips, E., & Johnson, C. (2022). *How to get a PhD: A handbook for students and their supervisors* (7th ed.). McGraw-Hill Education.

Radloff, A. (2010). The synergistic thesis: Students and supervisors' perspectives. *Journal for Higher and Further Education, 25*(1), 97–106.

Sayed, Y., Kruss, G., & Badat, S. (2006). Students' experience of postgraduate supervision at the University of Western Cape. *Journal for Further and Higher Education, 22*(3), 275–285.

Schulze, S. (2012). Empowering and disempowering students in the student-supervisor relationship. *Koers-Bulletin for Christian Scholarship, 77*(2), 1–8.

Smallwood, S. (2004, January 16). Doctor dropout: High attrition from PhD programs is sucking away time, talent, and money and breaking some hearts too. *The Chronicle of Higher Education.* https://www.chronicle.com/article/doctor-dropout/

Son, J., & Park, S. (2014). Academic experiences of international PhD students in Australian higher education: From an EAP program to a PhD program. *International Journal of Pedagogies and Learning, 9*(1), 26–37.

Sverdlik, A., Hall, N. C., McAlpine, L., & Hubbard, K. (2018). The PhD experience: A review of factors influencing doctoral students' completion, achievement, and well-being. *International Journal of Doctoral Studies, 13*, 361–388.

Taylor, P., & Medina, M. (2013). Educational research paradigms: From positivism to multiparadigmatic. *Journal for Meaning-Centered Education, 1*(2), 1–13.

Theron, L., Mitchel, C., Smith, A., & Stuart, J. (Eds.). (2011). *Picturing research: Drawing as visual methodology.* Sense.

Vladimir, J. (2010). Potential predictors of timely completion among dissertation research students at an Australian faculty of sciences. *International Journal of Doctoral Studies, 5*(1), 1–13.

Wubbels, T., & Mieke, B. (2006). Two decades of research on teacher-student relationship in class. *International Journal of Education Research, 43*(1), 6–24.

Zainal, A. (2007). Challenges in PhD studies: The case of arts student. *European Journal of Social Sciences, 5*(2), 83–93.

CHAPTER 7

Exploratory factor analysis of stakeholders' participation in school management and the enhancement of learners' academic achievement in public secondary schools in Uganda

Dorothy Nakiyaga, David Serem, Proscovia Namubiru Ssentamu, John Boit

Introduction

Effective stakeholder participation in school management is crucial for creating a collaborative and inclusive educational environment (Cheng, 2022). When stakeholders, such as parents, teachers, students, administrators, and community members, actively engage in school management, they can contribute valuable insights, diverse perspectives, and support to improve the overall educational experience (Cabardo, 2016; Bandur & Furinto, 2022).

The key strategies to promote effective stakeholder participation in school management include encouraging collaboration in developing school improvement plans, curriculum development, and other strategic initiatives (Zaid et al., 2022). By involving stakeholders in the planning process and regularly seeking their feedback on various aspects of school management, policies, and programmes, one can ensure that decisions align with the needs and aspirations of the entire school community (Cleminski, 2018; Naidoo, 2019).

Moreover, using surveys, focus groups, and other feedback mechanisms to evaluate the effectiveness of implemented changes can produce data-driven improvements, fostering a culture of open and transparent communication where all stakeholders feel comfortable expressing their ideas, concerns, and suggestions (Widodo, 2019); using various communication channels, such as regular meetings, newsletters, emails, and online platforms, to keep everyone informed and involved; actively involving stakeholders in decision-making processes that affect the school by creating committees or advisory groups comprising representatives of various stakeholder groups to participate in discussions and contribute to important decision-making; organizing regular meetings with different stakeholder groups to address pertinent issues, sharing updates, and seeking input on various aspects of school management (Tansiri & Bong, 2019).

The gatherings can include parent-teacher meetings, school board meetings, and student forums. Through participation, the school's stakeholders interact with management in the dimensions of school improvement planning, budgeting process, and coordinating academic activities (Bandur & Furinto, 2022).

However, generally, stakeholder participation in school management has been viewed mostly in terms of financial metrics such as school fee contribution, buying scholastic materials for learners, and providing food (Nakiyaga et al., 2021). Prior scholars focused on strengthening local stakeholders' governance of education and the effects they had on service delivery. Participation in the budgeting process has been reflected in the form of provision of funds, motivation of human resources, and physical infrastructural maintenance. Participation in coordinating the academic activities was reflected in the form of measures of school management quality in terms of student test scores, monitoring, and evaluation deemed as victimization. Scant literature addressed the extent of collective monitoring and evaluation of activities (Agbenyo et al., 2021; Nakiyaga et al., 2021).

However, effective stakeholder participation in school management also involves an oversight role in the strategic planning and implementation process that contributes to educational goals focused on the learner, the school, and the community (Sehrawat & Roy, 2021; Cheng, 2022).

Although stakeholder participation in school management has been proposed through school-based management (SBM) models, according to Ayeni and Ibukun (2013) and Ya et al. (2020), which aim to improve the quality of education by granting greater autonomy and decision-making power to individual schools and their stakeholders. Little is known about the validity and reliability of the underlying structures within each discrete dimension – planning, budgeting and coordinating the academic activities in which the stakeholders participate.

The existing policies in Uganda related to stakeholder participation in education management include:

- Education policy framework that emphasises stakeholder participation in education management. This framework recognises the importance of involving various stakeholders, including parents, teachers, local communities, and civil society organizations, in the planning, monitoring, and evaluation of education programmes (The Republic of Uganda Education Service Commission, 2008; Hassan & Macha, 2020).
- School Management Committees (SMCs) at the school level. SMCs are composed of parents, community members, and school staff. They are responsible for managing the affairs of individual schools, including financial management and decision-making (Serunjogi, 2022).
- Parent-Teacher Associations (PTAs) which play a significant role in Uganda's education system. They are comprised of parents and teachers, and are involved

in various school activities, including fundraising, infrastructure development, and providing feedback to school administrators (Media Officer, 2021).

- District Education Boards are responsible for overseeing and coordinating education activities. These boards are expected to engage with various stakeholders and ensure that education policies are effectively implemented at the local level (Wataba & Naifu, 2018).

Despite the policies in place to promote stakeholder participation in education management, there have been several perceived inefficiencies and challenges, namely:

- Limited capacity: Many stakeholders, especially at the community level, may lack the necessary knowledge and skills to effectively participate in education management.
- Corruption: There have been reports of corruption and mismanagement of funds at various levels of the education system, which can hinder the efficient utilization of resources.
- Inequality: There are disparities in stakeholder participation between urban and rural areas, with urban schools often having more active and resourceful PTAs.
- Limited resources: Inadequate funding and resources can hinder the ability of schools to implement policies effectively, limiting stakeholder participation opportunities.
- Political interference: Some stakeholders have expressed concerns about political interference in education management, which can impact decision-making processes.

Again, despite the functional policy framework that guides stakeholder participation in school management to enhance learners' academic achievement in public secondary schools, as well as the perceived inefficiencies in effective participation, little is known about the validity and reliability of the dimensions through which stakeholders participate in school management.

The study reported in this chapter aimed to validate three dimensions (school improvement planning, budgeting process, and coordinating the academic activities) of Ayeni & Ibukun's widely used school-based management model (Ayeni & Ibukun, 2013; The Republic of Uganda Education Service Commission, 2008) for the enhancement of learners' academic achievement (Figure 1). Specifically, the study sought to answer the research question, 'What are the underlying structures within each discrete domain – planning, budgeting, and coordinating the academic activities – of the school-based management model that support stakeholders' participation in school management to enhance learners' academic achievement in public secondary schools?'

Figure 1: *A Diagram Representing the Intended Granularity of the Exploratory Factor Analysis (EFA) within the Diverse Components of the SBMM*

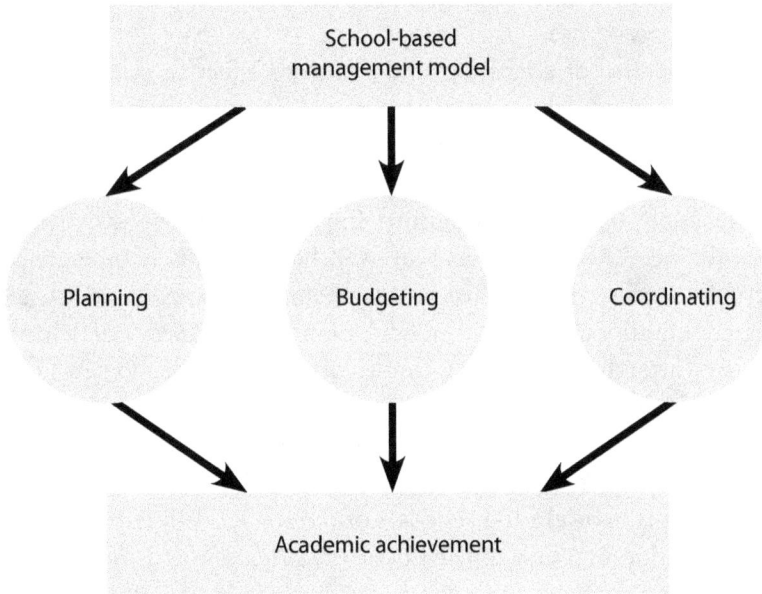

The study was carried out in four public secondary schools that were purposively selected. To compare their performance metrics, of the chosen schools, two were high-performing and the other two were low-performing public secondary schools in the Kampala District.

High-performance education indicators in academic achievement refer to the key measures that demonstrate outstanding educational outcomes and success for students, schools, or educational systems. These indicators can vary based on the level of education. For this study, the indicators were Standardised Test Scores used to assess students' academic performance and compare it to national benchmarks. The quantity grades attained in the Uganda Certificate of Education (UCE) is measured by the percentage of students who complete their educational programme within a specified time frame, usually the four-year academic cycle in ordinary levels based on the national grading system.

On the other hand, the quality of grades attained in UCE is measured by the assessments of students' proficiency in reading, writing, and mathematics, as these are foundational skills critical for academic success. Educational institutions and systems were ranked based on their academic performance in comparison to other institutions in the district. However, it should be noted that high-performance education is not solely measured by a single indicator, but rather by a combination of multiple factors that contribute to a comprehensive and successful learning environment. On the other hand, low-performing schools are the opposite of the latter, which have a performance percentage of 49%.

Uganda has recognised the importance of stakeholder participation in improving the quality of education and ensuring effective school management. Various policies and guidelines have been put in place to encourage and facilitate stakeholder involvement in education. School Management Committees (SMCs), Parent-Teachers' Associations (PTAs) (enshrined in the Education Act of 2008), District Education Boards, Community Engagement Programs: Training and Capacity Building. The involvement of stakeholders in school management is seen as crucial in fostering a sense of ownership and accountability, as well as promoting community engagement in education. Stakeholders' participation has a legal mandate through the statutory framework of the Education Act (2008). The strategy of participation includes creating a link between the Ministry of Education and Sports, founder members, school administrators, teachers, and parents, having joint decision-making, monitoring the implementation of priorities, and taking corrective measures to attain the set goals of the school. While prior studies show a positive correlation between stakeholders' participation and the development of quality learning outcomes if well set up, (Mahuro & Hungi, 2016), there is scant literature on the prioritization of stakeholders' participation in schools where learners' academic achievement is constantly declining. There are discrepancies in Uganda, whereby stakeholders' participation in school management does not reflect the quality education outcomes of the learners due to the continuous poor academic achievement in public secondary schools. The national trend of academic achievement in UCE examinations between 2015 to 2018 showed a steady decline in the realization of at least division 3 for easy selection and deployment in the next level of education. In 2015 the failure rate was 9.7% compared with 13.2% in 2016. In 2017 the failure rate was 14.2% compared with 2018, during which the failure rate was 15.4% (Uganda National Examinations Board, 2019). Could it be possible that the poor academic achievement among learners is attributed to the non-involvement of the stakeholders in the management of public schools?

The continuity of poor learners' academic achievement influences the attainment of knowledge, skills, and attitudes, which will affect their future academic and work opportunities. Additionally, most learners who drop out of school with low uptake skills affect the contribution to self-reliance and human capital required in the development of innovations for the social and economic growth of the country. Subsequently, this hinders the attainment of Sustainable Development Goals (SDG) which promote a more equitable, prosperous, and sustainable world for all, leaving no one behind (Barbier & Burgess, 2017).

Method

Participation and sampling procedure

The public secondary schools were stratified into five strata that constitute the five divisions of Kampala District. One stratum had no public secondary school, so this left the sample space with 4 strata. Thereafter, schools were ranked according to the national assessment metrics of the UCE. Schools that were considered as high performing had a percentage pass of 89%, while the pass of the low-performing was below 49%. A simple sampling procedure was applied to give equal opportunity to the schools based on the sampling frame. Data were collected using a questionnaire that was physically administered. The sample of 190 consisted of teachers, parents, and the Board of Governors; 139 (73%) were male, and 51 (27%) were female. The respondents' ages varied with 122 (64%) ranging between 45 to 63 years of age, 65 (34%) ranging between 40 to 45 years, and 4 (2%) being 64 years and older. Experience as either a stakeholder, Board of Governor member, or Parent-Teacher Association member ranged between more than 3 years: 103 (54%), between 5 to 8 years: 49 (26%), between 2 to 4 years: 27 (14%), and 1 year or less: 11 (6%).

Measures

As previously noted, the school-based management model proposed dimensions where stakeholders participate in school management. Effective participation refers to a collaborative and inclusive approach involving all relevant parties in the decision-making processes and overall governance of a school. This approach recognises that schools do not operate in isolation but are integral parts of their communities, and as such, they should engage with various stakeholders to ensure the best possible educational outcomes for learners.

Effective participation was measured through school improvement planning (a systematic and collaborative process that educational institutions use to enhance their overall effectiveness and student outcomes). It involves setting goals, identifying areas for improvement, and developing strategies to address those areas. The primary purpose of school improvement planning is to create a roadmap for achieving academic excellence, improving teaching and learning, and ensuring that schools provide a high-quality education to all students); budgeting processes refer to the involvement of individuals, groups, or organizations in the development of a budget. It ensures that a broader range of perspectives and interests are considered when formulating, reviewing, and approving budgets. It can lead to more informed and equitable budget decisions that better serve the needs of communities and society. Coordinating academic activities refers to involving various individuals and groups who have an interest or stake in the educational institution in the decision-making and planning processes related to academic activities. When done effectively, it can lead to improved academic programmes, greater community support, and more inclusive and accountable educational institutions. The aim was to enhance the learners' academic achievement in public secondary schools.

Participants were asked to indicate the extent to which they agreed with each of the observable items in the survey. The 61 observable items in the survey were measured using a 5-point Likert scale, ranging from (1) 'strongly disagree' to (5) 'strongly agree. The questionnaire was validated using the Content Validity Index (CVI) to generate the appropriateness and representation of the targeted attributes for the study. The researcher adopted Yusoff's (2019) six steps to calculate the CVI. The steps included preparing the content validation form, selecting the review panel, conducting the content validation, reviewing the domains and items, scoring each item, and calculating CVI. Before the calculation of CVI, the relevant items were rated and recorded as 1 (relevance scale of 3 or 4) or 0 (relevance scale of 1 or 2). The study adopted a Scale-level Content Validity Index based on the average method (S-CVI/Ave). S-CVI/Ave = (sum of proportion relevance rating)/ (number of items). The score for relevant items was 81. The sum of items in the questionnaire = 90. 81/90 = 0.9. A 0.90 value for two experts was considered evidence of good content validity of an instrument (Yusoff, 2019). Illustrations of items are shown in the results section.

Exploratory factor analysis (EFA)

The objective of this chapter is to examine the nature of EFA as it relates to stakeholders' participation in school management and the enhancement of learners' academic achievement in public secondary schools, a component missing from previous studies. Additionally, the factors and items identified through EFA are used as inputs for testing the outer model (regression model). The scope of this chapter, however, focuses on the inputs required for the outer model in the analysis of stakeholder participation in school management.

This section begins with the introduction to EFA, followed by its rationalization, the research question, the suitability of data required for factor analysis, and the principal component analysis (PCA). It then provides the primary factors for extraction and the specific techniques. The results of EFA with factor rotation, its methods, and labelling of identified factors are described and a comprehensive example of EFA focusing on stakeholders' perspectives on participation in school management is presented. The conclusion and limitations of the study are included at the end of the chapter.

The background of performing the procedures of EFA was that the adopted questionnaire used for the study had not been previously validated as it was developed from the literature reviewed. There was a need to explore the underlying structure of the study variables (Hair et al., 2019). The aim was to identify the patterns and relationships among observable items and group them into dimensions (Watkins, 2018; Hair et al., 2019; Willmer et al., 2019).

In this analysis, two variables were analysed, the exogenous (independent variable) and endogenous (dependent variable) to identify the structural relationships between the dimensions/factors and the latent (unobservable) items (Tavakol & Wetzel, 2020). Two phases are considered when conducting and interpreting EFA. In the first phase, the principal component analysis (PCA) examines the relationship between observed dimensions/factors and latent (unobserved) items to confirm construct validity and reliability (Watkins, 2018; Hair et al., 2019; Tavakol & Wetzel, 2020). The second phase confirmatory factor analysis (CFA) runs a theoretical correlation among the variables (Fan et al., 2016). This study adopted the PCA.

The validity (measuring what it intends to measure) and reliability (internal consistency) of the measurement model were assessed by observing the convergent validity, aiscriminant validity, individual item reliability, and reliability of the scales (Fan et al., 2016; Tavakol & Wetzel, 2020). To assess the validity and reliability of the outer model, variables that consistently co-varied were considered (Hadi et al., 2019).

The rationale for exploratory factor analysis

Dimension reduction: This simplifies complex data, helps identify latent variables, enhances interpretability, reduces data redundancy, facilitates hypothesis testing, improves visualization, and aids in model selection. It is a critical step in the process of uncovering the underlying structure of multivariate data and making it more meaningful and usable for further analysis and interpretation (Watkins, 2018).

Identifying hidden structure: EFA aims to uncover the hidden structure or shared variance among observed items. It is often used when there is a suspicion that the unobservable items influence the observed items, and there is a need to identify and name these dimensions/factors (Hair et al., 2019).

Construct validity: By identifying underlying factors, EFA provides evidence of construct validity as it helps to assess whether the observed variables indeed measure the intended constructs. If certain items within a construct do not load well on any factors or load on unexpected factors, it may suggest that these items are not contributing to the measurement of the construct effectively. Removing or revising such items can improve the construct's measurement. If the factor structure aligns with theoretical expectations (e.g. items related to budgeting load heavily on one factor), it provides support for the validity of the construct (Nakiyaga et al., 2021).

Simplification and interpretation: EFA transforms complex interrelationships between observable items into a smaller number of dimensions/factors, making it easier to understand and interpret the data. These factors often have clear meanings that can be labelled based on the items with high loadings. The correlation amongst a set of observed items is recognised and changed into small quantities of related factors (Hair et al., 2010; Willmer et al., 2019).

Data reduction: When working with a large number of observable items, EFA can reduce the dimensionality of the data, making it easier to work with and interpret the results. The data is reduced through either summated scales or factor scores and joins the items within each factor into a single score (Hair et al., 2019; Tavakol & Wetzel, 2020).

Model assessment: EFA allows researchers to assess the adequacy of the model fit to the data. Various fit indices and techniques can help in determining whether the identified factors adequately explain the correlations among the independent and dependent variables. In this process, the consistent movement of observed items is identified through factor extraction and factor rotation (Nakiyaga et al., 2021).

It is important to note that EFA is an exploratory technique, used when researchers do not have a pre-specified hypothesis about the number or nature of underlying factors, providing insights and generating hypotheses for further research. However, it neither confirms causal relationships nor establishes a definitive model. Nonetheless, it is an interdependency method whose primary aim is to define the underlying structure among the dimensions within the analysis.

Research question

'What are the underlying structures within each discrete domain – planning, budgeting, coordinating, and academic achievement – of the school-based management model that supports stakeholders' participation in school management to enhance learners' academic achievement in public secondary schools?'

The methodology for conducting EFA

Step 1: Checking the suitability of data for EFA

The vital assumptions for conducting EFA are more conceptual than statistical. The predominant concern focuses on the character and composition of the dimensions. The conceptual assumption states that there ought to be some underlying structure existing within the set of selected dimensions. In addition, the sample should be homogeneous to the underlying dimension or factor structure. This study focused on the conceptual composition of the stakeholders' participation in school management and the enhancement of the learners' academic achievement in public secondary schools in Uganda. The independent variable focused on school improvement planning, budgeting process, and coordinating the academic activities dimension, while the dependent variable dimension was academic achievement.

Step 2: Checking the reliability of the data

EFA requires a relatively large sample size to produce stable and reliable results. As a rule of thumb, a sample size of at least 200 observations is often recommended. However, the specific requirements can vary based on the complexity of one's data and the number of variables one is analysing (Watkins, 2018). The adequacy of the sampling size was tested through the Kaiser-Meyer-Olkin (KMO) test (Kaiser, 1970, 1974). while the strength of the relationship among variables was assessed through Bartlett's Test of Sphericity (Hadi et al., 2016). These tests assessed the adequacy of the data for factor extraction. It is worth noting that the items were measured at the interval level (Likert scale), and the level of significance, $p < 0.05$. Bartlett's test was applied to assess the factorability of the overall set of variables and individual variables. The null hypothesis of this test is that the variables are orthogonal (not correlated). In this study, the independent variables had to be orthogonal, implying that the correlation matrix had to be an identity matrix. An identity matrix is a matrix in which all of the diagonal values are one (1) and all off-diagonal elements are zero (0). The null hypothesis, 'The correlation matrix is not an identity matrix', ought to be rejected.

A rule of thumb for the sample size requirement is a bare minimum of 10 observations per variable (10:1) to avoid computational issues (Hair et al., 2019). The sample size obtained in this study was 190 observable items which exceeded the minimum requirement. This implied that the ratio of 63 per variable (63:1) was above the threshold to conduct EFA. KMO assessed the overall significance of the correlation matrix. This measure varies between 0 and 1, and values closer to 1 are better. According to Revelle (2022), the value of KMO which is above 0.6 is a suggested minimum. In this study, the KMO threshold was 0.6 (Table 1).

Table 1: *The KMO and Bartlett Test Results*

Variables	Kaiser-Meyer-Olkin of sampling adequacy	Barlett's Test of Sphericity approx. Chi-square	df	Sig.
Planning	0.638	1164.40	91	0.001
Budgeting	0.723	964.46	66	0.001
Coordinating	0.652	1417.64	91	0.000
Academic achievement	0.600	2901.48	703	0.000

Source: Primary data 2021

As shown in Table 1, the KMO of sampling adequacy and Bartlett's Test of Sphericity tests were appropriate and feasible for all the variables.

Step 3: Determine the technique for extraction

Once the conditions for performing FA were satisfied the subsequent step was to determine the technique for extracting the factors (either common factor analysis or principal components analysis) and the number of factors selected to represent the underlying structure in the data (Revelle, 2022).

Common factor analysis (CFA) focuses on understanding the common underlying factors that contribute to the observed correlations or covariances among a set of measured variables. These common factors are latent (hidden) variables that cannot be directly measured but are inferred from the observed variables. The goal is to explain the observed correlations or covariances between variables in terms of a smaller number of common factors, which can provide insights into the underlying structure or dimensions of the data (Hair et al., 2019).

Principal component analysis (PCA) analyses and explores complex datasets to extract important features from data, and to identify patterns and relationships that might not be immediately evident in the original high-dimensional space. All the variance of a score or variable is analysed, including its unique variance (Hair et al., 2010, 2019). It is assumed that the test used to assess the variable is reliable and error-free (Nakiyaga et al., 2021). The data obtained in this study were explored with Principal Components Analysis (PCA).

Step 4: Principal component analysis

The procedures for PCA included:

Data preparation: The dataset had three dimensions (variables) that describe each data point (school improvement planning, budgeting process, and coordinating the academic activities).

Standardisation: Data were standardised so that each feature had a mean of 0 and a standard deviation of 1. This step ensured that no single feature dominated the analysis solely due to its scale. The covariance matrix of the standardised data was computed to give an idea of how each dimension varied from the others. This showed the relationships between different pairs of features and helped in understanding how the matrix varied together.

Eigenvalue decomposition: The covariance matrix was decomposed into eigenvectors and eigenvalues. Eigenvectors represented directions in the original feature space, and eigenvalues quantified the amount of variance along those directions.

Selection of principal components: The eigenvectors were organized by their corresponding eigenvalues in decreasing order. The eigenvector with the highest eigenvalue is the first principal component; the one with the second-highest eigenvalue is the second principal component, and so on.

Factor rotation: Factor rotation involves applying a mathematical transformation to the original loadings (weights) of the variables on the extracted components or factors through PCA (Hair et al., 2019; Field, 2013; Warner, 2013). The goal of the rotation was to achieve a simpler and more interpretable structure that corresponded to the underlying theoretical or practical concepts of the data. The study applied the orthogonal rotation to acquire a simpler and theoretically more important factor solution since the goal was to reduce the data to a smaller number of observable items that were tapping into the generated factors. The VARIMAX approach, which focuses on simplifying the columns of the factor matrix was adopted since it maximizes the sum of the variance of the required loadings (IBM Corporation, 2021). Some high loadings (close to -1 or +1) indicated a clear positive or negative association between the variable and the factor. A factor loading of .40 was considered a significant threshold for interpretation purposes since the sample size for the study was 190 (Hair et al., 2010). This is indicated in Table 2.

Labelling of factors/components

The process of labelling components requires a combination of statistical analysis, domain expertise, and intuition to make sense of the underlying patterns in the data. Factors are labelled based on the factor loadings. Factor loadings represent the correlation between the item and the factor. The higher the loading, the stronger the relationship between the item and the factor. Items with the highest loadings on each factor are the most representative of the underlying factor. The content of these items represents a common theme or concept that ties them together. Based on the interpretation of the items with high loadings, each factor is given a meaningful and descriptive label. The label should reflect the common theme or concept that the items represent. The chosen labels should be clear and concise (Hair et al., 2019).

This study adopted a .40 threshold for retaining the items since the sample size needed for significance is 200. Since the sample size of the study was 190, it was deemed to use the approximation of 200 which is .40 the factor loading.

Projection: The final step involved projecting the original data onto the selected principal components to obtain the transformed data in the new coordinate system. Each new data point (dimension) represented was a combination of the selected principal components (Izquierdo et al., 2014).

Table 2: *Guidelines for Factor Loadings Based on the Sample Size*

Guidelines needed for identifying significant factor loadings based on the sample size	
Factor loading	The sample size needed for significance.
.30	350
.35	250
.40	200
.45	150
.50	120
.55	100
.60	85
.65	70
.70	60
.75	50

Note: Significance is based on a .05 significance level (α) at 80% and standard error assumed to be twice those of conventional correlation coefficients.

Practical example

Exploratory factor analysis for stakeholder participation in school management and the enhancement of learners' academic achievement in public secondary schools.

Participation in school management was conceptualised into three variables: participation in school improvement planning (had fourteen items) from the original questionnaire, participation in the budgeting process (had twelve items), and participation in coordinating the academic activities (had sixteen items). These were subjected to principal component analysis using SPSS.

Given that a minimum of three items is needed to reliably define a factor (Hair et al., 2019), the items for factors that had fewer than 3 items were not retained for further analysis. Similarly, items that had loadings < 0.4 or that were cross loaded across factors >0.4 were not retained for subsequent analyses (Hair et al., 2019).

The subsequent tables show that after deleting three item factors, items loading lower than 0.4, and three cross-loading items, a subsequent EFA yielded relatively clean factors, with no cross-loading items, explaining 81% of the variance. The 5-factor solutions consisted of performance indicators; school culture, budgeting, monitoring; and evaluation, as visually illustrated in Figure 2.

The factor loadings of the three respective dimensions after orthogonal rotation are illustrated in the tables below.

Figure 2: *Diagram Representing the Factor Solutions after EFA within the Diverse Components of the SBMM*

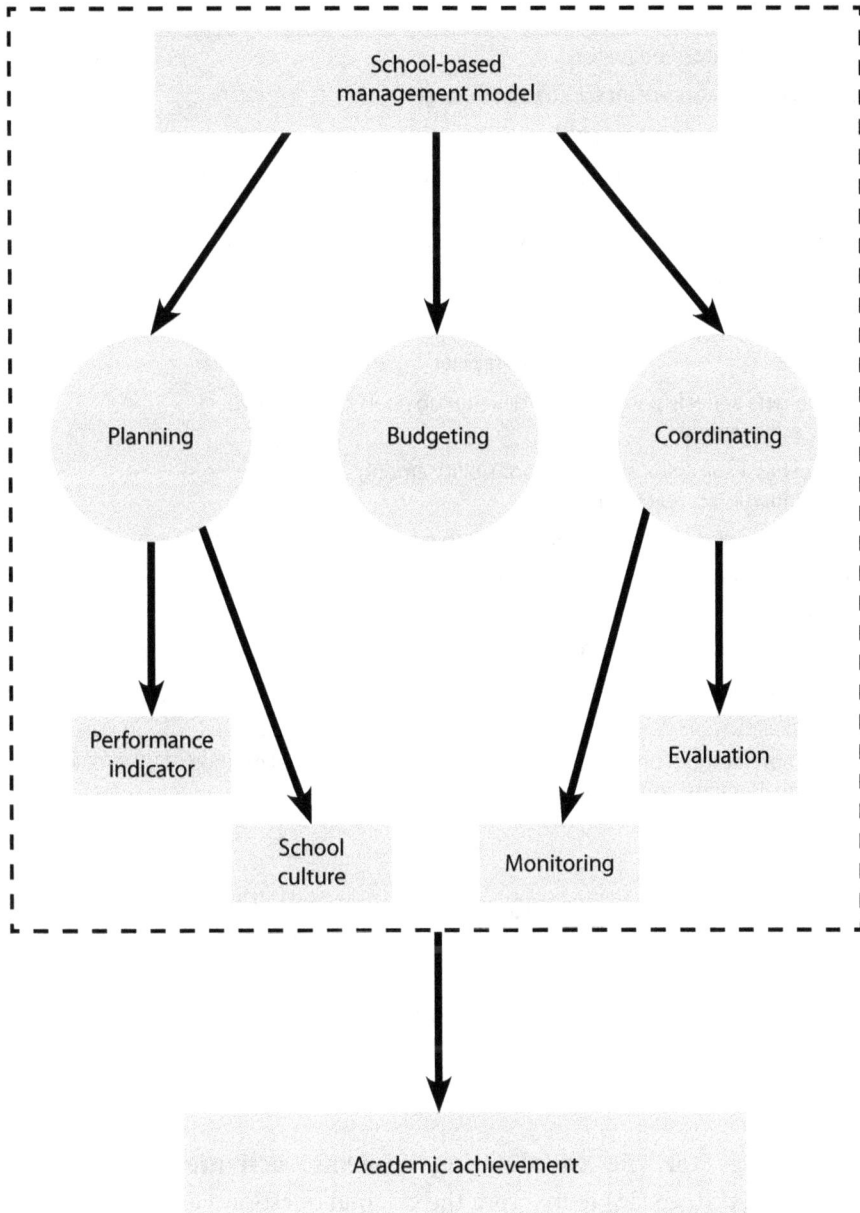

Table 3: *Factor Loadings of the School Improvement Planning Dimension*

Performance Indicator	Factor Loading	
	1	2
Performance indicators are realistic	0.850	
Performance indicators are attached to each target	0.824	
Performance indicators are achievable	0.816	
Learners actively participate in decision-making that improves their academic achievement.	0.666	
Standards of achievement are attached for each measurable indicator	0.485	
The academic targets to be achieved are well documented	0.438	
School Culture Predictor		
All stakeholders actively participate in developing goals that improve academic achievement		0.764
This school has a culture of shared responsibility among stakeholders to improve academic achievement		0.724
Stakeholders are given the responsibility to achieve the goals of the school		0.724
There is mutual support from the stakeholders to improve academic achievement		0.720
Parents/guardians check on the academic progress of the learners.		0.638
Parents actively participate in decision-making that improves academic achievement		0.602

Note: Extraction method: principal component analysis; rotational method: VARIMAX with Kaiser Normalization. Rotation converged in 3 iterations.

Source: Field data (2020)

Factor loadings for the budgeting process dimension. The dimension had twelve (12) items from the original questionnaire, these items were subjected to rotation and four (4) items were dropped as they did not meet the recommended threshold of 0.4 and above, according to Hair et al. (2010). The eight items that were retained had a loading ranging between .539 and .860. The factor was labelled 'budgeting' as indicated in Table 4.

Factor loadings for the coordinating academic activities dimension. The dimension had sixteen (16) items from the original questionnaire, these items were subjected to orthogonal rotation using the VARIMAX approach and four (4) items were dropped as they did not meet the recommended threshold of 0.4 and above (Hair et al., 2010). Two (2) factors were extracted resulting in two-factor solutions. Factor one (1) was labelled 'monitoring' using the highest loading item of .826 and the low loading item of .490. The second factor was labelled 'evaluation' with high loading item .765 and low loading item .612 whose findings are indicated in Table 5.

Table 4: *Rotated Component Matrix*

Budgeting	Factor Loading
	1
Academic activity inventory is done by the teaching staff as a basis for resource allocation and mobilization	0.860
An established system of monitoring and evaluation of the implementation of the budget is in place	0.779
Monitoring and evaluation of the budgeting process are jointly done by the stakeholders	0.736
Stakeholders use the accounted and audited reports as a basis to adjust resource allocations	0.715
Stakeholders are aware that regular academic inventory is used as a basis for resource allocation	0.711
Stakeholders participate in joint decision-making on resource allocation and mobilization	0.635
Academic inventory is communicated to the stakeholders and is used as a basis for resource allocation and mobilization	0.546
There are accounting and auditing systems that drive the effective use of resources	0.539

Note: Extraction method: principal component analysis; rotational method: VARIMAX with Kaiser Normalization. Rotation converged in 2 iterations.

Source: Field data (2020)

Table 5: *Rotated Component Matrix*

Monitoring	Factor Loading	
	1	2
There are monitoring systems to check on the implementation of academic interventions	0.826	
There are academic interventions to improve the learners' academic achievement	0.820	
Reports on the implementation of the intervention are periodically generated	0.803	
I am held accountable for the learner's performance	0.695	
Recommendations at points of action to improve performance are made	0.681	
The reports on the implementation of the intervention are jointly shared with all school stakeholders periodically	0.639	
The majority of stakeholders visit the school to ensure quality performance is achieved	0.586	
It is good practice to involve external stakeholders to improve the quality of academic performance in my school	0.49	

Evaluation

The stakeholders use these reports to inform decision-making on the intervention	0.765
A formative evaluation of the implementation of the intervention is done against the performance indicators	0.753
A summative evaluation of the implementation of the intervention is done against the performance indicators	0.681
There are tools with indicators used to monitor the intervention implementation.	0.612

Note: Extraction method: principal component analysis; rotational method: VARIMAX with Kaiser Normalization. Rotation converged in 2 iterations.

Source: Field data (2020)

Factor loadings for the academic achievement dimension. The dependent variable had nineteen (19) items from the original questionnaire, these items were subjected to extraction, and six (6) items were dropped and deleted as they did not meet the recommended threshold of 0.4 and above (Hair et al., 2010). A unidimensional factor was derived comprising thirteen (13) items with loading ranging between 0.440 and 0.839 as indicated in Table 6.

Table 6: *Rotated Component Matrix*

Academic Achievement	Factor Loadings
	1
Adequate exercises are given to the learners	0.839
Performance targets are realistic	0.810
Performance targets are achievable	0.789
Parents/guardians regularly check on their children's academic progress	0.779
Timely feedback is given after the assessment of learners' performance	0.747
Action points for academic improvement are made	0.736
Parents/guardians participate in joint decision-making toward academic improvement	0.726
I check regularly on the notes written by the learners	0.672
Parents/guardians participate in allocating financial resources that influence academic achievement	0.662
Parents/guardians assist their children with school work whenever possible	0.592
Performance targets are set by the school administration	0.526
Adequate equipment and learning materials are provided at school	0.472
Learners are held accountable for their performance	0.440

Note: Extraction method: principal component snalysis. 1 component was extracted.

Source: Field data (2020)

Construct reliability using Cronbach's alpha

The composite dimensions generated after EFA were tested for internal consistency using the Cronbach's alpha coefficient, this being the most widely used measure (Hair et al., 2019). The reliability coefficient was computed to test the internal consistency among the variables in a summated scale and select how the variables correlated among themselves. A high Cronbach's alpha (usually above 0.70) suggests good internal consistency, indicating that the items in the questionnaire after EFA were measuring the same underlying construct reliably. The results of Cronbach's alpha for the extracted variables are indicated in Table 7.

Table 7: *The Reliability Coefficient for the Extracted Variables*

	Scale Mean Item Deleted	Scale Variance if Item Deleted	Corrected Item-Total Correlated	Square Multiple Correlation	Cronbach's Alpha if Item Deleted Vari.
Performance Indicator	13.56	16.45	.734	.638	.814
School Culture	13.54	17.01	.694	.618	.825
Budgeting	13.40	16.81	.724	.549	.827
Monitoring	13.52	16.78	.681	.534	.834
Evaluation	13.44	16.83	.687	.508	.856
Academic Achievement	14.23	17.60	.553	.347	.867

Note: After the deletion of some items from the scale that had cross-loading or were below the threshold of 0.4, Cronbach's alpha was recalculated to assess the impact of the remaining items on the scale's internal reliability. Results are presented in Table 8.

Table 8: *The Reliability Coefficient after Extraction*

Variables	Cronbach's Alpha	Number of Items After Elimination
Performance Indicator	0.814	6
School Culture	0.825	6
Budgeting	0.827	8
Monitoring	0.834	8
Evaluation	0.856	4
Academic Achievement	0.867	13

Source: Field data (2020)

Discussion

The theoretical underpinnings for stakeholders' participation in school management to enhance learner' academic achievement were based on the stakeholder theory and school-based management model in school management. The theoretical framework recognises the various individuals and groups who have a vested interest in the operation and outcomes of a school. The primary goal of the theory in school management is to ensure that the school operates in a way that serves the best interests of all its stakeholders, rather than just focusing on the interests of one group, such as the administration or teachers. Through collaborative decision-making, emphasis is placed on transparency, accountability, and open communication between the school administration and the various stakeholder groups.

The findings indicate that by involving all relevant stakeholders in school improvement planning, budgeting processes, and coordinating academic activities, schools can work toward creating a more inclusive, responsive, and effective educational environment that better serves the needs of the entire school community. Decentralising decision-making and empowering stakeholders to have more control over their operations and resources in the respective schools would improve the quality of education.

The study aimed to validate the three dimensions of the widely used school-based management model in the enhancement of learners' academic achievement. Given that there has been limited empirical validation of measures of stakeholder participation in school management, the research contributes insights into the dimensions by which stakeholder participation can reliably be measured and therefore monitored, managed, and improved.

The measures were validated on a large scale using EFA analytical procedures. The results identified 5 dimensions and as such support the arguments that stakeholder participation is complex and multifaceted (UNESCO Education Sector, 2020). In support of their content validity, the 5 dimensions largely correspond to those previously identified by academics (Ayeni & Ibukun, 2013).

The results of the current study suggest a revised, more differentiated, and statistically defensible framework for evaluating the extent of stakeholder participation in school management to enhance learners' academic achievement. As previously noted, the current findings to a large extent confirm the existing conceptualisation of stakeholder participation in school management in relation to the enhancement of learners' academic achievement. Several factors were overlapping, hence alignment was expected, and cross-validation of the importance and generalisability of the 5 dimensions identified.

Practical implications

The development of a valid measure of stakeholder participation has clear practical implications.

- A valid and reliable measure can be used with confidence internally by school management to help them assess and improve their management effectiveness. The use of a reliable measure enables a confident assessment of whether stakeholder participation evaluations in school management change over time and identifies the directions in which they change.
- Similarly, school inspectors can use these dimensions to audit school management on the extent of collaborations as well as propose changes that can be adapted to contribute to the educational goals.
- Valid measures of stakeholder participation help school administrators and policymakers make more informed and inclusive decisions. When various stakeholders, such as parents, teachers, students, and community members, are actively involved in decision-making processes, the resulting decisions are likely to be more well-rounded and reflective of the needs and concerns of all parties.
- When stakeholders are actively engaged in school management, there is a higher degree of accountability. This accountability extends to school leaders, teachers, and even parents or community members who are involved. Knowing that their decisions and actions are subject to scrutiny encourages responsible behaviour and better governance.
- A valid measure can guide stakeholder participation in the identification of educational needs and priorities that might otherwise be overlooked. This can result in the allocation of resources and the implementation of policies and practices that directly benefit students and improve the overall quality of education.

Limitations of the study

While the current study has provided new insights into important elements contributing to stakeholder participation in school management to enhance learners' academic achievement, some limitations need to be acknowledged. The results relied on self-report measures and as such are subject to the threat of common method variance (CMV). This refers to the variance in data that is attributable to the measurement method itself rather than to the constructs being studied and it affects participants' responses across multiple items or measures (Kock et al., 2021). However, given that the measurement model demonstrated an acceptable fit to the data, given that the correlations between the measured constructs were moderate and varied quite considerably, given the very modest average reduction in the standardised loadings after a common methods factor was included, and given that all the factor loadings remained statistically significant after the common methods factor was modelled, the issue of CMV does not appear to be a significant concern. Nevertheless, future research could incorporate multi-rater or longitudinal data points to help address the risk of CMV.

In addition, no objective data were collected concerning the organizing and directing functions of the management of the schools sampled. Therefore, although the current model and measure suggest a range of dimensions that are important for effective stakeholder participation in school management to enhance learners' academic achievement, their impact or success in enhancing the learners' academic achievement or educational goals could not be determined. Furthermore, to answer the research question, 'What are the underlying structures within each discrete domain – planning, budgeting, coordinating, and academic achievement – of the school-based management model that support stakeholders' participation in school management to enhance learners' academic achievement in public secondary schools?', this study considered only EFA and found the involvement of 5 factor solutions from the 3 original constructs with 42 items.

Future research

Future research should employ confirmatory factor analysis (CFA) to validate the dimensions identified in this study. Such an approach would provide a more robust empirical basis for the constructs within the school-based management model (SBMM), thereby enhancing the generalisability and validity of these findings. It would perhaps be more expressive if the chapter confirmed the findings using oblique rotation.

The present results suggest that if reliable outcome measures can be accessed using the dimensions and measures described, then such future research can be conducted and interpreted with confidence.

Conclusion

This study aimed to validate the underlying structure of observed dimensions that support stakeholders' participation in school management to enhance learners' academic achievement in public secondary schools. Considering the total variance there was a need to reduce the linear correlated observed items of the dimensions to a smaller set of important independent composite dimensions. The EFA technique condensed the data into a smaller set of summary dimensions that were used to explore the underlying theoretical structures that enhance learners' academic achievement through stakeholder participation in school management. In totality, the findings make significant contributions to the literature on the multifaceted conceptualisation of the SBMM, which supports stakeholder participation in school management. The study presents empirically validated dimensions for the SBM model that can be used with confidence in support of stakeholder participation in school management. This can lead to more informed decision-making, increased accountability, improved educational quality, greater community support, enhanced inclusivity and equity, better teacher and staff morale, effective conflict resolution, long-term sustainability, and alignment with democratic values. These practical implications contribute to the overall success and effectiveness of the education system.

References

Agbenyo, F., Wisdom, N., & Akanbang, B. A. (2021). Stakeholder perspectives on participatory monitoring and evaluation in educational projects in upper West Region, Ghana. *Journal of Planning and Land Management, 2*(1), 50–64.

Ayeni, A. J., & Ibukun, W. O. (2013). A conceptual model for school-based management operation and quality assurance in Nigerian secondary schools. *Journal of Education and Learning, 2*(2), 36–43. https://doi.org/10.5539/jel.v2n2p36

Bandur, A. H., & Furinto, A. (2022). 21st-century experiences in the development of school-based management policy and practices in Indonesia. *Educational Research for Policy and Practice,* 1–23.

Barbier, E. B., & Burgess, J. C. (2017). The sustainable development goals and the systems approach to sustainability. *Economics, 11*(1), 20170028.

Cabardo, J. R. (2016). Levels of participation of the school stakeholders in the different school-initiated activities and the implementation of school-based management. *Journal of Inquiry and Action in Education, 8*(1), 81–94.

Cheng, Y. C. (2022). *School effectiveness and school-based management: A mechanism for development.* Taylor & Francis.

Cleminski, A. B. (2018). Practices that support leadership succession and principal retention. *Education Leadership Review, 19*(1), 21–41.

Fan, Y., Chen, J., Shirkey, G., John, R., Wu, S. R., Hogeun, P., & Shao, C. (2016). Applications of structural equation modeling (SEM) in ecological studies: An updated review. *Ecological Processes, 5*(1). https://doi.org/10.1186/s13717-016-0063-3

Field, A. (2013). *Discovering statistics using IBM SPSS statistics* (4th ed.). SAGE Publications.

Hadi, N. U., Abdullah, N., & Sentosa, I. (2016). An easy approach to exploratory factor analysis: Marketing perspective. *Journal of Educational and Social Research, 6*(1), 215–223.

Hair, J. F., Black, W. C., Babin, B. J., & Anderson, R. E. (2010). *Multivariate data analysis* (7th ed.). Pearson.

Hair, J. F., Black, W. C., Babin, B. J., & Anderson, R. E. (2019). *Multivariate data analysis* (8th ed.). Cengage Learning.

Hassan, R., & Macha, W. (2020, October 8). Education system profiles. *World Education News & Reviews.* https://wenr.wes.org

IBM Corporation. (2021). Exploratory factor analysis: Rotation. Search in SPSS Statistics Subscript. https://www.ibm.com/docs/en/spss-statistics/beta?topic=analysis-exploratory-factor-rotation

Izquierdo, I., Olea, J., & Abad, F. J. (2014). Exploratory factor analysis in validation studies: Uses and recommendations. *Psicothema, 26*(3), 395–400.

Kaiser, H. F. (1970). A second-generation little jiffy. *Psychometrika, 35*(4), 401–415.

Kaiser, H. F. (1974). An index of factorial simplicity. *Psychometrika, 39*(1), 31–36.

Kock, F., Berbekova, A., & Assaf, G. A. (2021). Understanding and managing the threat of common method bias: Detecting, prevention, and control. *Tourism Management, 86.* https://doi.org/10.1016/j.tourman.2021.104330

Mahuro, G. M., & Hungi, N. (2016). Parental participation improves student academic achievement: A case of Iganga and Mayuge districts in Uganda. *Cogent Education, 3*(1), 1264170. https://doi.org/10.1080/2331186X.2016.1264170

Media Officer. (2021, June 24). What do PTA do and why should you join one? PTA members answer your questions. *The Education Hub.* https://educationhub.blog.gov.uk/2021/06/24/what-do-ptas-do-and-why-should-you-join-one-pta-members-answer-your-questions/

Naidoo, P. (2019). Perceptions of teachers and school management teams of the leadership roles of public school principals. *South African Journal of Education, 39*(2). https://www.sajournalofeducation.co.za/index.php/saje/article/view/1534/861

Nakiyaga, D., Serem, D. K., & Namubiru, P. (2021). Stakeholder's participation in school management and the enhancement of learners' academic achievement in government-aided secondary schools in Uganda. *The International Journal of Business & Management, 9*(5). https://doi.org/10.24940/theijbm/2021/v9/i5/BM2105-049

Revelle, W. (2022). *How to: Use the psych package for factor analysis and data reduction.* Northwestern University.

Sehrawat, M., & Roy, M. M. (2021). Expected roles and functions of the school management committee: An investigation for effective functioning. *South Asian Journal of Social Sciences and Humanities, 2*(1), 79–92. https://doi.org/10.48165/sajssh.2021.2107

Serunjogi, C. D. (2022). The role of school management committees and head effectiveness in government-aided primary schools in Luweero District - Uganda. *American Journal of Leadership and Governance, 7*(1). https://doi.org/10.47672/ajlg.1036

Tansiri, I. Y., & Bong, Y. (2019, March). The analysis of school-based management (SBM) implementation to the educational quality service of state junior high school. In *2nd international conference on research of educational administration and management (ICREAM 2018).* Atlantis, Australia.

Tavakol, M., & Wetzel, A. (2020). Factor analysis: A means for theory and instrument development in support of construct validity. *International Journal of Medical Education, 11,* 245–247. https://doi.org/10.5116/ijme.5f96.0f4a

The Republic of Uganda Education Service Commission. (2008, August 29). Education (Pre-primary, primary and post-primary) Act. *Education Service Commission.* https://www.esc.go.ug/wp-content/uploads/2018/04/Education-Act-2008.pdf

Uganda National Examinations Board. (2019). *Uganda National Education Report.* https://www.monitor.co.ug/uganda/news/national/live-uneb-releases-2019-uce-results-1872522

UNESCO Education Sector. (2020). *Multi-stakeholder approaching education for sustainable development in local communities.* UNESCO Bangkok Office.

Warner, R. M. (2013). *Applied statistics: From bivariate through multivariate techniques* (2nd ed.). SAGE Publications.

Wataba, H., & Abiodun, N. L. (2018). Board of governors' roles and management of government-aided secondary schools in Kyenjojo District Uganda. *Interdisciplinary Journal of Education, 1*(2). https://journals.iuiu.ac.ug/index.php/ije/article/view/12

Watkins, M. W. (2018). Exploratory factor analysis: A guide to best practice. *Journal of Black Psychology, 44*(3), 219–246. https://doi.org/10.1177/0095798418771807

Widodo, H. (2019). The role of school culture in holistic education development in Muhammadiyah elementary school Sleman Yogyakarta. *Dinamika Ilmu, 19*(2), 265–285. https://doi.org/10.21093/di.v19i2.1742

Willmer, M., Jacobson, W. J., & Lindberg, M. (2019). Exploratory and confirmatory factor analysis of the 9-item Utrecht work engagement scale in a multi-occupational female sample: A cross-sectional study. *Frontiers in Psychology: Quantitative Psychology and Measurement,* 1–7. https://doi.org/10.3389/fpsyg.2019.02771

Ya, K. Z., Rizal, F., & Wulansari, R. E. (2020). Revisiting the school-based management recent studies. *Pedagogi: Jurnal Ilmu Pendidikan, 20*(2), 119–127.

Yusoff, M. S. (2019). ABC of content validation and content validity index calculation. *Education in Medicine Journal, 11*(2), 49–54.

Zaid, Z., Pettalongi, S. S., & Nurdin, N. (2022). Implementation of school-based management in improving the quality of state Islamic junior high school. *International Journal of Social Science and Human Research, 5*(8), 3448–3455. https://doi.org/10.47191/ijsshr/v5-i8-12

CHAPTER 8

Exploring the use of participatory visual methods in teaching sexuality education within the HIV and AIDS education programme in Kenyan secondary schools

Lily Yego, Violet Nabwire Opata, Heloise Sathorar, Mathabo Khau

Introduction

The study on which this chapter is based aimed at exploring the outcomes of integration of participatory visual methods (PVM) into sexuality, HIV and AIDS education in selected Kenyan secondary schools. There is generally a high degree of teacher discomfort when teaching these topics in Kenyan schools (Mukonyi, 2020; Ochieng et al., 2014). This challenge often stems from teachers' unease with delivering content related to HIV prevention (Ringisai, 2023; Gudyanga et al., 2019), necessitating the exploration of innovative teaching strategies to mitigate the pandemic's spread.

Robert et al. (2020) highlight that most new HIV infections in Kenya occur among adolescents aged 15 to 24 years, despite the introduction of the HIV and AIDS Education Programme into the curriculum in 2000. Despite its objectives to impart life skills, sexual reproductive health knowledge, and awareness of sexually transmitted infections (STIs) and HIV/AIDS, the programme's effectiveness remains questionable, with reports of continued risky sexual behaviours among youth (Manyibe, 2023; Muchiri & Omulema, 2020). Moreover, studies indicate that Kenyan learners still exhibit low levels of knowledge regarding sexuality, HIV and AIDS (Chory et al., 2021), with a significant gap between behavioural change objectives and actual outcomes (Njenga, 2019). This suggests either ineffective implementation of the programme or inadequacies in imparting the required knowledge, skills, and values. Notably, the predominant teaching method in Kenyan schools for HIV and AIDS education remains the lecture method, which is heavily reliant on textbooks (Chesaro, 2019), exacerbating teachers' discomfort in addressing the subject of responsible sexual behaviours with learners (Khan, 2019).

Despite the global inclusion of HIV and AIDS education in school curricula, there is still a paucity of studies exploring the integration of PVM as a pedagogical tool for the teaching of sexuality, and HIV and AIDS education in Kenyan secondary schools. Recognising the need for diverse pedagogical approaches to promote effective learning, particularly in sensitive subjects, such as sexuality education, this chapter presents a critical exploration of teachers' experiences with PVM within the HIV and AIDS Education Programme in Kenyan secondary schools. The study aims to elucidate how such methods impact the teaching of sexuality education in order to provide insights to inform future educational interventions.

HIV and AIDS education

Kenya ranks fourth globally in HIV epidemic prevalence, with 1.4 million individuals living with HIV in 2022 (UNAIDS, 2023; UNAIDS, 2023). Despite a decrease in new HIV infections, particularly in sub-Saharan countries like Kenya, young people aged 15 to 24 remain disproportionately affected (UNAIDS, 2023). Given the implications of HIV and AIDS on the future workforce and economy, addressing the pandemic is critical for the country's development (WHO, 2022). The Kenyan government has taken steps to combat the spread of HIV by setting targets to reduce infection rates, especially among youth (UNAIDS, 2023). However, effective HIV and AIDS education is essential for behaviour change, particularly among adolescents who are most affected.

While HIV and AIDS education is integrated into many national curricula, high infection rates persist in some countries due to teachers' discomfort in delivering prevention content (Ringisai, 2023; Gudyanga et al., 2019). Hence, there is a pressing need for innovative teaching approaches to mitigate the pandemic's spread. Participatory visual methods (PVM) are recognised as effective tools to engage both teachers and learners, fostering a conducive learning environment for sensitive topics like sexuality education (Hira et al., 2021). In Bangladesh and New Zealand, governments have invested in training teachers on diverse teaching methods, including PVM, to enhance learners' trust and participation in discussing HIV and AIDS (Sarma et al., 2017; Igbokwe et al., 2020).

Similarly, South Africa prioritizes HIV and AIDS education in schools, recognising them as ideal settings for promoting behaviour change and life skills among youth (Wood et al., 2013). However, challenges persist, such as inadequate time allocated for teaching sexuality education and its integration into other subjects (Daka et al., 2021). In India, despite initiatives like the Adolescent Education Programme, gaps in HIV knowledge among youth persist, underscoring the need for effective education strategies (National Art Education Association, 2009).

In countries like Thailand and Zambia, where HIV and AIDS education delivery is directive and selective, respectively, challenges in promoting learner participation and addressing comprehensive topics persist (Boonmongkon et al., 2019). Kenyan teachers, too, face challenges in delivering comprehensive HIV and AIDS education due to discomfort, inadequate training, and fear of promoting perceived immoral behaviour (Kiswili, 2021). Some resort to extracurricular activities or PVM to engage students in discussions on sexuality and HIV (Kiswili, 2021). However, research on the effectiveness of PVM in promoting behaviour change among Kenyan youth remains limited (Kafwa et al., 2015).

Addressing these challenges requires equipping teachers with adequate subject knowledge and engaging teaching methods to promote active learning and behaviour change (Kafwa et al., 2015). Given the dearth of proper PVM utilization in Kenyan schools, incorporating such methods into HIV and AIDS education could enhance teacher-student interaction and improve learning outcomes.

Challenges faced by Kenyan teachers in teaching sexuality, HIV and AIDS education

Despite efforts by the Kenyan government to integrate the HIV and AIDS programme into the school curriculum, challenges persist regarding its delivery and content. Kiswili (2021) highlights the inconsistency among teachers in delivering the programme, with many often focusing on comfortable topics like morals and abstinence, while neglecting sensitive aspects such as contraceptives and condom use. This discomfort stems from inadequate training and fear of promoting perceived immoral behaviour, leading some teachers to avoid teaching sexuality education altogether (Chavula et al., 2023; Kiswili, 2021; Machawira et al., 2020). Consequently, some teachers resort to discussing sexuality education during extracurricular activities, such as drama, music, and counselling sessions. Additionally, participatory visual methods (PVM), such as print media and folk tales, have been used by some teachers in Kenyan schools to address these challenges.

Despite the high prevalence of HIV among Kenyan youth, there is limited research on the effectiveness of PVM in promoting behaviour change and curbing HIV spread. Kafwa et al. (2015) emphasise the need for teachers to be well-versed in the subject matter and actively engage learners in the learning process. Hence, participatory visual methods have emerged as a suitable approach to facilitate teacher-student interaction and enhance learning outcomes.

Using participatory visual methods in teaching sexuality, HIV and AIDS education

Participatory approaches empower learners to express their perspectives on sexuality, HIV, and AIDS, fostering meaningful engagement (Johnson et al., 2020). Teachers play a crucial role in educating students about sexuality and HIV/AIDS before they become sexually active (Martin et al., 2020; Beyers, 2013). Participatory visual methods not only motivate teachers and learners to participate actively but also facilitate conversations and meaning making. Social interactions during these activities influence cognitive development and individual thinking processes (Vygotsky, 1978).

The liberalization of sexual norms exposes young people to various risks, such as unprotected sex and HIV infection (Johnson et al., 2020). PVM offer a simplified approach for teachers to provide guidance and enable learners to make informed choices about their lives. Through participatory strategies, learners share experiences, co-construct knowledge, and engage in critical dialogue (Johnson et al., 2020; Leshem et al., 2015; McTavish et al., 2012). By interacting with teachers and peers, learners develop a deeper understanding of sexuality, HIV and AIDS, empowering them to make informed decisions. Participatory learning environments facilitate secure and creative spaces for critical discussions, promoting hope among teachers and learners (Cherrington, 2017). Optimism is essential in teaching practices, as it fosters self-determination and promotes justice and equity (Kovach, 2021).

Materials and methods

The study presented in this chapter adopts a qualitative research approach, employing an interpretive paradigm and a phenomenological design to investigate methods of teaching sexuality education in schools, aiming to sensitize learners to make informed choices about sexuality, HIV and AIDS. According to Creswell and Poth (2018), a phenomenological study delves into individuals' experiences of a phenomenon, fundamentally seeking to describe its nature. Participants in this study were purposively selected to gather focused information from those directly involved. Purposive sampling involves deliberate selection of participants based on specific criteria. Participant teachers were chosen from county and sub-county school levels where the HIV and AIDS Education Programme is integrated into the curriculum. Three schools were selected, with three participant teachers per school, representing different subjects: biology, English/literature, and guidance and counselling. Purposive sampling often involves a small sample size, as it allows for in-depth exploration and detailed data collection. The selected schools included both co-educational and single-sex schools for girls and boys, situated in urban and semi-urban areas, providing a comprehensive understanding of diverse learner characteristics and experiences.

Data generation employed reflective journals and focus group discussions (FGDs). Prior to data collection, participants attended a one-day workshop facilitated by the researcher. The workshop, attended by eighteen teachers (nine of whom were study participants), introduced participatory visual methods (PVM) for teaching sexuality education, including drawings, collages, role-plays, songs, and poetry. Subsequently, participants implemented PVM in their classrooms, maintaining reflective journals to document classroom experiences. Reflective journals provide insights into participants' experiences, facilitating a deeper exploration of phenomena by bringing unconscious thoughts to light. During FGDs, meanings and insights emerging from discussions are socially constructed, offering a collective understanding of experiences. Focus groups are well-suited for exploring diverse perspectives and experiences, making them appropriate for this study. FGDs were used to gather teachers' views on their previous methods of teaching sexuality education and their experiences after adopting PVM. The discussions allowed participants to share varied experiences and perspectives, fostering a sense of support and empowerment.

Data analysis involved thematic analysis, aimed at identifying patterns across qualitative datasets. Initially, the researchers familiarized themselves with the data by reading transcripts multiple times, identifying units of meaning and generating initial codes. These codes were grouped into categories and used to develop themes, which were presented and discussed as study findings. Thematic analysis facilitates the extraction of themes directly from the data, providing concrete and tangible findings that contribute to advancing knowledge in social research.

Ethical considerations were meticulously observed throughout the study. Prior to data collection, ethical approval was obtained from the university's Ethics Committee and permission was obtained from the Education Department in Kenya and school principals. Participants provided informed consent, with full assurance of confidentiality and anonymity. Pseudonyms were used to protect participants' identities. Triangulation of data ensured credibility, while confirmability was established through rigorous data analysis processes. Transferability was ensured by providing a detailed context description and rationale for research methods. Confidentiality in FGDs was maintained through a confidentiality clause signed by participants, affirming their commitment not to disclose discussion content.

Findings

Findings related to teachers' experiences of using participatory visual methods in teaching sexuality education are presented. These were recorded in reflective journals by each teacher participant immediately after their try out lessons and were later discussed in a focus group discussion. Teachers' reflective journals are presented herein:

Tuti used poetry in his class. He asked the learners how HIV and AIDS spread and also the ways of curbing it. The learners engaged in group activities under the guidance of the teacher. The learners shared knowledge among themselves in the groups. They picked content words in a passage and composed poems. Their poems were about engaging in safe sexual practices and ways of protecting others from HIV infection in the event that one is infected, and one's partner is not. He also went further to guide the learners on the use of protection. Tuti noted that the discussion was impressive in that it encouraged hope, especially to those infected and affected by HIV. He wrote:

Tuti

After attending a training on the use of participatory methods in teaching sexuality education, I decided to implement it in my teaching as it was more of learner based and the students would come up with ideas as I was not the main source of the knowledge. I tried poetry. I went back to the same story in Literature on "When the sun goes down." I decided to use it for revision with the Form Four students who were about to sit for the national examination before they were free to face the world. I felt this came in time so that my students would brace themselves enough to face the world. I got to class so enthusiastic and asked the students if we could revise the story once more as I predicted would be the compulsory story in the national examination. After reading the story as a class, I asked the students to mention how HIV and AIDS are spread, and ways to curb the spread of HIV and AIDS. The students did that in groups and as I went round checking on what they had written in their groups; I was so impressed: the discussion was fruitful! Those who knew on the preventive measures discussed that with those who did not know about it. I asked them to further pick the content words and compose a poem using the words. They did. Being a young school, I had divided the class to two groups only. The first group in their poem recited how AIDS was a killer disease and it was affecting the young generation a lot in that they engaged in unsafe sexual practices and how hard it was for them to resist sexual pleasures. The second group recited on the fact that Veronica and Makanga lived together for so long and Makanga lived even after Veronica's death simply because they were using protection and therefore Makanga was not infected with AIDS. After the presentations I was able to guide them on the need of using protection- that's the use of condoms any time they engaged in sex if at all they couldn't wait for the right time. The students were so co-operative, as it was even simpler asking them other questions based on the story. We concluded the lesson by saying that actually when the sun goes down, one shouldn't cry for the tears will not let them see the stars to mean that even with HIV and AIDS, one can still have a partner, practise safe sex and live happily as a family and also on the need to accept those who are HIV positive in the society.

Tuti's and Enai's experiences share similarities, with both expressing admiration for the effectiveness and ease of use of participatory visual methods (PVM) in teaching. Enai highlighted that these methods facilitated a sense of comfort in her teaching approach. Following training on PVM, Enai felt a sense of obligation to impart knowledge to her students, recognising her responsibility in guiding them. Employing role-play, Enai engaged her students in discussions about socializing with peers outside of school. Their responses varied, with some expressing excitement about newfound freedoms while others expressed concerns about pregnancy. Notably, one student emphasised the importance of contraceptives and condoms, indicating a level of knowledge about responsible sexual behaviours among the learners. Enai then emphasised the reality of HIV and the necessity of protection and safe sexual practices. She found PVM to be more encouraging and engaging compared to traditional lecture methods, which often led to discomfort among students.

Enai

After going through training on using participatory methods in teaching, I decided to adopt a new way of teaching my learners. The training made me realize that I had to teach the learners as it was my responsibility and duty to do so. It was necessary for them to know about their sexuality as a guide to make informed choices. I chose to use Role-play with my Form Four learners. I asked them to stage a play on how they would behave immediately they finished their fourth form examination. They were so excited. Being a double lesson, I gave them the first lesson to prepare for the play. In the second lesson, some selected characters staged the play, [where they] would be meeting with their boyfriends every day. One of the characters was worried that school was better as she escaped being impregnated by her boyfriend as they did not have enough time over the holiday and one was quick to react that she would always be safe if she used contraceptives. By now I was getting amused how the girls had so much information. One character snapped in to say that contraceptives were good but that was only meant to control pregnancy, how about deadly diseases? The main character summed it up by saying she was so excited to be free from school at last but she was always careful to choose her friends and if possible, she would stay a virgin till she got married. After the play, I took them through a discussion on the need to have healthy relationships and that it was important to choose friends wisely. I also led them to understand that HIV and AIDS are real and they should take care of themselves, I also encouraged them to share that with their friends. I asked them of how they would go about it to protect them and their partners in case they were sexually active. They contributed in the discussion by saying that it was good to use condoms as it was known to be a barrier or stay cool till the ripe time. I was quick to tell them that even in marriage condoms can still work in case you feel you have a straying partner and of course you need to take care of the children. At the end of the lesson, I felt I had been wasting my learners' time a lot for not teaching them on what they needed to know about their sexuality. Using these participatory methods was so encouraging in that it was more of a discussion with the learners than the usual lecture method which to me I felt I owned the lesson and brought about some discomfort.

In the same way Enai wrote of the interactive nature of participatory visual methods, Krea admitted that she was more encouraged and equipped to teach than before when she used the lecture method of teaching. Furthermore, she wrote that her learners actively participated unlike before.

Krea admitted being more equipped than before in delivering sexuality education in her class. She used collages. The learners were grouped in three groups for the activities. In the collages, they expressed their awareness of the societal expectations of a family. Afterwards, Krea led them in a discussion on the biological functions of the body and in ways to avoid irresponsible sexual behaviour. Krea wrote that the method was very encouraging and helpful because it was learner-based. She wrote:

Krea

The training on participatory teaching methods was God sent to me because I now have better skills on how to cope with teaching topics related to sexuality. I employed the use of collage by asking the students to paste pictures that represent a family unit. After they did that, I asked them to explain their pictures. I had three groups: the first group had pictures of a father, a mother and three children together with their grandparents, the second group pasted pictures of a single mother with several children and lastly the last group had pictures of parents without children but had the extended family. In their explanation, the first group said that people get married and the society expects them to get children so as to continue the family lineage, so many cheeky girls came from this class and they even used my example that maybe the reason as to why I get children rapidly is because of the family expectation, especially my mother-in-law. Deep inside my heart, I was surprised that these learners were conversant with the customary expectations and somehow understood my situation. The second group explained that so many of them came from homes of single parents and their parents couldn't explain to them why they were so and the third said because of some biological reasons some parents were not blessed with children. I took their explanations to my advantage and explained to them the biological functions of our bodies and in depth of the hormones responsible for childbearing, and their rightful age to get children and be responsible parents. All along, I engaged them in my discussion, and I took advantage of the lesson to teach them of the irresponsible sexual behaviours. Using participatory methods are very helpful as you discuss with the learners rather than lecturing to them so they grasp it better.

Raed shared a similar experience with Krea. Just like in Krea's classroom, the learners in Raed's classroom actively participated for they owned the lesson; the method boosted their esteem in learning. Since the method was learner-based, Raed was encouraged to teach and she admitted that the learners were cooperative. Raed used poetry in her class to explore the students' understanding of human sexuality. She wrote that the learners exploited their talents in developing poems. They described what they saw in the picture presented to them. She noted that even the shy learners in her class participated actively. It was a fast way to learn as the learners owned the lesson:

Raed

I used poetry as a learning method to interpret one's understanding of what human sexuality is. A group of form 3 students were able to exploit their talent in development of poems. Having seen a photo of a couple spending time together, they could not hide their excitement. They moved closer to the photo with lots of description of what they saw. Even the known shy students were in the front line.

Writing of poetry was a fast way to learn or rather share an idea about human sexuality. They only see the positive side of life even when the negative is obvious. This means their understanding is that as sexual beings, love never ends. It was less involving for the teacher and the students took the methods and owned them.

Raed and Seng shared similar observations regarding their experiences in the classroom. Both found the method of using participatory visual methods (PVM) to be straightforward and conducive to rapid learning. They noted that this approach also had a positive impact on their students' self-esteem by encouraging them to address issues from a constructive perspective.

Seng's decision to incorporate collage into her teaching stemmed from a previous incident where a student felt negatively affected by the teaching method. To prevent such occurrences in the future, Seng adopted a learner-centred approach with the use of collage. She found this method to be both easy to implement and engaging for her students. Additionally, Seng utilized role-play in her lessons and observed that it led to significant improvements in her students' attitudes towards their bodies, fostering self-appreciation and confidence among them.

Seng

After being guided on participatory and visual ways of teaching sexuality, I decided to use collage so that I can see to what extent the students would think about themselves and the stages of development in both types of sexes. I tried this method because of my previous experience of being attacked by a student after handling this topic and giving them the details. I was very impressed when I used this method because this changed their perception and mine too. This was due to the fact that every detail came from them and not me hence this made my work easier, and it was also very interesting to the students. I also used them to do role-play whereby I watched great performances from them which made the lesson very enjoyable and students could now understand some details that are more real than the written documents in the textbooks. In this session, they turned the lack of hips and enlarged breasts to be an advantage like being an athlete.

In Seng and Tessy's classrooms, the learners easily expressed themselves by using the participatory methods. They were excited and positive about their sexuality. The two teachers' journal entries reflect that the method encouraged hope in teaching because of the cooperation of the learners.

Tessy used drawings in her classroom. She stated that the learners were still unaware of themselves as sexual beings. She further stated that this method was different from the lecture method that she had always used. The learners were excited and cooperative during the lesson.

Tessy

It was a cool afternoon having assembled my students, anxious as they were I asked them how they can express their sexual personality by use of a drawing (diagram). We had just completed a topic in Christian Religious Education called human sexuality. This was an awesome summary of the topic.

According to what they are told by friends. They are still unaware of whom they are as sexual beings. However, having taught them about human sexuality in class mostly using lecture method, this other approach was totally different. They were excited more co-operative, quick to respond and easy to express themselves.

There was a similarity in Tessy and Sue's experiences in using participatory methods. Their learners enjoyed working with the methodology. They wrote that the learners responded and expressed themselves easily; thus, the method was effective for use.

Sue used songs in her teaching. She asked the learners to compose songs and noted that they came up with lovely melodies and lyrics of how they saw themselves as sexual beings. They praised their sexuality. She also used drawings. The learners drew themselves in appreciation of themselves and how valuable they were. Sue wrote that the method was effective:

Sue

In my previous experience, I did not know how to approach and teach issues to do with sexuality. After the participatory methods were introduced, I engaged my students on the use of song; they were able to construct songs on sexuality and came up with very good melodies on how they saw themselves as sexual beings. The girls could praise themselves in a song referring to themselves as flowers. After the participatory methods were introduced, I went back to the same class and introduced the use of drawings and interestingly, the students were able to draw various pictures describing themselves as sexual beings some girls drew themselves as a pineapple illustrating that they are juicy but you cannot get them easily unless you ready to be pierced. Others drew themselves as sugarcane, coconut and many more. So the participatory methods of teaching sexuality are effective because students participate freely without fear of victimization.

Emar's experience with the participatory visual methods (PVM) mirrored that of Raed, Tessy, Seng, Sue, and Tuti's learners—excitement and engagement were prevalent in the classroom. Emar observed that his students thoroughly enjoyed using these methods, which made it effortless for him to guide them through interactive sessions comfortably.

Recognising Kenya's cultural context, Emar acknowledged that some parents might be apprehensive about their children gaining sexual knowledge. Initially, he assumed his students were naive in this regard, only to discover their awareness of sex and sexuality, largely influenced by peer interactions and social media exposure. Utilizing songs as a method, Emar observed that the compositions reflected the students' sense of freedom at home and hinted at their sexual activity and knowledge of contraceptives and condoms. Emar then took the opportunity to guide his students towards making informed decisions. Overall, Emar found the method exciting and enjoyable for both himself and his students.

Emar

During the training on the use of participatory methods in teaching, we were informed that it was necessary to guide our students on the need of healthy sexual practices. Based on the Kenyan culture, most parents would be mad to hear that their children are being taught about sex! Many at times we assume our children are naïve but they seem to know more than we would ever imagine. The training was a wakeup call to me as I realized I have not been guiding my learners in the right way. That question that I was once asked during one of the sessions made me realize that we as teachers and parents have been lying to ourselves that our children do not know anything about sex yet they learnt it from the peers or the social media. I decided to implement the participatory methods and change my way I delivered my guiding sessions. During this particular session, I asked the learners to compose songs of how they felt as young people, how useful the social media was to them and their relationships with their parents. As I listened to their presentations, I realised that the students were so enslaved to social media and were learning a lot. Another thing I learnt is that most of the students were given so much freedom at home and there was so much negligence from the parent's side as they highlighted of how they would always meet their friends in town or the house and how they always longed for holiday to catch-up with friends. I asked them if they were aware that HIV and AIDS was on the rise and that it was also affecting the youth and there was silence in the hall. I made them understand that it was good to spend time with their peers, but they also had to take care of themselves. Using the knowledge, I acquired in the training, I told the students that their songs suggested that some of them were sexually active, for once I told them that was not wrong but they needed to use protection. I asked them of the appropriate way to do so. I got responses like; using contraceptives and condoms. I then told them that condoms were the most appropriate as with those they would control pregnancy and HIV and AIDS. After our discussions, the learners commented that we should be having more of such sessions unlike the previous ones which I was always domineering.

The teachers' focus group discussions recording transcriptions are presented below:

Emar: The learners were able to have fun. At the end of the lesson, they were asking questions as compared to those other times. The students were able to recall because of using songs. And also on the role-play, although there wasn't enough time especially their performance plays, you know most of the time, they have not been incorporated to drama. I took care of one class and because of time, the teachers will be able to pick up from there. In the role-play, the students were able to bring out and remember most customs that they staged. For example, I gave them a bit of one scene, it was a set text and then I assigned them characters. With that play, so many were able to come out. The students were able to play roles, in the process learnt various ideas on their sexuality.

Raed: I teach English and literature. I used two methods; role-play and poems. The role-play: I used it when I was teaching poetry and I used some of the poems whereby I engaged the students to take up that role of being the persona and they recited the poems which have some words which when pronounced, when said in class, you see the students saying (surprise look). You mean the teacher can say that? So, I made them say those words so that they could know that it is something normal and we are in class. It's not that when you utter some words then that is what you do. It was very successful when it came to answering some questions in poetry. Then I used the poems. That one I used in comprehension. We read a comprehension, then I told the students to write some of the words and phrases they think had some content concerning some behaviour and later came up with a poem which enabled us to answer questions easily. Yes.

Enai: I also did the same: role-play and drawings. The students drew various things and I made them to be open. I told them they can draw anything. They did it. Some drew houses, some pencils, all sorts of drawings. They were happy, curious, and also wanted to know what the others were thinking. I also engaged in the role-play and they were able to. They made a play about child abuse. I recorded and it was fun. They really wanted to play again and again, only time could not allow. They just did one.

Tessy: I teach CRE and guidance and counselling. I tried out the use of drawings and poetry. For me I think this really came out the right time. After dealing with the Form Three; taking them through a topic on human sexuality. It was actually at the peak of the topic. I told them to draw themselves, what they understand, their general understanding on human sexuality, and the boys were really excited. For them, they wanted to express themselves, what they think about themselves. I just told them to express themselves, their sexual beings. None of them was negative. They were all positive. I realized that when they are given opportunities, they give you the ideas about themselves. Sometimes according to what they are told by others, what they hear, they believe that that is what they are. I did guide after teaching them about sexuality, there were some words that were difficult to mention and explain and at some point, I would chew some information because of being embarrassed especially being boys, my state, I am expectant. So, it was hard to teach them about sexuality, but when I now gave them that opportunity, I think they understood the topic better, those who were shy, I saw them really participate that was the drawing. There are a lot of drawings here. I teach the Form Three and the Form Four poetry. I gave them a picture, a photo and told them to make a poem of what they were seeing. They were able to come up with a poem; they could open up when I gave them a chance to.

Sue: Yes. I realized that when you are teaching such topics as sexuality, they actually come out. There is that something that comes out as compared to when we were teaching before. There is also something they have been hiding. I told them you are not talking about you but the drawing. You could see that openness; they were really open. In fact, when the bell rung, they were like aaah. In fact, they are asking for more lessons because we did not exhaust. And also, you capture their attention because everyone is involved. The responses were, I was happy. Then now the music. You see our students are very creative. They are really creative. Although we did not do much, it is really amazing; you could see that fear gone. Ask issues so openly as compared to those other times when they were reserved. Now students can stand and say, they have to protect their virginity, until marriage.

Seng: Good afternoon (response from group). ... I used two: the collage and role-play. I used in biology lessons. For sure there was a difference in how the students participated. In this case, I told them to use collage to explain characteristics of ladies and men. Like in class, you say there is the widening of the chest, muscles, but when they took magazines and saw pictures, cutting them, enjoying with all the fun, they really enjoyed it so much and in fact, it made it easy when explaining to them. When you talk of widening of the chest, you tell them, look at this man, then the hip. When you talk of the hips, they tell you, look at this lady the way she is and the rest. They really impressed me with how active they were. On the role-play, they worked. Of course there is that distinction, how those characteristics are portrayed amongst them. In fact, I really enjoyed teaching and they enjoyed the learning process.

Tuti: Yeah, I think the way we handle these students, for example, there are bad things we don't want them to do now. I think from what we have learnt here; it is better when we meet with teachers from other schools or even within the school. Then maybe we get time like one lesson to teach students especially on HIV and AIDS. So especially now that we teach them on the need to take care of themselves, control themselves and so on about these issues and handle the sexuality issues well.

Discussion of findings

The findings from the reflective journals of the participating teachers shed light on their experiences using participatory visual methods (PVM) in teaching sexuality education. Across the various classrooms, teachers employed methods such as poetry, role-play, collage, drawings, and songs to engage their students in discussions about sexuality, HIV and AIDS. The results indicate several key themes regarding the effectiveness and impact of these methods.

First, it is evident that teachers found PVM to be highly effective in facilitating student engagement and participation. Tuti, Enai, Raed, Krea, Sue, and Emar all noted the enthusiasm and cooperation of their students when using these methods. Students were actively involved in group activities, discussions, and creative tasks, demonstrating a genuine interest in the subject matter. This high level of engagement is crucial for effective learning, as it indicates that students are more likely to absorb and retain information when they are actively involved in the learning process.

Second, PVM was found to enhance students' understanding and awareness of sexuality-related issues. Teachers reported that their students demonstrated a deepened understanding of topics such as safe sexual practices, HIV prevention, and healthy relationships. Through activities like poetry composition, role-play, and drawing, students were able to express their thoughts and feelings about these issues in a creative and meaningful way. This suggests that PVM can serve as a powerful tool for facilitating open and honest discussions about sensitive topics, ultimately leading to greater awareness and knowledge among students.

Furthermore, the use of PVM was found to have a positive impact on students' self-esteem and confidence. Teachers like Raed, Seng, and Tessy observed that their students became more self-assured and willing to express themselves when using these methods. By providing students with opportunities to showcase their talents and creativity, PVM helped to boost students' confidence and self-esteem, creating a supportive and empowering learning environment.

Lastly, the findings from the focus group discussion further highlight the benefits of using PVM in teaching sexuality education. Teachers shared their experiences and insights, noting the effectiveness of PVM in promoting student learning and engagement. They also discussed the importance of collaboration and sharing best practice among teachers, suggesting that ongoing professional development and support are essential for effective implementation of PVM.

In conclusion, the findings of this study underscore the effectiveness of participatory visual methods in teaching sexuality education. By actively involving students in the learning process and providing opportunities for creative expression and discussion, PVM can enhance students' understanding, awareness, and self-esteem, ultimately leading to more informed and empowered individuals. Moving forward, it is essential for educators and policymakers to recognise the value of PVM and invest in training and resources to support its widespread implementation in schools.

Conclusion

The study outlined in this chapter aimed to investigate Kenyan secondary school teachers' experiences with using participatory visual methods (PVM) to teach sexuality education, focusing specifically on collages, role-play, music, poetry, and drawings. The effectiveness of PVM was evident in its facilitation of learner interaction and the teachers' comfort in fostering open dialogue in the classroom. Learners exhibited creativity, emerging as primary sources of knowledge, understanding more about their sexuality through interactive sessions guided by teachers. Teachers appreciated the simplicity, creativity, and enjoyment derived from guiding learners to deepen their understanding of sexuality.

PVM emerged as suitable for addressing sensitive topics like sexuality, HIV and AIDS, enabling teachers to simplify complex issues and foster an environment conducive to learning. Through collages, drawings, music, role-play, and poetry, learners developed comprehensive knowledge under teachers' guidance, thereby easing the teaching process and empowering learners to actively engage in their education. Consequently, PVM appears to be an effective pedagogical approach, providing a safe and inclusive space for effective teaching and meaningful learner expression, thereby facilitating behaviour change and promoting comprehensive sexuality education.

In summary, this chapter supports the efficacy of PVM in enhancing teaching effectiveness and promoting informed decision-making among learners. By prioritizing learners' needs and preparing them for life's challenges, the education system can contribute to the overarching goal of fostering a supportive environment for teaching and learning about sexuality, HIV and AIDS.

References

Beyers, C. (2013). In search of healthy sexuality: The gap between what youth want and what teachers think they need. *The Journal for Transdisciplinary Research in Southern Africa, 9*(3), 550–560.

Boonmongkon, P., Shrestha, M., Samoh, N., Kanchawee, K., Peerawarunun, P., Promnart, P., & Guadamuz, T. E. (2019). Comprehensive sexuality education in Thailand? A nationwide assessment of sexuality education implementation in Thai public secondary schools. *Sexual Health, 16*(3), 263–273. https://doi.org/10.1071/SH18121

Cherrington, A. (2017). Positioning a practice of hope in South African teacher education programmes. *Educational Research for Social Change, 6*(1). http://dx.doi.org/10.17159/2221-4070/2017/v6i1a6

Chory, A., Nyandiko, W., Martin, R., Aluoch, J., Scanlon, M., Ashimosi, C., Njoroge, T., McAteer, C., Apondi, E., & Vreeman, R. (2021). HIV-related knowledge, attitudes, behaviors, and experiences of Kenyan adolescents living with HIV revealed in WhatsApp group chats. *Journal of the International Association of Providers of AIDS Care (JIAPAC), 20*. https://doi.org/10.1177/2325958221999579

Creswell, J. W., & Poth, C. N. (2016). *Qualitative inquiry and research design: Choosing among five approaches.* Sage Publications.

Creswell, J. W., & Poth, C. N. (2018). *Qualitative inquiry and research design: Choosing among five approaches* (4th ed.). SAGE Publications Inc.

Daka, H., Jacob, W. J., Simeon, M., Mukuka Mulenga-Hagane, L., Kalisto, K., & Fumbani, M. (2021). Integration of HIV and AIDS into primary curriculum: Teacher training curriculum. *International Journal of Humanities Social Sciences and Education, 8*(2), 123–133.

Gudyanga, E., De Lange, N., & Khau, M. (2019). Zimbabwean secondary school guidance and counseling teachers teaching sexuality education in the HIV and AIDS education curriculum. *SAHARA-J: Journal of Social Aspects of HIV/AIDS, 16*(1), 35–50.

Hira, F. A., Singh, H., Moshiul, A. M., & Shahriar, A. S. (2021). How to curb the HIV/AIDS prevalence in Bangladesh? *International Journal of Academic Research in Business and Social Sciences, 11*(5), 300–309.

Igbokwe, U. L., Ogbonna, C. S., Ezegbe, B. N., Nnadi, E. M., & Eseadi, C. (2020). Viewpoint on family life and HIV education curriculum in Nigerian secondary schools. *Journal of International Medical Research, 48*(1). https://doi.org/10.1177/0300060519844663

Johnson, B., Flentje, J., & Bartholomaeus, C. (2020). Co-researching and designing innovative learning approaches in sexuality and relationships education. *Pastoral Care in Education, 38*(3), 191–207. https://www.tandfonline.com/doi/full/10.1080/02643944.2020.1773907

Kafwa, N. O., Obondo, G., & Kisaka, T. S. (2015). Teacher preparation practices in Kenya and the 21st century learning: A moral obligation. *Journal of Education and Practice, 6*(17). https://files.eric.ed.gov/fulltext/EJ1079789.pdf

Karten, J. (2010). *Inclusion strategies that work! Research-based methods for the classroom.* Corwin.

Khan, Z. (2019). Sexuality education and personal-efficacy in safe sexual behavior: *A study on secondary school girls in Chipata Zambia* [Unpublished master's degree]. Stockholm University.

Kiswili, K. (2021). Beyond the rhetoric: The case for the institutionalization of comprehensive sexuality education in Kenyan schools. *European Journal of Social Sciences Studies, 6*(4). https://oapub.org/soc/index.php/EJSSS/article/view/1092

Kovach, M. (2021). *Indigenous methodologies: Characteristics, conversations, and contexts.* University of Toronto Press.

Machawira, P., Castle, C., & Herat, J. (2020). Progress and challenges with comprehensive sexuality education: What does this mean for HIV prevention in the ESA region? *Preventing HIV among young people in Southern and Eastern Africa,* 261–279.

Manyibe, E. K. (2023). *Parenting styles and teenage sexual behaviors among teenage mothers in selected public secondary schools in Kajiado County, Kenya* [Doctoral dissertation, The Catholic University of Eastern Africa].

Martin, P., Cousin, L., Gottot, S., Bourmaud, A., de La Rochebrochard, E., & Alberti, C. (2020). Participatory interventions for sexual health promotion for adolescents and young adults on the internet: Systematic review. *Journal of Medical Internet Research, 22*(7), e15378. https://doi.org/10.2196/15378

Muchiri, P., & Omulema, B. (2020). Gender differences in relation to selected factors contributing to risky sexual behaviour among secondary school students in Molo Central Division, Kenya. *Journal of Humanities and Social Sciences, 1*(1), 1–12.

Mukonyi, P. W. (2020). *Socio-economic conflicts affecting students' participation in secondary school education in Kakamega County, Kenya* [Doctoral dissertation, MMUST].

National Art Education Association. (2009). *NAEA standards for art teacher preparation.* National Art Education Association.

Njenga, R. N. (2019). *The significance of secondary school life skills education in addressing the students' sexual and reproductive health information needs and knowledge gaps in Ruiru Sub-County, Kenya* [Unpublished doctoral dissertation]. University of Nairobi.

Ochieng, R. M., & Chege, F. N. (2014). Religious pluralism, conflict, and HIV/AIDS education in refugee-affected regions of North-Western Kenya. *Journal of Education and Practice, 5*(21), 11–22.

Ringisai, L., & Sutiningsih, D. (2023). Assessing the impact of teachers' training on teaching HIV/AIDS education in schools in KwaZulu-Natal, South Africa. In *E3S Web of conferences: The 8th international conference on energy, environment, epidemiology and information system* (Vol. 448, p. 05024). EDP Sciences. https://doi.org/10.1051/e3sconf/202344805024

Robert, K., Maryline, M., Jordan, K., Lina, D., Helgar, M., Annrita, I., & Lilian, O. (2020). Factors influencing access to HIV and sexual and reproductive health services among adolescent key populations in Kenya. *International Journal of Public Health, 65,* 425–432.

Sarma, H., Islam, M. A., Khan, J. R., Chowdhury, K. I. A., & Gazi, R. (2017). Impact of teachers' training on HIV/AIDS education program among secondary school students in Bangladesh: A cross-sectional survey. *PLoS ONE, 12*(7), e0181627.

UNAIDS. (2023). *UNAIDS global AIDS update: The path that ends AIDS.* https://thepath.unaids.org/

United Nations Educational, Scientific and Cultural Organization (UNESCO). (2014). *UNESCO roadmap for implementing the global action programme on education for sustainable development.* UNESCO. https://unesdoc.unesco.org/ark:/48223/pf0000230514

Vygotsky, L. (1978). *Mind in society: The development of higher psychological processes.* Harvard University Press.

Wood, L., De Lange, N., & Mkumbo, K. (2013). Drawing AIDS: Tanzanian teachers picture the pandemic. Implications for re-curriculation of teacher education programmes. *Perspectives in Education, 31*(2), 1–13.

World Health Organization. (2022). *Differentiated and simplified pre-exposure prophylaxis for HIV prevention: Update to WHO implementation guidance: Technical brief.* WHO.

CHAPTER 9
Barriers and enablers of educational inclusion of children in street situations in Uganda

Annah Atuhaire, Jonah Nyaga Kindiki, Stella Kyohairwe, Susan Kurgat

Introduction

Children in street situations pose a complex global challenge. They represent one of the most difficult-to-reach groups, facing exclusion from mainstream schools due to societal and health barriers (Uthayakumar & Vlamings, 2019). The United Nations' 2030 Agenda strives to ensure education for all, leaving no one behind. Despite global progress in primary school (estimated at 91% enrolment), information on the status of children in street situations remains largely unaccounted (Uthayakumar & Vlamings, 2019).

Children in street situations in Uganda, as elsewhere, need to be integrated into formal education if they are to benefit from 'education for all' frameworks. This requires a complex approach, exploring the perspectives of children in street situations and stakeholders involved in their lives regarding inclusion in education. Recognising the importance of barriers to the success of inclusive education programmes (Mutungi & Nderitu, 2014), this research seeks to shed light on the expectations of this marginalised group and other interested groups, in order to provide insights into how education can be leveraged to their advantage.

The challenges faced by children living in street situations, highlighted by Uthayakumar and Vlamings (2019), significantly impede their enrolment in formal education. Factors such as attitude, lack of a permanent address and legal identification contribute to these challenges. Even among those who manage to enrol, discrimination, stigmatisation, and marginalisation from both peers and teachers frequently disrupt their attendance and performance in class. Furthermore, the vulnerability of these children is compounded by exploitation, neglect, physical, and sexual abuse, which detrimentally affect their psychological development and overall health.

Children in street situations, like all other children, possess a fundamental right to education, a right guaranteed by various international declarations and inclusive education guidelines. For instance, the United Nations Convention on the Rights of the Child (1989) emphasises universal access to education for all children, including those in challenging circumstances. This commitment is echoed in ongoing initiatives such as UNESCO's Education for Sustainable Development, which advocates for educational policies addressing the needs of vulnerable and marginalised groups, including children in street situations.

However, despite these frameworks, the Ugandan government's contribution remains insufficient, with most children in street situations in Uganda not attending school (Retrak – Hope for Justice, 2017). Additionally, the African Charter on the Rights and Welfare of the Child emphasises the right to education for all children, a principle further reiterated in the African Union's Agenda 2063, envisioning accessible, inclusive, and high-quality education for all citizens. Despite Uganda's endorsement of these agendas, there is a dearth of information regarding the country's progress toward implementing SDG 4 (Initiative for Social and Economic Rights, 2019). Achieving equitable access to relevant and high-quality education and training at all levels is one of Uganda's goals outlined in the 2017–2020 Education Sector Strategic Plan (ESSP), aligning with the objectives of the 2008 Education Act, which aims for universal primary education.

Sustainable Development Goal 4 (SDG4) emphasises the achievement of inclusive, equitable, and quality education, along with lifelong learning opportunities by 2030. Uganda has ratified this goal, as reflected in the Education and Sports Sector Development Plan (2017) and the Uganda Education Act (2008). UNESCO (2017) underscores the necessity of safe, non-violent, and inclusive educational environments, stressing the responsibility of member states to address exclusion, disparity, vulnerability, marginalisation, and inequality in education.

Despite the existence of national and international laws, children in street situations receive minimal attention in inclusive education efforts. An estimated 80% to 30% of children living and working on the streets of Kampala are excluded from education (Retrak – Hope for Justice, 2017), and another 16 new children join them every day (Nabulya, 2013). Previous research has primarily focused on providing basic educational opportunities, yet there is a noticeable gap in understanding the expectations and rights of children in street situations concerning education (Nouri & Karimi, 2019).

Education plays a pivotal role in shaping fulfilling childhoods and improving economic prospects as adults. Inclusive education involves various stakeholders, but implementation challenges arise from unclear attitudes and perceptions (Okech et al., 2021). Cummings (2006) highlights a policy gap and inadequate response from educational authorities regarding the education of children in street situations. In contrast to developed countries like the United States, where the education of these children is a socio-economic and educational concern, many African countries lack investment in inclusive education, resulting in persistent vulnerability.

Mtaita (2015) reports that children in street situations face difficulties attending regular primary schools due to their preference for independence and engagement in street activities over formal education. Their unique values, shaped by their circumstances, pose challenges for enrolment and retention in school. Perceptions of these children emphasise their distinct needs, necessitating a shift in attitudes among stakeholders.

The influence of dysfunctional families and economic hardships, as highlighted by Kuparadze (2010), often leads to children dropping out of school. Initiatives like the Future Families Orphans and Vulnerable Children (OVC) programme in South Africa focus on supporting parents in stress management, parenting skills, and economic strengthening to promote stable families essential for children's access to education (Kris & David, 2020).

Mtaita (2015) emphasises that the self-perceptions of children in street situations shape their decisions regarding education. Strategies to address negative perceptions must be developed before their enrolment in schools. While researchers and scholars have emphasised inclusive education for children with disabilities and other special needs, educational inclusion for children in street situations has been neglected, resulting in scant empirical literature at both national and international levels. Overall, these insights underscore the multifaceted challenges faced by children in street situations and emphasise the need for comprehensive, targeted interventions to facilitate their access to education. This justifies the main research question for this chapter: 'What are the barriers and enablers of educational inclusion for children in street situations in Uganda?'

Design and methodology

This study employed a qualitative research approach to facilitate a comprehensive understanding of the phenomenon under investigation. Drawing on the work of various authors on the subject, including Creswell and Creswell (2017), Sharma (2020), Shakouri (2014), and Padilla-Díaz (2015), the qualitative approach was chosen for its capacity to delve deeply into how participants interpret experiences related to the phenomenon. Specifically, the approach aimed at addressing the main question; that is, 'What are the barriers and enablers of educational inclusion of children in street situations in Uganda?'

This qualitative method allowed the researchers to gather the perspectives of children who had dropped out of school but expressed an interest in re-enrolling, as well as insights from government and non-governmental officials directly involved with children in street situations. By obtaining multiple perspectives, the study aimed to gain a nuanced understanding of the challenges and opportunities associated with the inclusion of children in street situations in mainstream education.

Ethical approval for the study was obtained from the Uganda Christian University Research Ethics Committee. Further permissions were secured from the Commissioner of Youth and Children Affairs at the Ministry of Gender, Labour, and Social Development, which is responsible for the welfare of children in street situations. Given the study's focus on the Kampala District, additional clearance was sought from the Director of Education and Social Services at Kampala Capital City Authority and to guard against breaching the privacy and confidentiality of the participants, all the names mentioned in the results section are pseudonyms which were used to eliminate identifiers of the participants.

As noted earlier, the study was conducted in Kampala District, central Uganda, encompassing the five divisions of Rubaga, Kawempe, Makindye, Kampala Central, and Nakawa. A purposive sampling method was employed, resulting in the selection of 14 participants, including nine children in street situations, two government officials, and three non-governmental officials. Kampala District was chosen because of its high concentration of children on the street compared to other areas in Uganda in accordance with the enumeration report by Retrak – Hope for Justice (2017), where it was found that over 2,600 children were living on the streets of Kampala, 80% of whom were not attending school. Representative NGOs, acting in accordance with child protection policies, granted consent on behalf of the children and provided guidance to locate them in their respective retreats and safe places.

Semi-structured interviews were used to generate data in this study. Interviews with children in street situations were administered first and 9 children were interviewed one at a time in a local language with a guide tailored to their understanding. Questions regarding their school experience, factors that led to their drop-out, whether they preferred school or street, how they valued education, and their expectations from the school, government and the rest of the community were asked to gain insights into what the children perceived as barriers and enablers for their inclusion in mainstream education.

Research with children in street situations tends to raise ethical concerns because of their vulnerability. The present study guarded against this by contacting the Commissioner for Youth and Children Affairs under the Ministry of Gender, Labour and Social Development who guided on permissions for the children's participation and identified relevant bodies that could provide consent on behalf of the children to guard against breaching confidentiality, privacy and other ethical issues regarding the use of vulnerable persons in research. Two supporting NGOs provided assent on behalf of the children as well as consent forms for the children upon signing child protection policies.

Individual interviews with other five relevant stakeholders were later conducted in English with an alternative guide to supplement on the technical questions of the problem under investigation. Questions regarding their views towards including children in street situations in education; policy guidelines for educational inclusion of such children; their relationship, communication and collaboration with relevant stakeholders in including the children in education were asked. Interviews were only used to unveil the experiences of the children themselves as well gather views from relevant stakeholders to inform the problem since there was scant literature on inclusion of children in street situations in education. Collected data were recorded both in writing and using an audio recorder, with consent from the participants, and later transcribed for data processing, analysis, and reporting.

This study was limited by scant empirical literature relevant to inclusive education of children in street situations both at national and international level. In this case, the researchers reviewed literature related to inclusion but with other categories of children, especially those with disabilities, which explains the relatively brief discussion of findings. Moreover, the children interviewed in this study were between the ages of 6-12 which limited the study from capturing responses from older children. Some children did not respond to the interview questions and, of the data generated, the researchers only picked extracts which were relevant to the research objective.

Data in this study were analysed using Braun and Clarke's (2006), six-phase framework for doing thematic analysis. The Braun and Clarke framework is a widely used, flexible, and transparent approach to conducting thematic analysis, a qualitative research method for identifying and analysing patterns of meaning within qualitative data. The following is a breakdown of the framework and its application.

1. *Familiarization with data*: the researchers listened constantly to the recorded data to build a deep understanding of the recorded content and be prepared for coding.

2. *Initial coding*: words and phrases that were relevant to the perceptions (views and experiences) of the children and selected stakeholders in relation to the educational inclusion of street children in education were identified and labelled.

3. *Searching for themes:* identified and labelled codes were later grouped according to shared meaning.

4. *Reviewing themes:* mainly the perceptions revealed the barriers that hindered the children from being included in mainstream education and what could enable them to re-join.

5. *Defining and naming themes*: after refining, two main themes, barriers to inclusion and enablers to inclusion, were identified as broader themes.

6. *Reporting of findings*: findings were reported with supporting evidence such as quotations from transcripts, and at the end of each quotation, in brackets, the researchers indicated the type of interview that was administered, affiliation of the participant, name (pseudonyms), page of the transcript, line numbers of the transcript, and the date the interview was conducted. Below are the themes, supporting data, and interpretations.

Results

The children in street situations showed a strong preference for joining mainstream education. However, they mentioned barriers that hindered them from being included in education. The rest of the officials from government and non-governmental organizations also mentioned barriers and enablers for including children in street situations in mainstream education. The mentioned barriers were categorised as social, financial, environmental and inter-personal barriers whereas the enablers to inclusion in education were categorised as rehabilitation, reintegration and retention.

The children in street situations who were interviewed expressed a strong desire to enrol in mainstream education, despite identifying various barriers that hindered their inclusion in the educational system. Government and non-governmental organization officials also acknowledged both barriers and facilitators for incorporating children in street situations into mainstream education. These barriers were classified into social, financial, environmental, and interpersonal categories. The factors facilitating inclusion in education were categorized as rehabilitation, reintegration, and retention.

Barriers to inclusion

Social barriers

Children in street situations revealed that the community perception held towards them is negative. Children on the street are regarded as children with no morals originating from failed homes. Some children on the street attempt pickpocketing and use abusive language towards their peers. A few children on the street who are privileged to attend school expressed feelings of being marginalised by their teachers and fellow learners. This jeopardizes the chance of these children joining mainstream schools due to loss of confidence and self-esteem as well as suffering from depression. One of them said:

> "Teachers don't like us because they think we don't have the knowledge and skills to study, they think we are spoilt children. Even our fellow learners don't like associating with us, police and other people harass us because they think we have bad behaviours but not all of us are like that and that's why we don't like being at school." (Individual interview, street child, Keith, p. 18, line 1-3, 2022-01-28)

This kind of discrimination towards children from the street was validated by Anoline who revealed that it is a big challenge for children in vulnerable circumstances to access social services like health and education. Anoline works for Children at Risk Action Network (CRANE), which is a network of Christian organizations working together to support at-risk children in the greater Kampala region. In terms of joining mainstream education, Anoline revealed that children from the street have no responsible caregivers to register them at school, who are accountable for a child's well-being both at home and at school. She was quoted saying:

> "If a child from the street went to Mulago hospital to access health services, he or she would be automatically chased away because of how they looked like. Likewise, if a

street child went to a public school to be enrolled, he or she would not be welcomed because of the vulnerable status depicted by the child. Here in Kampala, teachers chase away children with no school uniform and other scholastic materials. This leaves a street child unable to continue learning with the rest of the children in mainstream education." (Individual interview, CRANE, Anoline, p. 7, line 33-37, 2022-02-12)

The above findings concur with the findings of Niboye (2013), and Friberg and Martinsson (2017) who reported that the community perceives children in street situations as dangerous and potential criminals. This leaves them traumatized and underprivileged in terms of interaction and social contact which is caused by shortcomings in their nurturing (Kuparadze, 2010). A few who can enrol in formal education often face unfairness, inequity, and stigmatisation by their teachers and peers which accelerates psychological health threats among the children, hence hindering their academic attainment and enrolment in schools (Uthayakumar, & Vlamings, 2019). This requires awareness to reduce discrimination (Bannink, 2016) and school's preparedness to play a major role in caring for them. In order to end social exclusion, the social pillar must work to create a clean, safe, and just society with social equality. It should also make sure that everyone has equal opportunity to engage in society, notwithstanding disparities in personal characteristics (Adoyo & Odeny, 2015).

Financial barriers

Children in street situations reported a range of financial barriers that hinder them from meaningful inclusion in mainstream schools, mainly reflected in the scarcity of financial and economic resources like scholastic materials, school fees, food, shelter, clothing, health care, among others, to survive. Both government and non-governmental representatives in this study revealed that Universal Primary Education in Uganda is not entirely as free as it is claimed, and public primary schools leave Parent and Teacher Association and development fees to be paid by learners. A high percentage of them revealed that children with or without families often cannot afford to pay school fees, which, along with scholastic materials and other demands of the school, are not affordable. Honest, a child on the street, was quoted saying:

"My mother did not have money to pay for my school fees and they kept chasing me at school. At home, we have no money to buy food so I come to the street to make some money so that I can give it to my mother and we buy food. If I get a sponsor to pay for my school fees, I can go back to school and study." (Individual interview, street child, Honest, p. 20, line 22-24, 2022-01-28)

The Global Citizenship Report (International Paper, 2019) asserts that, despite the abolition of school fees by many governments following the United Nations (UN) declaration of human rights, education costs remain too high for many of the least fortunate families, so kids have to stay at home and do household work themselves. Families remain locked in a cycle of poverty that goes on for generations. Education is free to the point of being theoretically available within most African countries. In practice, parents are being charged formal fees to buy essential items such as uniforms, books, pens, additional trainings, or money for maintaining the school buildings. In some places, parents are left with no choice but to send their children to private schools because of the lack of government support for public schools. The poorest families, who risk losing their lives in their efforts to improve their children's lives through education, are not even able to afford these schools, even if they are low cost.

Children in street situations mentioned the poor economic situation of their parents /caregivers as a barrier to inclusion in education. This was also reaffirmed by other respondents who acknowledged that the majority of the families of these children are below the poverty line and hence cannot provide adequate care to their children while at home and also meet the school requirements. The Global Citizen Report (2019) notes that children living in poverty lack funding for education and learning materials, which leads to their exclusion from education, particularly, those with disabilities. This means children in street situations attract little attention, not only on the side of the government, but also by scholars and researchers.

Children in street situations have unique financial needs depending on their lifestyles. In neighbouring Kenya, Kisirkoi and Mse (2016) assert that, despite children in street situations having been part of a category of orphans that benefitted from the government's policy on universal access to education, they were just enrolled in schools together with other children who live normal lives under the protection of adults. This is because their specific learning needs were not sufficiently addressed in order for them to be able to acquire the necessary skills, competences and attitudes that enable them to participate actively in societal activities they need to be made available.

Relevant agencies are unable to implement inclusive education in any meaningful way without funding. School administrators are often easily overwhelmed by the burden of implementation (Adoyo & Odeny, 2015), therefore, Uganda's Ministry of Education and Sports should assume responsibility for these duties to go forward, rather than leaving them solely in the hands of teachers and school administrators. That being said, the funding allocated to Uganda's Ministry of Education and Sports was cut which has left some of its programmes stagnant (BMAU, 2018).

Environmental barriers

In this study, the children showed that the COVID-19 pandemic exposed them to the street because of challenges that came alongside the pandemic and government's guidelines for limiting transmission. Many children in street situations lost street jobs that were earning them a living which forced them to drop out of school. The children also revealed that they had no homes which is a big challenge for them especially when they are attending school. They cannot bathe and wash their clothes after school and also, they encounter feeding challenges, hence some children arrive unprepared to learn (World Bank, 2018). Kato was quoted saying:

> *"We don't have a house and sometimes sleep in pipes when we go to school, no one cooks food for us to eat and we have no money to buy soap to wash our clothes and bathe. At school, is not like the street where you can be shirtless or even wear your dirty shirt because if you go with dirty clothes, other children will not sit with you and also teachers will push you out of class."* (Individual interview, street child, Kato, p. 18, line 21–24, 2022-01-28)

Children in street situations showed that the school environment is also unfriendly to them, and sometimes the subjects taught there are irrelevant to them. In other circumstances, children are below academic achievement by one or two or even more years, and they find joining lower classes at their older age inconvenient. They revealed how they do not fit into the school environment. Abdullah et al. (2018) acknowledge a conducive environment as a major determinant of academic achievement of such vulnerable learners. This was later confirmed by Fredrick, a government officer in the Commonwealth Youth Council (CYC), the official representative of young people in the Commonwealth. In this capacity, he has observed how teachers are not trained to handle children from vulnerable circumstances, therefore, they are not responsible for how a child from the street should fit in the mainstream class. Fredrick was quoted saying:

> *"Teachers are trained to handle children from normal circumstances not lampoons of the street and therefore the teacher's attitude towards children from the street is expected to be negative because accordingly, this teacher is risking the progress of the rest of the children because of one child and if at all children from the street are to be included in mainstream education, they should be rehabilitated first and teachers should be given adequate training on how to handle these kinds of children."* (Individual interview, CYC, Fredrick, p. 6, line 14-19, 2022-02-21)

Considering the above findings, Jamidulin et al. (2018) affirm that some children in street situations consider school as a waste of time and does not benefit them compared to street life. Nevertheless, they also had future aspirations of becoming teachers, doctors, engineers, among other professions. But they held that they lacked enough support to pursue the education that could lead them into such careers. Kisirkoi and Mse (2016) recommend development and implementation of a suitable curriculum for this category of vulnerable children. The curriculum should be flexible enough to make it possible for young people to take a non-formal approach to it that allows access to formal education systems and addresses their needs in terms of employment.

Interpersonal barriers

The children reported differing school preferences, including those who preferred vocational schooling to regular schooling. Some children preferred boarding to day schooling. Other children preferred being at school, whereas others prefer being on the street, and some children preferred learning with fellow children in mainstream classes, whereas others did not like learning at all. All this was reported based on the different circumstances of a child that exposed them to certain choices, dynamics that have to be understood in planning for the inclusion of children in street situation in education. Kisirkoi and Mse (2016) recommend that all children in street situations should be interviewed first to identify their varied categories as regards their health status, family links and to find out the level of psychosocial damage street life has wrought on each of them. It is necessary to treat each case individually.

Apart from differing preferences, children in street situations also reported that peer influence is the greatest vice on the street. It was indicated that some children will drop out of school because their friends dropped out of school. More so, even 'spoilt' children on the street influence others to behave contrary to societal norms and expectations. This leaves them with no chance of (re-)joining regular education because the community thinks it is useless to educate such children. A child was quoted saying:

"Some children drop out of school because they see their fellows are not attending school." (Individual interview, street child, Elen, p. 19, line 23-26, 2022-01-28)

Another interpersonal barrier that hinders children from joining mainstream education is the lack of parental support. NGO representatives reported that there is a lot of negligence and lack of accountability among parents or caregivers of children on the street. Jamiludin et al. (2018) acknowledge parental negligence, negative parent perception of education and broken families denying children in street situations a chance to attend education. This was also confirmed by some children, who shared that their high level of absenteeism from school was because of their caregivers forcing them to stay at home to help them with work. After missing enough school work, they end up being left behind in class which then ultimately leads to them leaving school for the street. This is evidenced in the extract below:

"My Aunty tells me to remain at home as she goes to the market. Sometimes she sends me on the street to beg for money from people on the street so that we can get what to eat." (Individual interview, street child, Rashid, p. 22, line 20-22, 2022-01-28)

Government representatives further revealed that caregivers neglect the responsibility of taking care of their children to the extent of sending them to do child labour in the streets which limits their opportunities of joining mainstream schooling. Accordingly, bad parenting, such as exposure to violence in homes, misbehaviour of parents, and societal neglect, influence children to leave their homes, drop out of school and opt for the streets. This is in accord with Sharma (2020), who mentions family-related problems as prime causes for pushing young children into the streets. Families are responsible for providing for the basic needs of a child's academic and social development.

In this study, both the children and their representatives also expressed their views and experiences on the way forward to the inclusion of children in street situations in mainstream education. This was after acknowledging the view that children in street situations should be included in mainstream education regardless of their challenges. They expressed their views on facilitators of educational inclusion of children in street situations and below is the main theme that emerged, labelled 'enablers to inclusion', where categories such as rehabilitation, re-integration and retention of children in street situations in schools were identified to explain the main theme.

Enablers of inclusion

Rehabilitation of children in street situations

In this study, participants perceived the NGO representatives of children in street situations as a key step before including children in street situations in mainstream education. According to representatives of the Kampala Capital City Authority (KCCA), children in street situations are subject to vulnerable conditions which result in low self-esteem and confidence, anxiety, and depression. On the street, the children are exposed to diverse behaviours that deviate from the norm, therefore, it would be imperative to consider their rehabilitation first. It was revealed that during this process of rehabilitation, the children are offered guidance and counselling, and adequate psychosocial support necessary for providing coping mechanisms to reintegrate back into normal social settings. This was evident in the ensuing below:

> "It is impossible to grab a child from the street and plant them in the mainstream class because it becomes a challenge to the teacher and poses a threat to other learners in a classroom since their behaviour can influence other learners." (Individual interview, PO- KCCA, Deborah, p. 13, line 3-5, 2022-02-25)

> "Rehabilitation of children from the street is very important before they join mainstream education. This is because teachers are trained to handle children from normal circumstances and normal family situations not lampoons of the street." (Individual interview, CYC, Fredrick, p. 6, line 2-6, 2022-02-21)

It would be necessary to rehabilitate all children in street situations in hygiene, games, sports, athletics, drama, basic numeracy and literacy, skills development, life skills, values acquisition, drug abuse and HIV/AIDS messaging; and religious education could be part of the rehabilitation course (Kisirkoi & Mse, 2016). The duration of this phase should be determined by the learners' needs. If the child is able to adjust to the learning environment, he or she should be moved to the next stage, where he or she should be ready for the development of academic and business skills.

Reintegration of children in street situations

NGO representatives reported that it is better to reintegrate children with their families because family is the best place for the child to grow and develop. For instance, for those who are homeless, it was reported that a safe space should be provided for them and they should be given options to choose what is good for their lives. It was revealed that at this point of reintegration, the need for sponsorship in terms of school fees and well-being is necessary so that children from the street are prepared for a life away from the streets. This was evident in the ensuing:

> "Reintegration of a street child first is what we take to be necessary here. We take children after rehabilitation to reunite them with their families whereas those who wish to join either mainstream education or vocational studies are given a chance to choose their interest and depending on the capacity of a child." (Individual interview, Education Officer, Brendah, p. 10, line 12-14, 2022-02-7)

> "In some other countries, children who are homeless are provided with a safe space where they sleep, bathe and wash which is not the case in Uganda." (Individual interview, CRANE, Anoline, p. 7, line 34-36, 2022-02-12)

Before effective education can be provided, therefore, relevant questions concerning the unique experiences of children in street situations need to be addressed. They are seeking a specialised curriculum that supports rehabilitation without relying on a formal approach, allowing students to transition in and out of traditional schools. The curriculum should be flexible and incorporate trade skills to help students build sustainable livelihoods (Kisirkoi & Mse, 2016).

Retention of children in street situations in education

Different studies have shown that with the introduction of Universal Primary Education, there was a significant increase in primary school enrolment, and among the children who were enrolled in primary schools were children in street situations. But in short order, these children drop out of school and are once again on the streets. The relevant authorities in this study were of the view that concrete actions be taken to ensure that children withdrawn from the street are retained in schools. One participant was quoted saying:

> "KCCA has always withdrawn those children from the street forcefully but they again re-appear on streets in a short while and as NGOs we also make some efforts to include some in school but when root causes are not addressed, we again lose these children to the streets." (Individual interview, Education Officer, Brendah, p. 10, line 15-17, 2022-02-7)

Among the actions that were suggested by government representatives, training both pre- and in-service teachers on how to handle this category of learners, providing activities that are socially attractive, designing flexible timetables to adopt several teaching strategies that facilitate individual differences, adequate staffing, and a flexible curriculum design for children in street situations that takes into account non-formal perspectives and learner needs for livelihoods were included. The ministry must assess instructors' readiness to instruct a diverse group of students in a single classroom before tackling implementation difficulties at the school level. Teachers must receive comprehensive training programmes in areas where they lack skills (Adoyo & Odeny, 2015).

To retain children in mainstream schools, Ainscow (2020) suggests that education departments should take the lead in promoting inclusion and equity as guiding principles for teachers across all schools. Policies should incorporate the knowledge and experience of all those involved in children's lives, including the children themselves. Definitions of inclusion and equity that are broadly accepted should serve as the foundation for policy. There should be a focus on whole-school approaches that help teachers in promoting inclusive practices. Strategies should be informed by evidence regarding the impact of current practices on the presence, engagement, and achievement of all children.

Discussion

The study identified various barriers to the inclusion of children in street situations in mainstream education, including social, financial, environmental, and interpersonal barriers. Social barriers, such as negative community perceptions and discrimination by teachers and peers, significantly hindered these children's access to education. Financial barriers, including the inability to afford school fees and essential materials, further exacerbated their exclusion. Environmental challenges, such as homelessness and unfriendly school environments, also contributed to the difficulty these children faced in attending school. Interpersonal barriers, such as peer influence and lack of parental support, further complicated their educational inclusion.

The findings align with existing literature highlighting the complex challenges faced by children in street situations regarding education. Similar studies have documented the negative attitudes of communities towards these children, the financial constraints they encounter, and the lack of appropriate support systems. Moreover, environmental factors such as homelessness and inadequate school facilities have been identified as significant obstacles to their education.

To address these barriers and facilitate the inclusion of children in street situations in mainstream education, several enablers were identified. Rehabilitation programmes aimed at addressing the psychological and social needs of these children were highlighted as essential first steps. Additionally, reintegration efforts to reunite children with their families and provide them with necessary support were deemed crucial. Finally, strategies to retain children in schools, such as teacher training and flexible curriculum design, were emphasised as necessary for sustained educational inclusion.

Conclusion

In conclusion, the study underscores the multifaceted challenges faced by children in street situations regarding their education. Social, financial, environmental, and interpersonal barriers collectively hinder their access to mainstream education. Addressing these barriers requires comprehensive strategies, including rehabilitation, reintegration, and retention efforts. By implementing these enablers, policymakers, educators, and relevant stakeholders can work towards creating inclusive educational environments that cater to the needs of children in street situations. Ultimately, ensuring the educational inclusion of these children is essential for promoting their well-being, fostering their development, and breaking the cycle of poverty and marginalisation.

References

Abdullah, M. F., Ahmad Shuhaimi, A. A., Mohamed Osman, M., & Suzilawati Rabe, N. (2018). Factors influencing parents in selecting school for children with special needs. *Journal of the Malaysian Institute of Planners, 16*(2), 207–216.

Adoyo, P. O., & Odeny, M. L. (2015). Emergent inclusive education in Kenya: Challenges and suggestions. *International Journal of Research in Humanities and Social Studies, 2*(6), 47–52.

Ainscow, M. (2020). Promoting inclusion and equity in education: Lessons from international experiences. *Nordic Journal of Studies in Educational Policy, 6*(1), 7–16.

Bannink, F. I. (2016). Teachers' and parents' perspectives on inclusive education for children with spina bifida in Uganda. *Journal of Childhood & Development Disorders, 2*(2), 2472–1789.

BMAU. (2018). *Provision of inclusive education in Uganda: What are the challenges?* Ministry of Finance, Planning and Economic Development.

Braun, V., & Clarke, V. (2006). Using thematic analysis in psychology. *Qualitative Research in Psychology, 3*(2), 77–101.

Creswell, J. W., & Creswell, J. D. (2017). *Research design: Qualitative, quantitative, and mixed methods approaches.* Sage Publications.

Cummings, P. A. (2016). *Factors related to the street phenomenon in major towns in Sierra Leone: A comparative study of the city's street children and children in normal family homes* [Unpublished doctoral dissertation]. St Clements University.

Friberg, A., & Martinsson, V. (2017). *Problems and solutions when dealing with street children: A qualitative study based on experiences from social workers in Bloemfontein, South Africa* [Unpublished candidate thesis]. Jönköping University, School of Health and Welfare.

Initiative for Social and Economic Rights. (2019). *Status of implementation of SDG 4 on education: Is Uganda on track?* ISER.

International Paper. (2019). *Global citizenship report.* https://www.internationalpaper.com/sites/default/files/file/2023-01/2019-ip-global-citizenship-report.pdf?cacheToken=XczmEGYURegLlDFU

Jamiludin, M., Darnawati, M., Uke, W., & Irawaty, D. (2018). Street children's problem in getting education: Economic and parental factors. *Mediterranean Journal of Social Sciences, 9*(1). https://doi.org/10.2478/mjss-2018-0010

Kisirkoi, F. (2016). Education access and retention for children in street situations: Perspectives from Kenya. *Journal of Education and Practice, 7*(2), 88–94.

Kris, E. E., & David, M. (2020). Perceptions of parents/guardians about the effectiveness of future orphans and vulnerable children programme in Olievenhoutbosch, South Africa. *Global Journal of Health Science, 12*, 20–36. https://doi.org/10.5539/gjhs.v12n4p20

Kuparadze, M. (2010). Education as a means of social integration of children in street situations in Georgia: Necessary reforms. *Problems of Education in the 21st Century, 23*, 105–123.

Mtaita, F. (2015). *Perceptions of street children and the role of community in supporting their access to education: A case study of Ilala Municipality, Tanzania* [Unpublished master's thesis]. Open University of Tanzania.

Mutungi, N. P., & Nderitu, M. N. (2014). Perceptions of teachers and head teachers on the effectiveness of inclusive education in public primary schools in Yatta Division Machakos County. *Journal of Educational and Social Research, 4*(1), 91–106.

Nabulya, R. (2013). Uganda street children number rises by 70 percent. *ChimpReports.* https://chimpreports.com/9358-uganda-street-children-number-rises-by-70-percent/

Niboye, E. P. (2013). Effectiveness of non-governmental organizations in the rehabilitation of street children – Experiences from selected NGOs in Dar es Salaam, Tanzania. *Journal of Education and Practice, 4*(1), 43–51.

Nouri, A., & Karimi, Y. (2019). A phenomenological study on the meaning of educational justice for street children. *Education, Citizenship and Social Justice, 14*(1), 57–67.

Okech, J. B., Yuwono, I., & Abdu, W. J. (2021). Implementation of inclusive education practices for children with disabilities and other special needs in Uganda. *Journal of Education and E-learning Research, 8*(1), 97–102.

Padilla-Díaz, M. (2015). Phenomenology in educational qualitative research: Philosophy as science or philosophical science. *International Journal of Educational Excellence, 1*(2), 101–110.

Retrak – Hope for Justice. (2017). *Enumeration of children on the streets in Uganda across four locations: Iganga, Jinja, Mbale, and Kampala.* Part of the Hope for Justice family.

Shakouri, N., & Nazari, O. (2014). Qualitative research: Incredulity toward metanarratives. *Journal of Education and Human Development, 3*(2), 671–680.

Sharma, M. K. (2020). Street children in Nepal: Causes and health status. *Journal of Health Promotion, 8*, 129–140.

UNESCO. (2017). *A guide for ensuring inclusion and equity in education.* https://doi.org/10.54675/MHHZ2237

UNESCO. (2020). Global education monitoring report summary: Inclusive and education: All means all. *UNESCO Digital Library.* https://unesdoc.unesco.org/ark:/48223/pf0000373721

United Nations Convention on the rights of the child, November 20, 1989, https://digitallibrary.un.org/record/80135?v=pdf

United Nations (UN). (2019). *Convention on the rights of the child (30th anniversary).* United Nations Publications.

Uthayakumar, C., & Vlamings, C. (2019). Realising street children's rights to education. *Consortium for Street Children.* https://www.streetchildren.org/news-and-updates/realising-street-childrens-right-to-education/

World Bank. (2018). *World Bank development report: Learning to realize education's promise.* World Bank. https://www.worldbank.org/en/publication/wdr2018

CHAPTER 10
Using participatory visual methods to teach character education in early childhood, Kenya

Evans Mos Olao, Bernard Misigo, Karsten Speck

Introduction

Among the ideals of character education is the inculcation of basic positive values such as respect, honesty, responsibility and fairness among learners (Osabwa, 2016). These ideals partly guide the education system of a country by being reflected in the aims, goals, content, instructional methods and policies of such a system. Battistich (2005) noted that teachers, as responsible adults, should use all the aspects of school life to foster optimal character development in learners. However, Osabwa (2016) argued that the objectives of character education in Kenya remain elusive as attempts to use the current teaching approaches appear less effective. He points out that:

> *After independence the main approach to character formation was instruction. This was administered through formal schooling, with moral values being taught through disciplines such as Religious Education, Social Ethics Education, Life Skills Education, and also through guidance and counselling, infusion and integration. There was little in terms of practical experiences [...] the said teachers mainly focused on attaining high grades in examinations as opposed to formation of good character among pupils. In the end, the objective of forming character remained elusive.* (Osabwa, 2016, p. 79)

Various alternative solutions to this issue have been proposed by previous studies. These include the need to teach character education in early childhood using the best teaching approaches and use of real life experiences (Battistich, 2005; Lee, 2013). Further, Akanga (2014) advocated for the use of child-centred methods in teaching character education, while Andiema (2016) suggests that participatory visual methods are effective when used with young children.

Based on these studies, the current study envisioned participatory visual methods (PVM) as innovative ways of teaching character education which might make a difference. The use of PVM in subjects like science, HIV/AIDS and sexuality education with older children in elementary and high schools has been documented sufficiently in the literature (e.g. De Lange & Stuart, 2008; Yego, 2017). However, there is limited empirical information on studies done on the use of participatory visual methods in teaching character education in Kenya. This lack of information formed the *raison d'etre* to explore teachers' experiences and views of using PVM to facilitate the teaching and learning of character education.

The concept of character education

According to Edgington (2002), character education (CE) is subjective and as such, it has not been able to acquire an all-encompassing definition. Berkowitz (2011) has described CE as an attempt within schools to craft pedagogical and supportive structures to foster the development of positive, ethical, pro-social inclinations and competencies in learners. The teaching of values has been a critical part of the Kenyan school curricula since pre-independence (Wamahiu, 2015). It was introduced in Kenya by missionaries linked to the Catholic and Anglican churches. These churches established schools with an aim of evangelizing and teaching of character that would enhance the religious beliefs of learners.

After independence the Kenyan government, through the Ministry of Education, Science and Technology (MoEST), developed reform documents that dealt with the institutionalization of character education in schools. This introduced the teaching of character education in formal schooling. Later it was recommended that character education be taught to students at all levels of education (Kamunge, 1988). However, the continued deviant behaviour that was observed among schoolgoing children led Akanga (2014) and other character education scholars to recommend the use of appropriate methods of teaching character education. The assertion by Muthamba (2017) that religious education lacked practicality, implied that character education required a more hands-on approach of teaching.

Teaching approaches in character education

Most of the traditional approaches to character education emphasised the role of modelling, instruction, imitation, rewards and punishment, and authority in the formation of character (Nucci et al., 2008). In contrast, heuristic educators present the benefits of utilizing child-centred approaches to foster character development (e.g. Dewey, 1952; Freire, 2017; Lanham, 2004). In Kenya, most teachers today apply learner-centred approaches of teaching so as to promote learners' interest, critical thinking and enjoyment during learning inside and outside of the classroom (Hesson & Shad, 2007). With particular regard to early childhood education, Andiema (2016) advocated for participatory teaching and learning methods that make children enjoy learning and apply what is learned to everyday life. De Lange and Stuart (2008) posited that, at the time, most practising teachers were not exposed to participatory strategies hence, they tended to teach the way they themselves were taught using didactic approaches.

Participatory visual methods

Participatory visual methods (PVM) are innovative teaching approaches that have been used successfully in addressing issues like HIV and AIDS, gender-based violence and sexuality education (Mitchell, 2008). They have also been widely used as research methodologies to enable participants to reflect on their knowledge of life and their daily experiences with the issue under investigation (De Lange et al., 2014). However, previous research has not mentioned the applicability of such methods in the teaching of moral values.

Participatory visual products can be handmade, digital media or performance-based in their design. The handmade products include drawings, story-boarding, collage, beading, quilting, memory boxes, body mapping, murals, installations and graffiti. The digital products are photovoice, digital story-telling, participatory videos, digital archiving, blogging and social media. The performance-based processes are dance, theatre-in-education, forum and image theatre, and role-plays. It must be noted at this point that these visual products can be used as teaching methods in the teaching-learning environment. Interestingly, they are being given more attention in Kenya which is experiencing curriculum reforms by way of adopting a Competency Based Curriculum (CBC). With the inception of CBC, it has become clear that children enjoy teaching approaches that are more practical and more visual such as in the use of photographs and videos (Griessel-Roux et al., 2005). Furthermore, visual material in teaching encourages maximum participation by learners and also provides avenues for free expression of understanding and experiences with little dependence on verbal communication (Van der Riet et al., 2005; Holderness, 2012; Wood & Wilmot, 2012).

Bearing the benefits of participatory visual methods in mind, it should be clear that most teachers are not really exposed to these methods. The teachers in Kenya are not an exception on this issue. Yego (2017) posits that participatory visual methods are effective for use by teachers and learners in the classroom to navigate issues around sexuality and HIV/AIDS education in Kenya. In her study, Yego summarized the pedagogical qualities of participatory visual methods as (1) being child-centred, (2) freeing learners to engage in learning, (3) simplifying teacher's role in the classroom, and (4) providing a free space for the teacher to deliver effectively.

Khau et al. (2013) concluded that participatory visual methods can transform classrooms into enabling and democratic spaces which are conducive for teaching and learning for all. Hence, it is imperative that teachers in all levels of education get exposed to the implementation of such methods in class. Berkowitz (2011) strongly advocated for the teaching of character education in early childhood, while Andiema (2016) recommended the use of participatory methods to teach in early childhood. Given these postulations, this study explored the use of participatory visual methods in the teaching of character education in early childhood, specifically focused on teacher experiences of using participatory visual methods upon implementation in class. An initial establishment of the methods used by teachers to teach CE in early childhood was also done.

Methodology

This study was located in the interpretivist paradigm that allowed for reliance on participants' views of their experiences using PVM. A qualitative approach was employed and a multiple-case study design utilized to enable the analysis of data within and across cases. This was helpful in establishing the value and reliability of findings (Baxter & Jack, 2008).

Sample and setting

A non-probability sampling technique was employed to obtain a purposive sample of eight Grade 3 teachers from 4 public primary schools that had two streams per level in Eldoret East Sub-County. The teachers selected were those that had been teaching the same set of learners from Grade 1 to Grade 3. It was presumed that this set of teachers had used a number of approaches to teach character education beforehand and would, therefore, be in a better position to report on the effectiveness of implementing participatory visual methods in class. All the learners from these teachers' classes were also chosen to take part in the study considering the reporting would be based on how the teacher participants worked with them specifically.

Data generation

Prior to the research, a three-day preparatory workshop was organized for the eight Grade 3 teacher participants. The main purpose of the workshop was to offer preliminary education on the use of participatory visual methods. The training practically covered the use of drawings and photovoice. Furthermore, the workshop aimed at making the teachers feel prepared and supported. They had a chance to meet and familiarize themselves with each other, and were also given the opportunity to talk about their expectations regarding the implementation of the participatory visual teaching methods. The sessions were conducted mainly in the English language, though occasionally participants would use Kiswahili. The discussions were recorded and later transcribed.

Data were generated through drawings, reflective journaling and face-to-face interviews that were conducted separately with each teacher participant. They were guided to make drawings about their experiences of implementing participatory visual methods in class, and provide captions describing their stories. They were also provided with writing pads which they used as reflective journals. In these journals, the teachers were expected to make notes representing their reflections of implementing participatory visual methods over a period of time. The teachers took part in face-to-face interviews that were semi-structured in design. They were interviewed to provide first-hand information on main issues around character education and its teaching. Notably, the PVM tools that were used included drawings and photovoice. The sampled teachers would prompt the learners on various character traits and allow them to engage in making drawings or taking photos which they would later describe. All the drawings and photovoice products would be displayed in the classroom for reference. To this end, it can be seen that drawings were used in two ways: as a data generation method, and as an approach to facilitate learning of character values.

Data analysis

The study employed thematic analysis to make meaning of the qualitative data generated. This was done in three stages: (1) open coding, (2) axial coding, and (3) selective coding. Initially, we began by listening to the audio transcripts obtained from the interviews and oral presentations of the drawings. This was followed by reading through the interview transcripts and the reflective journals. The data were then subjected to verbatim transcriptions that allowed me to read and re-read. In the open stage, data from the reflective journals, audio-recorded interviews and oral presentation of drawings was transcribed manually through typing. Spaces were then left to the right side of the transcript page margins for creation of memos. This enabled sorting of data for each school, and this was based on the uniqueness of the information.

During axial coding, I (first author) read through the memos while examining the commonalities between the data. A Microsoft Word programme called 'DocTools' was used to generate tables containing the data in text with their respective codes. This enabled me to see closely linked information and formed the basis of creating themes. After establishing the relationship between categories, the codes with the same labels were put together into one group. In the last stage, selective coding, I crosschecked for any missing information. At this point, the codes were also keenly reviewed and those that were overlapping and redundant were reduced.

Ethical considerations

Prior to data collection, the schools in the study area were visited to discuss the purpose of the study with the headteachers. After the initial permission was granted, I discussed the same with the teachers who later gave consent to participate in the study. The teachers volunteered to take part in the study and were assured that their responses would only be used for the purposes of the research. All the teachers who participated in semi-structured interviews signed written consent forms, as did the parents of the Grade 3 learners from the four schools. The participants' anonymity was maintained throughout the study through assigned pseudonyms. Ethical approval was obtained from the School of Education at Moi University, the Office of the County Commissioner and the National Commission for Science, Technology and Innovation (NACOSTI).

Results and discussion

The qualitative data generated in this study were discussed in line with the literature and the constructivism learning theory. I worked closely with the Grade 3 teachers in the incorporation of participatory visual methods in class. They particularly used drawings and photovoice to teach character education. However, there was the constraint of time considering the fact that character education was not indicated in the class timetable as a standalone subject. Hence, the teacher participants made time during Christian religious education and life skills lessons. They would teach the character values as indicated in the objectives of the individual lessons using drawings and photovoice.

Each teacher would create time to ensure that the drawings and photovoice were used as much as possible and at the end of the lesson, they were expected to reflect on their experiences as much as possible. Based on their reflections, the teacher participants were of the view that participatory visual methods were learner-centred and enhanced collaborative learning. These views formed the basis for creating the themes that were used to present the findings of this study as indicated in Table 1.

Table 1: *Summary of Findings*

Research Question	Themes	Categories (Sub-themes)
What views do teachers hold about using PVM to teach character education?	Learner-centred	• Active learning • Learning atmosphere • Excitement and motivation • Memory boost • Practical approach • Language barrier
	Collaborative learning	• Group work

Learner-centred learning

As explained by Gravoso et al. (2008), learner-centred learning involves putting the pupil at the centre of the learning process. Participants in this study argued that the use of drawings and photovoice carried many features of child-centred learning approaches.

"Use of drawings and photovoice is child-centred. It is more on the child. I didn't do the drawings. They drew themselves and it worked." (Oakley)

"Before attending the training on participatory visual methods of teaching, I used lecture method lessons which were teacher-centred." (Pina)

The teachers argued that through these methods, the learners were actively involved in class activities and that their degree of participation subsequently increased. Through their active participation in class, the children's thinking about character concepts widened. Teachers said that the children could be seen becoming critical

155

by asking each other questions and thinking deeply about how to present their work. This corroborates the constructivism learning theory which supports own creation of knowledge through critically asking questions and exploring existing knowledge.

> "Something like drawing, they are participating themselves, like the one we did, the photovoice, they are participating themselves. So that by the time you tell them we are going to something like respect, they come with different ideas themselves and not you giving them the ideas." (Becky)

This following drawing was made by Melissa. She indicated that with the use of drawings, the road ahead widens. This is because the children can now think broadly. Melissa noted that before the use of drawings, the learners could not think or do so normally, but now their thinking had widened. This observation is consistent with Mpho (2018) and Weimer (2013) who posit that active engagement in class activities by learners deepens learning and widens their thinking.

Knowledge retention also came up as an observed characteristic. It was found that active engagement and class participation enabled learners to exploit concepts first-hand hence leading to more knowledge retention. Karten (2015) posits that the use of child-centred teaching methods enables learners to accomplish tasks on their own with little guidance from the teacher. As a result, they are able to exploit their academic capabilities and increase the power of their knowledge retention.

> "Before, knowledge was not retained. Very few children could retain knowledge. But now that we've taken photos, they are on the walls, we've displayed them, they cannot forget. So, it makes knowledge to be retained for a long time." (Melissa)

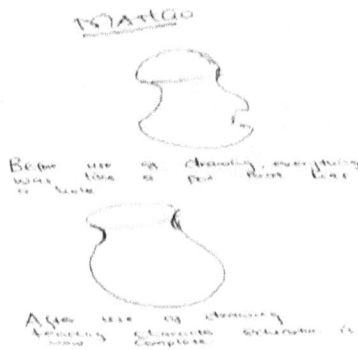

The drawing above was done by Melissa who pointed out that before the use of drawings everything (knowledge) was like a pot with a hole at the bottom. She argued that, in this example, knowledge was leaking out. But after the use of drawings, knowledge about values in character education stopped leaking out. She asserted that her learners could now retain knowledge. She also pointed out that with the use of drawings, she felt that the teaching of character education was made complete. This observation is consistent with Baker and Wang (2006) who assert that the use of participatory visual methods in teaching leads to long-term retention of knowledge.

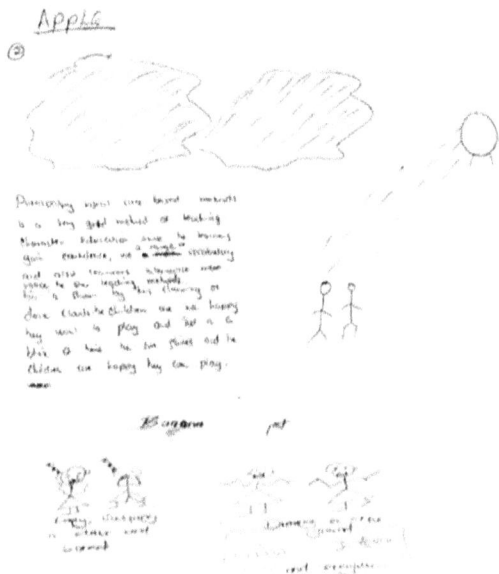

In the above drawings, the participants argued that the use of drawings and photovoice made learning more enjoyable. They indicated that the exciting nature of these methods made all learners want to participate, including the learners who were initially known to be less enthused. In agreement with Andiema (2016), this research found that the use of drawings and photovoice motivated learners to participate in the class learning activities. It was found that these methods were also exciting to the teachers. Back in the preparatory workshop, the teachers said that they had not been exposed to participatory visual methods initially. Because this came as a 'new' method to them, they said that they were eagerly waiting to see how it would work with their learners.

> *"The two methods are quite motivating. They are motivating first to the teacher and then to the learners. They are very interesting."* (Pauline)

> *"My learners were happy and not shy anymore. As a teacher, I also gained more out of their drawings. I put my thumbs up for drawing."* (Becky)

These teacher reports suggest that in the learning process, excitement begets motivation which enhances participation in class activities. However, it was the position of this study that teachers needed to take care that overexcitement on the part of the learners did not override the lesson objectives.

As claimed by the participants, the use of drawings and photovoice enabled them to transcend the language barrier. This in turn enhanced classroom interaction between the teachers and their learners. This study found that through these methods, learners did not have to struggle with vocabulary or language of communication as the drawings spoke for themselves. Also, when working in groups, the learners were able to step in for each other, hence covering for those that seemingly had poor language mastery for communication.

> *"If I find is somebody is stranded to explain him/herself, I just take a pencil or a piece of chalk. Go and draw whatever you want to talk about. And it will work."* (Becky)

> *"And it really helped my slower [learners] because even they never used to talk. They never used to smile, but when it came to drawings, it was like ... they were so excited."* (Lucy)

> *"There is richness of content and you can see the mind of that particular pupil. It is a better way of allowing people to say what they have in thoughts without having to struggle with limited vocabulary. I will recommend these methods for the learners in the lower and mid classes because they have not yet acquired much vocabulary and this can limit them in the way they can write about a particular topic given to them."* (Oakley)

Closely linked to the issue of transcending barriers, the teachers felt that the use of participatory visual methods created a conducive learning environment where learners were free to express their thoughts and ideas with ease.

> *"You find that child who was not able to talk, was silent all the time now can talk, can even ask questions, is free to mingle with the rest."* (Agnes)

> *"I also came to realize that pupils like to work in a free atmosphere where not much supervision is done."* (Pauline)

In this case, the learners were able to interact freely with each other and with their teachers through the use of drawings and photovoice thus improving the student-teacher relationship. The teachers maintained that the use of participatory visual methods to teach character education was timely as it enabled them to realize that all learners are unique and need friendly learning environments to be able to work well and learn better as individuals and as members of a group.

From a constructivist learning perspective, teachers are encouraged to provide reflective activities that engage both the minds and hands of the learners (Dewey, 1929). These activities should as well provide something to think about and something to touch. It was revealed that through drawings and photovoice, learners got a practical experience of learning about character values within the process of character education.

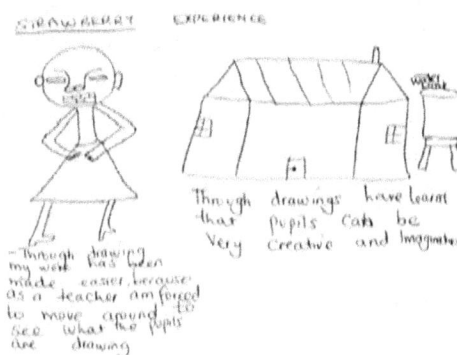

The above was a drawing by Stacy where she pointed out that, through participatory visual methods, her work in class was made easier. She was left to move around the class and see how the pupils were immersed in the action of drawing. Stacy argued that the use of participatory visual methods is practical and not theoretical. The practical nature of using drawings and photovoice encouraged the learning of character values in a manner that was more concrete. This finding is consistent with Griessel-Roux et al. (2005), who posit that children desire teaching approaches to be more practical and visual to enhance learning processes.

Collaborative learning

The teachers felt that using drawings and photovoice in class helped the learners to work together hence learning from each other. It was clear in this research that all teachers and learners were new to the use of participatory visual methods in teaching and learning character education. For this reason, there was a need to work as a team for guidance and direction.

> "The children were able to discuss and tell situations depicting hard work. Some went as far as telling their experiences of hard work in school and at home. The children grouped themselves and started taking photos depicting hard work." (Agnes)

"After the lesson I came to realize that my learners have developed some values like sharing, love and others. They have developed in their language in that they can communicate and collaborate by sharing ideas, working together. I really was happy because each group had different ideas and the photos that came out and they also learnt from other." (Pauline)

When learners engage in group learning, as seen in the highlighted responses, as a form of a participatory strategy, they are able to construct knowledge through reflection and dialogue. Through group work, the learners were able to engage in critical discussion of concepts and ideas pertaining to character values (Cherrington & Shuker, 2012).

Up to the completion of this research, it was found that teachers experienced some constraints that had the potential of impeding the implementation of participatory visual methods in class. Their main concerns were around their preparedness and competency in incorporating these methods in class. They also argued that these methods took more time in class during teaching and, therefore, were not suited to the strict class timetables that they had. They felt that if the challenges they faced were appropriately addressed, then these methods would be successful in the teaching of character education and other subjects.

Connecting to constructivism learning theory

Constructivism learning theory (CLT) foregrounds the learner as the centre of focus in all learning activities. It then follows that classrooms which subscribe to the principles of this theory set a constructivist learning environment (Bada & Olusegun, 2015). The findings of this study revealed that using participatory visual methods gave learners the opportunity to learn concepts on their own through self-discovery and reflection. Teachers also revealed that in their teaching using drawings and photovoice, everything was done by the learners and they only facilitated the process. This is supported by CLT which advocates the use of learner-centred approaches (Gravoso et al., 2008).

Furthermore, the teacher provides pupils with opportunities to learn independently and from one another and coaches in the skills they need to do so effectively (Collins & O'Brien, 2011). This was evident in the findings of this study as teachers reported that learners could be seen asking each other questions and seeking answers on their own. The teachers acknowledged that participatory visual methods enhanced peer teaching. Dewey (1929), in his contribution towards the constructivism learning theory, emphasised the need for practical, concrete, participatory and experiential learning. Similarly, this study revealed that the use of drawings and photovoice enabled children to share their experiences bearing different character values. They were also able to practically express the different character values in the drawings they made and the photos they took.

Discussion

The qualitative data analysis in this study illuminated the perspectives of Grade 3 teachers regarding the integration of participatory visual methods (PVM) in teaching character education. Grounded in constructivism learning theory, which emphasises learner-centred approaches, the findings underscored the efficacy of using drawings and photovoice to facilitate character education. Despite logistical challenges, such as time constraints within the curriculum, teachers creatively integrated PVM into Christian religious education and life skills lessons.

Learner-centred learning emerged as a prominent theme, aligning with scholarly literature and the pedagogical principles of child-centred approaches. Participants noted that PVM encouraged active engagement, expanded thinking about character concepts, and fostered collaborative learning environments. This resonates with constructivism theory, which posits that learners construct knowledge through active participation and exploration. By allowing students to generate their own ideas and interpretations, PVM facilitated deeper understanding and memory retention of character values.

Moreover, PVM were found to enhance motivation and enjoyment in learning, both for students and teachers. The novelty and excitement of these methods motivated even previously disengaged learners, contributing to a more dynamic classroom atmosphere. However, it's essential for educators to ensure that excitement aligns with lesson objectives to maintain focus and effectiveness.

One notable advantage of PVM highlighted by participants was its ability to transcend language barriers, promoting inclusive classroom interactions. By allowing students to express themselves visually, regardless of language proficiency, PVM facilitated communication and participation among diverse learners. Additionally, PVM created a conducive learning environment where students felt empowered to express their thoughts and ideas freely, improving student-teacher relationships and promoting individualized learning experiences.

The practical nature of PVM was also emphasised, providing tangible experiences for students to explore character values first-hand. Through drawings and photovoice, students were able to actively participate in the learning process, leading to a more concrete understanding of abstract concepts. This aligns with constructivist principles advocating for experiential and hands-on learning opportunities.

Conclusion

The findings of this study suggest that participatory visual methods in teaching character education within Grade 3 classrooms is effective. Grounded in constructivism learning theory, the integration of drawings and photovoice promoted learner-centred approaches, collaborative learning environments, and practical learning experiences. Despite challenges such as time constraints, teachers creatively incorporated PVM into existing curriculum frameworks, enhancing student engagement, motivation, and understanding of character values.

Moving forward, addressing logistical challenges and enhancing teacher preparedness will be important for the successful implementation of PVM in classroom settings. By embracing participatory visual methods, educators can foster inclusive, dynamic, and experiential learning environments that empower students to construct their own knowledge and develop essential character values.

References

Akanga, J. O. (2014). *Character development through education in Kenya: A pragmatic perspective* [Unpublished doctoral dissertation]. University of Nairobi.

Andiema, N. C. (2016). Effect of child-centred methods on teaching and learning of science activities in pre-schools in Kenya. *Journal of Education and Practice, 7*(27), 1–9.

Bada, S. O., & Olusegun, S. (2015). Constructivism learning theory: A paradigm for teaching and learning. *Journal of Research & Method in Education, 5*(6), 66–70.

Baker, T. A., & Wang, C. C. (2006). Photovoice: Use of a participatory action research method to explore the chronic pain experience in older adults. *Qualitative Health Research, 16*(10), 1405–1413.

Battistich, V. (2005). *Character education, prevention, and positive youth development.* Character Education Partnership.

Baxter, P., & Jack, S. (2008). Qualitative case study methodology: Study design and implementation for novice researchers. *The Qualitative Report, 13*(4), 544–559.

Berkowitz, M. W. (2011). What works in values education. *International Journal of Educational Research, 50*(3), 153–158.

Cherrington, S., & Shuker, M. (2012) Diversity amongst New Zealand early childhood educators. *New Zealand Journal of Teachers' Work, 9*(2), 76–94.

Collins, J. W., & O'Brien, N. P. (2011). *The Greenwood dictionary of education.* ABC-CLIO.

De Lange, N., & Stuart, J. (2008). Innovative teaching strategies for HIV & AIDS prevention and education. In L. Wood (Ed.), *Dealing with HIV and AIDS in the classroom* (pp. 35–50). Juta & Company Ltd.

De Lange, N., Khau, M., & Athiemoolam, L. (2014). Teaching practice at a rural school? 'And why should we go there?' Part 1: Exploration of the critical relationship between higher education and the development of democracy in South Africa. *South African Journal of Higher Education, 28*(3), 748–766.

Dewey, J. (1929). *The quest for certainty.* Minton, Balch.

Edgington, W. D. (2002). To promote character education, use literature for children and adolescents. *The Social Studies, 93*(3), 113–116.

Freire, P. (2017). *Pedagogy of the oppressed.* Penguin Classics.

Gillies, V., Harden, A., Johnson, K., Reavey, P., Strange, V., & Willig, C. (2005). Painting pictures of embodied experience: The use of nonverbal data production for the study of embodiment. *Qualitative Research in Psychology, 2*(3), 199–212.

Gravoso, R., Pasa, A., Labra, J., & Mori, T. (2008). Design and use of instructional materials for student-centered learning: A case in learning ecological concepts. *The Asia-Pacific Education Researcher, 17*(1), 109–120. https://ejournals.ph/article.php?id=3880

Griessel-Roux, E., Ebersohn, L., Smit, B., & Eloff, I. (2005). HIV/AIDS programmes: What do learners want? *South African Journal of Education, 25*(4), 253–257.

Hesson, M., & Shad, K. F. (2007). A student-centered learning model. *American Journal of Applied Sciences, 4*(9), 628–636. https://doi.org/10.3844/ajassp.2007.628.636

Holderness, W. (2012). Equipping educators to address HIV and AIDS: A review of selected teacher education initiatives. *SAHARA-J: Journal of Social Aspects of HIV/AIDS, 9*(sup1), S48–S55. https://www.tandfonline.com/doi/full/10.1080/17290376.2012.744901

Kamunge, J. (1988). *Report of the commission of inquiry into the education system of Kenya.* Government Printer.

Karten, T. J. (2015). *Inclusion strategies that work! Research-based methods for the classroom.* Corwin Press.

Khau, M., De Lange, N., & Athiemoolam, L. (2013). Using participatory and visual arts-based methodologies to promote sustainable teaching and learning ecologies: Through the eyes of pre-service teachers. *TD: The Journal for Transdisciplinary Research in Southern Africa, 9*(3), 401–412.

Lanham, M. D. (2004). *The Montessori method: The origins of an educational innovation.* Rowman & Littlefield Publishers.

Lee, G.-L. (2013). Re-emphasizing character education in early childhood programs: Korean children's experiences. *Childhood Education, 89*(5), 315–322.

Lickona, T. (1996). Eleven principles of effective character education. *Journal of Moral Education, 25*(1), 93–100.

Mitchell, C. (2008). Getting the picture and changing the picture: Visual methodologies and educational research in South Africa. *South African Journal of Education, 28*(3), 365–383.

Mpho, O. (2018). Teacher-centered dominated approaches: Their implications for today's inclusive classrooms. *International Journal of Psychology and Counselling,10*(2), 11–21.

Muthamba, J. (2017*). Implementation of moral education in Kenyan schools: A study of selected Catholic schools from Kitui Central Deanery* [Unpublished master's thesis]. Strathmore University.

Mwaka, M., Nabwire, V., & Musamas, J. (2014). *Essentials of instruction: A handbook for teachers.* Eldoret Moi University Press.

Nucci, L., Krettenauer, T., Nucci, L. P., & Narvaez, D. (2008). Traditional approaches to character education in Britain and America. In L. P. Nucci & D. Narvaez (Eds.), *Handbook of moral and character education* (pp. 96–114). Routledge.

Osabwa, W. (2016). An analysis of the pedagogical approaches to character formation in Kenyan schools: In search of an alternative. *Journal of Education and Practice, 7*(14), 41–50.

UNICEF. (2002). *The state of the world's children.* Oxford University Press for UNICEF.

Van der Riet, M., Hough, A., & Killian, B. (2005). Mapping HIV/AIDS as a barrier to education: A reflection on the methodological and ethical challenges to child participation. *Journal of Education, 35*(1), 75–98.

Wamahiu, S. (2015). *Value-based education in Kenya: An exploration of meanings and practices.* Republic of Kenya Ministry of Education and Women Educational Researchers of Kenya.

Watz, M. (2011). An historical analysis of character education. *Journal of Inquiry and Action in Education, 4*(2), 3–24.

Weed, S. (1995). *Report to the Thrasher Foundation: Alternative strategies for behavioral risk reduction in children: A character education approach to healthy behavior.* Institute for Research and Evaluation.

Weimer, M. (2013). *Learner-centered teaching: Five key changes to practice.* John Wiley & Sons.

Wentzel, K. R. (2002). Are effective teachers like good parents? Teaching styles and student adjustment in early adolescence. *Child Development, 73*(1), 287–301.

Wood, L., & Wilmot, D. (2012). In search of an enabling pedagogy for HIV and AIDS education in initial teacher education. *South African Journal of Higher Education, 26*(5), 1112–1130.

Yego, L. J. (2017). *Exploring the use of participatory visual methods in teaching sexuality education within the HIV and AIDS education programme in selected Kenyan secondary schools* [Unpublished master's thesis]. Nelson Mandela University.

CHAPTER 11

A focus on drawing as method: Insights from a novice participatory visual methodologies researcher

Naomi Mworia

Supervisors: Dr Felicity W. Githinji and Professor Naydene De Lange

Introduction

> *I want to understand the world from your point of view. I want to know what you know*
> *in the way you know it. I want to understand the meaning of your experience, to walk*
> *in your shoes, to feel things as you feel them, to explain things as you explain them.*
> (Spradley, 2016, p. 34)

The above classic statement by Spradley describes the essence of my study as a qualitative researcher. It depicts the relationship I wished to have with my participants, being sensitive to understand the world from their eyes. This desire as well as the study objectives, led me to employ drawing as method, to generate data with girls who had seen, heard, or experienced GBV. This then enabled me to conceptualise and understand the GBV experiences of the girls from their lens. The methodology of my study is the focus of this chapter. I will share my general research process and experience using drawing as method, the challenges I encountered as a novice participatory visual methods (PVM) researcher, as well as my fears and successes.

Violence against schoolgirls is a daily reality. Unfortunately, most literature is mainly focused on GBV among adult females (Morof et al., 2014; Mutinta, 2022), yet the vice can be traced in the early years of female lives. My study thus sought to explore the forms of GBV secondary schoolgirls experience in informal settlements and to find out from them the ways in which secondary schools can improve their support systems for secondary schoolgirls who experience GBV. GBV is part of the hard realities of living in an informal settlement. The United Nations (2006) reports it as one of the most serious human rights violations, with more than 30% of females worldwide experiencing GBV. Vulnerability to GBV in informal settlements is increased when one is younger, as is the case with secondary schoolgirls, with statistics indicating that they have the highest recorded number of cases of GBV (Mahlangu et al., 2014). Both globally and locally in Kenya, numerous policies to mitigate GBV are in place, yet the vice remains on the increase. Such policies include the Constitution of Kenya (2010), the Children's Act (2001); the Sexual Offence Act (2006); the Sexual Offences Regulations (2008). Although research on GBV is vast, and much of the literature is mainly focused on GBV among adult females (Crooks et al., 2019), the research around GBV and girls is on the increase. This qualitative research, using a girl-friendly approach to explore the problem and possible solutions, could further contribute to understanding GBV in the lives of girls. In that way, immediate intervention measures could be put in place to deal with this vice. And who better to provide what is needed, than the schoolgirls themselves?

As such, the study set out to explore secondary schoolgirls' experiences of GBV in informal settlements in Nairobi, Kenya. The objectives of the study were to explore the forms of GBV experienced by girls in secondary schools and to find out from them how support systems for secondary schoolgirls who experience GBV might be improved. The following research questions were formulated:

- What forms of GBV did secondary schoolgirls experience in informal settlements?
- How could secondary schools improve their support systems for secondary schoolgirls who experience GBV in informal settlements?

This chapter is derived from a previous study (Mworia, 2023), with a focus on how drawing as method was used to generate data with the girls on such a sensitive topic, ensuring that it led to "most good and least harm" to them (Mitchell et al., 2011).

Methodology

Kumar (2011, p. 33) posits that "it is the purpose for which a research activity is undertaken that should determine the mode of enquiry, hence the paradigm". The study, as guided by its objectives, was located within the interpretivist paradigm. Interpretivist approaches have the intent of understanding the world of human experience while suggesting that reality is socially constructed (Van der Walt, 2020). The interpretive researcher relies on the participants' views of the situation being studied (Creswell & Creswell, 2017) and attempts to interpret social reality through the subjective viewpoints of the participants within the context where the reality is situated. Further, this paradigm's ontological perspective is based on the notion that multiple realities exist. This study, therefore, recognised the numerous and varied participants' realities. Therefore, the interpretivist paradigm was used as the basis of this study. My focus as a researcher was on describing the experiences of participants, assuming multiple meanings rather than a single 'truth', and holding onto the fact that reality is subjective and can differ based on the perspectives of different individuals. The choice of the interpretivist paradigm led to the generation of rich, in-depth data as it is based on personal contributions with consideration of different constructs. Furthermore, the interpretivist paradigm enabled me, as a researcher, to treat each girl's experience as unique considering her given circumstances as well as the individual girl involved, abstaining from generalisation as a given in the positivist paradigm.

The study embraced a phenomenological research design. Neubauer et al. (2019) described phenomenology as a form of qualitative research that focuses on the study of an individual's lived experiences within the world. The goal of this study was to describe the meaning of the girls' experiences, understanding it in terms of both what was experienced and how it was experienced. Therefore, phenomenology was a powerful well-suited research design in this study as it sought to describe the GBV experiences among the girls, thus creating a platform for them to air their concerns, fears, and/or unmet needs.

Sampling and participants

The study was conducted in two selected public secondary schools in informal settlements in Nairobi County, Kenya. Purposive sampling was used in the selection of schools. This study targeted the largest and centrally located secondary schools as they potentially had a higher chance of having more girls who have seen, heard of, or experienced GBV. Two schools were selected. Snowball sampling was used in the selection of individual girls who served as 'seeds', which means that one participant is recruited who in turn recruits another, and the cycle continues. Snowball refers to a technique in which existing participants are asked to suggest more participants (Taherdoost, 2016). The target population was all the secondary schoolgirls who had seen, heard of, or experienced GBV and were studying in selected schools in informal settlements.

This technique enabled me to identify girls from the general school population who had seen, heard of or experienced GBV and could share their experiences and thoughts with ample depth and clarity. Once I identified one girl in each school, with the help of the guidance and counselling teacher, the girl was requested to help locate other girls who had also experienced GBV. Factors such as availability and willingness to participate, ability to recall and relate real-life experiences as well as the capacity to communicate were considered. It was important in this study because it enabled me to arrive at information-rich cases for an in-depth study. Fourteen girls from each of the two schools were selected to participate in the study. Thus, twenty-eight girls in total were selected. Their ages ranged from 13 to 18 years. This sample size was arrived at after data saturation was reached. Saturation is reached based on the data that had been collected and analysed up to a given point in time, indicating further data collection and/or analysis was unnecessary (Braun & Clarke, 2021; Saunders et al., 2018) on the basis of the data that had been collected or analysed hitherto. However, there appears to be uncertainty as to how saturation should be conceptualised, and inconsistencies in its use. In this chapter, we look to clarify the nature, purposes and uses of saturation, and in doing so add to theoretical debate on the role of saturation across different methodologies. We identify four distinct approaches to saturation, which differ in terms of the extent to which an inductive or a deductive logic is adopted, and the relative emphasis on data collection, data analysis, and theorizing. We explore the purposes saturation might serve in relation to these different approaches, and the implications for how and when saturation will be sought. In examining these issues, we highlight the uncertain logic underlying saturation—as essentially a predictive statement about the unobserved based on the observed, a judgement that, we argue, results in equivocation, and may in part explain the confusion surrounding its use. We conclude that saturation should be operationalized in a way that is consistent with the research question(s).

Method

The study used a PVM drawing to produce data with the participants. Over the years, PVM has gained popularity among researchers and practitioners. PVM is used as an umbrella term, capturing a wide range of methods including, but not limited to photovoice, digital storytelling, participatory video, and drawing (Mitchell, 2008). The purpose of using these methods was to help bring the ideas, and voices of marginalised groups to the public and to try to concentrate the priorities of the research closer to the needs of those that it is envisioned to benefit (Hergenrather et al., 2009). They have a common aim of enabling ordinary people to be active contributors in decisions that affect their lives, rather than be mere objects of research (Coyne & Carter, 2018), from inception to implementation and beyond.

Engagement of children and young people requires the use of creative, participatory methods, tools and involvement strategies to reveal their competencies. This chapter shares knowledge about creative participatory techniques that can enable and promote children's ways of expressing their views and experiences. The chapter provides guidance on appropriate techniques that reduce the power differential in the adult-child relationship and which optimise children's abilities to participate in research. This chapter is targeted at researchers, academics, and practitioners who need guidance on what tools are available, how the tools can be used, advantages and challenges, and how best to involve children in all stages of a research project. It will provide several examples of how children can have an active participatory role in research. There is increasing interest in involving children as co-researchers but little guidance on how this can be done.

This chapter addresses these issues by providing practical examples from leading researchers and academics, utilising participatory visual methodologies. These methods use creative techniques to ensure that people are not only listened to but genuinely heard, with their input shaping the outcomes (Dockery, 2020). The chapter also explores the crucial question of why participatory visual methodologies should be used at all—what sets them apart from conventional research, who benefits from participating in the research process, and who holds the power? It's not about offering a toolkit or a set of techniques that guarantee quick or easy solutions for effective outcomes, nor is it an automatic alternative to conventional research approaches. In fact it may be inappropriate in certain contexts. Supporting or enabling participation in its fullest sense is a political act, establishing partnerships between researchers and participants where ownership, empowerment, and accountability are shared throughout the research process. Participatory visual methodologies can play a key role in fostering community activism both at the individual and collective levels (Dockery, 2020). The use of both word- and image-based research methods provides a way to explore the multiplicity and complexity that underpins social research focused on human experience (Guillemin, 2004).

In this study drawing as a method was employed. Brailas (2020) posits that participant-produced drawings provide access to non-verbal meanings and facilitate participants sharing their feelings, thoughts, and experiences which are not easily communicated otherwise. Drawing as method was an ethical methodology as it enabled the girls who found it difficult to speak about their GBV experiences to share them in a non-threatening way. Drawing as method has two phases, draw and tell. The first session involves the participants drawing an image of the phenomenon at hand while the second session involves them elaborating on their drawings. In this case, drawings can serve as icebreakers and effective prompts to catalyse verbal communication (Ellis et al., 2011)

Drawing as method has been used in various types of research the world over. It has been used in Russia, to study social representations of intelligence (Räty et al., 2012). It has been used with women in the United States of America, to explore women's perspectives on why people might decline HIV testing (Mays et al., 2011). It has been used in rural north-west Uganda to explore the challenges girls face with respect to unequal educational opportunities (Jones, 2019). Further, it has also been used with girls to discuss their safety and security in slums in and around Nairobi, Kenya (Chege et al., 2014).

In this study, I first formulated a drawing prompt. This was a simple guide informing the participants of the phenomenon at hand and what I expected of them as they drew. It included phrases such as "the quality of the drawing is not important, rather the meaning of the same". I also asked them to choose a pseudonym, and requested the participants not to include any identifiers on the drawing paper. On the data generation day, the girls were invited to complete drawings on blank paper, using pencils and colouring crayons, that symbolized how they see GBV and to explain in writing what they wished to communicate via these drawings. Here, I provided a prompt such as, "Draw how you see GBV and how it has affected you". During the drawing sessions, each girl was given at least 15 minutes to draw and write a caption individually. This was done separately for each girl, in a private space.

The second session of the drawing was the tell session, where girls were requested to verbally explain or give further information on their drawings to the researcher, and what they symbolized. They were then asked to talk about their drawings individually with the researcher. Thereafter, the girls shared their drawings with each other, in a group setting. This session took around four hours cumulatively.

Here, I encouraged the girls to verbally describe their drawings by using phrases such as "tell me about it" and asking further clarification and probing questions. The drawings and captions were later digitized by scanning and the girls' explanations were recorded using an audio recorder and then transcribed. All oral data were tape-recorded and transcribed verbatim afterward since this protected against bias and provided a permanent record of what was and was not said. Sensitive issues were always approached with care to minimize distress, while allowing the girls to tell their stories.

Data presentation

In this study, a set of 28 drawings were submitted. They were on A4 white paper, made with coloured pencils with pseudonyms written on them. At the back, the girls wrote a caption of the drawing they had made. I then digitized them by scanning and labelled them using the girls' selected pseudonyms. It is important to note that since the participants' first language was Kiswahili, most of them chose to write in it because it allowed them to express themselves fully. For the girls who wrote in Kiswahili, I retyped the caption in Kiswahili, translated it to English, and finally gave a summary of the captions as well as the tell session.

Of the 28 drawings the girls made, three are offered below, one for each form sampled. In some cases, the convergence of multiple forms of abuse directed at individual girls can be observed:

Figure 1: *Olive's Drawing and Caption (Mworia, 2023, p. 36)*

"This man is this girl's stepfather. The man started advancing toward her eldest daughter, touching her inappropriately and having sex with her. He threatened that he would beat or stab her".

Figure 2: *Shamizah's Drawing and Caption (Mworia, 2023, p. 109)*

"This girl is about to join secondary school, but her guardians want her to get married. They organized for an old rich man to marry her. She tried to resist but they overpowered her and she got married forcefully".

Figure 3: *Ceane Clara's Drawing and Caption (Mworia, 2023, p. 120)*

"A girl coming home with exams and she passed but she is not appreciated at all. Coming home from school, finding a lot of work waiting for the girl. Accusation and being beaten every time. The boy passing exams and being appreciated at school and loved but the girl passing exams and not being appreciated at all simply because you are a girl".

In Figure 1 Olive drew a bedroom with a bed in their home. Probably the mother and stepfather's bedroom, where the stepfather made advances to her, revealing that physical and sexual violence are often intertwined.

Olive's explanation translated from Kiswahili:

> "This father is this girl's stepfather. I mean that the last born in that family is born of this man. So, the mother was living with this man as her husband. The girl was the first born followed by two boys. The mother respected this man and did not know what was happening. So, the girl decided to report to her grandmother, as she was living close by. The grandmother advised her to move in with her as she planned on questioning the mother. When the mother heard the case, she denied it and said that her husband cannot do such a thing. When the mother finally discovered the truth, she chased away the man and apologized to her daughter. The daughter forgave her mother and she returned home."

While the drawing was simply of a room with a double bed in the house, the drawing enabled her to tell the story the way she constructed it. The drawing depicts sexual abuse.

In Figure 2 Shamizah drew a girl in agony as she is faced with forced marriage. Her guardians are forcing her to marry a rich, old man. This was evidence of psychological abuse, as Shamizah shared that she felt and saw that she was being treated as a commodity for 'sale'.

Shamizah's explanation translated from Kiswahili:

> "This girl lives with her guardians because her parents died a long time ago. She is about to join secondary school, but her guardians want her to get married. They believe that a girl is useless, even if she completes her studies. Further, they wished to get money from the dowry. They thus organized for an old rich man to marry her. As much as she tried to resist, they overpowered her and she got married forcefully."

This drawing revealed that forced marriage is an issue that faces schoolgirls. Globally, it is estimated that 82 million girls between the ages of 10–17 years will be married off before their eighteenth birthday, before they are able to consent (Save the Children Alliance, 2005). This is an unfolding disaster that we must act now to bring to an end. Drawing as method, provided a channel for Shamizah to share her experiences in means that would not further traumatize her. This is consistent with Guillemin and Westall (2008), who posit that visual methods can facilitate the communication of painful and difficult experiences in a non-threatening way.

In Figure 3 Ceane Clara drew a brother and sister who were unequally treated by their parents. The girl was side-lined and abused both verbally and physically, while the boy was praised outright.

Ceane Clara's explanation translated from Kiswahili:

> "A girl coming home with exams and she passed but she is not appreciated at all. Coming home from school, finding a lot of work waiting for the girl. Accusation and being beaten every time. The boy passing exams and being appreciated at school and loved but the girl passing exams and not being appreciated at all simply because you are a girl."

The drawing depicted a patriarchal society where the girl's effort is not rewarded by her guardian, while the boy is praised and encouraged for the same effort input. Further, it portrays the physical and verbal abuse the girl undergoes. Drawing as method allowed Ceane Clara to share her experience through a non-threatening approach.

Data analysis

Qualitative data analysis refers to the process of description, classification, and interconnection of phenomena with the researcher's concepts, with a general aim of developing an explanation of the phenomenon under study (Graue, 2015). This study was qualitative in nature and thus yielded mainly unstructured text-based data from the explanation of the drawings, other field notes, pictorial captions, and audio recordings. From these primary sources, it is worth reiterating the argument by Taylor and Ussher (2001) that themes do not just sit waiting to be discovered, they do not simply appear, but must be actively sought out.

In this study, I did not analyse the drawings, but only what the girls wrote and said about their drawings. This is because I did not want to make up my own meanings of the drawings. This is consistent with Rech (2013), who posits that drawing as a research method includes analysis by both the researcher and the participant. In this way, the research becomes collaborative and the analysis cannot take place without the participant.

Data generation and analysis were done concomitantly, allowing for the investigation of emerging themes and issues. Immediately after data had been collected, data transcription commenced. Transcription can be described as "the process of reproducing spoken words, such as recorded data from an interview, and converting it into written form so the data can be analysed" (McGrath et al., 2019, p. 8). Data were then analysed immediately, to guide me on what further data needed to be improved or generated to satisfy the study objectives.

The schoolgirls drew, wrote a caption, and explained their drawings and these explanations served as a first layer of analysis. This study, then, employed thematic analysis as a second layer of analysis to tease out these themes from the dataset. Thematic analysis refers to a method of identifying, analysing, and reporting patterns and themes within data (Braun & Clarke, 2006).

Data were coded and organized into categories and themes. Coding refers to the identification of issues, differences, and similarities that are discovered in the participants' narratives as interpreted by the researcher (Sutton & Austin, 2015). In this study, this involved analysing the data and identifying themes and topics which represent gender-relevant themes and presenting them in narratives showing excerpts from participants, as guided by the objectives set.

The three seminal coding steps by Strauss and Corbin (1990, 2014) – open, axial, and selective coding; combined with the six steps by Braun and Clarke (2006) were used to analyse text data in this study.

Phase 1: Data familiarization: I began by examining the drawings and transcribing draw-and-tell sessions. This helped me get acquainted with the data. Then, I analysed the raw text line by line to identify relevant concepts related to gender-based violence (GBV) experienced by the schoolgirls.

Phase 2: Initial code generation: I generated initial codes from the data, noting interesting segments and potential patterns. Using MS Word, I linked each code to specific text portions and color-coded them based on research questions.

Figure 4: *Image of Initial Code Generation*

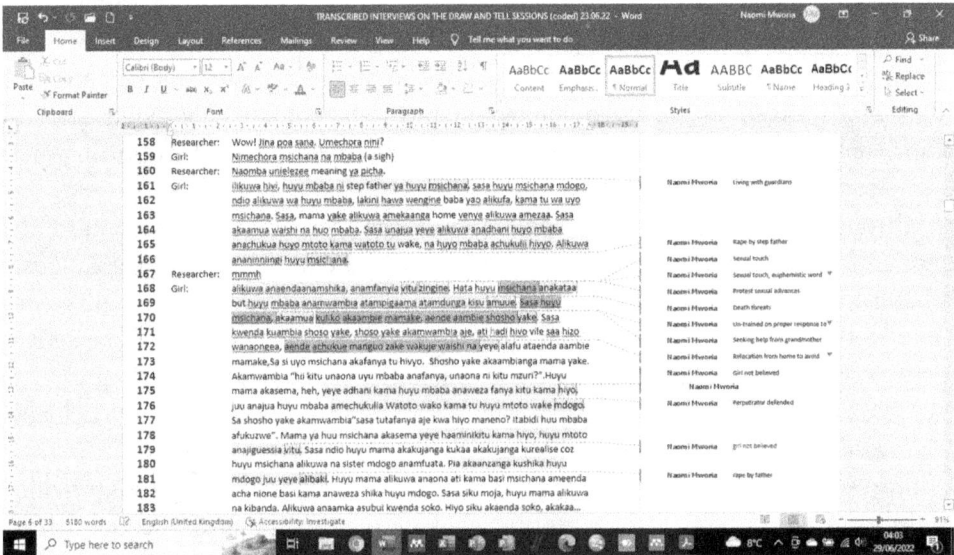

Phase 3: Theme search: I sorted codes into potential themes, establishing relationships between them visually and hierarchically.

Phase 4: Theme review: Themes were refined to ensure clarity and distinction, with additional data checked for emerging categories. Themes were consolidated or eliminated until data saturation was reached.

Phase 5: Theme definition: Final themes were defined, capturing the essence of the data within them. Appropriate labels were given to each theme.

Phase 6: Analysis report production: I crafted a thematic analysis report, presenting a coherent account of the data story within and across themes. The narrative was guided by research questions, supported by evidence from data extracts, and continually refined throughout the analysis process.

Ethical considerations

According to Creswell and Creswell (2017), research ethics is a codification of scientific morality in practice. Researching GBV against schoolgirls is similar to researching any other sensitive topic. Therefore, it was key that the research was conducted ethically from beginning to end. The ethical considerations that were observed in the study are elaborated below:

Before embarking on the fieldwork, I navigated the ethical landscape. This involved securing research approval from the university, obtaining clearance from the National Commission for Science, Technology, and Innovation (NACOSTI), and seeking authorization from the respective school principals. Prioritizing the welfare and autonomy of participants, I procured informed consent from parents, school principals, and assent from the girls themselves. Each participant was thoroughly briefed on the research purpose, methods, potential consequences, and associated risks. They were empowered to make voluntary decisions regarding their participation, free from coercion or deception.

Throughout the research process, utmost care was taken to safeguard the anonymity and confidentiality of all participants. Identifiers were meticulously removed, and pseudonyms were employed to shield identities. Sensitive language was conscientiously utilized during data collection, and only participants' perspectives were recorded to ensure the integrity and credibility of the research findings.

Ensuring participant safety remained paramount at every stage. Participants were assured of their right to withdraw from the study at any point, and their comfort with audio recording was acknowledged, with withdrawal options provided if discomfort arose. For participants under the age of 18, parental and school written consent was sought.

By initially focusing on broader topics to avoid re-traumatization, participants' emotional welfare was safeguarded. Counselling support was arranged for those in need, emphasising proactive measures to address any potential distress.

Methodologically, drawing upon participatory visual methods offered a delicate balance between information generation and participant protection. This approach minimized risk while facilitating authentic documentation of experiences. Throughout the research journey, visual ethics and participant anonymity remained steadfast priorities, ensuring the integrity and ethical conduct of the study.

Findings: Fears, successes, and challenges

In this section I only offer a summary of the findings (see Mworia, 2023). These were as follows.

Fears on conducting research using drawing as method

I experienced several fears when I selected drawing as method for my research. First, I feared that my participants would be uncomfortable drawing their experiences. This was especially for those who believed they did not have a drawing talent or those who lacked self-confidence in their ability to draw. However, I was able to overcome this fear by reassuring the girls that the quality of their drawings was not paramount (Mitchell et al., 2011). Further, a few months before the onset of data generation, I attended a research school centred on research methodologies. Here, I tried out drawing as a method of data generation. This enabled me to get the skill and confidence to use drawing as method and further, use it as a means of expression. Consequently, this was very beneficial during data generation with my participants, as I could guide them on the process of drawing.

Second, I was puzzled by the prospect of participants drawing something abstract. I wondered how they would make the thoughts they had tangible and visible on paper. This fear was eased as I delved more into literature. Mitchell et al. (2017) posit that while older participants may feel daunted by the idea of drawing, it is in the process of drawing that their thoughts on the phenomenon might become clarified. I then realized that in the drawing process, the participants would gradually get a clearer mental picture of the topic at hand. Truly, this was confirmed when I went into the field. Even those participants who struggled to draw at first, in the process, were able to make clear drawings and captions.

Successes in using drawing as method

When I was headed into the field for data generation, one question lingered on my mind, 'With such a sensitive topic, would the girls open up to me?' As much as I was prepared in all ways possible, I still had this fear. By the end of my data generation process, I knew better! Drawing as method, true to its word, had repositioned ethics to doing least harm and doing most good (Theron, 2012). The girls did not seem (re-)traumatized by sharing their experiences. Instead, it created a moment for them to share their feelings and suggestions on creation of better support systems for girls who experience GBV in school. Some girls found the method very playful and really enjoyed the entire process of sharing their experiences.

Another success I experienced was drawing as method allowing me to engage with participants who found it hard to verbalize their experiences and thoughts. Mitchell et al. (2011), emphasise this by pointing to Weber's argument that: "artistic images can help us access those elusive hard-to-put-into-words aspects of knowledge that might otherwise remain hidden or ignored" (Weber, 2008, p. 44). The drawings revealed experiences and explanations that were often not explicitly spoken about before. An example of this is the sexual abuse by stepfathers that some girls shared. It seemingly became easier for participants to explain their experiences – seen, heard or experienced – and to remember tiny details, when they visualized them. The method also allowed some girls to share painful memories by drawing, which they found to be a better option than speech. They could choose what to communicate via drawing and what they wished to share verbally during the tell session.

Challenges encountered using drawing as method and suggested ways to overcome them

The main challenge I experienced was that different girls had different reactions to drawing as method. While some expressed joy at the thought of drawing, others displayed dissatisfaction. Those who were used to drawing saw it as an opportunity to feel more comfortable than simply talking. On the other hand, some felt uncomfortable, finding it unusual. Some were unwilling to produce a drawing, while others said they did not know what to draw.

To deal with this challenge, I suggest that the researcher emphasise to the participants from the very beginning that the quality of their drawings is not important. What is important is the message it portrays, the content, and how drawing enables talking about it. This will encourage participants to draw as directed, no matter their abilities. Also, the researcher can allow the participant time to think through what is to be drawn. However, despite the researcher's effort, some participants may still be hesitant to draw (Horstman et al., 2008), thus a need for an alternative plan. A good plan may be to sit with them and also make a drawing on the subject matter at hand, and also tell them about your drawing. Another alternative could be for the participant to find a picture from a magazine or from the internet, then write a caption, and talk about it.

Discussion

The study findings, for research question one, revealed that the girls experienced physical, sexual, verbal, and psychological abuse. Physical abuse would occur alone or intertwined with sexual abuse. Psychological abuse encapsulated rejection and being treated as commodities. The girls were also verbally abused, taking the form of harsh words and gender-discriminative speech. The results of this study align with Nyamanhindi (2015) who asserts that schoolgirls experience different forms of GBV. Perpetrators included teachers, relatives, fellow students, and gangs in the community.

The findings, for research question two, revealed that girls offered several suggestions on ways in which support could be improved for them. They shared that the school could introduce clear reporting strategies by putting up clear mechanisms to report. They could also provide safe places for girls to report, as well as teach them how to report. The findings also revealed that the girls hoped for a whole school approach where both boys and girls could be trained on what GBV is and how it can be prevented. They also thought that teachers could be trained on how to respond to cases of GBV. These findings are congruent with Parkes et al. (2017) who point out the need for using a multi-dimensional approach in tackling GBV issues, such as innovative teaching and learning as well as curriculum modification. The study concluded that girls experienced varied forms of abuse, which most of the time were neither reported nor even noticed, thus urgent intervention is needed.

Conclusion

In conclusion, the study underscores the importance of considering both the benefits and challenges of using drawing as a research method, particularly when exploring sensitive topics like GBV. While drawing facilitates communication and empowers participants, researchers must be mindful of individual preferences and provide alternative avenues for expression. By acknowledging these nuances, researchers can enhance the effectiveness of their studies while ensuring participant comfort and ethical integrity.

Pink notes that "there is more to human experience than can be captured in words" (2013, p. 11). This sentiment is affirmed in terms of research by Weber (2008, p. 44) who states that "the use of visual images is not a luxury or add-on to scholarship, but in many cases, essential". Participatory visual methodologies combine the strength of spoken word and drawing (Guillemin, 2004). Using drawings helped me to capture some of the non-verbal aspect of human experience and provided me with a platform for the discussion of an otherwise difficult topic. As such, I encourage emerging researchers to try this research method when encountering difficult cultural and social issues.

References

Brailas, A. (2020). Using drawings in qualitative interviews: An introduction to the practice. *The Qualitative Report, 25*(12), 4447–4460. https://doi.org/10.46743/2160-3715/2020.4585

Braun, V., & Clarke, V. (2006). Using thematic analysis in psychology. *Qualitative Research in Psychology, 3*(2), 77–101. https://doi.org/10.1191/1478088706qp063oa

Braun, V., & Clarke, V. (2021). To saturate or not to saturate? Questioning data saturation as a useful concept for thematic analysis and sample-size rationales. *Qualitative Research in Sport, Exercise and Health, 13*(2), 201–216. https://doi.org/10.1080/2159676X.2019.1704846

Chege, F., Maina, L., Mitchell, C., & Rothman, M. (2014). A safe house? Girls' drawings on safety and security in slums in and around Nairobi. *Girlhood Studies, 7*(2). https://doi.org/10.3167/ghs.2014.070209

Coyne, N., & Carter, B. (Eds.). (2018). *Being participatory: Researching with children and young people: Co-constructing knowledge using creative techniques.* Springer.

Creswell, W., & Creswell, D. (2017). *Research design: Qualitative, quantitative, and mixed methods approaches* (5th ed.). Sage Publications.

Crooks, C. V., Jaffe, P., Dunlop, C., Kerry, A., & Exner-Cortens, D. (2019). Preventing gender-based violence among adolescents and young adults: Lessons from 25 years of program development and evaluation. *Violence Against Women, 25*(1), 29–55.

Dockery, G. (2020). Participatory research. Whose roles, whose responsibilities? In *Research and inequality* (1st ed., pp. 95–110). Routledge.

Ellis, J., Amjad, A., & Deng, J. (2011). Interviewing participants about past events: The helpful role of pre-interview activities. *In Education, 17*(2), 61–73.

Graue, C. (2015). Qualitative data analysis. *International Journal of Sales, Retailing & Marketing, 4*(9), 5–14.

Guillemin, M. (2004). Understanding illness: Using drawings as a research method. *Qualitative Health Research, 14*(2), 272–289. https://doi.org/10.1177/1049732303260445

Guillemin, M., & Westall, C. (2008). Gaining insight into women's knowing of postnatal depression using drawings. In P. Liamputtong & J. Rumbold (Eds.), *Knowing differently: Arts-based and collaborative research methods* (pp. 121–140). Nova Science Publishers.

Hergenrather, K. C., Rhodes, S. D., C., C. A., Bardhoshi, G., & Pula, S. (2009). Photovoice as community-based participatory research: A qualitative review. *American Journal of Health Behavior, 33*(6), 686–698. https://doi.org/10.5993/ajhb.33.6.6

Horstman, M., Aldiss, S., Richardson, A., & Gibson, F. (2008). Methodological issues when using the draw and write technique with children aged 6 to 12 years. *Qualitative Health Research, 18*(7), 1001–1011. https://doi.org/10.1177/1049732308318230

Jones, S. (2019). Drawing gender equality: A participatory action research project with educators in Northern Uganda. *Engaged Scholar Journal: Community-Engaged Research, Teaching, and Learning, 5*(2), 135–160. https://doi.org/10.15402/esj.v5i2.68340

Kumar, R. (2011). *Research methodology: A step-by-step guide for beginners* (3rd ed.). Sage Publications. https://www.sociology.kpi.ua/wp-content/uploads/2014/06/Ranjit_Kumar-Research_Methodology_A_Step-by-Step_G.pdf

Mahlangu, P., Gevers, A., & De Lannoy, A. (2014). Adolescents: Preventing interpersonal and gender-based violence. *Child Gauge, 73*.

Mays, R. M., Sturm, L. A., Rasche, J. C., Cox, D. S., Cox, A. D., & Zimet, G. D. (2011). Use of drawings to explore U.S. women's perspectives on why people might decline HIV testing. *Health Care for Women International, 32*(4), 328–343.

McGrath, C., Palmgren, P. J., & Liljedahl, M. (2019). Twelve tips for conducting qualitative research interviews. *Medical Teacher, 41*(9), 1002–1006.

Mitchell, C. (2008). Getting the picture and changing the picture: Visual methodologies and educational research in South Africa. *South African Journal of Education, 28*(3).

Mitchell, C., De Lange, N., & Moletsane, R. (2017). *Participatory visual methodologies: Social change, community and policy.* Sage Publications.

Mitchell, C., Theron, L., Smith, A., Stuart, J., & Zachariah, C. (2011). Drawings as research method. In L. Theron, C. Mitchell, A. Smith & J. Stuart (Eds.), *Picturing research: Drawing as visual methodology* (pp. 17–36). Brill Sense.

Moletsane, R., Wiebesiek, L., Treffry-Goatly, A., & Mandrona, A. (Eds.). (2021). *Ethical practice in participatory visual research with girls: Transnational approaches* (pp. 31–51). Berghahn.

Morof, D. F., Sami, S., Mangeni, M., Blanton, C., Cardozo, B. L., & Tomczyk, B. (2014). A cross-sectional survey on gender-based violence and mental health among female urban refugees and asylum seekers in Kampala, Uganda. *International Journal of Gynecology & Obstetrics, 127*(2), 138–143.

Mutinta, G. (2022). Gender-based violence among female students and implications for health intervention programmes in public universities in Eastern Cape, South Africa. *Cogent Social Sciences, 8*(1). https://doi.org/10.1080/23311886.2022.2079212

Mworia, N. (2023). *Exploring the gender-based violence experiences of secondary schoolgirls in Mathare informal settlements, Nairobi County, Kenya.* [Unpublished master's thesis]. Moi University.

Neubauer, B. E., Witkop, C. T., & Varpio, L. (2019). How phenomenology can help us learn from the experiences of others. *Perspectives on Medical Education, 8*, 90–97.

Nyamanhindi, R. (2015, February 4). Hidden in plain sight: Child sexual abuse in Zimbabwe. *The Herald*. https://www.herald.co.zw/hidden-in-plain-sight-child-sexual-abuse-in-zimbabwe/

Parkes, J., Johnson Ross, F., Heslop, J., Westerveld, R., & Unterhalter, E. (2017). *Addressing school-related gender-based violence in Côte d'Ivoire, Togo, Zambia and Ethiopia: A cross-country report*. UCL Institute of Education. https://www.researchgate.net/publication/321125266_Addressing_School-Related_Gender-Based_Violence_in_Cote_d%27Ivoire_Togo_Zambia_and_Ethiopia_A_Cross-country_Report

Pink, S. (2013). *Doing visual ethnography* (3rd ed.). SAGE Publications.

Räty, H., Komulainen, K., & Paajanen, T. (2012). Portraying intelligence: Children's drawings of intelligent men and women in Finnish and Russian Karelia. *Educational Studies, 38*(5), 573–586. https://doi.org/10.1080/03055698.2012.661928

Rech, L. (2013). Picturing research: A review essay. *International Journal of Education & the Arts*. http://www.ijea.org/v14r6/

Saunders, B., Sim, J., Kingstone, T., Baker, S., Waterfield, J., Bartlam, B., Burroughs, H., & Jinks, C. (2018). Saturation in qualitative research: Exploring its conceptualization and operationalization. *Quality & Quantity, 52*(4), 1893–1907.

Save the Children Alliance. (2005). *Listen and speak out against sexual abuse of girls and boys: 10 essential learning points*. Global presentation by the International Save the Children Alliance to the UN Secretary-General's study on violence against children. Save the Children International. https://resourcecentre.savethechildren.net/document/listen-and-speak-out-against-sexual-abuse-boys-and-girls-10-essential-learning-points-global/

Spradley, J. (2016). *The ethnographic interview*. Waveland Press.

Strauss, A., & Corbin, J. (1990). *Basics of qualitative research: Grounded theory procedures and techniques*. Sage Publications.

Strauss, A., & Corbin, J. (2014). *Basics of qualitative research: Techniques and procedures for developing grounded theory*. Sage Publications.

Sutton, J., & Austin, Z. (2015). Qualitative research: Data collection, analysis, and management. *The Canadian Journal of Hospital Pharmacy, 68*(3), 226–231.

Taherdoost, H. (2016). Sampling methods in research methodology: How to choose a sampling technique for research. *International Journal of Academic Research in Management (IJARM), 5*(2), 18–27.

Taylor, G., & Ussher, J. (2001). Making sense of S&M: A discourse analytic account. *Sexualities, 4*(3), 293–314. https://doi.org/10.1177/136346001004003002

Theron, L. C. (2012). Does visual participatory research have resilience-promoting value? Teacher experiences of generating and interpreting drawings. *South African Journal of Education, 32*(4), 381–392. https://doi.org/10.15700/saje.v32n4a656

United Nations. (2006). *World report on violence against children*. UN. https://violenceagainstchildren.un.org/content/un-study-violence-against-children

Van der Walt, J. L. (2020). Interpretivism-constructivism as a research method in the humanities and social sciences: More to it than meets the eye. *International Journal of Philosophy and Theology, 8*(1), 59–68. https://pdf4pro.com/view/interpretivism-constructivism-as-a-research-method-in-the-654676.html

Weber, S. (2008). Visual images in research. In J. G. Knowles & A. L. Cole (Eds.), *Handbook of the arts in qualitative research: Perspectives, methodologies, examples and issues* (pp. 41–54). Sage Publications.

CHAPTER 12

Using gender-atypical Kiswahili children's stories to deconstruct gender-stereotyped roles among learners

Simon Ekiru, Mathabo Khau, Sammy Chumba

Introduction

Gender stereotypes impact negatively on children when exposed to them during the early stages of their socialization (Onyango, 2007; Floyd, 2012; Toçi & Aliu, 2013). They shape children's conceptualisation of gender roles and can influence in them the development of notions that one gender is weaker in certain societal spheres of influence (Floyd, 2012). When this notion is consistently propagated in their lifetimes, there is a danger of creating a society where individuals discriminate against others based on their gender identities. Despite this fact, few studies on gender have focused on children, even though childhood is an important stage in human development.

A number of studies in child psychology (Kohlberg, 1966; Gottfredson, 1981; Eccles, 1994) have revealed that fixation in adulthood can be traced back to childhood. It is in light of the above that global strategies to address gender stereotypes were formulated. One of the proposed strategies was to deconstruct gender stereotypes using children's books. This is due to the fact that books play a significant role in the socialization process of a child because, like other human beings, children acquire a lot of knowledge from books which enable them to form certain patterns of behaviours, perceptions, thinking and beliefs. Fox (1993) says that everything human beings read constructs them and makes them who they are, enabling them to present the image of themselves as girls and women and as boys and men. Mpesha (2007, 1996) and Mbuthia (2018) also affirm that children's literature is not just a record of social events but also an instrument for socialization. A number of studies have shown that a reading culture and skills are significant to the child's cognitive development.

Singh (1998) argues that, apart from being a significant resource for developing language skills among children, children's books play an important role in transmitting societal culture to children. Gender roles are an important part of this culture. How genders are portrayed in children's books contributes to the images children develop of their own roles and that of their genders in society (Onyango, 2006). It is in light of the above that this chapter examines how exposure to gender-atypical Kiswahili children's stories influenced learners' understandings of gender roles.

Background

This section of the chapter presents global interventions to curb gender stereotypes, rationale to deconstruct gender-stereotyped roles, and empirical studies on the deconstruction of gender-stereotyped roles among learners.

Global interventions to curb gender-stereotyped roles

The pursuit of eliminating gender stereotyping has been a focal point in global discourse for decades (Tabassum, & Nayak, 2021). This has led to the development of global strategies such as Sustainable Development Goal 5 on gender equality and continental frameworks like the African Union's Agenda 2063, specifically Target 5 on gender equality and women's empowerment (African Union, 2015). These initiatives aim to foster equality and empowerment for all individuals regardless of gender. Furthermore, various countries, including Norway and Zimbabwe, have devised national strategies to combat gender stereotyping.

Norway and Zimbabwe have endeavoured to address gender-stereotyped roles by implementing action plans for gender equity (Floyd, 2012). For instance, Norway introduced the Action Plan for Gender Equity (2008) to tackle long-standing gender stereotypes prevalent in their kindergartens. The objective of this plan was to ensure that kindergartens and basic education systems foster a society where individuals can utilize their interests and abilities irrespective of gender. Floyd (2012) emphasises the importance of promoting gender equity in early education, noting the stance of the 'Gender Equality in the Kindergartens' (2008) position:

> Preschools must remain places where boys and girls have the same opportunities to participate in activities and work together. Early education should focus these activities on preparing young children to live in a society that is based on gender equality and avoid stereotyping children based on gender expectations. (Floyd, 2012, p. 8)

She believes that preschools must serve as environments where boys and girls have equal opportunities to engage in activities and collaborate. Early education should orient these activities towards preparing young children for a society grounded in gender equality, avoiding the pigeonholing of children based on gender expectations (Floyd, 2012, p. 8).

In Zimbabwe, Nhundu (2007), highlighted the establishment of Gender Equity Initiatives (GEI) to tackle gender stereotyping. This initiative was founded in 1995 following the Fourth World Conference on Women in Beijing. Zimbabwe developed a policy on gender equity and established a dedicated ministry to empower women and girls facing vulnerability due to gender inequality pervasive across all spheres. Additionally, the Zimbabwean government enacted an Education Act advocating for the gradual integration of gender education into curricula and teacher training. The Ministry of Education introduced the Gender Equity in Education Initiative

(GEEI) to address gender disparities in education. Under GEEI, the Role Model Reader Project (RMRP) was launched to counter traditional gender role stereotypes by using children's literature to inspire girls in primary schools to cultivate positive, non-stereotypical career aspirations

Why deconstructing gender stereotypes is important

When children encounter stereotypical notions and behaviours early on, they often internalise and conform to them. This impact is compounded when they are exposed to negative stereotypes, hindering, and adversely affecting their learning processes (Ambady et al., 2001).

Research by Golshirazian et al. (2015) indicates that gender stereotyping introduced during preschool can have long-term effects, extending beyond adolescence into adulthood. They argue that such patterns persist, with girls often relegated to supportive roles, while boys take centre stage in society. Children who diverge from these gender stereotypes risk feeling isolated and ridiculed, impacting their ability to learn (Fagot, 1977; Fagot & Leinbach, 1987; Thorne, 1993; Kao et al., 2014). Thus, addressing gender stereotyping early in a child's development is essential, as it occurs during an important stage of socialization and knowledge construction.

Miller (2013) suggests various methods to address gender stereotyping in young children. One approach is for parents, teachers, and authors to convey non-sexist messages. She advocates nurturing children in environments that foster diversity in gender roles, providing equal opportunities regardless of gender. Miller proposes exposing children to gender-neutral career puzzles and images depicting women and men in non-traditional roles. For instance, women and girls can be portrayed as physically strong leaders in fields like science, mechanics, and sports, while boys can be depicted expressing emotions beyond anger, participating in domestic chores, caring for families, and pursuing careers in nursing, dance, and cooking. In a gender-neutral environment, children can freely explore their ideas without gender constraints, laying a positive foundation for their future gender identity development (Derman-Sparks & Edwards, 2010; Miller, 2013).

It is in light of these considerations that this study explores how gender-atypical Kiswahili children's stories can be utilized to address gender-role stereotyping among young learners. Specifically, the study seeks to answer the question: How do learners construct gender roles when exposed to gender-atypical Kiswahili stories?

Empirical studies on deconstruction of gender-stereotyped roles among learners

According to Liben et al. (2001), young children have preconceived notions about what roles are suitable for females and males, and have a tendency of selecting roles that are stereotypically associated with their gender when inquired about their future careers (Morgan, 2008). However, 5-6-year-old children are more likely to remember individuals displaying gender-atypical roles and activities, than those portraying gender-stereotyped activities (Wilbourn & Kee, 2010). Furthermore, children still attribute knowledge about roles or activities to individuals portraying gender-atypical roles (Gregg & Dobson, 1980; Shenouda & Danovitch, 2013). For example, when children are presented with a female mechanic and male nurse and asked who knows more about a number of occupation-related items, children would attribute mechanic-related knowledge to a woman and nurse-related knowledge to a man, despite the fact that their occupations defied stereotypes.

In light of the above arguments, empirical studies (e.g. Scott & Feldman-Summers, 1979; Trepanier-Street & Romatowski, 1999; Nhundu, 2007; Karniol & Gal-Disegni, 2009) have shown that, reading gender-atypical storybooks changes children's stereotypes notions about gender appropriate occupation and activities. The above studies suggest that, when children are exposed to storybooks with female central characters displaying atypical gender roles (i.e. occupations, activities), their belief in the number of occupations appropriate for women is likely to increase.

For instance, the study conducted by Scott and Feldman-Summers (1979) on third and fourth grade children who read gender-atypical stories, in which female main characters were involved in gender-atypical roles and activities (e.g. a story about a female explorer). Those children who were exposed to those significantly reported that girls could participate in the gender-atypical activities depicted in the stories. Another similar study to this was an experiment study done by Trepanier-Street and Romatowski (1999) on 4–6-year-old children to examine their gender attitudes concerning occupation roles. At the pre-test of the study, children distinguished occupations appropriate for male and female. Later in the study, children were carefully read selected books of males and females portraying gender-atypical occupational roles by their teacher. After reading and engaging in teacher-guided activities related to the gender-atypical stories, more children judged the occupations as suitable for both male and female.

Similarly, studies on young children by Karniol and Gal-Disegni (2009) also revealed that gender-atypical books shape children's notions of occupational roles and activities. The study involved first graders who were categorised into two groups. The first group was assigned gender-fair basal readers while the second group was given gender-stereotyped readers. At the end of the study, the evaluation results of the two groups indicated that those children who were exposed to gender-fair basal readers judged more activities (e.g. baking a cake, playing in mud) as suitable for both females and males than those children assigned gender-stereotyped basal readers. The above studies suggest that children's exposure to gender-atypical stories defy children's stereotypes about gender-appropriate activities and occupation.

Nhundu's (2007) study of Zimbabwean girls is considered one of the most exciting results in children's stories and gender-stereotyped literature (Abad & Pruden, 2013). This study was conducted on young Zimbabweans' girls enrolled in the fourth grade until their completion of the seventh grade. The study used an experiment design where girls were put into two groups (the experiment and control groups). In the experiment group, girls were exposed to biographical stories of women succeeding in non-traditional careers, while the control group was not exposed to those stories. During the pre-test, girls in both groups showed an interest in gender-stereotyped careers and occupations. However, during post-test, the girls who were in the experiment group reported that all jobs were equally appropriate for both female and male. When asked to mention the careers they aspired towards in future, they mentioned gender-atypical careers similar to those done by the successful women in the biographical stories. In contrast, almost all the girls in the control group, who had not been exposed to gender-atypical biographical stories, still showed desire for stereotypically traditional careers rather than gender-atypical careers. Hence, this finding indicated that reading gender-atypical stories can shape young girls' future career goals and ambitions. Nhundu's study is similar to the current study because they both explore the use of children's stories with characters engaged in gender-atypical roles. However, Nhundu's study adopted an experimental design, while the current study adopted the participatory visual methodologies (PVM) design. Moreover, Nhundu's study was limited to female learners as its participants, while the current study used both male and female participants.

In conclusion, it is evident from the reviewed literature that there is still a deficiency in empirical research, despite the urgent need to combat gender stereotyping in learners' constructions of gender roles during the early years of their socialization. This is more surprising in Kiswahili children's literature, given the fact of its swift growth and popularity among Kiswahili literary scholars (Bakize, 2017). Therefore, this study sought to fill the empirical gap in research done in Kiswahili children's literature and awaken future scholarship debates in pursuit of addressing gender stereotyping.

Research design and methodology

As noted earlier, the study sought to answer the question: how does exposure to gender-atypical Kiswahili children's stories influence learners' understanding of gender roles and how do learners construct gender roles when exposed to gender-atypical Kiswahili stories? With the help of experts in Kiswahili children's literature from the Department of Kiswahili & African Languages at Moi University, we carefully selected gender-atypical Kiswahili children's stories that were used in the study. The selected Kiswahili children's stories were those stories which had themes and content that exhibited gender-atypical roles. Moreover, these stories were found in storybooks that were recommended by the Kenya Institute of Curriculum Development (KICD) to be used in primary schools for reading lessons. The selected gender-atypical storybooks were: *Sungura Mjanja* (Islam, 2003), *Atoke*

Asitoke? (Mwangi, 2009), *Siku za Juma la* (Nyakeri, 2006), *Mama Mwizi* (Mutuku, 2014), *Kombo Arudi Shule* (Lewela, 2008), *Zawadi ya Rangi* (Karan, 2005), *Tuzo ya Baba* (Zawadi, 2013), *Vitendo vya Jamila* (Mogambi, 2006), and *Furaha ya Arope* (Walibora, 2013).

The study was grounded in the interpretivist paradigm with a qualitative research approach. It adopted the participatory visual methodologies (PVM) design. Data were generated using drawings and discussions with Grade 3 learners from a purposively selected primary school. The drawing method was used because it is the simplest method of data generation in social science research involving children and other individuals in society who may have difficulties in expressing themselves due to language or other constraints that encompass the topic of discussion (Mitchell et al., 2011; Mitchell et al., 2017). Drawings were suitable for this study because they not only gave children aesthetic pleasure, but also crystalized their thoughts to produce artefacts that could be drawn on to tease them into a discussion of their viewpoints (Mitchell et al., 2011; Mitchell et al., 2017).

The school was selected because it had active reading classes from Grade 1 to Grade 3 which were properly monitored and supervised by the teachers. The school also had a library which had enough Kiswahili children's storybooks that learners read during their reading lessons and also in their leisure time. The participants of the study were Grade 3 pupils of the selected primary school. The study focus was on exploring the use of gender-atypical (GA) Kiswahili children's stories to deconstruct gender-stereotyped roles among Grade 3 learners in the selected primary school. The study used learners at this level because, according to the school enrolment policy by the Ministry of Education in Kenya, children aged 9 years are supposed to be in this grade (Muthara, 2012). This study also incorporated learners at this age based on Kohlberg's (1966) ideas of cognitive development, namely that at this age, children would have formed a stable gender identity and sexuality and start adopting gender-stereotyped behaviours, activities, preferences, etc., exhibited to them either in their environment or by social models (Gooden & Gooden, 2001; Clarke & Stermac, 2011). Bender and Leone (1989) reported that the development of gender identities in children occurs alongside the desire and passion to read and re-read their favourite storybooks. This occurs when children are between the ages of 8 and 10. They begin to integrate abstract notions and concepts, such as the concept of femininity and masculinity, into their representations (Eisenberg et al., 1996). The selected school had fifteen Grade 3 learners (ten girls and five boys) who willingly showed interest in participating in the study. They also had good reading, writing and communication skills, which made them suitable for this study.

We gave our participant Grade 3 learners drawing prompts during the pre-exposure evaluation to make drawings of work and activities they like doing at home and school. We also asked them to draw their future career goals and aspirations. After the drawings, we asked each participant to give an oral explanation for each drawing he/she had made. Thereafter, we exposed the participants to gender-atypical Kiswahili children's stories for a period of 4 weeks. After the exposure to gender-atypical Kiswahili children's stories, we conducted a post-exposure evaluation of the participants. We advised the participants to use pseudonyms in their drawings to protect their true identities. This ensured that all the information they gave, which included drawings and discussions, was protected and concealed. We labelled our participants' data using their pseudonyms, when data were generated (i.e. pre-exposure or post-exposure), page number (i.e. p. 1), date, month, and year (i.e 18/7/2018). Data review and analysis were done thematically and concurrently with data generation.

Research findings and discussion

After analysing the pre- and post-exposure evaluation drawings and their explanations, we came up with a table that summarized the 30 drawings presented by the learners. The drawings depicted how learners constructed gender roles in two ways. First, the drawings showed how they constructed work and activities they normally do at school and at home, and second, how they constructed their future career aspirations.

Table 1: *Categories of Gender Roles Portrayed by the Participants during the Pre-exposure Evaluation and the Post-exposure Evaluation*

Participant	Age	Gender	Pre-exposure Drawing on Gender Role: Work & Activities	Post-exposure Drawing on Gender Role: Work & Activities	Pre-exposure Drawing on Gender Role: Future Career Goals	Post-exposure Drawing on Gender Role: Future Career Goals
1. Jack	9 years	Male	Playing football	Farming	Teacher	Soldier
2. Maureen	10 years	Female	Fetching water	Looking after sheep	Doctor	Doctor
3. Pogba	10 years	Male	Washing utensils Playing football	Cooking food Washing utensils	Soldier	Soldier
4. Shantel	11 years	Female	Washing utensils Fetching water	Looking after the cow Farming	Teacher	Police officer
5. Brown	8 years	Male	Playing football Drawing a car	Fetching water Slashing grass	Footballer	Pilot

6. Annete	11 years	Female	Watering flowers Weeding plants	Looking after the sheep	Doctor Teacher	Police officer
7. Fatuma	11 years	Female	Washing clothes Singing Playing 'kati'	Fetching water Washing utensils	Doctor	Teacher
8. Evelyne	11 years	Female	Washing clothes Picking up litters	Cooking food Washing clothes	Driver	Teacher
9. Maria	10 years	Female	Farming Cooking food	Washing clothes Watering plants	Doctor	Teacher Police officer
10. Princess	11 years	Female	Sweeping Washing clothes Fetching water Farming	Fetching water Cleaning the environment Watering plants	Doctor	Bus driver
11. Rehema	8 years	Female	Washing clothes Fetching water Skipping a rope	Looking after a cow Sweeping the house	Doctor	Police officer
12. Pinky	10 years	Female	Singing Washing clothes Skipping a rope Reading a book Planting maize	Looking after a cow Collecting and burning rubbish	Police officer	Soldier
13. Mos	10 years	Male	Farming	Washing utensils	Pilot	Police officer
14. Specks	10 years	Male	Fetching water	Fetching water	Soldier	Singer / musician
15. Precious	11 years	Female	Sweeping	Watering plants	Police officer	Doctor

Source: Primary data (2019)

Learners' construction of gender roles

The tabulated summary of findings (Table 1) demonstrates how learners constructed gender roles. The construction of gender roles entails work and activities they like doing at home as well as their future career goals and aspirations. Table 1 presents a summary and categories of gender roles constructed by the learners during the pre- and post-exposure evaluations. The learners, both boys and girls, constructed their gender roles by drawing what they liked doing at home and also their future career goals. Work and activities that were most preferred by boys in the pre-exposure evaluation, as shown in Table 1, were drawing a car, farming, washing utensils and fetching water. On the other side, girls reported in the pre-exposure evaluation that they preferred doing tasks such as fetching water, washing utensils, watering flowers, weeding plants, washing clothes, picking up litter, cooking food, sweeping the house, reading a book, and planting maize.

However, after being exposed to GA Kiswahili children's stories, boys seemed to present work and tasks in their post-exposure evaluation which were similar to what they presented during pre-exposure evaluation. These works were farming, fetching water, and slashing grass. Interestingly, two participants (Pogba and Mos) presented different findings in their post-exposure evaluation from what they had presented in their pre-exposure evaluation. Mos, for example reported in the pre-exposure drawing that he likes farming but later, in the post-exposure drawing, he changed his work of preference to washing utensils. Pogba on the other hand changed his preferred work from washing utensils to cooking food even though he still reported in the post-exposure drawing that he still likes washing utensils.

On the other side of girls, the results presented during their post-exposure evaluation indicated a majority of them had changed from their previous work of preference during the pre-exposure to different work in the post-exposure, even though some of the work they reported in the post-exposure evaluation was earlier mentioned in the pre-exposure evaluation of other female participants. The preferred tasks among the girls in the post-exposure evaluation were farming, looking after sheep, looking after cow, fetching water, washing utensils, cooking food, washing clothes, sweeping house, collecting and burning rubbish and watering plants.

Regarding their future career goals and aspirations, most boys in the pre-exposure evaluation reported their preferences for careers such as teacher, soldier, footballer, pilot and police officer, while girls indicated their partiality towards careers such as doctor, teacher, driver, and police officer. During the post-exposure evaluation most boys' future career preferences revolved around soldier, pilot and police officer. It was only one male participant (Specks) who aspired to be a musician. On the girls' side, the post-exposure results indicated that a majority of them reported different future career choices from what they had presented earlier in the pre-exposure. The most preferred careers among girls were doctor, police officer, bus driver and soldier.

The findings show that the majority of the participants showed gender-stereotyped role preferences during the pre-exposure evaluation. The gender roles presented above in the pre-exposure evaluation correspond to what previous scholars from different African backgrounds termed as traditional stereotyped roles. For example, a study conducted by Mosley (2004) in Ethiopia reported that cleaning the house, fetching water and cooking are perceived as feminine roles, while agricultural activities such as ploughing are believed to be masculine. In South Africa, a study conducted by Mwaba (1992) reported that most boys and girls in South African secondary schools considered that nursing, housecleaning, and sweeping as primarily jobs for women. In another study conducted in Kenya, Wanjeri (2006) reported that gender dictated the division of roles among the Kikuyu communities. Boys were taught and expected to undertake masculine roles such as herding cattle, hunting, building houses, ploughing, among others. On the other hand, girls were taught and expected to perform 'womanly' roles such as cleaning, cooking, and taking care of their younger siblings.

In the current findings, few boys during the pre-exposure evaluation presented drawings that showed a deviation from the traditional gender-stereotyped roles for men. These participants (Pogba and Mos) reported that they liked washing utensils and fetching water, respectively. Accounting for their preferences for work that is predominantly considered for girls and women within the societal context in which the research was conducted, this is what they said:

Pogba: *I have drawn myself washing utensils.*

Researcher: *It seems you like washing utensils?*

Pogba: *Yes.*

Researcher: *That is good. Why do you like washing them?*

Pogba: *I don't like dirty utensils. I wash them so that they become clean.*

Researcher: *Are you the only one who washes utensils at home?*

Pogba: *No. All of us wash. Each one of us has a duty to wash the utensils.*

(Oral explanation, Pogba, pre-exposure, p. 1, [15/6/2018])

Researcher: *I can see you have drawn a good picture. What have you drawn?*

Mos: *It's me. I am weeding crops.*

Researcher: *Do you weed crops alone or you are helped by other people?*

Mos: *My brothers and sisters help me. We have duties to weed crops.*

(Oral explanation, Mos, pre-exposure, p. 1, [15/6/2018])

From the explanation above, it is revealed that the participants developed interest in those roles because they are used to doing them at home as required by their respective home duty routine, which dictates gender roles in their homes. This means that gender roles are not innate but rather a product constructed by the society. The society then socializes children to acquire those gender roles. Quite a number of girls showed preferences for farming during the pre-exposure evaluation though their interest was only limited to watering flowers, weeding, planting crops but not digging and ploughing. Girls reported that they do not like digging because it makes them tired as evident in the following sample extracts:

Researcher: *Okay. Apart from fetching water what other activity do you like doing?*

Maureen: *I also like sweeping, moping,*

Researcher: *Okay. What are those activities that you don't like doing?*

Maureen: *I don't like digging. It makes me feel tired.*

Researcher: *Who then does digging at home?*

Maureen: *My brothers.*

Researcher: *Don't they as well get tired like you?*

Maureen: *No.*

(Oral explanation, Maureen, pre-exposure, p. 3, [15/6/2018])

Some reported that they would rather do other activities for the boys in exchange for them doing the digging task on their behalf as revealed by the girl participant Annete below in her oral drawing explanation.

Researcher: *How do you divide activities that you do at home?*

Annete: *My brothers usually farm at the shamba while my sister and I washes clothes for them.*

Researcher: *Okay.*

(Oral explanation, Annete, pre-exposure, p. 3, [15/6/2018])

Another interesting finding is that a majority of the girls changed their preferred tasks after the exposure to gender-atypical Kiswahili children's stories which corresponded to the tasks exhibited by the female characters in those stories. These tasks were: looking after the cows, looking after the sheep, collecting garbage/litter and burning them. The above-mentioned tasks, for example, looking after the cows were portrayed by female characters such as Maria (*Siku za Juma*), Arope (*Furaha ya Arope*) and Jamila (*Vitendo vya Jamila*). Similarly, participants Mos and Jack presented task preferences in the post-exposure evaluation that resembled the task that was undertaken by the male character, Baraka (*Tuzo ya Baba*). The above-mentioned tasks that those girls showed interest in after being exposed to GA Kiswahili children's stories are predominantly perceived to be male gender roles. In the same way, those tasks preferred by a minority of the male participants (Pogba and Mos) are stereotypically considered to be tasks meant for girls and women. However, during their oral explanations, the participants attributed the change to their desire to emulate the characters in the stories as highlighted in the excerpts below.

Researcher:	*Apart from seeing that girl looking after the sheep what else motivated you or is there any movie or story you read about looking after the cattle?*
Maureen:	*Yes. I read about the girl looking after the sheep.*
Researcher:	*Which story?*
Maureen:	*Ndoto ya Arope.*
Researcher:	*What was the story about?*
Maureen:	*The story was about a girl called Arope who helped her mother to look after sheep, goats and cattle.*
Researcher:	*When you saw her looking after the sheep, how did you feel?*
Maureen:	*I felt good.*
Researcher:	*Does it mean that you have drawn this picture as result of seeing Arope looking after the sheep?*
Maureen:	*Yes.*
Researcher:	*Do you think you can do the same as her?*
Maureen:	*Yes*

(Oral explanation, Maureen, post-exposure, p. 1, [18/7/2018])

Annete and Rehema share the same sentiment as Maureen, saying that seeing fellow girls in the stories (Maria and Arope) inspired them to develop an interest in looking after the cattle.

Researcher:	*How did you feel, seeing small girls like you looking after the cattle?*
Annete:	*I felt good. I felt I can also look after the cattle like them. (Smiling)*

(Oral explanation, Annete, post-exposure, p. 3, [18/7/2018])

Researcher:	*How did you feel when you read the story?*

Rehema: *I felt good (Smiling). I was happy to see Maria looking after the cow.*

Researcher: *Could she have inspired you to look after the cow?*

Rehema: *Yes.*

(Oral explanation, Rehema, post-exposure, p. 1, [18/7/2018])

The findings on future career goals and aspirations also revealed that boys preferred careers such as being a teacher, a soldier, a footballer, and a pilot during the pre-exposure evaluation. According to Nhundu (2007) the above listed careers over the decades have been stereotyped to be male-gendered occupations. This therefore suggested that boys' choice of future careers echoed societal gender stereotypes. Insignificant change was seen in their post-exposure evaluation since the previous career choices (e.g. soldier, pilot and police officer) were replicated. It was only one boy participant (Specks) who presented a different career aspiration of being a musician in future. Conversely, the story was different with girls. The most preferred career choices among girls during the pre- and post-exposure were doctor, teacher, driver and police officer. During the post-exposure evaluation, a majority of the girls aspired to be policewomen, soldiers, doctors, and teachers.

The above data reveal that participants gave varied responses related to gender-role construction after exposure to GA Kiswahili children stories. The majority of the girls adopted gender-atypical roles, while the boys still conformed to gender-typical roles even after being exposed to GA Kiswahili children's stories.

Adoption of gender-atypical roles

The above findings revealed that a majority of the girls, as compared to the boys, adopted gender-atypical roles. The adopted gender roles by girls corresponded with the atypical roles displayed by model characters in the stories (e.g. policewomen, soldier, drivers, doctor, looking after the cows, collecting and burning rubbish, farming, etc.). The only atypical roles adopted by boys were washing utensils and cooking food. These results therefore suggest that the girls found roles perceived to be predominantly male much more appealing to them than the boys found the female-stereotyped roles. This may mean that girls identified more with the role models in the stories than boys did. This indicates that the attraction to and admiration of the role model characters in the story was more prevalent in girls than in boys, and that the stories influenced them to adopt gender-atypical roles. These findings are supported by previous studies on gender-role preference (Nhundu, 2007). These results could have two possible explanations.

First, the fact that all of the role model characters in the stories, except one, were girls and women who were engaging in gender roles traditionally conceived of as male might have made it easier for girls than boys to identify with them and imitate their behaviours. According to the social learning theory, sexual similarities between the child and model play an important role in learning and imitating behaviours (Bandura, 1986; McLeod, 2016). The child is more likely to pay more attention to those people it perceives as similar to itself and imitate their behaviours. Hence, this could be the possible reason why more girls imitated the gender-atypical roles displayed by the models in the stories who were girls and women.

Second, previous studies (e.g. Bussey, 1983; Green et al., 2004) that explored rigidity and variability of gender roles among boys and girls showed that boys conform more rigidly to gender-stereotyped roles than girls. The reluctance among boys to detach themselves from male gender-stereotyped roles is due to the fear of the consequences that befall them when they counter stereotypical gender roles. Prior research has revealed that boys are treated more harshly than girls by peers (Fagot, 1977) and adults (Langlois & Downs, 1980) for engaging in behaviours and activities that go against the 'gender-appropriate' roles constructed by the society. This is why girls find it easier to adopt gender-atypical roles than boys because society shows more tolerance for 'tomboys' than for 'sissies' (Fagot & Leinbach, 1987). The intolerance and pressure put on boys by society discourages them from imitating and adopting gender-atypical roles. Perhaps this is what could have discouraged one of our boy participants (Mos) who had tried to engage in a gender-atypical role and received severe criticism and discouragement from his grandmother.

> "… one day my grandmother and my sister were not at home, so I decided to go to the kitchen and cook 'ugali' for them. When they came back at home, my grandmother was angry at me and said that the 'ugali' was badly cooked and being a boy, I was not supposed to go to the kitchen to cook because it is women's responsibility to prepare food for men. She cautioned me from going to the kitchen." (Oral explanation, Mos, pre-exposure, p. 1, [16/6/2018])

According to the social learning theory (Bandura et al., 1977), the responses of the people around the child toward an imitated behaviour will also influence their imitation and internalisation of those behaviours. The people around will either reinforce (encourage) or punish (discourage) the child from imitating their models. If a child copies a model's behaviour and the consequences are rewarding or encouraging, the child is likely to continue engaging in that behaviour. However, if the consequences are harsh, the child stops or becomes reluctant to perform that behaviour.

Therefore, the case for the two boy participants (Specks and Pogba) who challenged gender stereotypes by adopting gender-atypical roles after being exposed to gender-atypical stories could have been influenced by the gender role structures at home and school as well as the reinforcement of the male role model in the story

(Baraka, a boy character in the story, 'Tuzo ya Baba'). During their oral explanations of their drawings, the two participants said that they preferred to do those roles (washing utensils and washing clothes) because that is what they normally do at home and school. They said that at their respective homes and at school, they have a chore routine where all children participate in household duties such as washing utensils and washing clothes irrespective of the gender, as shown in the interaction below.

Researcher: *That is good. Why do you like washing them?*

Pogba: *I don't like dirty utensils. I wash them so that they become clean.*

Researcher: *Are you the only one who washes utensils at home?*

Pogba: *No. All of us wash. Each one of us has a duty to wash the utensils.*

(Oral explanation, Pogba, pre-exposure, p. 1, [15/6/2018])

Researcher: *Here you also said that you like washing clothes?*

Specks: *Yes, I like washing my clothes.*

Researcher: *Do you wash them here in school or at home?*

Specks: *In school. It is always mandatory for everybody to wash his/her clothes on Saturday before we go home.*

(Oral explanation, Specks, post-exposure, p. 1, [18/7/2018])

Conforming to gender-stereotyped roles

Table 1 reveals that all the boys conformed to predominantly male gender-coded careers. Their future career choices during the post-exposure evaluation entailed careers such as soldier, pilot and policeman. It is only one of them who chose to be a musician, a career that can also be categorised as one of those occupations that enjoys male dominance. These findings are similar to the findings of a study conducted by Nhundu (2007) in Zimbabwe which showed that boys conformed to gender stereotyped roles even after being exposed to Role Model Readers which contained stories of role models engaging in gender-atypical roles. When we asked the participants for reasons behind their choices of those careers, most boy participants preferred those careers because they believed they would give them higher status in society such as being custodians that provided security in the society. This was contrary to girl participants who asserted that the motivation behind their choices in future careers was influenced by their aspiration to help the society. Prior studies have demonstrated that boys tend to prefer more 'self-oriented careers', while girls prefer 'people-oriented careers' (Levy et al., 2000; Morgan, 2008). Self-oriented careers are those careers that enable one to have a higher status and value in the society, while people-oriented careers are associated with working with people, serving others and helping others in the society.

From their explanations of the drawings, boys choose those careers which would enable them to have higher status, value and respect in the society such as soldier, policeman, musician and pilot. In many African societies, Kenya included, the police forces and the army are one of the most feared and respected groups by the members of the society because of the consequence that may befall any member of the public who disrespects a police officer or a soldier. This fear could be attributed to the colonial imperialism in Africa, where colonial police forces used coercive means to exert rule over Africans. After independence, African police forces emerged which conformed to their predecessors' ideology of using coercive means (Ndege, 2009). However, these traits are usually understood by children, especially boys as heroic, courageous, superhuman, among others which they find attractive to (Evans & Davies, 2000). This could be the possible reason why some of the boy participants aspired to be police officers and soldiers so that they can provide security as well as terrorize criminals or those participating in antisocial behaviours, and by doing so, they would gain more status and value in the society. Another wanted to be a musician so that he could go far and have adventure. All the above career choices centre personal status development as opposed to societal development as evident in the following extracts:

"When I grow up, I would like to be a soldier so that I can protect my country."

(Written explanation, Pogba, Drawing caption 5 on gender roles: Future career goals)

'I would like to be a footballer because I normally see footballers being given presents.

(Written explanation, Brown, Drawing caption 9 on gender roles: Future career goals)

"I would like to be a soldier because I would be helping my country to catch robbers and thieves."

(Written explanation, Specks, Drawing caption 15 on gender roles: Future career goals)

"I would like to be a musician because I believe it would take me far like Tanzania and America. I am an artist."

(Written explanation, Specks, Drawing caption 16 on gender roles: Future career goals)

Source: Primary data (2019)

Contrary to boys, most of the girl participants' choices of career were driven by their motives to help society as opposed to status-development that was witnessed in boys.

This is similar to the previous studies (Levy et al., 2000; Morgan, 2008; Nhundu, 2007) which found that girls and women expressed greater preference for helping careers, such as those of nurse, teacher, secretary and doctor, among others. Even from their written explanations in their drawing captions, their interest in helping society was evident.

"I would like to be a doctor so that I can help different types of sick people."

(Written explanation, Maureen, Drawing caption 3 on gender roles: Future career goals)

"When I grow up, I would like to be a teacher so that I can teach my students the way I was taught."

(Written explanation, Shantel, Drawing caption 7 on gender roles: Future career goals)

"I am a doctor. I am helping the sick people so that they cannot die early."'

(Written explanation, Annete, Drawing caption 11 on gender roles: Future career goals)

"I would like to be a doctor when I complete school so that I can help sick people including my father."

(Written explanation, Fatuma, Drawing caption 13 on gender roles: Future career goals)

Scholars (e.g. Liben et al., 2001) have argued that boys are reluctant to adopt feminine activities such as gender roles because they see lower value in them and associate that lower value with them. Hence this demotivates them as they do not satisfy their quest of achieving a higher status and value in the society. This little or no motivation, according to social learning theorists (Bussey & Bandura, 1992), discourages them from adopting those behaviours and activities.

Nevertheless, even though in the current study most of the boys conformed to gender-stereotyped roles in their drawings, they still showed change in their perspective towards feminine roles. During their oral explanations, most boys expressed their personal feelings and desire to perform the feminine roles. They also supported the view that girls were capable of doing the masculine roles effectively. Similar views were expressed by girls who believed that just like the male characters in the stories (Juma and Baraka in the stories, *Siku za Juma* and *Tuzo ya Baba*), boys can also perform domestic activities such as cooking food, washing utensils and fetching water. Even though this is what they purport to believe, most of them (both boys and girls) still presented drawings of themselves and their friends doing gender-stereotyped roles. This resembles the findings of previous studies done by Gregg and Dobson's (1980) and Nhundu (2007) who found that children expressed liberal views of what they could do but were more gender-stereotypical in their choice of future occupations. As discussed earlier, the long period of their socialization to gender-stereotypes and the societal pressure for them to conform to gender-stereotyped roles could be the possible reason for the above. However, the change in their views and perspectives towards gender-atypical roles during the post-exposure evaluation is an indication of the influence of the gender-atypical Kiswahili stories to deconstruct gender stereotyped roles.

Conclusions

The study examined how exposure to gender-atypical Kiswahili children's stories influenced learners' understanding of gender roles. By analysing drawings and explanations from the learners before and after exposure to the stories, the researchers found that the stories did have an impact.

Girls, for the most part, began to see themselves as capable of traditionally masculine tasks like caring for cows and sheep. This suggests that the stories challenged their earlier ideas about what activities were appropriate for each gender. Boys, on the other hand, were more consistent with traditional gender roles in their drawings. However, during discussions about their drawings, some boys expressed a willingness to do tasks typically seen as feminine. This hints at a potential change in attitudes even if their drawings reflected more traditional views.

There are possible reasons why girls might have been more open to adopting new ideas about gender roles. Social learning theory suggests that people are more likely to imitate behaviours of those they see as similar to themselves. The girls might have identified more closely with the female characters in the stories, making them more likely to want to be like them. Additionally, societal pressure might be stronger on boys to conform to traditional masculinity. This pressure could discourage them from trying out behaviours that go against gender stereotypes.

Interestingly, boys' career aspirations remained mostly focused on traditionally masculine careers like soldier or pilot. Their reasons for wanting these careers seemed to be about achieving status and respect in society. Girls, on the other hand, were more drawn to careers that allowed them to help others, like doctor or teacher. This aligns with what other researchers have found about how girls and boys tend to gravitate towards different career paths.

Overall, exposure to the gender-atypical stories appears to have the potential to challenge traditional gender roles, particularly for girls. While boys' actions still largely reflected stereotypes, their expressed willingness to do feminine tasks suggests a shift in attitudes. More research is needed to see how long-term exposure to these stories might influence behaviour and how societal pressures interact with these influences.

References

Abad, C., & Pruden, S. M. (2013). Do storybooks really break children's gender stereotypes? *Frontiers in Psychology, 4*, 986. https://doi.org/10.3389/fpsyg.2013.00986

African Union. (2015). *Agenda 2063: The Africa we want.* African Union.

Ambady, N., Shih, M., Kim, A., & Pittinsky, T. L. (2001). Stereotype susceptibility in children: Effects of identity activation on quantitative performance. *Psychological Science, 12*(5), 385–390.

Bakize, L. (2017). Gender balance struggles in Tanzanian Swahili children's literature. *Kiswahili, 78*(1). https://www.ajol.info/index.php/ksh/article/view/159397

Bandura, A. (1986). *Social foundations of thought and action: A social cognitive theory.* Prentice-Hall, Inc.

Bandura, A., Adams, N. E., & Beyer, J. (1977). Cognitive processes mediating behavioral change. *Journal of Personality and Social Psychology, 35*(3), 125–139.

Bender, D. L., & Leone, B. (1989). *Human sexuality: 1989 annual.* Greenhaven.

Bussey, K. (1983). A social-cognitive appraisal of sex-role development. *Australian Journal of Psychology, 35*(2), 135–143.

Bussey, K., & Bandura, A. (1992). Self-regulatory mechanisms governing gender development. *Child Development, 63*(5), 1236–1250.

Clarke, A. K., & Stermac, L. (2011). The influence of stereotypical beliefs, participant gender, and survivor weight on sexual assault response. *Journal of Interpersonal Violence, 26*(11), 2285–2302.

Derman-Sparks, L., & Edwards, J. O. (2010). *Anti-bias education for young children and ourselves.* National Association for the Education of Young Children.

Eccles, J. S. (1994). Understanding women's educational and occupational choices. *Psychology of Women Quarterly, 18*(4), 585–609.

Eisenberg, N., Fabes, R. A., & Murphy, B. C. (1996). Parents' reactions to children's negative emotions: Relations to children's social competence and comforting behavior. *Child Development, 67*(5), 2227–2247.

Ekiru, S. E. (2019). *Exploring the use of gender-atypical Kiswahili children's stories to address gender stereotyping among learners in a selected primary school in Trans-Nzoia County, Kenya* [Unpublished master's dissertation]. Moi University.

Evans, L., & Davies, K. (2000). No sissy boys here: A content analysis of the representation of masculinity in elementary school reading textbooks. *Sex Roles: A Journal of Research, 42*(3–4), 255–270.

Fagot, B. I. (1977). Consequences of moderate cross-gender behavior in preschool children. *Child Development, 48*(3), 902–907.

Fagot, B. I., & Leinbach, M. D. (1987). Socialization of sex roles within the family. In D. B. Carter (Ed.), *Current conceptions of sex roles and sex typing: Theory and research* (pp. 89–100). Praeger Publishers.

Floyd, C. A. (2012). *Gender depiction in preschool books: A comparison between early care and education classrooms in the United States and Norway.* [Doctoral dissertation, University of Denver]. Digital Commons @ DU. https://digitalcommons.du.edu/etd/203

Fox, M. (1993). Men who weep, boys who dance: The gender agenda between the lines in children's literature. *Language Arts, 70*(2), 84–88.

Golshirazian, S., Dhillon, M., Maltz, S., Payne, K. E., & Rabow, J. (2015). The effect of peer groups on gender identity and expression. *International Journal of Research in Humanities and Social Studies, 2*(10), 9–17.

Gooden, A. M., & Gooden, M. A. (2001). Gender representation in notable children's picture books: 1995–1999. *Sex Roles: A Journal of Research, 45*(1–2), 89–101.

Gottfredson, L. S. (1981). Circumscription and compromise: A developmental theory of occupational aspirations. *Journal of Counseling Psychology, 28*(6), 545–579.

Green, V. A., Bigler, R., & Catherwood, D. (2004). The variability and flexibility of gender-typed toy play: A close look at children's behavioral responses to counterstereotypic models. *Sex Roles: A Journal of Research, 51*(7–8), 371–386.

Gregg, C. H., & Dobson, K. (1980). Occupational sex role stereotyping and occupational interests in children. *Elementary School Guidance & Counseling, 15*(1), 66–75.

Islam, K. (2003). *Sungura Mjanja Mjanja*. Oxford University Press.

Kao, K.-Y., Rogers, A., Spitzmueller, C., Lin, M.-T., & Lin, C.-H. (2014). Who should serve as my mentor? The effects of mentor's gender and supervisory status on resilience in mentoring relationships. *Journal of Vocational Behavior, 85*(2), 191–203.

Karan, W. (2005). *Zawadi ya Rangi*. Phonex Publishers.

Karniol, R., & Gal-Disegni, M. (2009). The impact of gender-fair versus gender-stereotyped basal readers on 1st-grade children's gender stereotypes: A natural experiment. *Journal of Research in Childhood Education, 23*(4), 411–420.

Kohlberg, L. (1966). Moral education in the schools: A developmental view. *The School Review, 74*(1), 1–30.

Langlouis, J. H., & Downs, C. A. (1980). Mothers, fathers, and peers as socialization agents of sex-typed play behaviors in young children. *Child Development, 51*(4), 1237–1247.

Leaper, C. (2000). Gender, affiliation, assertion, and the interactive context of parent-child play. *Developmental Psychology, 36*(3), 381–393.

Levy, G. D., Sadovsky, A. L., & Troseth, G. L. (2000). Aspects of young children's perceptions of gender-typed occupations. *Sex Roles: A Journal of Research, 42*(11–12), 993–1006.

Lewela, M. (2008). *Kombo Arudi Shule*. East Africa Educational Publishers.

Liben, L. S., Bigler, R. S., & Krogh, H. R. (2001). Pink- and blue-collar jobs: Children's judgments of job status and job aspirations in relation to sex of worker. *Journal of Experimental Child Psychology, 79*(4), 346–363.

Mbuthia, D. E. M. (2018). The role of Kiswahili children's literature in formulating their worldview. *International Journal of Educational Research, 6*(2), 129–140.

McLeod, S. A. (2016). Albert Bandura's social learning theory. *SimplyPsychology*. http://www.simplypsychology.org/bandura.html.

Miller, D. (2013). *Reading in the wild: The book whisperer's keys to cultivating lifelong reading habits*. John Wiley & Sons.

Mitchell, C., De Lange, N., & Moletsane, R. (2017). *Participatory visual methodologies: Social change, community and policy*. SAGE Publications Ltd.

Mitchell, C., Theron, L., Stuart, J., Smith, A., & Campbell, Z. (2011). Drawings as research method. In L. Theron, C. Mitchell, A. Smith & J. Stuart (Eds.), *Picturing research: Drawing as visual methodology* (pp. 19–36). Sense Publishers.

Mogambi, H. (2006). *Vitendo vya Jamila*. Moran Publishers.

Morgan, L. A. (2008). Major matters: A comparison of the within-major gender pay gap across college majors for early-career graduates. *Industrial Relations: A Journal of Economy and Society, 47*(4), 625–650.

Mosley, J. (2004). Gender and daily life in Ethiopia. *Contemporary Review, 285*(1663), 97–101.

Mpesha, N. (2007). African children's literature: A bibliography. *CiNii Research.* https://cir.nii.ac.jp/crid/1130014171864914069

Mpesha, N. G. A. (1996). *Children's literature in Tanzania: A literary appreciation of its growth and development* (Publication No. 10091.A1M65) [Doctoral thesis, Kenyatta University]. DSpace. http://ir-library.ku.ac.ke/handle/123456789/13816

Muthara, K. K. (2012). Effect of free primary education on the enrolment of boys and girls in Kenya. *International Journal of Humanities and Social Science, 2*(16), 135–144.

Mutuku, Y. (2014). *Mama Mwizi.* Moran Publishers.

Mutunda, S. N. (2009). *Through a female lens: Aspects of masculinity in Francophone African women's writing* [Doctoral thesis, The University of Arizona]. UA Campus Repository. https://repository.arizona.edu/bitstream/handle/10150/194161/azu_etd_10646_sip1_m.pdf?sequence=1

Mwaba, K. (1992). Batswana children's career aspirations and views of sex roles. *The Journal of Social Psychology, 133*, 587–588. https://doi.org/10.1080/00224545.1993.9712187

Mwangi, W. (2009). *Atoke Asitoke?* Oxford University Press.

Ndege, P. O. (2009). *Colonialism and its legacies in Kenya* [Lecture]. Fulbright–Hays Group Project Abroad Program.

Neuville, E., & Croizet, J. C. (2007). Can salience of gender identity impair math performance among 7–8 years old girls? The moderating role of task difficulty. *European Journal of Psychology of Education, 22*(3), 307–316. https://psycnet.apa.org/doi/10.1007/BF03173428

Nhundu, T. J. (2007). Mitigating gender-typed occupational preferences of Zimbabwean primary school children: The use of biographical sketches and portrayals of female role models. *Sex Roles: A Journal of Research, 56*(9–10), 639–649.

Norwegian Ministry of Foreign Affairs. (2008). *Action plan for gender equity: St.meld. nr.11 (2007-2008).* På Like Vilkår: Kvinners.

Nyakeri, F. (2006). *Siku za Juma 1a.* Oxford University Press.

Onyango, J. O. (2007). Masculinities in Kiswahili children's literature in Kenya. *Swahili Forum, 14*(2007), 245–254.

Onyango, O. (2006). Dark shadow of masculinities and women emancipation agenda. *CODESRIA Bulletin: Special issue on the African woman*, 36–38.

Scott, K. P., & Feldman-Summers, S. (1979). Children's reactions to textbook stories in which females are portrayed in traditionally male roles. *Journal of Educational Psychology, 71*(3), 396–402. https://psycnet.apa.org/doi/10.1037/0022-0663.71.3.396

Shenouda, C. K., & Danovitch, J. H. (2013). Does a male nurse know about football? American and Egyptian children's understanding of gender and expertise. *Journal of Cognition and Culture, 13*(3–4), 231–254.

Singh, R. (1998). *Gender autonomy in Western Europe.* Springer.

Tabassum, N., & Nayak, B. S. (2021). Gender stereotypes and their impact on women's career progressions from a managerial perspective. *IIM Kozhikode Society & Management Review, 10*(2), 192–208. https://doi.org/10.1177/2277975220975513

Thorne, B. (1993). *Gender play: Girls and boys in school.* Rutgers University Press.

Toçi, A., & Aliu, M. (2013). Gender stereotypes in current children's English books used in elementary schools in the Republic of Macedonia. *American International Journal of Contemporary Research, 3*(12), 32–38.

Trepanier-Street, M. L., & Romatowski, J. A. (1999). The influence of children's literature on gender role perceptions: A reexamination. *Early Childhood Education Journal, 26*(3), 155–159.

Walibora, K. (2013). *Furaha ya Arope.* Oxford University Press.

Wanjeri, M. M. (2006). *Language and gender: Male domination among the Kikuyu of Kenya, East Africa* [Unpublished student thesis]. Karlstad University. Digital Vetenskapliga Arkivet. http://www.diva-portal.org/smash/record.jsf?pid=diva2%3A5920&dswid=6087

Wilbourn, M. P., & Kee, D. W. (2010). Henry the nurse is a doctor too: Implicitly examining children's gender stereotypes for male and female occupational roles. *Sex Roles: A Journal of Research, 62*(9–10), 670–683.

Zawadi, R. (2013). *Tuzo ya Baba*. Queenex Publisher Limited.

CHAPTER 13

A 'play way' method for developing digital literacy among pupils in primary schools in Nandi sub-county, Kenya

Sarah Jemutai

Introduction

Play has been recognised as a fundamental factor in early learning and its implications for subsequent academic achievement. As such, play has gained global awareness and prominence (Ansari et al., 2019). A report by UNICEF underscored the significant role of play in a child's learning process, emphasising that play enables learners to engage in day-to-day activities, paving the way for learning (UNICEF, 2018). According to Donald et al. (2010, p. 53), "development does not just happen to pupils. It is also based on their active engagement with and exploration of their physical and social world". Thus, through play, pupils learn to engage analytically with each other's ideas (Ansari et al., 2019; Lipsey et al., 2018). Play also contributes to the development of various domains, including cognitive, intellectual, linguistic, physical, socio-emotional, creative, and visual perception (Jemutai & Webb, 2019; Smith & Pellegrini, 2013). Furthermore, play is directly related to children's development, as it promotes the acquisition of pre-academic skills necessary for early education and academic achievement (Whitebread et al., 2017). Its connection to early literacy and numeracy acquisition, as well as later academic achievement, has gained widespread recognition (Whitebread et al., 2017).

Play actively encourages the acquisition of a wide range of knowledge and abilities, such as verbalization, vocabulary development, language comprehension, attention span, creativity, focus, impulse management, visuo-spatial abilities, scepticism, problem-solving techniques, collaboration, compassion, and cooperation (NAEYC, 2020; Jemutai & Webb, 2019; Hassinger-Das et al., 2017; Whitebread et al., 2017; Linder et al., 2011; Kimbell-Lopez et al., 2016; Nath & Szücs, 2014). While substantial evidence exists regarding learning through play, there is a relative dearth of evidence on teaching digital literacy through play. This study aims to explore the utilization of play-based approaches using tablets provided by the Government of Kenya, as a teaching strategy to enhance digital literacy. The government's expectation is to integrate digital literacy into teaching and learning starting from Grade 1 (Republic of Kenya, 2017, as cited in Kerkhoff & Makubuya, 2021).

In this context, the study employs play as a means to develop digital literacy in order to meet the expectations of a competency-based curriculum. Play is recognised as an engaging way for learners to acquire and display their potential and cognitive development (Piaget, 1962; Vygotsky, 1978). Play is a universal phenomenon, deeply rooted in children's development (Csikszentmihalyi, 1990; Smith & Pellegrini, 2013). The United Nations Convention on the Rights of the Child (1989) acknowledges play as a fundamental right of children. The International Play Association (2016) recognises play as a recreational activity inherent in children's lives. Play is a serious, thought-provoking process that encompasses aspects of knowledge, growth, and advancement (Gauntlett et al., 2010).

Digital play, according to Salonius-Pasternak and Gelfond (2005), represents a fundamentally distinct type of learning. Digital play is important as it offers interactive and engaging experiences, providing immediate feedback to reinforce concepts. Its adaptability tailors learning to individual needs, while fostering collaboration and social interaction. Simulations allow for real-world application in a safe environment, and intrinsic motivation is enhanced through game elements like rewards and competition. Digital play employs multimodal learning, incorporating various media types, and offers continuous learning opportunities beyond traditional settings. It possesses specific qualities that can be cultivated, such as promoting the discovery of passions, collaboration, independence, motivation, sincere praise, autonomy, patience, respect, choice, and decision-making. When used effectively, play opens up new avenues for research and discovery, providing a unique approach to learning (Mudra, 2020).

Play and digital literacy: A path to enhancing learning

The integration of information and communication technology (ICT) in education and training is essential for enhancing learning experiences. It provides innovative methods for teaching and learning, promotes student engagement, and fosters critical thinking skills. Moreover, ICT can help bridge educational gaps and ensure access to quality education for all students. By incorporating technology into the curriculum, educators can create more dynamic and interactive learning environments that cater to diverse learning needs (Ministry of Education, Kenya, 2021). Despite the acknowledgement of digital literacy's importance, there is limited knowledge about the development of digital literacy skills in primary schools (Kennedy et al., 2012; Kerkhoff & Makubuya, 2021). What is known is that digital literacy enhances the effectiveness of instruction, improve learning outcomes, self-efficacy, and learner capabilities (Aslan, 2021; Erwin & Mohammed, 2022), making it a critical component of contemporary education.

However, a notable gap exists in understanding how teachers and educational institutions are expected to actively integrate digital literacy into their teaching methods. Given these considerations, it becomes evident that educational institutions should incorporate digital literacy tools and resources into their teaching practices for learners to thrive in the digital era. In alignment with this vision, Ntorukiri et al. (2022) assert that every learning institution, teacher, and learner should be equipped with the necessary digital skills and relevant infrastructure. Nevertheless, the integration of digital literacy into the Kenyan school curriculum presents challenges, as only a fraction of students has access to digital devices. This study explores a specific approach to the integration of digital literacy through digital play activities, with a focus on perceptions, experiences, skills development, and challenges faced by teachers and learners.

The primary school syllabus in Kenya proposes the development of digital literacy competence, with teachers taking the lead in utilizing technology to emphasise specific concepts during teaching. For instance, in Grade 1, where digital literacy is supposed to commence, there are programmes installed in digital devices covering subjects such as mathematics, English, Kiswahili, science, and social studies for both Grades 1 and 2, along with different play programmes. Although these learning areas contain topics that can be effectively taught electronically, school visits suggest that in schools that have been provided with computers by the Kenyan Education Ministry, teachers have been slow to embrace technology for teaching and learning.

The incorporation of digital literacy into classrooms is believed to offer numerous benefits for students. It promotes individual-centred learning, allowing students to choose, organize, and assess information, while also providing easy access to electronic information and concept comprehension (Mudra, 2020). Furthermore, digital literacy enhances the effectiveness of instruction and learning and enhances learning outcomes and learner competences (Buabeng-Andoh, 2012). Consequently, digital literacy is indispensable for contemporary teaching and learning.

The use of computers in small groups fosters collaboration and teamwork, enhancing peer relationships (Freeman & Somerindyke, 2001). Tablets empower learners, allowing them to perform tasks autonomously and make choices. Pupils view these devices as under their control, offering a safe space for learning, free from criticism. Tablets encourage pupils to inspect their achievements, receive immediate feedback, and build independence (Bolstad, 2004; Anderson, 1997). In this approach, learners' autonomy and independence are increased, and they gain the ability to evaluate their accomplishments immediately. For teachers to guide learners effectively in this digital environment, they must be well-versed in digital media.

The integration of digital play activities into teaching practices offers a promising approach to accelerating the implementation of digital literacy in primary schools. This study aims to explore the perceptions, experiences, and skills development associated with this approach, shedding light on the challenges faced by both teachers and learners. The digital era requires educators to embrace innovative teaching methods that utilize digital resources and technologies, ultimately equipping pupils with the digital skills needed for the future.

The intervention used in this study

The 'play way' approach, often referred to as 'play-based learning' or 'learning through play,' is an educational method that promotes the use of playful activities, games, and hands-on experiences as a primary way to teach various subjects (Hirsh-Pasek et al., 2009). This approach is particularly popular in early childhood education, where young learners engage in activities that resemble play but are designed to foster the development of skills and concepts in a fun and interactive manner (Clements & Sarama, 2008).

This study focused on digital literacy using 'play way' mathematical and language games that are available to the participating schools. Play way is based on the idea that children learn best through direct experiences. It emphasises active engagement and interaction with mathematical concepts and language competence rather than rote memorization (Dewey, 1938).

In the context of this study, play-based learning used interactive computer-based activities games, puzzles, and playful activities that present learning as fun (Benesch, 2010) while requiring digital literacy. The play approach is child-centred, meaning that it tailors learning activities to the interests and developmental level of each child (Vygotsky, 1978). Play-based learning also helps children develop social and emotional skills, such as cooperation, communication, problem-solving, and perseverance (Bodrova & Leong, 2007), skills that promote digital learning.

While the play way approach has been shown to be effective in promoting a deep and lasting understanding of mathematical concepts, it has not been used to explore children's natural curiosity in terms of fostering digital literacy. It is for this reason that a digital play way approach was used to explore the development of digital literacy.

Research design and methods

This study employed a case study research design, which incorporates multiple data collection methods. Data were gathered through interviews, observations, and teacher reflective journals. The researcher conducted classroom observations to examine how digital literacy was promoted within the classroom. This approach aimed to analyse and describe the events, actions, pupil activities and institutional strategies (Thomas, 2011; Yin, 2014) while providing an understanding of specific occurrences (Yin, 2018; Rashid et al., 2019). The hermeneutic tradition of research, emphasising viewing situations through participants' perspectives, was widely followed in this case study (Cohen et al., 2018).

The objectives of this study were to examine the classroom promotion of digital skills, observe teachers' and pupils' engagement in digital play, gather teachers' experiences with digital devices, and record their views on digital play within reflective journals. A case study design offers the advantage of exploring how various elements influence a specific phenomenon (Hyett et al., 2014), providing detailed insights into the experiences of participants (Aggarwal et al., 2019). However, case studies are often criticised for their reliance on specific cases, limiting generalisability (Hyett et al., 2014; Cohen et al., 2018).

Nonetheless, in the context of technology-based cases, such as the one in this study, the emphasis is on understanding how technology can be used to transform education practices (Kozma & Anderson, 2002). The aim is not to generalise but to gain an in-depth understanding of the situation under study to improve teaching methods and teacher training. Although generalisation is challenging in case studies, the results are relevant to the specific case and other similar contexts.

The study included participants from various schools, which allows for cross-case verification and the identification of variations or inconsistencies related to specific aspects (Yin, 2014; 2018). The study was a single case study that aimed to explore play-based strategies for developing digital literacy in primary schools and the challenges faced in developing digital literacy through this method.

Sample and setting

The research was conducted in the peri-urban Mutwot zone of the Chesumei constituencies near Eldoret, located in Nandi County, Kenya. Twelve public schools were selected for the study due to their geographic proximity to one another, which facilitated the researcher's movement within the area. Importantly, initial investigations showed that the promotion of digital literacy in teaching and learning was relatively limited in this region, making it a suitable context for investigation.

The decision to work with a small sample size in this qualitative research was deliberate, as it enables a more in-depth exploration of the primary concept or phenomenon under study (Creswell & Creswell, 2018). Moreover, this particular study area was chosen to optimise the efficient use of time and available human resources. It is noteworthy that research of this nature had not been previously conducted in Nandi County.

As noted earlier, the study encompassed 12 public primary schools in Nandi County, including one officer responsible for quality assurance at the sub-county level, the head teachers at these schools, 24 Grade 1 teachers and a total of 480 pupils. The selection of Grade 1 teachers was purposive, focusing on existing classes and ensuring that the chosen population was reliable for the research (Campbell et al., 2020). To protect the privacy and anonymity of the schools and individuals involved, pseudonyms were assigned to the selected schools, and the teachers' names were not disclosed. All Grade 1 pupils from the participating schools were considered for inclusion in the study and all volunteered to be part of the process. All of the participating schools were equipped with functional computer laboratories and had received government-provided tablets.

The intervention

The participating schools were visited, the study was introduced to the school principals, and letters of introduction and permission to conduct the study were handed to them. The Grade 1 teachers were informed about the research and the digital play activities and invited to participate in the intervention that they would be expected to conduct in their classrooms.

All of the Grade 1 teachers who were invited volunteered to participate (none refused) and were introduced to the objectives of the study and the research instruments that the researcher would use as part of the research process. They then underwent a one-day training session on the play way method using the tablets and activities on them at their disposal. To introduce the concept of digital guided play, all the participating Grade 1 teachers were trained to use the available tablets in the schools. School tablets featuring play programmes were utilized during the study to explore the impact of this teaching approach on digital literacy development.

The school administrators provided access to the tablets that were gathering dust in the cupboards. Some of the teachers had not switched on a tablet before. The devices were brought to a classroom/laboratory and charged. Once the tablets were charged, the group was guided through activities to be able to guide their pupils, including switching on and shutting down, how to get to the plays installed and how to search for a game on the search bar. After the teachers had fully familiarized themselves with the tablets, they began play activities with the children in class.

Together the researcher and the Grade 1 teachers created a scheduled timetable for digital play activities. The schools that retained afternoon remedial work time used these sessions for digital play, while other schools used one lesson per week for the intervention for a period of four months (August to November 2021). These interventions were scheduled into a regular timetable, with some schools incorporating digital play during afternoon remedial sessions and others dedicating one English lesson per week to the intervention.

Data collection procedure

Classroom observations were conducted, and open-ended field notes were recorded during visits and transcribed. Observations focused on how pupils followed instructions, completed tasks, sought clarification when needed, and shared ideas with classmates. These observations provided first-hand data from within naturally occurring social settings.

Additionally, semi-structured interviews were conducted with teachers, the officer responsible for quality assurance at the sub-county level, the head teachers at these schools, to gather data on how digital play activities were conducted. Interviews offered insights that could not be obtained through observations alone. Open-ended questions were used to enable participants to express their views and experiences without researcher bias. Teacher reflective journals were also used to capture the teachers' thoughts, feelings, experiences, and challenges regarding computer use.

Data analysis

Data from all sources were transcribed, coded, and categorised into themes. The coding process utilized participants' or researchers' exact words to create phrases (Creswell & Plano, 2011). Teacher reflective journals were also analysed, and themes were developed from them. Data collection and analysis were concurrent, with each phase building on the other in this qualitative study. The researcher used thematic analysis to organize the data systematically, identify recurring patterns, and produce meaningful, in-depth analyses (Watts, 2014). Thematic analysis was chosen for its flexibility, capacity to handle complex and extensive data, and emphasis on understanding participants' perspectives.

Ethical considerations

Prior to the commencement of data collection, the researcher visited the participating schools to engage in discussions with school principals and Grade 1 teachers. These discussions covered the study's objectives, research design, and methodology. It was made clear to the teachers that their participation in the study was entirely voluntary, and they were assured that the information they provided would be used solely for the purpose of this research.

To ensure ethical standards and informed consent, both teachers and parents of the learners involved in the study were required to sign consent forms. This step helped to ensure that all participants, including the children, had their rights and privacy respected. Throughout the study, the anonymity of the participants was rigorously maintained. Their identities and personal information were kept confidential to protect their privacy and rights.

This research was conducted with the necessary ethics approval from the National Commission for Science, Technology, and Innovation (NACOSTI), which permitted the researcher to conduct the research within the school setting. Ethics approval ensures that research is conducted in an ethical and responsible manner, upholding the rights and well-being of the participants.

Results

Qualitative data were obtained from the journal reflection sheets, observation schedule, and semi-structured interviews.

"This is a different form of play where the children use the tablets to play. They share ideas together and play together in turns in a collaborative manner. Pupils learn to search and scroll. What pleased me the most is the fact that learners enjoyed the play sessions so much and they were very cooperative and enthusiastic every time I entered the classroom! This method led to collaborative learning and enjoyment on the side of the learners."

Quotes such as the one above represent the type of data generated by teachers. Commentary like this resonates with other findings that, during play, pupils became engaged actors, aligning with the expectations of educators (Fluck et al., 2020). The integration of digital play into the learning process empowers students, contributing to their development as conscientious and compassionate individuals (Abu Zahra, 2020).

More examples of teachers' responses to the play way method can be found in the author's doctoral thesis on the topic and her paper on teachers' perceptions of the 'play way' method (Jemutai et al., 2023).

Themes were derived from the study findings related to three objectives: teachers' perceptions of play-based strategies for developing digital literacy in primary schools, primary school children's digital literacy competencies demonstrated through play-based learning, and the challenges faced in developing digital literacy through this method.

The findings highlight three key themes in response to teachers' perceptions of play-based learning strategies for developing digital literacy:

- Participants in this study perceived play-based learning as a means for learners to acquire digital skills through enjoyable interactions with digital devices. This approach is believed to lead to knowledge creation (Erwin & Mohammed, 2022).
- Teachers regarded digital play as a child-centred method that placed pupils at the core of the educational process. This is seen to be a departure from traditional teaching methods, fostering high levels of learner motivation (Mudra, 2020).
- The teachers felt that their role had been transformed into that of a facilitator of the learning process. Many researchers note that this method challenges existing educational beliefs and emphasise the influence of educators' ideas on their professional decisions (Rubach & Lazarides, 2021).

The second objective of the study aimed to examine primary school children's digital literacy competencies demonstrated as they went through the play-based learning strategy. The resulting themes are presented in Figure 1. This figure reveals a theme around manipulating the tablet menu leading to better navigation of the activities. A second theme developed around finding digital content which included improvement in search and reading skills. A third theme included booting up the devices and the ability to switch on and shut down the devices safely, with the third theme highlighting the use of icons and search engines, in other words developing an understanding of computer language usage.

Figure 1: *Primary School Digital Literacy Competencies as Developed through the 'Play Way' Process*

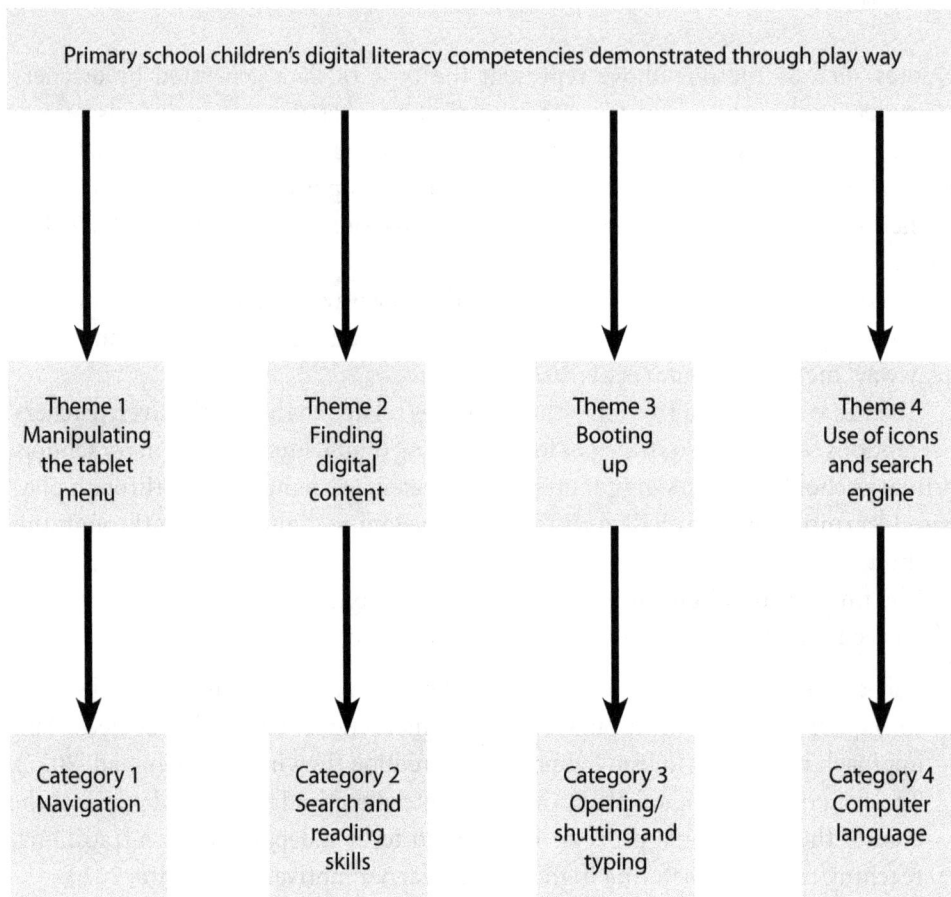

Primary school children's digital literacy competencies demonstrated through play way

| Theme 1 Manipulating the tablet menu | Theme 2 Finding digital content | Theme 3 Booting up | Theme 4 Use of icons and search engine |

| Category 1 Navigation | Category 2 Search and reading skills | Category 3 Opening/ shutting and typing | Category 4 Computer language |

Source: Jemutai et al. (2023)

Four major themes of the challenges faced by teachers in developing digital literacy through play-based methods were:

- Improper storage and handling led to some tablets malfunctioning.
- Schools received digital resources without clear usage guidelines and limited administrative support (Kristiawan & Muhaimin, 2019).
- Pupils initially lacked confidence in using tablets.
- The curriculum did not allocate time for teaching digital literacy, leading to its neglect.

Based on these findings, the researcher devised a model that connects play-based learning strategies with the development of digital literacy competencies among primary schools learners (Figure 2).

Figure 2: *Pupils' Digital Play Model for Digital Literacy Development*

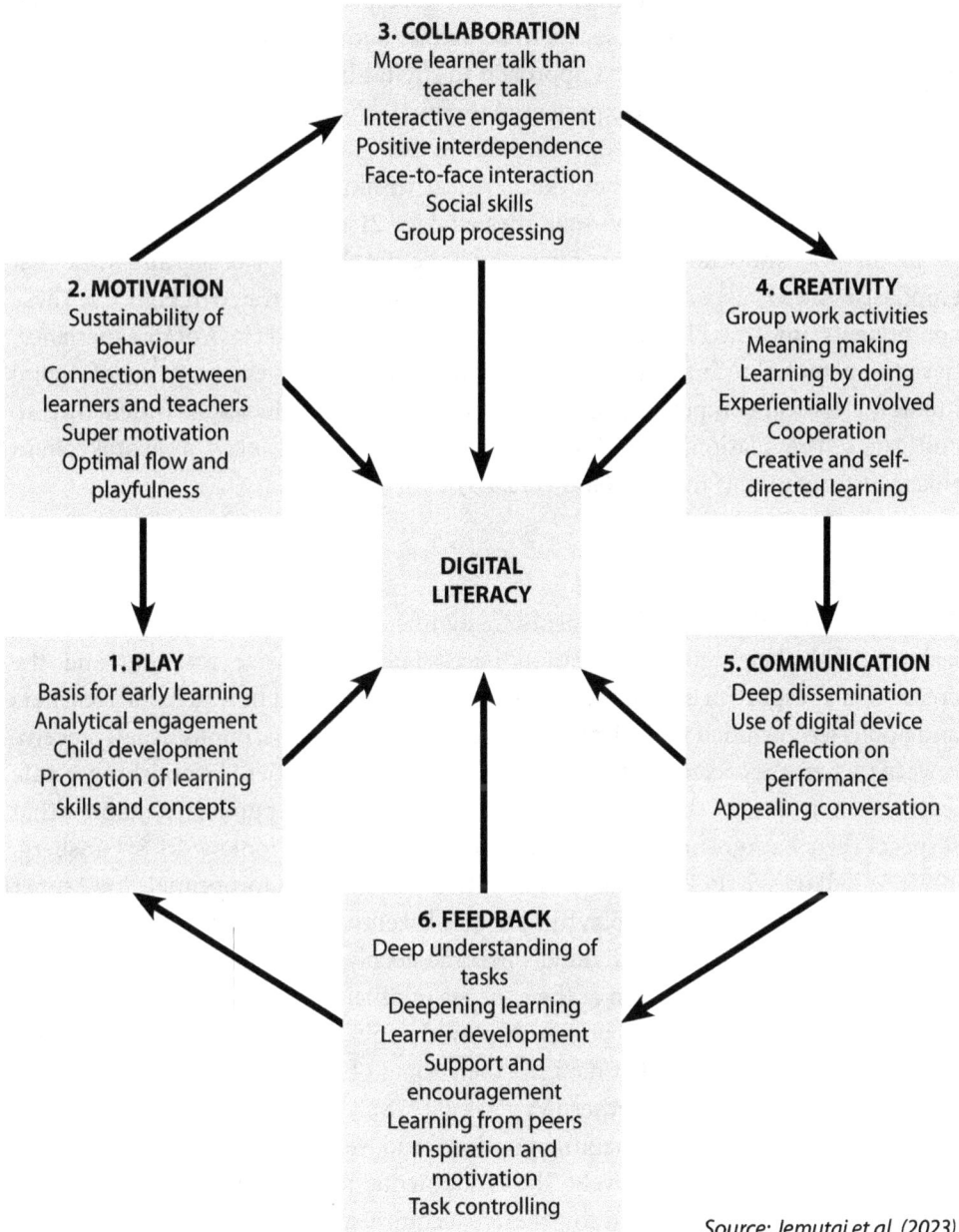

3. COLLABORATION
More learner talk than teacher talk
Interactive engagement
Positive interdependence
Face-to-face interaction
Social skills
Group processing

2. MOTIVATION
Sustainability of behaviour
Connection between learners and teachers
Super motivation
Optimal flow and playfulness

4. CREATIVITY
Group work activities
Meaning making
Learning by doing
Experientially involved
Cooperation
Creative and self-directed learning

DIGITAL LITERACY

1. PLAY
Basis for early learning
Analytical engagement
Child development
Promotion of learning skills and concepts

5. COMMUNICATION
Deep dissemination
Use of digital device
Reflection on performance
Appealing conversation

6. FEEDBACK
Deep understanding of tasks
Deepening learning
Learner development
Support and encouragement
Learning from peers
Inspiration and motivation
Task controlling

Source: Jemutai et al. (2023)

This model, called the 'pupils' digital play model for digital literacy development', positions the learner at the centre of the learning process, a departure from models that predominantly focus on the teacher's role. Moreover, this model underscores the essential role of hands-on, experiential learning in technology acquisition (Sefton-Green et al., 2016).

As digital literacy remains a critical challenge, especially in the field of education, the pupils' digital play model seems to be able to address some of these challenges by promoting a learner-centred approach to digital literacy. This model shifts the focus from memorization to experiential learning, challenging pupils and teaching them how to acquire knowledge through active participation in class. A move aimed at fostering peer collaboration, critical thinking, leadership, digital skills, communication, and creativity—qualities vital for 21st-century learning.

In this way the study may contribute to the development of a framework that emphasises six key aspects of teaching digital literacy, as illustrated in Figure 2. These components, informed by literature, case study analysis, and classroom experience, have the potential to inform basic education and enhance the acquisition of digital literacy, a critical competency for the 21st century. Basic education, which aims to cultivate self-regulation, self-criticism, and goal attainment, plays a pivotal role in this transformation (Jansen & Grance, 2011).

Discussion

The pupils' digital play model appears to significantly enhance motivation among learners. This heightened motivation necessitates responsive teaching and the creation of a respectful and supportive learning environment in which both teachers and pupils feel included in the learning process. As part of this, pupils usually receive rewards when they excel in their digital play-based activities. Establishing a safe learning environment through teachers engaging with their pupils in a manner that respects their backgrounds, viewpoints, and skill levels (Wlodkowski & Ginsberg, 1995; Wlodkowski, 1999) leads to motivation which leads to optimal flow, super motivation, ideal flow, and playfulness (Csikszentmihalyi, 1990). Optimal flow refers to the state in which individuals become deeply absorbed in a task, finding it pleasurable and engaging, even at the expense of other activities.

During this intervention, pupils displayed high levels of collaboration, with participants helping each other navigate their zones of proximal development (ZPD) as they learned and grew together (Vygotsky, 1978). Group activities on the tablets provided a creative context, enabling pupils to read, search, navigate, discuss, share, and solve problems collaboratively. The fundamental tenet of the pupils' digital play model is that pupils are guided to generate, acquire, and apply knowledge through engaging activities, sparking their curiosity and encouraging deep thought. When teachers facilitate this process, pupils evolve into active evaluators of their own learning.

The play-based approach also appeared to sharpen communication skills as it fostered engaging conversations that unveiled hidden thoughts and ideas within each individual's mind. Furthermore, feedback was provided involving constructive criticism during or after a thorough examination of the pupils' work on the tablets. Pupils had opportunities to express their tacit knowledge, experiences, triumphs, and aspirations within groups or in front of the entire class. Feedback is a powerful tool for promoting deep understanding of tasks, focusing on the learning objectives and success criteria. The teachers played a supportive role, viewing pupils as individuals who need guidance to progress. When peers are seen as valuable sources of knowledge, learners are more likely to seek assistance from one another.

Vygotsky's (1978) insights into the role of play as a leading activity in cognitive and imaginative development was evident, as the children interacted with content in an enjoyable and constructive way (Rahman & Yunus, 2020). Teachers' perceptions of the digital play strategy revealed that they understood that information can be found not only in books but also in digital devices, where knowledge can be imparted in an enjoyable manner. This perspective aligns with Rahman and Yunus (2020), who emphasise that the implementers of an activity are the beneficiaries when the activity is performed. As such, the 'play way' intervention might be seen to an extent as a teacher development programme.

The fact that the Grade 1 pupils appeared to benefit from technology by playing on their tablets supports Tan's (2019) notion that a computer serves as a mind-extension cognitive tool, with learners contributing intelligence (Erbas et al., 2021). Active participation, such as successfully using icons, signified that learning took place, and that it evolved into a process of active construction of content and concepts (Jonassen, 2002; Sailin & Mahmor, 2018). The digital play learning strategy also promoted interactions between pupils as well as between pupils and the teachers (Sabiri, 2020).

Conclusion and recommendations

In conclusion, this study underscores the effectiveness of the play-based method of learning as a catalyst for the development of digital literacy skills among primary school pupils. This approach, characterised by its child-centred and hands-on nature, should contribute to the acquisition of digital literacy competencies. However, a notable challenge to this goal is the inadequate supply of digital devices in many schools in Kenya and the absence of a comprehensive integration strategy for digital content in school curricula.

Based on the findings of this study, the following recommendations can be made:

- Teachers should be encouraged to embrace digital play strategies. The pupils' digital play model proposed in this study could help attain this goal. This model, designed to enhance the acquisition of digital literacy competencies, positions learners at the centre of the learning process. By implementing this model, educators can foster a more interactive and engaging digital learning environment.
- The consistent supply of digital devices to schools should be prioritized and curricula should provide more focus on the integration of a wide range of digital content for educational purposes. By providing a diverse and comprehensive array of digital resources, teachers will be more inclined to incorporate technology into their teaching methods.
- Curriculum designers should consider allocating time within curriculum designs specifically dedicated to teaching digital skills. Including digital literacy as an integrated subject will ensure that the development of these skills is prioritized and formally recognised within the educational framework.

By implementing these recommendations, educators, policymakers, and curriculum designers could work together to foster a more technologically proficient generation of learners. This, in turn, will better equip students to meet the challenges of the digital age, promoting digital literacy as a core competency in the 21st century.

References

Abu Zahra, H. (2020). *The management of digital technology towards equipping students with 21st century skills: Its implementation in lower primary pedagogy* [Unpublished doctoral dissertation]. The British University in Dubai (BUiD).

Aggarwal, R., & Ranganathan, P. (2019). Study designs: Part 2 – Descriptive studies. *Perspectives in Clinical Research, 10*(1), 34–36. https://doi.org/10.4103/picr.PICR_154_18

Anderson, H. (1997). *Conversation, language, and possibilities: A postmodern approach to therapy.* Basic Books.

Ansari, A., Pianta, R. C., Whittaker, J. V., Vitiello, V. E., & Ruzek, E. A. (2019). Starting early: The benefits of attending early childhood education programs at age 3. *American Educational Research Journal, 56*(4), 1495–1523.

Aslan, S. (2021). Analysis of digital literacy self-efficacy levels of pre-service teachers. *International Journal of Technology in Education (IJTE), 4*(1), 57–67. https://doi.org/10.46328/ijte.47

Benesch, J. (2010). Mathematics through play in the early years. In A. Anning, J. Cullen, & M. Fleer (Eds.), *Early childhood education: Society and culture* (2nd ed., pp. 93–106). SAGE Publications.

Bodrova, E., & Leong, D. J. (2007). *Tools of the mind: The Vygotskian approach to early childhood education* (2nd ed.). Pearson.

Bolstad, R. (2004). *The role and potential of ICT in early childhood education: A review of New Zealand and international literature* – Prepared for the Ministry of Education. Ministry of Education, New Zealand.

Buabeng-Andoh, C. (2012). Factors influencing teachers' adoption and integration of information and communication technology into teaching: A review of the literature. *International*

Journal of Education and Development using Information and Communication Technology (IJEDICT), 8, 136–155.

Campbell, S., Greenwood, M., Prior, S., Shearer, T., Walkem, K., Young, S., Bywaters, D., & Walker, K. (2020). Purposive sampling: Complex or simple? Research case examples. *Journal of Research in Nursing, 25*(8), 652–661. https://journals.sagepub.com/doi/10.1177/1744987120927206

Clements, D. H., & Sarama, J. (2008). Experimental evaluation of the effects of a research-based preschool mathematics curriculum. *American Educational Research Journal, 45*(2), 443–494.

Cohen, L., Manion, L., & Morrison, K. (2018). *Research methods in education* (8th ed.). Routledge. https://doi.org/10.4324/9781315456539

Creswell, J. W., & Creswell, J. D. (2018). *Research design: Qualitative, quantitative, and mixed methods approaches.* Sage.

Creswell, J. W., & Plano Clark, V. L. (2011). *Designing and conducting mixed methods research* (2nd ed.). Sage Publications.

Csikszentmihalyi, M. (1990). *Flow: The psychology of optimal experience.* Harper & Row.

Dewey, J. (1938). *Experience and education.* Kappa Delta Pi.

Donald, D., Lazarus, S., & Lolwana, P. (2010). *Educational psychology in social context.* Oxford University Press.

Erbas, İ., Çipuri, R., & Joni, A. (2021). The impact of technology on teaching and teaching English to elementary school students. *Linguistics and Culture Review, 5*(S3), 1316–1336.

Erwin, K., & Mohammed, S. (2022). Digital literacy skills instruction and increased skills proficiency. *International Journal of Technology in Education and Science (IJTES), 6*(2), 323–332. https://doi.org/10.46328/ijtes.364

Fluck, A. E., Ranmuthugala, D., Chin, C. K. H., Penesis, I., Chong, J., Yang, Y., & Ghous, A. (2020). Transforming learning with computers: Calculus for kids. *Education and Information Technologies, 25*(5), 3779–3796.

Freeman, N. K., & Somerindyke, J. (2001). Social play at the computer: Preschoolers scaffold and support peers' computer competence. *Information Technology in Childhood Education Annual, 12,* 203–213.

Gauntlett, D., Ackermann, E., Whitebread, D., Wolbers, T., & Wekstrom, C. (2010). *The future of play.* LEGO Learning Institute.

Hassinger-Das, B., Toub, T. S., Zosh, J. M., Michnick, J., Golinkoff, R., & Hirsh-Pasek, K. (2017). More than just fun: A place for games in playful learning. *Infancia y Aprendizaje: Journal for the Study of Education and Development, 40*(2), 191–218.

Hirsh-Pasek, K., Golinkoff, R. M., Berk, L. E., & Singer, D. G. (2009). *A mandate for playful learning in preschool: Presenting the evidence.* Oxford University Press.

Hyett, N., Kenny, A., & Dickson-Swift, V. (2014). Methodology or method? A critical review of qualitative case study reports. *International Journal of Qualitative Studies on Health and Well-Being, 9,* 23606. https://doi.org/10.3402/qhw.v9.23606

International Play Association. (2016). *Children's right to play and the environment: A discussion paper prepared for the UN Committee on the Rights of the Child Day of General Discussion.* International Play Association: Promoting the Child's Right to Play. chrome-extension://efaidnbmnnnibpcajpcglclefindmkaj/https://ipaworld.org/wp-content/uploads/2016/05/IPA-Play-Environment-Discussion-Paper.pdf

Jansen, W., & Grance, T. (2011). Guidelines on security and privacy in public cloud computing. *NIST Technical Report-SP-800-144.*

Jemutai, S., Kemboi, M., & Nabwire, V. (2023). Teachers' perceptions of play way strategies of learning in developing digital literacy among pupils in primary school. *European Journal of Education Studies, 10*(11). https://doi.org/10.46827/ejes.v10i11.5090

Jemutai, S., & Webb, P. (2019). Effects of a 6 Brick Duplo block guided play intervention on pre-literate learners' visual perception. *South African Journal of Childhood Education, 9*(1), a634. https://doi.org/10.4102/sajce.v9i1.634

Jonassen, D. H. (2002). Engaging and supporting problem solving in online learning. *Quarterly Review of Distance Education, 3*, 1–13.

Kennedy, E. L., Greene, J., & Cameron, R. J. (2012). Transitions in the early years: Educational and child psychologists working to reduce the impact of school culture shock. *Educational and Child Psychology, 29*(1), 19–31.

Kerkhoff, S., & Makubuya, T. (2021). Professional development on digital literacy and transformative teaching in a low-income country: A case study of rural Kenya. *Reading Research Quarterly, 57*(1), 287–305.

Kimbell-Lopez, K., Manning, E., & Cummins, C. (2016). Developing digital literacy in the middle school classroom. *Computers in the Schools, 33*(4), 211–226.

Kozma, R., & Anderson, R. E. (2002). Qualitative case studies of innovative pedagogical practices using ICT. *Journal of Computer Assisted Learning, 18*, 387–394.

Kristiawan, M., & Muhaimin, M. (2019). Teachers' obstacles in utilizing information and communication technology. *International Journal of Educational Review, 1*(2), 56–61.

Linder, S. M., Powers-Costello, B., & Stegelin, D. A. (2011). Mathematics in early childhood: Research-based rationale and practical strategies. *Early Childhood Education Journal, 39*(1), 29–37.

Lipsey, M. W., Farran, D. C., & Durkin, K. (2018). Effects of the Tennessee Prekindergarten Program on children's achievement and behavior through third grade. *Early Childhood Research Quarterly, 45*, 155–176. https://doi.org/10.1016/j.ecresq.2018.03.005

Ministry of Education, Kenya. (2021). *Information and communication technology in education and training.* Ministry of Education.

Mudra, H. (2020). Digital literacy among young learners: How do EFL teachers and learners view its benefits and barriers? *Teaching English with Technology, 20*(3), 3–24.

NAEYC. (2020). *Developmentally appropriate practice (DAP) position statement.* NAEYC. www.naeyc.org/resources/position-statements/dap

Nath, S., & Szücs, D. (2014). Construction play and cognitive skills associated with the development of mathematical abilities in 7-year-old children. *Learning and Instruction, 32*, 73–80.

Ntorukiri, T. B., Chun, X., & Boudouaia, A. (2022). Influence of teachers' competencies on ICT implementation in Kenyan universities. *Education Research International, 2022*(3), 1–11.

Piaget, J. (1962). The stages of the intellectual development of the child. *Bulletin of the Menninger Clinic, 26*(3), 120–128.

Rahman, Q., & Yunus, T. (2020). Role of students learning through education technology in the communication process. *Journal of Education and Development, 10*(20), 56–68.

Rashid, Y., Rashid, A., Warraich, M. A., Sabir, S. S., & Waseem, A. (2019). Case study method: A step-by-step guide for business researchers. *International Journal of Qualitative Methods, 18*. https://doi.org/10.1177/1609406919862424

Rubach, C., & Lazarides, R. (2021). Addressing 21st-century digital skills in schools: Development and validation of an instrument to measure teachers' basic ICT competence beliefs. *Computers in Human Behavior, 118*(1). https://doi.org/10.1016/j.chb.2020.106636

Sabiri, K. A. (2020). ICT in EFL teaching and learning: A systematic literature review. *Contemporary Educational Technology, 11*(2), 177–195.

Sailin, S. N., & Mahmor, N. A. (2018). Improving student teachers' digital pedagogy through meaningful learning activities. *Malaysian Journal of Learning and Instruction, 15*(2), 143–173.

Salonius-Pasternak, D. E., & Gelfond, H. S. (2005). The next level of research on electronic play: Potential benefits and contextual influences for children and adolescents. *Human Technology, 1*(1), 5–22.

Sefton-Green, J., Marsh, J., Erstad, O., & Flewitt, R. (2016). *Establishing a research agenda for the digital literacy practices of young children: A white paper for COST Action IS1410.* https://www.lse.ac.uk/media-and-communications/assets/documents/research/projects/p4df/COST-2016.pdf

Smith, P., & Pellegrini, A. (2013). Learning through play. In *Encyclopedia on early childhood development.* http://www.child-encyclopedia.com/documents/Smith-PellegriniANGxp2.pdf

Tan, S. C. (2019). Learning with computers: Generating insights into the development of cognitive tools using cultural historical activity theory. *Australasian Journal of Educational Technology, 35*(2).

Thomas, G. (2011). A typology for the case study in social science following a review of definition, discourse, and structure. *Qualitative Inquiry, 17,* 511–521.

UNICEF. (2018). *Learning through play: Strengthening learning through play in early childhood education programs.* UNICEF Education Section, Programme Division.

United Nations Convention on the Rights of the Child, November 20, 1989, https://www.ohchr.org/en/instruments-mechanisms/instruments/convention-rights-child

Vygotsky, L. S. (1978). *Mind in society: The development of higher psychological processes* (M. Cole, V. John-Steiner, S. Scribner, & E. Souberman, Eds.). Harvard University Press.

Watts, S. (2014). User skills for qualitative analysis: Perspective, interpretation, and the delivery of impact. *Qualitative Research in Psychology, 11*(1), 1–14.

Whitebread, D., Neale, D., Jensen, H., Liu, C., Solis, S. L., Hopkins, E., Hirsh-Pasek, K., & Zosh, J. M. (2017). *The role of play in children's development: A review of the evidence (Research Summary).* The LEGO Foundation.

Wlodkowski, R. J. (1999). *Enhancing adult motivation to learn.* Jossey-Bass Publishers.

Wlodkowski, R. J., & Ginsberg, M. B. (1995). A framework for culturally responsive teaching. *Educational Leadership: Journal of the Department of Supervision and Curriculum Development, 53*(1), 17–21.

Yin, R. (2014). *Case study research: Design and methods* (5th ed.). Sage Publications.

Yin, R. (2018). *Case study research: Design and methods* (6th ed.). SAGE.

CHAPTER 14
Culturally appropriate linguistic responses to taboo issues when teaching biology

Ayanda Simayi, Paul Webb

Introduction

Global discourse on science education has increasingly called for the expansion of its scope through the development of culturally responsive strategies (Abrams et al., 2014). A growing body of literature, including works by Abrams et al. (2014), Gay (2013), Gee (2015), and Mhakure and Otulaja (2017), has underscored the importance of these strategies, particularly within diverse cultural contexts. These scholars advocate for a pedagogical approach that takes into account the cultural backgrounds of teachers and students.

Furthermore, within this discourse, there is a recurring emphasis on the fundamental role of language in the effective teaching of science. Gay (2013), Lewthwaite et al. (2014), and Mpofu et al. (2014) have all highlighted the pivotal role of language in conveying the unique terminology and concepts inherent to various scientific disciplines. As Hodson (2009, p. 242) succinctly put it, "a subject is its language", emphasising the inseparable connection between language and the subject matter.

Yore and Treagust (2006, p. 296) extend this notion by introducing the concept of a "three-language problem". They contend that science education involves an intricate interplay of three distinct language domains: the students' home language (L1), the language of instruction in school (L2), and the specialised language of science disciplines (L3). This perspective provides a comprehensive framework for understanding the complexities of language in conveying scientific concepts.

Additionally, a fourth dimension of the language issue (L4) arises when children are educated in a language that is not their native or home language (Webb, 2013, 2017). This situation is prevalent in Africa as a majority of the countries on the continent were colonised and due to their education systems being established in this period, they have inherited systems of education in the languages of their colonisers. This is still the case in most African countries, including South Africa (Maluleke, 2019). The challenges posed by this multilingual and multicultural context underscore the critical need for culturally responsive and linguistically inclusive approaches to science education (Msimanga et al., 2017), which is the focal point of this chapter, with an emphasis on heteroglossia, polyphony, metonyms, and taboos.

There is evidence that the language used when teaching sexual concepts in culturally homogenous communities such as the Xhosa people is constrained, and certain words and phrases are culturally taboo. For example, Doidge and Lelliott (2016) state that there are cultural taboo problems with language used when naming genitalia and sexual language which may not be part of the normal, everyday language of that group of individuals. Using such language may raise conflict between teachers, learners, and parents, bringing to the fore a need to directly confront the connection between culture, ethnic grouping and learning between individuals and groups (Gee, 2015; Kral & Schwab, 2016; Odora Hoppers, 2009)

Such taboos are common in rural areas where traditional culture persists most strongly (Deyi, 2016; Simayi & Webb, 2020). As such, the phenomenon of how cultural taboos influence language use when teaching aspects of human sexual reproduction has led to an interest in how, when teaching culturally sensitive issues in culturally homogenous classes, these metonyms, words and phrases can be used to alleviate this problem.

African teachers of Xhosa culture experience similar inhibitions when talking about sexual reproduction terms and processes in the schools where they teach and have difficulties providing a culturally appropriate response to these challenges. We also know that teachers perceive these inhibitions and language issues as taboos when teaching children of their own culture, and do not know how to alleviate them. As such, in this chapter, which is based on portions of Simayi's doctoral thesis (2021), we examine linguistic issues of polyphonies, metonyms, and taboos surrounding menstruation where strong traditional Xhosa culture persists, that is in rural areas of the Transkei, South Africa.

Language and taboos

In the film *We Still Live Here – âs nutayuneân* (Newell, 2011) which documents the efforts of the Wampanoag people to revive their indigenous language, the renowned linguist, Noam Chomsky, reminds the viewer that "a language is not just words. It's a culture, a tradition, a unification of a community, a whole history that creates what a community is. It's all embodied in a language" (Hajek, 2021). First-nation peoples and those communities whose languages are in danger of extinction understand better than most how language encapsulates cultural heritage and history, acting as a core element of communal identity. Language is an effective communication tool, but intracultural epistemic access requires intracultural communication (Kecskes, 2015, 2018). However, there is the issue of lexical ambiguity that exists within the same culture, concepts referred to as heteroglossia, polyphony and metonyms by linguistic scholars (Akuno, 2017; Mtintsilana, 1990).

Heteroglossia is a concept introduced by Russian linguist and literary theorist Mikhail Bakhtin (Todorov, 1984). It refers to the coexistence of multiple voices, languages, and discourses within a single linguistic or cultural space. In other words, heteroglossia acknowledges that language and culture are dynamic and constantly evolving, with various voices and perspectives interacting and influencing one another.

Polyphony is a literary and linguistic concept that is closely related to heteroglossia. It refers to the existence of multiple voices or perspectives within a text or discourse (Bakhtin, 1984, 2010). In polyphonic texts, different characters or speakers may express their own viewpoints and ideologies, creating a rich and complex narrative. Polyphony is a manifestation of heteroglossia in literature.

Metonyms are figures of speech in which one word or phrase is substituted with another closely related word or phrase to represent a larger concept or idea (Akuno, 2017; Hutchison, 1998). Metonyms rely on the idea that words are connected to broader cultural and social contexts. In a heteroglossic environment, metonyms can take on various meanings and connotations, as different voices and discourses influence their interpretation.

Teaching and talking about content of a sexual nature is a problem in many parts of the world (Buni, 2013; Kral & Schwab, 2016). There are studies on culture and human reproduction in sub-Saharan Africa such as Doidge and Lelliott's (2016) research on metaphorical language and sexuality education but generally, African research projects focus mainly on HIV and sexuality (Gudyanga et al., 2019; Mpondo et al., 2018; Ngabaza & Shefer, 2019). In particular, MacEntee (2020) cites Masinire et al. (2014), emphasising a paucity of research on the existence and influence of cultural taboos in African contexts. However, we do know that intracultural communication is a foundational element for effective teaching and discussions surrounding sensitive/taboo topics in communities that have deeply rooted conservative cultural views.

Taboos are social or cultural restrictions or prohibitions related to certain topics or behaviours. They vary across cultures and can include restrictions on discussing or teaching certain subjects, such as sexuality and menstruation. In a heteroglossic context, taboos may be upheld by some voices or communities while challenged or reinterpreted by others.

As noted above, heteroglossia is a concept that highlights the diversity of voices and perspectives within language and culture. In the context of teaching sexual concepts in culturally conservative communities, heteroglossia highlights the complexity of balancing traditional taboos with contemporary educational goals and values.

There is evidence of such taboos in Xhosa rural communities (Simayi & Webb, 2019). In classes where isiXhosa speaking children are taught what may be considered to be sensitive sexual content by isiXhosa first-language teachers in the English language in rural schools, these taboos persist and negatively affect any meaningful teaching and learning of the topic.

Such a taboo is the teaching of sexual concepts in culturally conservative communities like the Xhosa cultures in South Africa, it appears that in such communities there can be a clash of heteroglossic voices and perspectives. On one hand, there may be traditional or conservative voices that adhere to long-standing taboos surrounding the discussion of sexual concepts and menstruation. These taboos could stem from cultural, religious, or social beliefs that consider these topics as sensitive or inappropriate for open discussion, especially in educational settings.

On the other hand, there may be voices advocating for a more inclusive and informative approach to sex education, recognising the importance of providing accurate information about sexual health, menstruation, and related topics to young learners. These voices may draw from global or contemporary discourses on comprehensive sex education, human rights, and gender equality.

The coexistence of these diverse voices and discourses within the community creates a heteroglossic environment. It is within this context that educators and policymakers must navigate and make decisions about the curriculum and teaching methods in schools. They have to address and potentially challenge certain taboos while respecting the cultural values and beliefs of the community.

Design and methodology

In Simayi's (2021) original doctoral study, polyphonies, metonyms, and taboos surrounding menstruation were explored as part of the research with teachers of Grade 12 biology. A preliminary semi-structured questionnaire was administered using pen and paper to 30 participants. The questionnaires included demographic questions aimed at establishing relevant sampling based on cultural grouping, subject taught, and rural location of the schools during the initial data collection session. The second data set was captured from focus group questions aimed at establishing use of polyphonies and metonyms by teachers or learners during teaching. The third data set was generated from a flow-chart which was sourced as personal reflections by the teachers.

Thematic data analysis was conducted on the generated data by identifying similarities through colour-coded themes and key terms (Braun & Clarke, 2019; Clarke & Braun, 2014). Following the translation and transcription processes, data were analysed by organization into patterns and themes through manual coding involving sorting, writing, and labelling techniques (Creswell & Plano-Clark, 2007; Denzin, 2012). In phase one, the exploratory study consisted of 18 female and 12 male participants, making a total of 30 participants as the first phase of critical participatory action learning and action research (CPALAR) design. Results of data analysis from open-ended questions revealed cultural avoidances and no use of Xhosa terms in explaining menstruation due to Xhosa cultural restrictions. Focus group interviews revealed the following: that there are multiple terms used for menstruation by Xhosa teachers; even the teachers indicated that they do not teach menstruation due to poor learner behaviour when sexual topics are taught.

Heteroglossia was used as the theoretical underpinning to comprehend the intricacies of intracultural communication within the context of sensitive/ taboo topics in this study, and a linguistic framework using Bakhtin's theory of heteroglossia was applied using the topic of menstruation within the Xhosa culture to offer insights into the language-related issues examined in this study, namely heteroglossia, or polyphony, which represent diverse language discourses where nuanced variations in meaning emerge within specific social contexts. An illustrative example of polyphonies in isiXhosa is illustrated where menstruation is termed '*engceni*,' signifying 'on the grass,' and '*exesheni*,' connoting 'on time.' The notion of polyphony denotes multiple voices or discourses within a social grouping, which is also referred to as multi-voicedness (Bakhtin, 2010).

This exploratory study sought to unravel the potential of heteroglossic terms within a seemingly homogenous culture, with a specific focus on the Xhosa culture. However, it was found that even individuals within the same culture residing in different geographical regions exhibit subtle variations in the terminology they use. As such, this chapter endeavours to uncover and analyse the presence of diverse linguistic expressions and their implications within the context of intracultural communication within Xhosa culture.

Results and findings

Results of data analysis from open-ended questions revealed that participants avoided talking about sexual concepts in their biology classes and in community settings due to Xhosa cultural restrictions. Counting of participants' responses indicate that all 30 participants responded with "*no*" to the question of whether they thought that human reproduction topics such as menstruation, ejaculation, fertilization, pregnancy and childbirth are part of the normal cultural conversation among young and old members of their culture. Out of the 30 participants, 10 participants did not give explanations for their *no* responses.

Based on translation and coding of the transcripts using Atlas ti. 8 software, two dominant patterns that emerged from the responses were: "*Asibizi*" around sexual concepts. A Xhosa term meaning avoidance of talking about something, signifying how cultural taboos restrict teaching of sexual concepts due to innate Xhosa cultural beliefs. Results of data analysis indicated that 20 out of 30 participants responded with explanations indicating that they avoided explaining sexual topics in isiXhosa as their culture prevented talk about sex matters such as vagina, penis and menstruation.

Verbatim responses were as follows (the original identifiers are presented on the left and on the right further down):

P29:	*Asibizi, not allowed in our culture.*
P9:	*According to our culture, it is seen as a sign of disrespect and looking down at our culture.*
P20:	*We don't say these things, siyahlonipha, asibizi.*
P30:	*Yhoo! Even menstruation is difficult to talk about, it is a No-No! We talk sex things with friends. Boys are very naughty and uncontrollable in class.*
P7:	*Traditionally we don't talk about it.*
P23:	*Tradition dictates silence on sex language or talk.*

Data analysis showed additional support for the development of *asibizi* was provided by the "groundedness" (Friese, 2019, p. 14) of the code, showing the number of times that a particular written text was connected to a particular code. For example, results show in vivo coding that generated the code *asibizi, not allowed in our culture,* had a grounding of 17. This means that 17 text passages were connected to the code *asibizi,* 'it's not allowed in our culture'.

Supporting comments for the general description of the cultural aspect of *asibizi* was shown by statements that did not disclose specifically what was being avoided in sexual talk. For example, participants gave general statements such as *"gender and age restrict sex talk"* and *"people respect sex (ukuhlonipha) topics"*. There were also direct statements that named the sexual concepts they avoided and how they felt about the avoidance, such as *"Menstruation talk is culturally taboo"* and *"Penis talk is taboo in presence of circumcised boys"*.

Supporting statements for cultural limitation on talking about sexual concepts was derived from the participants' written responses:

P1:	*I was raised in a community of Xhosa people who respected private parts and never called them with their real names. Even now, we don't talk about sexual parts and sexuality openly.*
P4:	*No, it's called 'amanyala/izimanga'(vulgar) in isiXhosa, so we don't talk about these sex things, parents used to hit us and said we are using vulgar language when we asked anything close to sex.*
P5:	*My culture does not allow talking about sex matters, we respect instructions of older people as forbearers of our Xhosa tradition.*

Further data analysis indicated an expression of a common text in the vernacular of 'siyahlonipha', meaning 'We are respectful' in English. Again, cultural value was coded as central to the avoidance of naming sexual concepts. A theme emerged indicating that there were common cultural taboos expressed as 'siyahlonipha', meaning that participants avoided naming sexual concepts out of respect for their cultural values as indicated by the participants' comments:

P10:   *Talking about sex, reproduction, parts or organs is not normal in our culture, siyahlonipha.*

P22:   *My family values don't allow sex talk.*

Various responses indicated that Xhosa language was not used to clarify sexual concepts, only English was used:

"It is difficult for me to call vagina in isiXhosa, even in English. Instead, I use substitute terms … I end up using slang and call vagina 'usisi'." (1A)

"Explaining and teaching fertilization in learners seems as if you say they must do sexual intercourse." (1B)

"Learners disrespect me as if we are of the same age." (1C)

"It is easy to say it in English, but I don't feel comfortable to say it in my own language." (1F)

Xhosa beliefs acted as a barrier as female teachers were held back by Xhosa cultural beliefs related to circumcised men, that is, boys who had undergone the rite of passage (usually at eighteen years of age) to become considered as men:

"According to our culture, as a woman you have to respect men especially those who have reached 'manhood' (circumcised)." (1G)

"I feel like culture is a barrier in teaching reproduction." (1G)

'Teaching about the penis is very difficult. It seems as if you are invading the privacy of men." (1B)

"My Xhosa culture stops me and does not allow the pronunciation of these terms." (1D)

"It becomes difficult for me to call vagina; I use substitute terms to call it. Terms that are acceptable to use in my culture." (1A)

The unexpected gender trend continued to develop from data analysis as results showed that male teachers felt uncomfortable and disrespected when teaching sexual concepts, particularly when teaching sexual concepts related to typical male anatomy. Male participants felt naked, as if learners could see the anatomy of the male reproductive system through their clothes while presenting the topic:

"I am a male teacher, and these parts are in me and kids start to see these parts in me. It made me feel uncomfortable to disclose some of the sensitive parts such as testis. Learners want me to explain their personal issues because they start talking about their male and female problems." (1E)

"Testes, it is easy to draw and label both the testes. It is difficult to explain in Xhosa language. I do not feel comfortable to say it (penis) in my own Xhosa language." (1F)

In addition, male participants feared being disrespected by learners when having to teach both male and female sexual concepts. Male participants feared losing their respected status as men when having to explain the structure and functions of sexual concepts:

"The kids disrespect me as a male teacher because I have disclosed some of my private parts such as penis and testis and these kids look at me that way (funny and disrespectful way)." (1E)

"I am unable to call sexual terms by their name in my language. I explain in English as I am uncomfortable to explain in Xhosa." (1F)

Male participants were also scared of being viewed as having disclosed secret Xhosa cultural practices that occur in male rites of passage to manhood such as circumcision:

"Kids start to doubt that I am a Xhosa guy because I am disclosing everything in front of the female kids, and they doubt that I am a man. It made me feel uncomfortable to disclose some of the sensitive parts such as testis." (1E)

"Because of culture, I am unable to call (parts of) the female reproductive system by their name using my own Xhosa language." (1F)

There were moments of excitement emanating from the use of the vernacular *"yiyeke kanjalo mam, yibamb' apho"*, meaning 'stop there, just there' (PF2) in addressing the issue of female teachers being stopped by male learners in class, observed from simultaneous talk as more female participants continued talking while PF2 was still talking:

"When you start talking about circumcision they say, 'No, stop there Mam, stop just there (yiyeke kanjalo mam, yibamba' apho' (immediately) there is a confirmation from others while the speaker is on of 'heeke' and laughter from others and excited talk amongst each other." (PF2)

The reported negative responses of male learners towards female teachers was exacerbated by their living in the same rural village as the learners:

"Heey! It is more difficult to teach these sexual things as we are staying in the same vicinity with them, and you also see the manner they look at you that it is totally disrespectful and different than before the sexual lesson." (PF1)

Heteroglossia and terms for sexual concepts

Probing for the actual Xhosa terms used in simplifying sexual concepts was key to getting the language used by the teachers to clarify sexual concepts to Grade 12 learners of Xhosa cultural background in rural secondary schools. However, it started on a negative footing as teachers kept quiet and did not respond to the question. Participants were required to say these Xhosa sexual terms aloud in the focus group session. There was total silence, nobody was talking, and men looked down at the desk in front of them after I had posed this question. This was followed by unintelligible murmurs, some fidgeting with a pen, others looking down at the desk in front of them, coupled with turning and tossing on swivel chairs. I could sense that my question had created some tension as participants kept quiet.

Generating data proved difficult as participants continued to share their challenges instead of giving specific responses to the direct question requiring examples of Xhosa terms used in clarifying sexual concepts. The teachers kept deflecting questions on the naming of Xhosa sexual concepts expressing their frustration. Even though I felt anxious that I was not addressing the research question, I allowed the participants to communicate their views as allowed by the selected research design. For example, a participant reported on the difficulty of being labelled as non-Christian for teaching sexual concepts (PF4):

> "In my school, I used to teach human reproduction and had learners who labelled me. Learners who were saved by Jesus labelled me as a person who was no longer part of the Christian brethren, not 100% saved because of what I was saying in class." (PF4)

I was stressed a bit as I thought that my study was about to fail due to a lack of responses. At the same time, I thought the participants required guidance as they remained seated and continued to be part of the study. Probing the participants to say out loud (to name) Xhosa concepts that are known and used in their mother tongue when referring to sexual concepts, I elaborated on the question and used specific Xhosa substitute terms such as 'inkomo' (cow), 'igusha' (sheep) when referring to the vagina.

I had to alleviate tension as the teachers could not share openly the specific terms that they use to explain how they teach sexual concepts. Silence and occasional unintelligible sighs and shock mumbling in isiXhosa like 'Mnxccxx' (a mostly involuntary sound and action made in frustration, known in English as 'sucking one's teeth'), indicating helplessness and frustration, emerged from the data. I had to think quickly and made an inoffensive joke about specific sexual concepts, this exercise helped to break the ice, and they all laughed. I had to identify with them and really be an insider and they openly shared their isiXhosa terms after this playful activity.

An inoffensive joke about the penis was the icebreaker in this tense situation. Saying the real Xhosa word for penis aloud, 'umthondo', without using nicknames or substitutes, produced emotions of shock such as 'Yhuuu' in Xhosa, mingled with laughter, broke the silence. 'Yhuuu' is an exclamation term in isiXhosa therefore, the results show that the participants were shocked at first on the use of the term 'umthondo'. However, the shock was followed immediately by laughter and participants shared their views (PF4):

> "I, in my personal teaching experience, I would never explain in isiXhosa such that I use simple English that I think they can understand because I am avoiding to say these things. I get scared of saying these scary things. (There is an emotional minute where participants spontaneously talk, some saying 'yhuu' (shock) and helplessness, mxxcm (disdain) and hands thrown in the air to show loss of hope)." (PF4)

Barriers about pronouncing Xhosa names were broken as participants joined in, in a jovial atmosphere and shared Xhosa substitute terms that they used for sexual concepts. A male participant revealed that, to him, the penis is a "kettle (iketile)", and this substitute word was used to avoid saying "vulgar terms like penis":

> "On my side I use my home experience for example, the kettle is a substitute for the penis. So, when teaching, I use the kettle instead of using penis as a substitute as a way of avoiding the use of repeated English vulgar terms like penis." (PM6)

Data analysis showed that there were less suitable substitute Xhosa terms as some sexual concepts have more than one substitute for the concept. A different substitute name for a penis was given by another participant, calling it a "tososo". The tososo produced laughter among the participants:

> "The penis is also a 'tososo' (laughter from all the participants)." (PF4)

No additional substitute terms were given as participants shared only the two substitute terms for the penis (ketile and tososo).

However, the Xhosa cultural time period used by the model teacher explained the menstrual process using 'gentle' Xhosa concepts for fertilization and active sex days for women wanting to fall pregnant:

> "We know that ovulation from the science curriculum is the release of the egg cell. Therefore, we can integrate the period of 'jumping the fireplace after being on the grass or on time' as equivalent to having sex after menstruation and that is the ovulation period." [T: 00:03:00:00]

A cognitive shift was reported by the model teacher and confirmed by the teachers as:

> "We have integrated our cultural terms which were used by the elderly as we use them now in our menstruation talk. We have moved to what is called ... chorus response from colleagues ... equipollent cognition." [T: 00:02:30:00]

There is a Xhosa culture counting programme that compared similarities in the counting of the number of days in the 28-day menstrual cycle, using Xhosa euphemistic concepts. Ovulation was counted from day 11 of the menstrual cycle and was regarded as the *free time* for copulation (jumping the fireplace) for families that wanted a pregnancy:

> "*After 10 days, from day 11 it's free time to jump the fireplace and is regarded as ovulation because the egg cell has been released, although old people did not have this term of ovulation.*" (PF1)

Thickening of the endometrium (*grass*) and nourishment by the blood capillaries (*soil*) was known as a preparation for receiving a fertilized egg cell that would be implanted in the readily prepared grass (endometrium):

> "*As our teacher explained just now, the grass which is the endometrium and its soil which is the blood vessels, have become thicker and ready to receive something new for attachment, that's a fertilized egg cell that will be implanted inside the fertile grass which is the womb or endometrium.*" (PF1)

The importance of an endometrium that was reported as becoming *thicker like a thick carpet*, signified that historical Xhosa women, although they were reportedly unlearned, instinctively knew about developmental challenges that took place inside a young woman's body. Moreover, knowing that the thickening of the endometrium takes place on completion of menstruation and a thickened endometrium represents a state of readiness for fertilization is important for integrating IK into the teaching of sexual concepts:

> "*Once menstruation or 'being on grass' stops, the endometrium inside the womb grows and grows thicker just like a thick carpet for the attachment of the embryo while the soil (capillaries), get ready to provide nourishment for the growing embryo.*" (PF1)

There was a change from avoidance to naming of sexual concepts, to using the euphemistic Xhosa words first before using the 'avoided' scientific sexual concepts. Participants reported feeling less frustrated as they shared ideas and they could not believe that they were talking amongst each other openly about concepts such as copulation and fertilization "*without stress*":

> "*Can't believe that I'm saying these things like copulation, fertilization and menstruation without stress … laughter … seriously this IK and CAT information has made saying and using these terms lighter.*" (PF1)

> "*Yes.*" (group members agree in unison)

Participants revealed that before the research discussions, teaching sexual concepts would make them feel like *"dying inside because of pain"* of having to talk about sexual concepts to learners:

> *"To me, feeling like a wilted flower means that I feel like dying inside because of pain of saying these sexual words. These things that we teach strip us of our humanity so much and kills the self-respect that we have deep down inside just like this wilted flower."* (PF4)

Discussion and conclusions

It was revealed early in the research process that the teachers did not know of any form of culturally responsive teaching strategies that they could use to teach sexual concepts. They reported that *"we do not know any culturally responsive strategies, we simply teach these things in English"*. This lack of existing culturally responsive strategies is affirmed by research studies that reveal that professional development strategies are scarce (Desimone, 2009). Adedeji and Olaniyan (2011) comment on this general lack of knowledge about IK-based strategies, citing that there is little to no direction on how to teach IK by departments of education. The participants' lack of knowledge is thus not confined to the context of this study but is supported by literature.

Considering that the different isiXhosa speakers used polyphonies and metonyms for sexual terms enabled the improved teaching of sexual terms via this research intervention, the following broad recommendations can be made for stakeholders with an interest in developing culturally responsive strategies in rural schools. They are to conduct regular professional development (Desimone & Pak, 2017) sessions on IK and science teaching where teachers can develop a bank of Xhosa terms that can be used as substitutes for sensitive concepts. Extending the professional development to include officials of the Department of Education so that the new knowledge is used by the governing education sections in school material and empowering rural-based teachers through science content-based sessions which are linked with their IK so that they can develop culturally responsive strategies (Budge, 2006, 2010; Nkambule et al., 2011).

Although the substitute terms referred to in this study are specific to, and were drawn from, Xhosa history used long ago by unlearned yet authoritative women elders, the methods are probably transferrable to other aspects of teaching and learning in communities located in rural spaces (Gay, 2013). This claim is made because this small-scale research intervention with rural teachers in a deeply culturally determined community has been shown to be effective where there are local linguistic heteroglots who know the cultural history still known by many deeply rural Xhosa people (Mda, 2007).

In short, this study suggests that the use of culturally responsive teaching strategies developed by isiXhosa speaking teachers who teach children of the same culture has a meaningful prospect of success. The issue of familiar language is regarded as a fundamental form of communication and as a means of empowering teachers working in marginalised, rural and indigenous Xhosa communities. Not only is the claim made that using local linguistic heteroglossia and cultural history is an effective strategy among rural Xhosa communities that are steeped in their indigenous culture, but that it may also be an effective strategy for many indigenous people worldwide (Hodson, 2010).

References

Abrams, E., Yore, L. D., Bang, M., Brayboy, B. M. J., Castagno, A., Kidman, J., Lee, H., Villanueva, M. G., Wang, M. H., & Webb, P. (2014). Culturally relevant schooling in science for indigenous learners worldwide: Stressing the all in science literacy for all. In *Handbook of research on science education* (Vol. 2, pp. 685–710). Routledge.

Adedeji, S. O., & Olaniyan, O. (2011). *Improving the conditions of teachers and teaching in rural schools across African countries.* UNESCO-IICBA.

Akuno, L. A. (2017). *A comparative analysis of conceptual metaphors and metonymies of love in selected Dholuo Benga songs by Ochieng Kabaselle and Atomi Sifa* [Master's thesis, Maseno University]. Maseno University Institutional Repository. http://repository.maseno.ac.ke/handle/123456789/904

Bakhtin, M. (1994). *The Bakhtin reader* (P. Morris, Ed.). Oxford University Press.

Bakhtin, M. (2010). *The dialogic imagination: Four essays* (Vol. 1). University of Texas Press.

Braun, V., & Clarke, V. (2019). Reflecting on reflexive thematic analysis. *Qualitative Research in Sport, Exercise and Health, 11*(4), 589–597.

Budge, K. (2006). Rural leaders, rural places: Problem, privilege, and possibility. *Journal of Research in Rural Education, 21*(13), 1–10.

Budge, K. (2010). Why shouldn't rural kids have it all? Place-conscious leadership in an era of extralocal reform policy. *Education Policy Analysis Archives, 18,* 1. https://doi.org/10.14507/epaa.v18n1.2010

Buni, C. (2013, April 15). The case for teaching kids 'vagina,' 'penis,' and 'vulva'. *Atlantic.* http://www.theatlantic.com/health/archive/2013/04/the-case-for-teaching-kids-vagina-penis-and-vulva/274969/

Clarke, V., & Braun, V. (2014). Thematic analysis. In *Encyclopedia of critical psychology* (pp. 1947–1952). Springer.

Creswell, J. W., & Plano-Clark, V. (2007). *Designing and conducting mixed methods research.* SAGE.

Denzin, N. K. (2012). Triangulation 2.0. *Journal of Mixed Methods Research, 6*(2), 80–88.

Desimone, L. M. (2009). Improving impact studies of teachers' professional development: Toward better conceptualizations and measures. *Educational Researcher, 38*(3), 181–199.

Desimone, L. M., & Pak, K. (2017). Instructional coaching as high-quality professional development. *Theory Into Practice, 56*(1), 3–12.

Deyi, S. (2016). Significance of offering a context-specific language teaching in contexts persistent of cultural constraints. *International Journal of Scientific Research and Innovative Technology, 3*(11), 40–47.

Doidge, M., & Lelliott, A. (2016). Language choices in the teaching of human reproduction. *Journal of Biological Education, 51*(2), 186–196. http://doi.org/10.1080/00219266.2016.1177577

Friese, S. (2019). *Qualitative data analysis with ATLAS.ti.* SAGE Publications Limited.

Gay, G. (2013). Teaching to and through cultural diversity. *Curriculum Inquiry, 43*(1), 48–70.

Gee, J. (2015*). Social linguistics and literacies: Ideology in discourses* (3rd ed.). Routledge.

Gudyanga, E., de Lange, N., & Khau, M. (2019). Zimbabwean secondary school guidance and counseling teachers teaching sexuality education in the HIV and AIDS education curriculum. *SAHARA-J: Journal of Social Aspects of HIV/AIDS, 16*(1), 35–50.

Hajek, I. (2021, November 23). Language matters, especially when it was here first. *The Charger Bulletin.* https://chargerbulletin.com/language-matters-especially-when-it-was-here-first/

Hodson, D. (2009). *Teaching and learning about science: Language, theories, methods, history, traditions and values.* Brill Sense.

Hodson, D. (2010). Science education as a call to action. *Canadian Journal of Science, Mathematics and Technology Education, 10*(3), 197–206.

Hutchison, J. P. (1998). *Power, marginality and African oral literature* [Review]. *The International Journal of African Historical Studies, 31*(2), 409–412. https://www.jstor.org/stable/221118

Kecskes, I. (2015). Is the idiom principle blocked in bilingual L2 production? In R. R. Heredia & A. B. Cieślicka (Eds.), *Bilingual figurative language processing* (pp. 28–53). Cambridge University Press.

Kecskes, I. (2018). *Intercultural pragmatics.* Oxford University Press.

Kral, I., & Schwab, R. (2016). A space to learn: A community-based approach to meaningful adult learning and literacy in remote Indigenous Australia. *Prospects, 46*(3–4), 465–477.

Lewthwaite, B., Owen, T., Doiron, A., Renaud, R., & McMillan, B. (2014). Culturally responsive teaching in Yukon First Nation settings: What does it look like and what is its influence? *Canadian Journal of Educational Administration and Policy, (155),* 1–34.

MacEntee, K. (2020). Participatory visual methods and school-based responses to HIV in rural South Africa: Insights from youth, preservice and inservice teachers. *Sex Education, 20*(3), 316–333.

Maluleke, T. (2019). Using code-switching as an empowerment strategy in teaching mathematics to learners with limited proficiency in English in South African schools. *South African Journal of Education, 39*(3), 1–9.

Mda, Z. (2007). *The heart of redness: A novel.* Farrar, Straus and Giroux.

Mhakure, D., & Otulaja, F. S. (2017). Culturally-responsive pedagogy in science education: Narrowing the divide between indigenous and scientific knowledge. In F. S. Otulaja & M. B. Ogunniyi (Eds.), *The world of science: Handbook of research in science education in Sub-Saharan Africa* (Vol. 6, pp. 66–81). Sense.

Mpofu, V., Otulaja, F. S., & Mushayikwa, E. (2014). Towards culturally relevant classroom science: A theoretical framework focusing on traditional plant healing. *Cultural Studies of Science Education, 9*(1), 221–242.

Mpondo, F., Ruiter, R. A., Schaafsma, D., Van Den Borne, B., & Reddy, P. S. (2018). Understanding the role played by parents, culture and the school curriculum in socializing young women on sexual health issues in rural South African communities. *SAHARA-J: Journal of Social Aspects of HIV/AIDS, 15*(1), 42–49.

Msimanga, A., Denley, P., & Gumede, N. (2017). The pedagogical role of language in science teaching and learning in South Africa: A review of research 1990–2015. *African Journal of Research in Mathematics, Science and Technology Education, 21*(3), 245–255.

Mtintsilana, P. N. (1990). Polysemy, homonymy and hyponymy in Xhosa bilingual dictionaries. *South African Journal of African Languages, 10*(2), 69–73.

Newell, A. (Director). (2011). *We still live here – âs nutayuneân* [Film]. Makepeace Productions.

Ngabaza, S., & Shefer, T. (2019). Sexuality education in South African schools: Deconstructing the dominant response to young people's sexualities in contemporary schooling contexts. *Sex Education, 19*(4), 422–435.

Nkambule, T., Balfour, R., Pillay, G., & Moletsane, R. (2011). Rurality and rural education: Discourses underpinning rurality and rural education research in South African postgraduate education research 1994–2004. *South African Journal of Higher Education, 25*(2), 341–357.

Odora Hoppers, C. A. (2009). Education, culture and society in a globalizing world: Implications for comparative and international education. *Compare, 39*(5), 601–614.

Simayi, A. (2021). *A culturally responsive strategy for teaching sexual concepts in rural Xhosa secondary schools* (Publication No. vital:59660) [Doctoral thesis, Nelson Mandela University]. South East Academic Learners System Digital Commons. http://hdl.handle.net/10948/58519

Simayi, A., & Webb, P. (2020, January 3–6). *Asibizi: Teaching human reproduction in rural Eastern Cape schools* [Paper presentation]. Eighth international conference to review research in science, technology and mathematics education, Mumbai, India. https://episteme8.hbcse. tifr.res.in/proceedings/"ASIBIZI"- TEACHING HUMAN REPRODUCTION IN RURAL EASTERN CAPE SCHOOLS.pdf

Todorov, T. (1984). *Mikhail Bakhtin: The dialogical principle.* Manchester University Press.

Webb, P. (2013). Xhosa indigenous knowledge: Stakeholder awareness, value and choice. *International Journal of Science and Mathematics Education, 11*, 89–110.

Webb, P. (2017). Science education in South Africa. In F. S. Otulaja & M. B. Ogunniyi (Eds.), *The world of science education: Handbook of research in science education in Sub-Saharan Africa* (pp. 119–131). Sense Publishers.

Yore, L., & Treagust, D. (2006). Current realities and future possibilities: Language and science literacy empowering research and informing instruction. *International Journal of Science Education, 28*(2–3), 291–314.

CHAPTER 15
Beyond saviour research: A critical synthesis of the CERM-ESA project celebration

Michael Anthony Samuel

This chapter critiques the staging of Africa as a space in need of a saviours. Indeed, the saviours have already risen in the hearts and minds, and commitments of projects which move beyond the promotion of econometric markets, disguised elitist agendas or expansionist imitations of strategies crafted elsewhere. As a critical synthesis of the project of the anthology as a whole, this chapter attempts to open up questions about *how* research projects in the field of education research come to be designed, *by whom*, and with *what intentions*. The focus of these questions directs an analysis towards *whose interests* are being served by the agenda of the research being undertaken. *Who* are the ultimate beneficiaries of the research design we conduct? The chapter emphasises that the terrain of educational research is embedded within contestations and possibilities of collaborative efforts across many interlocuting partners both at the systemic macro-level and at the micro- and meso-level of personalised and localised classroom institutional spaces within different levels of the education system: primary, secondary and higher education. Hence the chapter is organized to reflect two overarching, interrelated sections.

The first (Part A) locates the review of the anthology *Education Research in African Contexts: Traditions and New Beginnings for Knowledge and Impact* within a broader **macro-systemic continental space** where the motivation for an upscaling of the production of African research is presented. The broad African Union's *Agenda 2063* provides the overarching idealism of research development expectations. This present chapter demonstrates how the ten-year CERM-ESA project offers pragmatic commentary on how the African Union (AU) agenda is indeed already being enacted, showing what has been achieved and what still needs to be done for continental transformation. A parallel to the CERM-ESA project is another prospective continental project: the African Research Universities Alliance (ARUA) agenda foregrounding its commitment to African research development. Both these initiatives (AU and ARUA) are seen as sounding boards to juxtapose the unique features of the CERM-ESA project showing why and how the promotion of educational research is a complex and messy terrain, requiring many levels of theoretical and practical interventions.

The second part of the chapter (Part B) deals with **meso and micro-research space**, inside the CERM-ESA programmes and institutional research studies produced. It begins by reflecting on the CERM-ESA initiative on its decade anniversary by critically reviewing two sub-sections of the anthology's broad focused research studies: on researching the *higher education space* (B1), and on researching the *school and society space* (B2)

A: Macro-systemic policy reform: A space for educational research

Agenda 2063: An African Union initiative

"The Africa we want" is a slogan underpinning the ambitious Agenda 2063 of the African Union (AU). This intra-continental masterplan aims to activate, over 50 years from 2013 to 2063, a vision to cultivate a unified, thriving, and harmonious Africa, shaped by its own people and playing a significant role on the global stage. Amongst its strategies is the need to activate social, developmental and economic policies that are people-centred, promote gender equity and youth empowerment, and re-examine African responses to increasing globalisation and the ICT revolution. Education is considered one of the key commodities to galvanise the potential to realize this agenda. Agenda 2063 marked the Golden Jubilee celebration of the Organisation of African Unity (OAU) which was first established in 1963. Whereas the original OAU agenda campaigned attainment of political independence and critiques of regime injustices like the South African apartheid system, the new AU strategy reprioritizes inclusive social and economic growth and development, integrating partnerships across continental and regional structures within a climate of democratic governance, peace and security. One of the key challenges noted in the AU's first ten-year implementation plan (FTYIP) review of Agenda 2063 is the creation of appropriate and robust systems for monitoring and evaluating the outcomes of these strategies. Institutionalized evidence-based reporting provides a research foundation from which progress can be monitored successfully, key milestones reviewed, and outcomes of projects defined and shared. This sets the benchmarks for prospective future-oriented research.

Progress on Agenda 2063 is reportedly robustly supported ideologically, but concerns are repeatedly raised about the lack of human, physical and institutional infrastructure to enact the vision in many contexts within the African continent. It is somewhat disappointing that these high-level systemic reporting protocols often remain in the realm of policy spaces in the national and continental arena, and seldom inform directly the agenda of research within higher education academic spaces. Paradoxically, it is the higher education research systems that are expected to provide the resources to engage in such monitoring and evaluation research designs. The AU target is to produce 100,000 PhDs over 10 years to address how higher education can contribute to social and economic development. What collaborations could be fostered between the varied levels of the socio-political and academic realms to foster shared, mutually reinforcing agendas?

Collaborative doctoral programmes: An African Research Universities Alliance (ARUA) initiative

The African Research Universities Alliance (ARUA) has chosen to move beyond the talk and take the necessary actions to redress the low levels of research productivity outputs. As secretary general of the ARUA, Aryeetey (2024) argues that their strategy of revolutionising doctoral training in Africa is motivated by the worrisome data which show that Africa produces less than 3% of the global generation of knowledge, that fewer than 50% of academic staff at most African universities have a PhD, and that many African universities do not offer more than just undergraduate programmes. Their template is to harness the existing doctoral programmes of 15 African universities (considered ARUA Centres of Excellence) to offer harmonised doctoral degrees to promote inter-disciplinary networking and mobility across partnership institutions. The strategic plan of ARUA is to provide enhanced research support and training, build research management capabilities and advocate the value of doctoral education. Exploration for joint-badged degrees is being explored.

At face value, the ARUA agenda seems laudable, that is until one delves deeper into the pragmatics of realizing these ideals in practice. First, the model is overambitious in its belief that its small contribution of 1,000 PhDs over ten years would make a significant dent against the systemic foundational infrastructure that characterises the widespread and diverse under-resourced African university system.[1] However, the ARUA agenda is not necessarily focused on providing a systemic engagement with the inequities across the whole African higher education system (as is perhaps the AU agenda). Instead, it prefers to work with only the already privileged institutions within the African context. It could be argued that the agenda is indirectly elitist since it protects and expands the worldview of the already privileged. Second, the ARUA agenda needs to declare more overtly who the partner institutions are, especially those international partnerships from outside of Africa being brought to activate the agendas of reconstruction of the doctoral education system. Whilst initial seed funding for ARUA is drawn from the Kresge Foundation and Carnegie Corporation of New York, the partner institutions themselves are expected to sustain the long-term funding. Will African universities be able to afford to invest in transnational agendas especially as financial budget cuts are endemic challenges within the national contexts?

---

1 The pilot inter-institutional doctoral programme will be launched in January 2026.

Beyond saviour research

Fredua-Kwarteng (2023), a Canadian policy researcher, cautions against policy staging in which Africa is positioned as "in need of development from outside". Samuel and Mariaye (2023, p. 3) argue that "the agenda of external deficit framings of the African context could be also understood as creating a marketplace of spaces where 'saviours' from the outside world might intervene to rescue the African context". Sometimes, and fuelled by the ARUA logic, the 'saviours' are the privileged African institutions themselves. Often the intervention is already pre-packaged with an *a priori* solution which needs to find an expanded market.

Many of the partnership universities (both the powerful and the perceived as disempowered, and the local, continental and global partners too) publicly kowtow to the declared organizers: the involvement in the project is a guaranteed source of income and market possibilities for a 'foray into Africa'. For the relatively under-resourced institutions, any involvement in large-scale continental programmes is likely to be simply another valued source of financial injection into already cash-strapped university coffers. Recipient universities tend to be complicit in this saviour research agenda, seemingly clutching at straws rather than powerfully contributing to systemic and sustainable development. Ironically, creating economic markets for higher education exploration and importation across Africa is considered 'developmental'. A new knowledge colonialism (albeit an internal continental one) is at play.

African higher education specificities and complexities: A non-homogenous terrain

Finally, a critique of the above macro-systemic agendas does not realistically acknowledge the lack of higher education infrastructural and supervisory resources that are needed to activate the agenda of expanding postgraduate education on the African continent. For example, Odhiambo (2024), reflecting on the University Statistics Report (2017-2018) released by the Commission of University Education (CUE) in Kenya, laments the trials that both students and supervisors have to endure:

> *Kenya is one of several countries in the region that is struggling to meet its research demand. Fewer than 1,000 professors are expected to meet the needs of more than half a million students across the country's 68 universities. This means the professor-student ratio is 1:500.* (Odhiambo, 2024)

This reflective report elaborates on the lived experiences of the pragmatic challenges of a doctoral student from Ghana who is studying in Kenya. The report highlights Odhiambo's negotiations of cultural crossing over between West and East African contexts, revealing the complexities of 'putting one's life on hold' to achieve the targeted doctorate. Moreover, it underscores that Africa is not a homogenous edu-terrain wherein models can be easily transposed from one context to another. The psychological and emotional support required to endure studies abroad is exacerbated by the limited supervisory academic guidance afforded.[2] The experiences of doctoral students not receiving examination reports for over a year are explained in the report as related to the lack of finances within institutions to pay for external examiners. These pragmatic realities underscore critical sensitivity beyond the political and econometric rhetoric when designing and proposing macro-systemic postgraduate educational reform for the African continent.

B: Meso-/micro-research reform: A space for educational research

Reflections on the ten-year implementation: The Centre for Educational Research Methodologies and Management in East and South Africa (CERM-ESA) initiative

The opportunity to reflect on the CERM-ESA initiative serves as a foil to examine the prospects of both the AU and the ARUA agendas. It serves to examine how macro-systemic plans need to be translated operationally and conceptually at local meso- and micro-levels. Within literary narrative traditions, the foil is often a cameo character who comments or provides the audience with the means to make more noticeable the foibles and merits of the lead character/s. For example, the court jester in Shakespearean dramas (such as the Fool in *King Lear*, or the gravediggers in *Hamlet*) does not merely provide comic relief to the audience; instead, the fool is no fool at all but serves as a poignant commentator, a friend and speaker of truths to the audience. It is the fool who overtly communicates the themes of the play directly commenting on actions, even when they are derided by the general congregation of actors.

This synthesis chapter serves to offer a critical reflection on the celebratory agenda of the CERM-ESA project. Besides commentating on the actions of others, it looks inwardly. Like the AU project, the CERM-ESA project too, in its first ten-year implementation of the plan, chose to document the key milestones of the project, surveying the evidence of the outcome of its efforts. The anthology, within which this present chapter is located, outlines the bricolage of perspectives on undertaking postgraduate educational research within the East and South African context in collaboration with a partner institution from the German context.

B1: Researching the higher education space

The agenda of creating the platforms involved working across funders, project leaders, policymakers, government officials, higher education institutions, academics and teachers, and with schooling systems in an ongoing iterative relationship of building trust, collegiality and respect for local contexts. Shared open-access online resources by collaborating research experts were created to provide a database

---

2   Odhiambo (2024) hints that this prevails due the over-intensification of the work responsibilities of supervisors under pressure to support their assigned supervisees.

of resources to support partnership institutions to activate the research agenda. These projects continue to the present day. Doctoral and master's research studies were commissioned to draw students and supervisors from across the African and German partner collaborators. Japheth, Chang'ach, Kurgat and Chemutai Barasa (2024) (Chapter 1) explore how these co-supervision and peer mentorship programmes promoted an exchange of diverse knowledge and practical skills with mutual reciprocal learning for all partners. Historical situatedness was emphasised by challenging a simplistic importation of models from one context into another. A respect for localised knowledge-making was promoted with the Capacity Building Programme for Lecturers and Supervisors (CABLES). This included the exchange of interpersonal skills for pedagogical approaches for schoolteachers exploring the activation of emotional relationships with students. The supervision models included highlighting interpersonal skills, as well as diversification of educational expertise in the range of quantitative and qualitative methodologies in promoting education research.

Researching university-community partnerships around research: Case study research

Chapter 1 argues that a *triadic relationship* was being developed through the CERM-ESA initiative: between the promotion of education *research*, the broader *schooling context* and the *local cultural context*. This became the architecture for the book which foregrounds the context of the higher education space, the social collaborations between school and the broader society embedded in unique cultural interpretations of education.

Methodologically, Chapter 1 accents the dominance of *case study research* which permeates the book's research topics selected by the chapter authors. Such small-scale research studies are characteristic of educational studies that rely on relatively diminished budgets. Novice researchers, like most masters and doctoral students, whose studies are reported on in this anthology, rely on the limited access to the fields within which they operate, constrained by exigencies of time and monetary resources; also, many such researchers have other working responsibilities that constrain long-term fieldwork studies. Snapshot insights of the field and the phenomena are likely to characterise their study designs. However, this should not detract from the overall goals of case study research. Unlike large-scale quantitative research, or longitudinal studies which trace the evolutions of a phenomenon across time and space, or aim to provide predictable outcomes for large systems, the aim of case study research is not to be generalised and create universal claims to truth. Instead, small case study research aims to be generative: to activate provocative, insightful questions about the phenomenon they study. Generativity rather than generalisability is the goal of case study research.

Nevertheless, the case study researcher ought to provide thick descriptions of the contextual spaces they explore. Multiple methods and sources of data should be the goal of the research design to ensure a rich *triangulated trustworthy dataset* (Peels & Bouter, 2023). Perhaps there is an overreliance in the case studies within this anthology on self-reported evaluations of project interventions. A small range of methods of data production (even when they are relatively provocative or innovative) are adopted. Additionally, it is surely likely that research participants who have been offered an innovative intervention (whatever the source or the content) are likely to report a high degree of satisfaction with the product, especially when their daily diet is relatively under-nourished intellectually. They are also likely to agree on project implementation targets met, especially when they (the respondents to evaluation survey questionnaires or focus group discussions) are considered beneficiaries of funding and intellectual resources provided courtesy of the evaluators/researchers.

On a broader – rather than study – methodological design micro-level focus, and true to the overarching goals of the project collaborative effort, most of the chapters in this anthology draw on a *writing collaboration* between authors from varying contexts, and across diverse countries and student-supervisory contexts. The act of writing the chapters, and the construction of a shared anthology itself is exemplary of the capacity-building and promotion of education research dissemination and communication, sadly lacking on the African continent. Previous studies from the African context decry the abusive unethical conduct of supervisors who exploit publications drawing on their students' works (Aidonojie et al., 2022; Muthanna & Alduais, 2021). The writing and publication collaborations reflect the goals of respectful interchange and exchange of expertise and resources, celebrated in the anthology.

Ronoh and Webb (2024) in Chapter 2 expand the triad between educational research, schooling and the broader society. By focusing on teacher educators' views of *relevant indigenous knowledge* (IK) for inclusion in the school curriculum, the researchers adopt what they consider to be a culturally appropriate form of a modified focus group discussion, referred to as the *Imbizo/Baraza* method. The data production in a South African and a Kenyan teacher education context was conducted in the participants' home languages. Short local contentious historical stories provided a stimulus to facilitate dialogue probing participants' views on the type, place and position of IK to be incorporated into the school curriculum. While participants positively reported on the *Imbizo/Baraza* data production strategy, the researchers commented on the limitations created by the distortion of cultural nuances and expressions when translating education research data, findings and analysis into a second language like English. A further question may be asked whether the two data production sites tend to commodify IK as a static essentialist form of knowledge and whether the perspective of IK promoted a touristic notion of culture as an exotic nostalgic remembering of past historical conceptions of the society that no longer exists in a 'pure' form. In promoting a prospective agenda for cultural studies, one should embrace the notions that all cultures evolve in relation to varied external and internal combative and contested forces. Romanticising IK stereotypes a bounded singular African knowledge system that is past, rather than present and future-oriented. This conceptualising of the enduring effect of a past-oriented view of knowledge and culture recurs in other studies (see discussion later).

Two further studies under the sub-grouping of studies within the space of the higher education context deal with the matter of the relationship between *knowledge produced* within the university research space, and how it finds expression in the lives and worlds of the societies surrounding them, with their attendant *cultural values, beliefs and practices*. First, Ssekamatte, Speck, and Siebenhüner (2024) in Chapter 4 document the *training and research interventions* related to climate change and sustainability at a selected university in Uganda. Their participants were staff and students within the university who reported on their wide range of climate change science initiatives, mitigation and policy research projects in various sectors and ecosystems, including weather-related predictions and modelling for different sectors within the country. The descriptive case study revealed that faculty and students actively engaged in research relevant to local communities: including on agriculture (crop and animal livestock) farming in dry arid regions, and climate resilience in the cattle corridor revealing strategies for livestock farmers to adapt to scarcity of water and pasture.

Second, Mandela, Ssekamatte, and Kyalo Wambua (2024) in Chapter 5 extend the *university-community partnership* to include matters related to the gender injustices prevalent in and the management of climate change research interventions. The study participants in this chapter were students, university staff and community leaders. This chapter represents a strong presentation of a theoretical feminist lens to examine why women's experiences and practices of managing climate change were not fully embraced in conservative patriarchal community contexts. Women often have no say on environmental issues, land ownership and decision-making. The cultural rather than the scientific interpretations of mitigating climate change are emphasised in this study.

These above studies may be critiqued for not expanding the research design strategies to broaden the sample size and diversity to include a range of other stakeholders such as policymakers, non-governmental organizations (NGOs) and other universities to offer a comparative perspective of different communities and institutional responses to the same topic. Future research should trace the long-term effect of the sensitization efforts undertaken by the researchers, and review over time the local evolving adaption strategies adopted in the researched sites. The influence of these studies on the activation of system-wide policy development arising from the small-scale research case studies would potentially be beneficial. This would move the research agenda away from exotic exceptional celebratory discourses into the terrain of critical engagements on a systemic level of both the macro and micro-cultural systems that impede change.

Researching student experiences

Two studies in the section on higher education terrain involve the focus on *students' experiences*: the first (Chapter 3) deals with *student resilience* in an engineering degree in South Africa (Mapaling, Webb & du Plooy, 2024) and the second (Chapter 5) deals with *student–supervisor relationships* in an African doctoral studies programme (Rugut, 2024).

Chapter 3 represents one of two chapters in the anthology which foregrounds *quantitative* research approaches (see discussion on Chapter 7 later). The authors, however, declare that the chapter itself is a sub-report of a larger mixed-method study, which identifies the interplay between quantitative and qualitative data gathered. The study claims to explore the factors affecting the *psychological well-being* of students. It chooses to look at the impact of "academic success workshops" conducted by the institution to support students navigate their academic journeys, whilst also probing perceptions of students related to the online learning emergency strategy that was introduced during COVID-19. The study reports on the multifaceted nature of resilience and the mental health of students, especially at the senior stages of the undergraduate degree. Only self-reported data is generated, largely from those who choose the institutional support strategies and do not drop out of university.[3] The study underestimates how its participant sample, at the time of data production, represents those who have already crafted ways of surviving the transition from schooling into a university environment, as well as adapted to academic literacy discourses of engineering faculties. They ought to be more resilient and represent already successful academic candidates. Nevertheless, the study highlights the need to address reducing depression, anger and sleep problems, as well as promote perseverance strategies and reflective self-help-seeking strategies. The study would be advised to expand the exploration of the wider institutional context outside of Engineering for comparative perspectives of other fields or disciplines and their students. Specific gender trends should be explored comparatively for deeper theorization. The broader university-wide environment space, its institutional ethos and turbulence influencing unrest, disruptions and contestations may also be examined to understand what enables or constrains academic and personal resilience. An interdisciplinary lens of gender, psychological and sociological analyses is needed.

Chapter 6 draws on a wide literature review of past studies challenging the quality of *supervisory-student partnerships* and their influence on the completion rates of doctoral students. The literature constitutes a mix of studies from both Western contexts and research focused on African universities; it also shares both positive and negative experiences of doctoral students with their supervisors. The literature highlights fulfilling relationships as characterised by inspiration, bonding,

---

3   Perhaps the qualitative dimension of the study, not reported in this chapter, attends to matters of the critique offered below.

and effective scaffolding provided by supervisors, while unfulfilling relationships lead to disengagement, neglect and sometimes bullying or imposition of unrealistic demands by supervisors. The latter produces feelings of discontent and frustration that influence not only the academic and professional development of doctoral students but also their personal growth and well-being. Communication and support were regarded as foundational for fostering productive student–supervisor relationships. Methodologically, the study employs drawing as a data collection tool to capture visually the nuanced experiences of participants, offering deep insights into the complexities of these relationships within the African academic context. The drawing enabled the revelation of conscious and unconscious issues and experiences, potentially bringing to light hidden or unknown perceptions or views.

While the study endorsed the extant literature cited, it tends to remain at the level of describing the relationships only on personal, psychological dimensions linked to the unique identities of the academics and their students. There are some instances of acknowledgement of the intense work environment of higher education where supervisors are often overwhelmed with administrative and teaching responsibilities or having too many students to supervise. This meso-systemic institutional, contextual analysis of the higher education system offers the possibility of expanding beyond descriptive data to engage in explanatory evaluations of the nature of the specific quality of relationships activated. Another examination of the dominance of hierarchical patterns of doctoral supervisory relationships linked to cultural expectations of deference required in patriarchal societies, or as a product of respect for seniority or perceived authority status, could have provided more theoretical analysis. The spaces for crafting relationships across varied fields of doctoral study also could be linked to reinforcing signature disciplinary practices, such as negotiation of the managed, surveilled team use of laboratory spaces in the natural sciences, or more exploratory individual fieldwork studies in social sciences.

The small sample of this chapter's study, however, opens methodological innovations to generate further research into theoretical and explanatory studies about other university student–supervisor patterns. It is acknowledged that future studies should harness the perspectives of supervisors which could provide a more balanced view, revealing their challenges, expectations and perceptions of areas for improvement in the supervision practices and their need for further training. Perhaps the study could have been enhanced by offering more insight into how university policies could be used to mediate and monitor conflict resolution mechanisms. Both the meso-systemic institutional contexts and the micro-personal contexts co-affect each other.

Reflections: Research *in* higher education and research *of* higher education

The above studies are perhaps characterised by a reporting of research studies within the higher education space. This research *in* higher education is varied, focusing on elements of curriculum programmes offering, support structures for students, and analysis of partnerships produced in the research space between supervisor and students, or between researchers and the wider community. It infers that the authors are interested in assessing the impact of their work on the broader cultural sphere within higher education, and within the communities.

However, a missing gap in this section of the anthology is the research *of* the higher education system in more overt ways. For example, the studies are driven not primarily by an examination of the senior governance and management systems that characterise African higher education as part of a broader systemic national, regional, continental and global level. No direct studies examine in-depth the financial management of African universities, nor specifically the policy development opportunities and challenges. Financial analysis is limited to only the requests for extended support for localised programmatic offerings and practices. Additionally, little analysis is afforded to examining academic and professional services staff development initiatives to address higher education's resource potential. The effect is to celebrate the incompleteness of staff who are seen as in need of some rescue/ saviour intervention (see earlier discussion in the introduction to this chapter). The systemic critique of the present resources of staff is not fully explored. Human, physical and financial resource planning is not foregrounded. The studies only refer tangentially to the administrative, management, and human resources of leadership. Perhaps future studies would benefit from expanding higher education studies not just in parochial, technical and operational terms, but also on institutional and national systems levels as an emerging field of study. The contribution to theorizing African higher education studies as a field of study would be most resourceful.

B2: Researching the school and society space

The second section of the anthology focuses on research (by higher education researchers: the supervisors and the supervised) conducted within the schooling space. The studies aim to explore the relationship between schools, their curriculum and management structures, and the broader cultural context of the social environments within which the study is conducted. Two broad groups of *quantitative* confirmatory research designs and *qualitative* exploratory research alternatives are the focus of this section.

Quantitative ways of knowing: Using replication study methodological approaches

Chapter 7 by Nakiyaga, Serem, Namubiru Ssentamu and Boit (2024) constitutes the second study in this anthology using a *quantitative* methodological study design (see the analysis of Chapter 3 above). The study design is inspired by positivist empirical research traditions that aim to pursue what is considered to be a universalist truth, that can be generalised across varying contexts. This study represents an anomaly to the other study designs of the anthology.

The study seems aimed to validate the already established findings of a Nigerian study by Ayeni and Ibukun (2013) in which a conceptual model for school-based management operations and quality assurance was promulgated. The researchers of Chapter 7 used the framework of this school-based management model (SBMM) to look at how the Ugandan schools' adoption of the stakeholder theory of governance could influence the involvement of participants when dealing with enhancing learners' academic achievement. The findings reinforce and confirm the ones established by the Nigerian study: learner achievement is underpinned by major challenges facing effective operation of SBMCs. The five factors influencing the efficacy of the SBMC were identified as the low capacity of key members of the SBMCs; poor attendance of members at meetings due to lack of incentives and financial support from the government; lack of cooperation from the schools; and Parents Teacher Association resistance to the SBMC initiatives. These collectively resulted in ineffective school management and a low level of student academic achievement. The study may be considered to have come to the same conclusion that SBMCs matter and that the involvement of stakeholders is important to activate learner achievement. The study reinforces the need for inclusive, responsive and effective educational environments that bring varied stakeholders in developing school improvement planning, budgeting and coordinating of academic activities.

Qualitative ways of knowing: Using innovative methods of data generation

The next set of chapters in this sub-section consciously chose to create alternative pathways to dominant research methods for data production. Chapters 9, 10, 11 and 12 constitute a strong case for using participatory visual methodologies (PVM) to produce different data differently. All these studies are located within the Kenyan context where the external influence of supervisors and co-supervisors from contexts in South Africa and Germany could be noted. PVM as a creative methodological approach formed part of the repertoire of new methodologies offered during the CABLES programme and constituted part of the Research Schools adopted during the CERM-ESA project duration. This constitutes another form of borrowing which is motivated not by replication (as in Chapter 7) but by *disruption of the conventionalised ways of doing data production* in the field. The studies foreground doing research *with* participants rather than *on* participants. Moreover, the research success relies on the relational, dialogical, iterative and emotional rapport that the researchers establish *with* their participants. Both the researcher and the researched are regarded as co-producers (generators) of the insights being developed without fear of the 'corruption of the field' since the embodied interactive presence of both interlocutors is granted respectful acknowledgement.

The studies span a range of topics and contexts of data activation like researching the teaching of *sexuality education* in secondary schools (Yego & Khau, 2024, Chapter 8); the development of *character education* in early childhood education (Olao, Misigo & Speck, 2024, Chapter 10); the reviewing of *gender-based violence* amongst secondary school girls in an informal settlement (Mworia, Githinji & De Lange, 2024, Chapter 11); and challenging *gender stereotypes* through exposure to gender-atypical Kiswahili stories in primary schools (Ekiru, Khau & Chumba, 2024, Chapter 12). The studies draw on the discussion around participants' constructed visual drawings and caption notations related to the phenomenon of the study. Given their labour-intensive and closely responsive verbal questioning interviews akin to clinical interviewing (Brailas, 2020), these studies adopted a case study approach aiming to provide an in-depth interpretation of a few participants. Depth rather than breadth of understanding was the goal.

Sexuality education (Chapter 8) is a sensitive topic due to the discomfort among teachers in delivering such programmes. Teachers were more comfortable talking about topics like morals and abstinence but shied away from discussing contraceptives and condom use. Teachers perceived that talking about uncomfortable topics promoted perceived immoral behaviour, leading some of them to avoid teaching sexuality education altogether. The chapter reports on promoting student participation through poetry, role play, collage-making, drawings and songs. The findings suggest that the pedagogical strategy of PVM boosted students' self-confidence to talk confidently about topics such as safe sexual practices, HIV prevention and healthy relationships. Moreover, the study reports positive enjoyment and creative expression by the participant teachers. This study reinforces sexuality education which emphasises constructing *knowledge* about safe sex practices and HIV transmission. However, other studies such as Bhana et al. (2021) advance the need to recognise the complexities of negotiating sexualities which expose how gender relations intersect with other material and social contextual factors that impede or enable safe or risky behaviours. Knowledge alone is a necessary but insufficient condition. This chapter, nevertheless, is motivated not by looking at the long-term impact of the pedagogical intervention on changing knowledge, attitudes and behaviours. Instead, it emphasises creating an alternative creative environment within classrooms that is usually teacher-led and dominated by non-participatory pedagogies of teaching and learning. The introduction of the PVM strategies could therefore be a teacher development exercise. Future studies on how students themselves interpreted the value or lack thereof of the activity should elaborate not just on the enjoyment of the classroom but on how this approach influences (or does not) learners' future choices relating to sexual practice.

Similarly, Chapter 10 responds to the dominant traditions of teaching *character education* (CE) which have tended to foreground the model of imitation, modelling, instruction, teacher-centred pedagogies of reward, punishments and deference to authority. Working with primary school teachers and their learners, the study reports on the uses of PVM as a strategy to promote learner interests, critical thinking and enjoyment as they dealt with building positive, ethical, pro-social inclinations and competences. This study reports on self-study reflection by the teachers on the use of drawings and photovoice to promote collaborative learning. The study extends to produce data through engagement with learners in their classrooms. A broader question is directed towards the cultural assumptions about the role of the teacher as the authority figure in primary school classroom spaces. The intervention of the study is perhaps a singular intervention that needs to be sustained over time, to activate pedagogical approaches that challenge the power dynamics that are unconsciously inculcated in the learners. The undeclared underlying issue is whether this alternative is indeed culturally valued. The learners' enjoyment reported in the study might be a function of the innovation and their freedom to express themselves which is not normally permitted in such classrooms.

Chapter 11 might be considered to be a gathering of the cases of physical, sexual, verbal and forms of *gender-based violence* (GBV) that is experienced by girls in an informal settlement. In an ethically sensitive manner, drawings were used to represent what is often unarticulated by victims of abuse. While the study revealed the range of experiences of rejection and being treated as commodities by familiar perpetrators (teachers, relatives, fellow students and community gangs), the girls struggled to articulate their reactions enthusiastically. Despite its therapeutic intentionality, the methodology of drawing was seen as an uncomfortable experience pointing to a lack of clarity of what the participants believed they could draw. To counter this, the messaging of the drawing rather than the aesthetics of the representation of the drawing was reinforced by the researcher. Nevertheless, the study yielded the girls' conceptions of what support strategies could be enacted including mechanisms for clear reporting strategies, safe places for reporting, education on GBV for boys and girls and training for teachers on how to respond to GBV cases. The study points towards recommended action, yet it is worth examining in future research whether these proposed intervention strategies remain merely at the level of description by researchers, instead of leveraging concerted policy and pragmatic action to resolve this scourge.

Disrupting *gender stereotypes* is addressed as a methodological strategy adopted by Chapter 12, focused on the use of atypical stories in which gender roles are consciously reconfigured in the stimulus story material which was presented to a small sample of Grade 3 learners. Further drawings were used to depict children's representation of themselves in response to the stories read. The use of PVM was reported by the researchers as providing children with not only the aesthetic pleasure of creating a visual presentation of themselves but also crystalized their thoughts to produce an artefact that could be drawn on to engage children in their discussion of gender stereotypes. The findings reveal the deep-seated social/cultural constraints imposed by socializing agents like teachers, parents and peers who reinforce gender stereotypes. Children reported that those who resisted these stereotypes faced harsh treatment, which pressured them to conform to societal expectations of gender roles, hindering equality and potential individual development. Despite the exposure to gender-atypical roles through stories, both girls and boys still depicted themselves in stereotypical roles in their drawings. The stories opened spaces for discussion about why males still aspire to traditional male roles. The discussion revealed that girls were far more prepared to adopt a broader range of non-typical future career aspirations. The study seems to suggest that tackling gender stereotypes cannot be confined to only the school/ formal learning spaces, but should also consciously work with how the home, family and community reinforce culturally normative behaviour. The study opens questions about whether researchers have a right to be disruptive of what they perceive to be iniquitous, while the broader social system is comfortable with current social practices.

While strictly not a PVM strategy, in Chapter 13 by Jemutai (2024) the researcher adopted a multiple data production strategy that included triangulation of interviews, observations and the use of teacher reflective journals. The aim was to understand how a 'play way' approach contributed to the *development of digital literacy skills* amongst primary school learners. The study represents one of the studies of this sub-section that attends to adopting various methods and sources of data production to examine a single phenomenon by providing an in-depth, thick description of the contextual spaces where the study is conducted. The respondents of the study interviews were teachers, the officer responsible for quality assurance at the sub-county level, and the head teacher of the school where data were produced. Reflective journals captured more of the teachers' thoughts, feelings, experiences and challenges regarding computer use. The dataset was complemented by observing how digital literacy was promoted within the classroom, providing resources for describing events, actions, learner activities and institutional strategies comprehensively. Rather than being advocatory of singular methods of intervention, the study seeks to examine the worthwhileness of the alternative 'play way' method. As a method, 'play way' draws on early childhood child-centred pedagogical theoretical foundations which suggest the value of playful activities and games to stimulate learning; this is reinforced with puzzles and games in computer-based programmes. The claim of whether social and emotional development are activated is the focus of the study.

The study reports high levels of enjoyment for the learners who engaged meaningfully through games yet simultaneously acquired digital skills. However, the study identified that the child-centred and hands-on nature of the intervention was possible because of the availability of digital devices to promote digital literacy. Many schools outside the sampled site do not have an adequate supply of digital devices. A more comprehensive district-wide digital integrated strategy was proposed to tackle the systemic resourcing to affect the use of this alternative approach. The researcher notes that at the core of the intervention is the need to reposition the role of teachers as facilitators of learning and the need to reinforce teacher professional development and training that emphasises learner and learning-centred pedagogies. However, pedagogical strategies alone without human, physical and financial resourcing were insufficient as levers of change.

Chapter 14 by Simayi and Webb (2024) points to another study that looks at the teaching of topics that are considered *cultural taboos*. This chapter reflects a similar agenda to the Kenyan study reported in Chapter 8. A comparative analysis could be made to review these two studies since Chapter 14 is located within the isiXhosa cultural setting in rural South Africa. The 30 participants were high school biology teachers. A preliminary semi-structured questionnaire was administered to establish the uses of specific linguistic polyphonies and metonyms that are used by teachers and learners when talking about sexual concepts such as menstruation, copulation and fertilization. In the context of cultural avoidance of dialogue between adults and children about sexual concepts, the study further probed through focused interviews with teachers their reflections on teaching sexual concepts. A flowchart represented the personal reflections of teachers which were then analysed and coded to reveal dominant trends.

Teachers reported that topics of menstruation and fertilization, or sexual concepts more broadly, were not a normal part of cultural conversations amongst members of their culture. However, teachers expressed that when euphemistic isiXhosa words were used before introducing sexual concepts, interlocutors (like teachers and their learners) were less frustrated and more comfortable discussing these concepts. The use of isiXhosa rather than English words was considered a more culturally sensitive pedagogical strategy. Nevertheless, the study revealed a lack of knowledge among the teachers regarding culturally responsive teaching strategies for sexual concepts, indicating a general absence of professional development strategies in this area. Their inability to share a sufficient database of alternative terminologies in isiXhosa is concerning.

The study highlights the intersection of several issues: the need for building linguistic terminology databases and discourses about culturally taboo topics for use in pedagogical settings, the role of inclusive culturally sensitive language pedagogies and the examination of what produces comfortable or uncomfortable pedagogies. Additionally, the study pointed to the difficulty of data collection which could have been impacted by the nature of the gender, age, culture or racial grouping of the interviewers. Outsiders probing into and challenging the cultural contexts of the Xhosa world might be considered obtrusive or interfering, especially in a dominantly patriarchal setting. Paradoxically, while the linguistic practices were the focus of the study, the participants hesitated to offer adequate language examples, providing pragmatic barriers to the research in this sensitive area. Perhaps a broader critical anthropological study is required to explore the cultural constraints and taboos surrounding sexual education within the Xhosa community. By definition, culture is malleable, and can be open to new possibilities for growth and development. But who decides when that direction should proceed, and how? Such a theoretical analysis would be appropriate as a future direction for this study.

Chapter 9 constitutes a Uganda study conducted by Atuhaire, Nyaga Kindiki, Kyohairwe and Kurgat (2024) looking at the importance of addressing the challenges and possibilities of mainstreaming children in the street into formal schooling settings. The study draws on traditional semi-structured interviews with nine 6-12-year-old *'children in the street'*, and five relevant government and non-government organization stakeholders. The study findings confirmed other cited literature of past studies that document the barriers and enablers for their inclusion in formal schooling. Barriers included social, financial, environmental and interpersonal factors, while rehabilitation, reintegration strategies and focus on school retention programmes were considered as enablers. The children tended to report the experiential barriers more, whilst the adult participants foregrounded how the structural formal systems should be imposed onto the presenting problem.

The challenge with the data of this study was that the young children were not forthcoming in providing in-depth reflection. Researching vulnerable groups (like the girls reporting GBV in the informal settlement study of Chapter 11) requires specific kinds of methodologies beyond the traditional ask-response interaction. Despite official ethical clearance being obtained from the Commission of Youth and Children Affairs, the researchers should have expanded their interests methodologically on how to protect, nurture and support the comfort of these vulnerable groups during data production. The full scope of the worldview of these children cannot be understood without a deeper involvement of data provided by other caregivers in the homes, families and communities within which these children are embedded.

Paul (2020) in a related study of out-of-school youth in the Mauritian context, suggested that probing the life history[4] of these vulnerable children reveals that dropping out of schooling involves a recurring process of absorption, push-out and pull-in factors that simultaneously are interpreted and reinterpreted by youth throughout their development. His study looked at a wider and older age range of out-of-school youth and showed that these drop-out/drop-in patterns recur across

---

4   This life history tradition suggests a challenge to the short bursts of interviewing strategies which draw data from the field in particular singular moments in time. Instead, life history interviewing strategies aim to expand to review different stages in the career/lifespan of the individuals whom one researches. The aim is not just to describe their lives, but to expose theoretical insights in what complexities are being negotiated and where these forces originate. The intersection across biographical, institutional, curricular and programmatic forces become more evident in this tradition (see Dhunpath & Samuel, 2009).

different stages of childhood and adolescence in response to the evolving nature of vulnerable children's homes, families, peers and official structural support of government (such as formal schooling) and non-government agencies (such as street-children shelter programmes). Further, he cautions that the public media tend to report on the exceptional case of individuals who escape the pattern of recurring absorption and withdrawal of out-of-school youth. He advocates that a more systemic analysis of factors should challenge naïve hope (the former strategy of celebrating exceptionality). Instead, he promotes the notion of *critical hope* which constitutes the analysis of how formal institutionalized systems themselves might be the source of the problem (Bozaleck et al., 2014b).

These critiques of the research study of Chapter 9 of this vulnerable group suggest that alternative pedagogical approaches outside conventional school and formal structures should be considered. Street children cannot simply be re-institutionalised into spaces from which they have chosen to escape. For example, education technological inclusive strategies such as online platforms, educational apps and other digital resources could be considered more appropriate to deal with those children who have lost faith in formal structures.

As a conclusion to this sub-section, the above critiques and critical syntheses suggest that schooling research cannot be simply confined to habituating learners through conventional pedagogical approaches and operational systems. A much more concerted effort is required to examine the theoretical foundation upon which the present pedagogical strategies are built. However, it is not the action of the alternative future pedagogy alone that requires analysis; instead, it is the intentionality of what the action theoretically hopes to achieve that should become the agenda of schooling researchers. One cannot confine oneself to the celebratory potential of otherness (a challenge to the habituated norms) or the belief in the 'innovativeness' of one's new approaches. These approaches require deeper theoretical and philosophical elaboration which opens alternative avenues for contestation. Theoretical commentary, such as that offered on critical hope by Bozaleck et al. (2014a), shows that new ways of seeing across both schooling and higher education settings are needed. Theoretical tools rather than only descriptive pedagogical practices are a potentially valuable resource to challenge the unconsciousness of seeing schooling as 'spaces for producing enjoyment and happiness'. Critical hope is much more expansive than protecting cultural boundaries or promoting enjoyment and happiness. Schooling education is also deeply connected to the social-cultural world within which it operates. It is a product of and produces the nature of the society we inhabit in its fullness: morally, ethically, politically, psychologically and systemically. Additionally, the existence of adequate human, physical and financial resources to underpin the introduction of these alternative school-based approaches is paramount.

Closing thoughts: Working beyond saviour research

It is worth cross-referencing again the macro-system goals outlined by Agenda 2063 presented in Part A of this chapter. The critical synthesis of the programmes and studies of the CERM-ESA project as outlined in Part B of the chapter (sections B1 on *higher education* and B2 on *schools and society*) reveal that many of the Agenda 2063 goals already have been and are being tackled courageously by the collaborative network partnership of the CERM-ESA project. The multiple-country engagement across Africa in the research agenda is already evident. Lessons have been learnt through a respect for evidence-based reporting, and the book itself is a testimony to the range of methodological approaches required to do so. Overall, the project is indeed a people-centred approach which affirms the efforts of local African partners working in interactive and iterative dialogue across varied heterogenous research traditions and contexts. Perhaps the CERM-ESA project has challenged the AU's romantic notion that a singular homogenous African worldview exists. The studies reported in this book point to diverse and contestable traditions of pedagogy, of habituated research edifices, and of societal cultural values, beliefs and practices that are worth affirming, and also some that are worth disrupting.

The search for new interpretations is not simply a naïve celebratory fetish of an institution or disciplinary preservation endeavour but acknowledges the need to locate its scholarship endeavours on a continental and global scale. Respectful, fulfilling partnerships between supervisors, co-supervisors, writers and co-writers across the project enhance the exchange of alternative ways of seeing and doing research. This constitutes deep development discourses. The studies' topics selected by the project partners tackled issues related to developing gender equity and youth empowerment, a declared focus of Agenda 2063. Some of the studies have incorporated the challenges facing the embracing of ICT into the world of schooling and higher education as expected on the continental masterplan. The case studies demonstrated that to track the trajectory of development of their research and project efforts, detailed research monitoring and evaluation of the contextual factors on the ground are needed. These commitments might be misunderstood to have emanated from the AU's agenda whereas they have infused independently the CERM-ESA project's values and strategies since its inception.

All the studies reported on in this anthology show the deep accountability and commitment to seeking alternative ways that challenge habituated practices and set the terms of reference for prospective future-oriented research. These alternatives should be founded on deep theoretical justification. Perhaps the next stages of the project's unfolding will attune more attentively to whose and what new theoretical insights they themselves have and are producing prospectively.

However, all the studies, while dominated by a descriptive account of the on-the-ground realities, point to the challenges of operating in a vacuum without the necessary physical, human and institutional resources required as a supportive baseline from which alternatives may be operationalized. The studies' small-scale descriptive accounts show that potential is available within the African continent itself. Nevertheless, a shortcoming of the project is that it does not consciously delve into how wider-level institutional, political and programmatic interventions must be harnessed to tackle broad-based systemic change. The present studies are parochially fixated on the change agents being localised practitioners in small spaces. They under-report the accountability that macro-systemic partners need to make to the agenda of social transformation. A focus only on the meso-micro system (Part B) whilst capable of activating the initial stages of redirection is unlikely to be sustained in the absence of funders, resources and infrastructure directed by the macro-systemic forces which have greater leverage power (Part A). Many of the obstacles to broadening the research footprints of the project's studies also have to tackle the deeply embedded normative values that are sustained by societal cultural beliefs and practices.

The anthology as a whole would have benefitted from a greater discursive dialogue not just with its project partners but also with actors at the macro-system level. More studies should have been included that research the political offices and administrative/ management/ leadership spaces within institutional, provincial and national contexts. Africa is littered with ghosts of past projects which withered and faded into oblivion when external funding resources ceased to sustain operations. Put differently, the road to failed change is paved with good intentions. Policy declarations alone cannot activate change: they represent symbolic redirection that can only be experienced concretely when practitioners on the ground feel and experience systemic support. The practitioners seem ready to understand the intersection between the localised and the broader systemic levers of change (at least from within the CERM-ESA project). The challenge is redirected to political leaders and heads of government to question how Agenda 2063 can indeed be activated not just by rhetoric but by commitment of financial resources, governance planning, and management and leadership at macro-levels. It is acknowledged that financial budget priorities are constrained, yet collective systems need to question where our public financial resources are being directed and whose interests these indeed serve. Many more CERM-ESAs should be activated and sustained so long as they are not simply fashionable 'political projects' to solicit votes or buy favour amongst the electorate.

This chapter has attempted to outline why African scholars and research need to move beyond merely imitative and expansionist research which borrows models and patterns of designing, conducting, analysing, and reporting research (epistemologies, methodologies and representations) that draw on traditions and customs that have emanated from outside the localised context. The chapter has suggested that when research borrows uncritically from beyond its borders, it runs the risk of elevating and reinforcing the source of the theorists from elsewhere, and undercuts the potential of activating relevant, appropriate and worthwhile questions and analyses from within the local context. This kind of critical distance between and across all micro-, meso- and macro-levels constitutes working *beyond saviour research* where the solutions to current challenges are drawn through lenses not circumscribed by deference to saviours who aim to proliferate their products in evangelical ways. This does not mean that one does not examine the patterns and perspectives of others for their potential value. Instead, a critical research stance critiques the embedded external hegemonic discourse as well as one's own valuing and belief systems. From where did our ways of knowing originate? Could these also be interrupted, contested or disrupted? We, too, should be critical of our parochial and localised ways of being and becoming.

There are no pre-packaged products that should be paraded in the marketplace of higher education or school development spaces. Robust and resilient ways of activating respectful dialogues by, within, in and through the African continent should be our priority in constructing the locally appropriate strategies that could be introduced. This will entail not simply accepting current normative practices, traditions in the higher education research space, or unconscious perpetuation of pedagogies that oppress schoolteachers and their learners simultaneously. Our agendas of deep transformation equally will be directed towards challenging notions of patriarchy, inequity and social injustices. This will involve tackling not just our grandmothers' and grandfathers' interpretations but also our own inherited new alternatives, always asking questions about whose interests all the alternatives might serve. Thankfully, the CERM-ESA project has contributed a cadre of potentially committed individuals who will likely rise into the echelons as defenders of new appropriate pedagogies, alternative meaningful and provocative programmes, and new sustaining institutional policy spaces. Our hope is not a naïve one that will fade when these individuals graduate into positions of power. With critical hope, they will be able to redirect resources to meaningfully promote deep change. Instead, our hope is born when the graduation celebrations and exploratory research campaigns have served their purpose. The time for continued action is now.

References

Aidonojie, P. A., Okuonghae, N., Agbale, O. P., & Idahosa, M. E. (2022). Supervisor and supervisee relationship: The legal and ethical issues concerning academic theft in Nigeria tertiary institutions. *Euromentor, 13*(1), 113–138.

Aryeetey, E. (2024, March 21). ARUA plans to revolutionise doctoral training in Africa. *University World News: Africa Edition.* https://www.universityworldnews.com/post.php?story=2024031822421416

Ayeni, A. J., & Ibukun, W. O. (2013). A conceptual model for school-based management operation and quality assurance in Nigerian secondary schools. *Journal of Education and Learning*, 2(2), 36–43. http://dx.doi.org/10.5539/jel.v2n2p36

Bhana, D., Singh, S., & Msibi, T. (2021). Introduction: Gender, sexuality, and violence in education—A three-ply yarn approach. In D. Bhana, S. Singh & T. Msibi (Eds.), *Gender, sexuality and violence in South African educational spaces* (pp. 1–46). Palgrave Macmillan.

Bozalek, V., Leibowitz, B., Carolissen, R., & Boler, M. (Eds.). (2014a). *Discerning critical hope in educational practices*. Routledge.

Bozalek, V. G., McMillan, W., Marshall, D. E., November, M., Daniels, A., & Sylvester, T. (2014b). Analysing the professional development of teaching and learning from a political ethics of care perspective. *Teaching in Higher Education*, 19(5), 447–458.

Brailas, A. (2020). Using drawings in qualitative interviews: An introduction to the practice. *The Qualitative Report, 25*(12), 4447–4460.

Dhunpath, R., & Samuel, M. (Eds.). (2009). *Life history research: Epistemology, methodology and representation*. Sense.

Fredua-Kwarteng, F. (2023, May 10). PhD cannot alone solve Africa's developmental challenges. *University World News*. https://www.universityworldnews.com/post.php?story=20230509120343196

Muthanna, A., & Alduais, A. (2021). A thematic review on research integrity and research supervision: Relationships, crises and critical messages. *Journal of Academic Ethics, 19*, 95–113.

Odhiambo, W. (2024, March 28). Putting your life on hold: The reality of being a PhD student. *University World News: Africa Edition*. https://www.universityworldnews.com/post.php?story=20240324195627754

Paul, J. L. L. (2020). *Out-of-school children: Life experiences of Mauritian learners* [Unpublished doctoral thesis]. University of KwaZulu-Natal.

Peels, R., & Bouter, L. (2023). *Replicability, reproducibility, and transparency in research: A philosophical and ethical analysis*. Springer.

Samuel, M. A., & Mariaye, H. (2023). Exploring the postgraduate education space. In J. A. Smit & N. Ndimande-Hlongwa (Eds.), *Transforming postgraduate education in Africa* (pp. 1–32). Alternation African Scholarship Book Series.

The following list of references constitutes the chapters of the anthology reviewed:

Anthology: Webb, P., Khau, M., & Namubiru Ssentamu, P. (Eds.). (2024). *Education research in African contexts: Traditions and new beginnings for knowledge and impact*. African Minds.

Chapter #	Authors	Chapter title
Chapter 1	Japheth, N., Chang'ach, J. K., Kurgat, S., Chemutai Barasa, M.	A reflection on collaborative teaching and learning in higher education: The case of the East and South African-German Centre of Excellence for Educational Research Methodologies and Management
Higher Education		
Chapter 2	Ronoh, J., Webb, P.	Exploring teacher educator views on place and position of indigenous knowledge in the school curriculum using an indigenous methodology

About the authors

Annah Atuhaire is a former master's scholarship holder in the in-country/in-region DAAD/CERM-ESA scholarship programme and graduated in December 2023. She is currently serving as a Research Ethics Committee administrator at Bishop Stuart University, under the Directorate of Graduate Studies, Research and Innovations. She is a lecturer and research supervisor in the Department of Economics, Management, and Tourism at Bishop Stuart University. Her research interests revolve around sustainable development issues, specifically inclusive education of children in vulnerable situations, gender equality and climate action.

Ayanda Simayi is a science lecturer in the Faculty of Education at Nelson Mandela University in South Africa. She is a former PhD scholarship holder in the CERM-ESA programme and graduated with a PhD in 2021 from Nelson Mandela University under the supervision of Professor Paul Webb. Her main research interests are critical participatory action research methodologies, indigenous knowledge, decolonised science education, taboo sexual concepts, cultural studies, rural education and language issues in science teaching.

Belinda du Plooy holds qualifications in Public Relations and Communication Studies (NDip: PR Management, PET) and in Literary Studies and Philosophy (BA, BA Hons, MA and DLitt et Phil, UNISA). She worked in the fields of public relations, media and rural community development before joining the higher education sector, where she has worked as administrator, manager, lecturer, postgraduate supervisor, researcher and published author for nearly 30 years, across various disciplines and faculties. She is currently employed as senior manager: engagement at Nelson Mandela University in Gqeberha. She collaborated with CERM-ESA as a doctoral supervisor and researcher.

Benjamin Kyalo Wambua is a seasoned associate professor with over twenty years in research, training, consultancy, and university teaching. He holds a PhD in Educational Research and Evaluation. He is a multi-skilled and versatile leader and academic with extensive experience and expertise in research, evaluation, and education policy.

Bernard Lushya Misigo is an associate professor of Educational Psychology and associate dean in the School of Postgraduate Studies, Research and Innovation at Moi University, Eldoret. He is a research supervisor in the CERM-ESA programme with interests in mental health, stress and resilience.

Bernd Siebenhüner is a professor of Ecological Economics at the Carl von Ossietzky University of Oldenburg, Germany. His academic interest centres on social learning and sustainability, socio-ecological transformations, climate adaptation and governance, sustainable rural and urban development in Africa, governance of marine biodiversity, sustainable coastal zone management and international environmental policy.

Cornelius Kipleting Rugut holds a PhD in curriculum studies from Moi University and holds a master's degree in education research from Nelson Mandela University. He has participated in several international conferences, workshops and research schools held in different countries. Rugut has taught in secondary school for several years and participated in different co-curricular activities. He is currently a teaching practice mentor for students at Kenyatta University, a senior teacher and examiner of the Kenya national examinational council. His research interest is in topics of higher education and issues in curriculum development, instruction and implementation. He has widely published on issues of curriculum in higher education, particularly on supervision and research in higher education.

Curwyn Mapaling, a senior lecturer and clinical psychologist in the Department of Psychology at the University of Johannesburg, South Africa, is an alumnus of the CERM-ESA programme, having earned his PhD in Education from Nelson Mandela University in 2023. He currently contributes as an external research supervisor for Moi University within the same programme. His research focuses on integrating psychological principles into higher education to enhance well-being and improve teaching and learning experiences.

David Serem holds a Doctor of Education in Administration of Higher Education degree from the University of Wyoming, USA. He has held numerous leadership positions in Kenyan universities, including head of department, dean, principal, deputy vice chancellor, and acting vice chancellor. As the pioneer principal of Narok University College, he guided the development of the young institution until it received its charter in 2013. He was also instrumental in establishing Maseno University College. He is a member of several professional associations, including the Kenya Institute of Management. Currently, he is the chairman of the Mount Kenya University Council and serves as a professor at Moi University.

David Ssekamatte is a lecturer in Monitoring and Evaluation at Uganda Management Institute with more than eighteen years of experience in programme management, monitoring and evaluation, participatory research, and strategy management. He has published extensively and consulted on various development projects. His research focuses on sustainability and climate change education, environmental citizenship, and higher education management. A former NAFSA senior fellow, Ssekamatte is currently a postdoctoral fellow with the FAR-LeaF Future Africa Programme, studying climate change education in Ugandan universities. He holds a PhD from Carl von Ossietzky University and an MA in Economics from the University of Lucknow.

Dorothy Nakiyaga is an advocate for positive change in education, recently completing a doctorate in Education Management and Policy Studies. Her research focuses on stakeholder participation in school management and enhancing learners' academic achievement in public secondary schools. Passionate about inclusivity and diversity in school management, she has supported master's and doctoral students, represented educators on the Board of Governors, enforced quality assurance, administered curriculum implementation, and managed sports activities. A former CERM-ESA PhD scholarship holder from Moi University, she is currently an associate consultant in Educational Leadership and Management at Uganda Management Institute, Kampala.

Evans Mos Olao is currently a PhD student at Moi University in Kenya, whose programme is focused on Curriculum Studies. He is also a holder of a Master of Education in Research degree. He is an alumnus of the East and South African German Centre of Excellence in Educational Research and Research Management (CERM-ESA) and a member of the African Excellence Network (AEN). His academic interests are in research methods, early childhood pedagogy and curriculum design.

Felicity W. Githinji is a senior lecturer in the School of Education at Moi University, and completed her PhD in Sociology of Education at Kenyatta University in 2013. Currently, she is the chair of the Department of Educational Foundations and a research supervisor and facilitator in the CERM-ESA programme for both master's and PhD students.

Heloise Sathorar is a professor at Nelson Mandela University's Faculty of Education, of which she is currently dean. Her research interests focus on accounting education, economics education, business and entrepreneurship education, humanising pedagogy, critical pedagogy, decolonisation, teacher education and higher education.

Janet Ronoh is a teacher by profession. She was among the first cohort of master's scholarship holders in the CERM-ESA programme and received her degree from the Nelson Mandela University, South Africa. Her area of interest is in teacher preparation regarding indigenous knowledge in the African context.

John K. Chang'ach is a professor of History at Moi University, with over eighteen years of experience in teaching, research, and consultancy in public organizations. Specialising in history and history of education, he has participated in numerous international and national research collaborations. He is the former project leader of CERM-ESA and served as dean of the School of Education at Moi University (2017–2022). With vast experience in personnel mobilization, placement, and management, he is highly adaptable to technological advancements. Currently, he is the acting deputy vice chancellor of Alupe University, Kenya.

Jonah Nyaga Kindiki earned his PhD from the University of Birmingham, UK, in 2004. He is a full professor of International Education and Policy at Moi University with 117 publications and has supervised over 41 PhD and 175 master's candidates. He is the former coordinator of various educational programmes, head of the Department of Educational Management and Policy Studies, dean of the School of Education, and project leader for CERM-ESA. He is a consultant, member of several professional bodies, and an external examiner, having attended numerous international and local conferences, courses, and seminars.

Karsten Speck is a professor of Research Methods in the Department of Education at the Carl of Ossietzky University of Oldenburg in Germany. His current research focuses include multi-professional cooperation, school absenteeism, cooperation between youth welfare and schools, school social work, participation and volunteer work, university research and inquiry-based learning and teaching.

Lily Yego is pursuing a PhD in Educational Communication and Technology at Moi University, Kenya. She advocates for using participatory visual methodologies to enhance young people's knowledge of sexuality, HIV/AIDS, and contemporary issues. Currently a teacher, Lily's experience has inspired her to explore collaborative research to improve teaching skills among African educators. She is passionate about addressing learners' issues and helping them develop better behaviours for social change.

Mathabo Khau is an associate professor in Education at Nelson Mandela University, with a PhD from the University of Kwa-Zulu Natal. Editor-in-chief of *Educational Research for Social Change*, she is also a fellow of GEXcel International Collegium, the Nordic Africa Institute, and the South African Department of Higher Education and Training's Future Professors' Programme. Khau received the 2020 Faculty of Education Researcher of the Year award. Her research employs participatory visual methodologies to address gender, sexuality, and HIV/AIDS in education, focusing on integrating HIV/AIDS into higher education curricula. Using 'intersectionality' and 'research as social change' frameworks, she includes marginalised people in her work.

Mercy Chemutai Barasa holds a bachelor's degree in science education from Mbarara University of Science and Technology, Uganda, and a master's degree in Educational Leadership from Pan Africa Christian University, Kenya. Currently, she is working towards her doctorate in Educational Research and Evaluation at Moi University, Kenya, under a CERM-ESA scholarship grant. Until the commencement of her PhD studies, she served as a headteacher and a teacher of Biology and Chemistry at the secondary level in Uganda. Her research interests include educational leadership, educational policy, and teacher professional development.

Michael Anthony Samuel is a professor in the School of Education at the University of KwaZulu-Natal. He holds a Doctorate in Education from the University of Durban-Westville, focusing on a force field model of teacher development. He has designed innovative master's and doctoral programmes, and contributed to national teacher education policy in South Africa. Formerly dean at UKZN, his research interests include teacher professional development, higher education, and narrative inquiry. His books, such as the *Life History Research* and *Disrupting Higher Education Curriculum*, are highly regarded. He received the Turquoise Harmony Institute's National Ubuntu Award for his contributions to education.

Naomi Mworia is a teacher of English and Literature, having pursued a BEd (Arts) from Moi University. She is greatly honoured to also be a former scholarship holder in the CERM-ESA programme towards the completion of a Master of Education in Research, with which she graduated in 2023 from Moi University. Her main research interests are in the areas of education and gender studies.

Naydene de Lange is professor emerita in the Faculty of Education at the Nelson Mandela University, Gqeberha, South Africa. Her educational psychology background and interest in inclusivity provide a frame for working towards including those who are marginalised – using a 'research as social change' theoretical framework. Her research therefore focuses on using participatory visual methodologies in researching with participants in addressing gender inequalities and integrating gender into higher education curricula.

Nelson Mandela, a Ugandan student at Moi University's School of Education, is pursuing a Doctor of Philosophy in educational research and evaluation under a DAAD and CERM-ESA scholarship. He earned a master's in Educational Research from Moi University in 2019 under a similar scholarship. Nelson's research focuses on higher education engagement and climate change action, building on his master's work on school-community engagement. His current research explores university-community engagement opportunities to address climate change in Africa, aiming to guide African universities in integrating institutional contexts like history, culture, and indigenous knowledge into their climate change education strategies.

Noel Japheth holds a Bachelor of Arts in Education from Kabale University, a Master of Education in Educational Psychology from Mbarara University of Science and Technology, and a Master of Education in Research from Moi University. As a former CERM-ESA scholarship holder, he worked as a research assistant at the East and South African-German Centre of Excellence for Educational Research Methodologies and Management. Currently, he is a research fellow at the International Centre for Higher Education Research (INCHER) in Kassel, Germany. His research interests include inclusive higher education, education for minority social groups, postgraduate education, and higher education governance.

Paul Webb is emeritus professor of Science Education at the Nelson Mandela University in Gqeberha, South Africa. He earned his PhD at Curtin University, Australia. His interests lie in the promotion of scientific literacy, alternative worldviews and science, and language issues in science teaching and learning.

These interests have led to research in productive discussion, use of technology in science education, and the development of thinking skills and visuo-spatial abilities. Over four decades his work has encompassed pure science, science education, and educational psychology.

Proscovia Namubiru Ssentamu is an associate professor of Education and head of the Quality Assurance Department at Uganda Management Institute. She is the project leader of the CERM-ESA Uganda chapter, as well as research supervisor. Her main research interests are in teaching and learning, curriculum, and quality assurance in education.

Sammy Chumba holds a PhD in Educational Management and is a professor at Moi University. He taught Chemistry and Mathematics and served as high school principal in various schools before joining Moi University in 2008. Since then, he has taught Educational Management and Research courses both at undergraduate and postgraduate level. He is a research supervisor in the CERM-ESA programme and has interests in quantitative and mixed-methods studies. Currently, he is the chairman of the School Graduate Studies Committee in the School of Education.

Sarah Jemutai is a teacher by profession and an administrator. She is also a former PhD scholarship holder in the CERM-ESA programme at Moi University School of Education in Eldoret, Kenya. She specialises in curriculum instruction and educational media and her major area in research is early year education.

Simon Esekon Ekiru is an alumnus of the second CERM-ESA scholarship cohort. Currently, he is a lecturer in the Teacher Education Department at Turkana University College, where he teaches courses on Kiswahili Linguistics, Kiswahili Literature and Kiswahili Research Methods. His research interest is in gender and sexuality issues in popular and children's literature.

Stella Kyohairwe is a senior lecturer in public administration and management and head of the Department for Political and Administrative Sciences at Uganda Management Institute. She is a scholar, researcher, and consultant in public administration, public policy, institutional leadership, organizational development, HR management, and local governance. She holds a PhD and an MPhil in Public Administration from the University of Bergen, Norway, a BA in Social Sciences from Makerere University, and a Postgraduate Diploma in HR Management from Uganda Management Institute. She is also a research supervisor in the CERM-ESA programme.

Susan Kurgat is currently an associate professor in the Curriculum Instruction and Educational Media Department, School of Education, and the project coordinator of the East and South-African German Centre of Excellence in Educational Research Methodologies and Management (CERM-ESA) at Moi University. She is a member of the African Network for Internationalization of Education (ANIE). Her research interests are in teacher education and specifically in promotion of modern methods of teaching, new research methods and research supervision, development of thinking skills, alternative worldviews, and the use of technology in education.

Violet Nabwire Opata is an associate professor at Open University of Kenya (OUK) and formerly at Moi University, School of Education. She specialises in curriculum development, educational technology, and online assessment. Currently the acting head of department and programme leader for Learning Design and Technology at OUK, she holds a PhD and MPhil in Educational Communication and Technology from Moi University and a Bachelor of Education (Arts) from Kenyatta University. Her research focuses on teacher education, HIV/AIDS, gender issues, and eLearning. She has authored several journal articles, book chapters, and books on education.

www.ingramcontent.com/pod-product-compliance
Lightning Source LLC
Chambersburg PA
CBHW080550270326
41929CB00019B/3256